Census

THE EXPERT GUIDE

Peter Christian and David Annal

The National Archives

First published in 2008 by

The National Archives
Kew, Richmond
Surrey, TW9 4DU, UK

www.nationalarchives.gov.uk

The National Archives brings together the Public Record Office, Historical Manuscripts Commission, Office of Public Sector Information and Her Majesty's Stationery Office.

A catalogue card for this book is available from the British Library.

ISBN 978 1 905615 34 6

Design by Goldust Design
Printed in the UK by The Cromwell Press Ltd, Trowbridge, Wiltshire

Cover illustrations: Miss Fitzroy, 1903 (COPY 1/459); J. Brown, 1901 (COPY 1/452); unknown Victorian lady (courtesy of Robert Pols); John Webb, 1873 (PCOM 2/290); Samuel Coleridge-Taylor, 1901 (COPY 1/451); a lady of Porthcawl, 1901 (COPY 1/452); boy on a wall, Yorkshire 1906 (COPY 1/497).

Photographic credits: **1** © Crown copyright UK Government Art Collection; **4**, **18** and **26**, The Mary Evans Picture Library; **8**, **11** and **36**, *The Illustrated London News* (which can be seen at The National Archives in ZPER 34/98). All other images are from The National Archives and are © Crown copyright.

Census

The publishers would like to thank Audrey Collins at the National Archives for her valuable contribution to the writing and production of this book.

The website for this book is at <**www.spub.co.uk/census**>.

CONTENTS

PREFACE

What you'll find in this book

Why is such importance attached to census returns? Why does the release of another set of records provoke such avid, some might even say obsessive, interest? What is it about the census that has led to questions being asked on a number of occasions in the House of Commons? This book will attempt to answer these questions as well as explaining what the census is, how and why it was taken, and most importantly how researchers can use, understand and access the returns today – with the focus on online research.

Census returns are one of the key nineteenth-century sources for family historians, delivering a wealth of information about their ancestors including names, addresses, ages, family relationships and occupations. The documents may appear on the surface to be quite straightforward, but the process by which they were compiled means that the unwary researcher can easily fall foul of them – this book also aims to help you navigate your way through the census returns and show you how to avoid the major pitfalls.

We begin with an exploration of the census itself. The returns for the years 1841 (the first that recorded our ancestors' names) to 1901 are fully open, and we take a detailed look at these remarkable records in Chapter 1. The 1911 census is treated separately in Chapter 2. This is not just because it is newly available: although there are broad similarities between it and its Victorian predecessors, the layout of the schedules, the range of questions asked and, perhaps most importantly, the process that led to the creation of the records are different enough to warrant a separate chapter.

In Chapter 3 we explain why finding your ancestors in the returns isn't always as easy as it might be and we'll offer some advice to help you to untangle these problems.

The book then goes on to explain how to access the census returns. Chapters 4 to 6 cover the census online, what you can access for free, and the best techniques to maximize your search. Chapters 7 to 13 take you on a guided tour of the most important census websites, concluding with a comparison in Chapter 14, which looks at the pros and cons of each of the sites and helps you to decide which best suits you.

For the most part, the book deals with the census returns for England and Wales, the Channel Islands and the Isle of Man, which were taken every ten years from 1841 to 1911 – essentially the records held by the National Archives. The Scottish census is treated with the English one because it is similar in many respects; Ireland is covered in Chapter 15.

Chapters 16 and 17 cover topics that may seem old-fashioned, but will still be incredibly useful for some researchers. Chapter 16 is about the census products available on CD-ROM, and in Chapter 17 we'll take a brief look at some of the 'offline' finding aids available to help you to access the census on microfilm. Some people prefer to access the returns this way and in certain cases it might be the best option.

Lastly, the book assumes that most readers are interested in census returns from a family history perspective, but we need to remember some important points here. Firstly, the census was not taken with family historians in mind – the arrangement of the returns and the information they record may sometimes make us feel that this *was* the case but we have to put that idea out of our minds. The census returns were taken by the government of the day for a variety of social and political reasons, which we'll explore below. Also, although family historians may form the main body of users today, we mustn't ignore the requirements of academics and local historians; the census returns can be vital to their research and this book is aimed at them too.

Websites

The chapters devoted to the main census websites describe them as they were in June and July 2008, but these services are subject to the occasional facelift so you shouldn't be surprised if what appears on your screen is slightly different from our screenshots. Also, commercial data services are constantly making improvements, whether to enhance existing features or to add new facilities. For this reason, you may also encounter less superficial differences when you access sites yourself.

The chapters on the major data services are in many cases the most detailed discussions of census records on these sites ever published. Nonetheless, the coverage is not and could not be exhaustive. Ancestry, for example, has 35 different census datasets for the British Isles, while TheGenealogist has over 300. Needless to say, we have not checked every single database offered by these sites and nor could we explore absolutely every search option.

In the discussion of individual sites, we have given a number of examples of errors in indexing and transcription. However, with any luck, some of them will have been corrected by the time you read this. You may, therefore, not be able to locate the errors cited, but they retain their value as example of the *types* of error found in online censuses.

While we have attempted to give you all the information you need to decide which of the commercial services (if any) best meet your needs, there is one aspect of them we have not attempted to test: the response to customer support requests. The various companies have differing reputations in this regard, but since the comments found in the online discussion groups have only anecdotal value, we felt it was inappropriate to take them into account. If you want to find out what others think of a particular data service, a question in a suitable discussion forum will undoubtedly elicit a range of responses. You can easily find past comments from users in the archives of relevant mailing lists. The archives of GENBRIT at <**lists.rootsweb.com/index/other/Newsgroup_Gateways/GENBRIT.html**> or <**groups.google.com/group/soc.genealogy.britain/**> would be a good place to start.

When evaluating sites, we have used Firefox 3.0 and Internet Explorer 7.0 running on Windows XP systems, and have drawn attention to one or two browser problems encountered. However, we have not attempted to test the sites for browser compatibility, nor to check how these sites look with Macintosh or Linux browsers.

The traditional caveat about the longevity of internet resources applies. Web addresses for the commercial sites are not very likely to change (though the location of individual pages may well do). But one or two of the smaller websites mentioned in the text, particularly those run by individuals or informal volunteer groups, are bound to move or even, alas, close down in the lifetime of this book. However, information on such changes will be found on the website for this book at <**www.spub.co.uk/census/updates/**>.

Diagrams

In general, all the websites offering census data and images of the original records work the same way. You complete a search form and click on the search button. This brings up a list of matching individuals, from which you select the one you want to see the full details of. From there you can choose to look at a digital image of the original census enumeration schedule. Beyond this commonality, though, there are usually many more options and they differ considerably from site to site. For this reason, we have provided flowcharts showing you how all the main screens and options interrelate. The census images usually pop up in a separate browser window (with controls for zooming, panning and saving the image), and this is indicated by the rounded corners on the box. For pay-per-view sites, the flowchart will also indicate which steps you pay for and how much each costs.

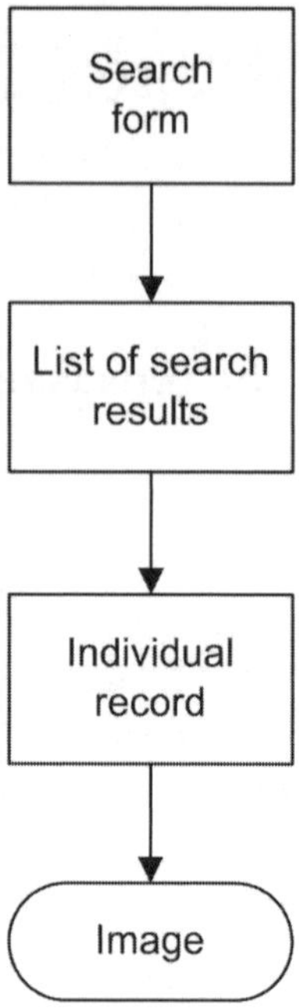

Acknowledgements

The authors would like to thank Audrey Collins for her major contribution to the writing of this book. Her in-depth knowledge of the workings of the General Register Office in the nineteenth and early twentieth centuries was invaluable. The works of Eddy Higgs and Matthew Woollard also proved an invaluble source of information and are essential reading for any serious students of census returns.

We are indebted to those data services which provided free access so that we could explore and test their facilities in depth. We would like to thank Nigel Bayley, Elaine Collins, Ian Galbraith, Steve Waters and Simon Ziviani for answering countless questions and for providing details of future plans. Steve Archer provided useful information on surname matching. A special mention must go to Jeanne Bunting and John Hanson, the 'Census Detectives', who have done much to identify the types of error in the online censuses and to analyse the problems of finding individuals.

INTRODUCTION

The census revolution

On 2 January 2002 a remarkable event occurred, which thrust the previously quiet and peaceful world of family history research into the glare of the national media. An ambitious plan to make the records of the 1901 census for England and Wales available online proved a victim of its own success when thousands of family historians who had been waiting ten years for its release and many others, inspired by press coverage but with perhaps no more than a passing interest in the subject, logged onto to the 1901 census website – causing it to crash within hours of its launch. The 1901 census included the details of more than 30 million people, and this was the first time that an attempt had been made to provide access to such a large volume of family history data via the World Wide Web. Earlier censuses had been made available on microfilm and although each successive release had provoked excitement and interest in the family history community, no previous census release had captured the attention of the national press in quite the same way.

We're fast approaching the release of the next decennial census. As a result of a ruling made under the Freedom of Information Act, the National Archives is releasing the 1911 census early – that is, before the customary 100 years have passed. The returns will begin to be made publicly available in 2009. The population of England and Wales increased by three and a half million between 1901 and 1911 – an enormous number of people will appear on the census for the first time, both as young children and as immigrants from Europe and other far flung corners of the world. As with the releases of other censuses, a whole new generation of researchers will no doubt be inspired to start researching their own family history. You may be one of them; or perhaps you're an experienced researcher hoping against hope that the answer to your age-old family history problem will be found amongst the 1911 census returns.

An introduction to census access

The internet has revolutionized the way that we look at census returns. Online access to the census returns, together with comprehensive indexes, has without question improved our ability to find particular individuals in the records – in fact, as anyone who spent hours on end back in the 1970s and 1980s winding through microfilms, waiting for a name to jump off the page at them, would no doubt tell you, it's improved beyond recognition.

Just ten years ago, anyone looking for their ancestors in the census would have had to visit an archive, a record office or a local library to view the records on microfilm. The only complete collection covering the whole of England, Wales, the Channel Islands and the Isle of Man was held by the Public Record Office (PRO). Public access to the collection was provided at a succession of locations: Portugal Street, Chancery Lane and latterly at the Family Records Centre.

There were some alternatives. Most county record offices and many of the larger local libraries had microfilm copies of the censuses for their own areas of interest, but the biggest problem wasn't getting access to the records: the challenge facing family historians in this pre-digital age was actually finding their ancestors in the returns.

As we'll see in Chapter 1, the census returns are arranged by place and not by name. So unless your ancestors were amongst the minority who spent the whole of their lives living in the same place, tracking them down in successive censuses was difficult. To stand a good chance of finding a particular individual or family in the census you really needed to know where they were living at the time. Ideally, you had to know the name of the village or, if they were living in an urban area, the name of the street and preferably the house number.

The census is of course a snapshot – taken once every ten years on a particular date. Sunday nights were chosen, as this increased the chance of finding people at their usual place of residence, but it was no guarantee. People working away from home, visiting relatives or simply travelling from one place to another will not be recorded where you would expect to find them.

The number of people who fell into this category was in fact quite small, and thus unlikely to have a noticeably negative impact on your research. But what did have an impact was the fact that the vast majority of the Victorian urban population lived in rented accommodation: our ancestors moved from one address to another at a rate which is quite difficult for our twenty-first-century minds to come to terms with. The moonlight flit when the rent was due was no urban myth!

So even if you had a copy of a certificate recording a birth or a death in the family occurring within a few weeks of the date of the census, there was no guarantee that you would find them in the returns living at the address shown on the certificate. It was likely that the family would be somewhere in the same general area, possibly quite nearby, but in the most heavily populated areas of the larger industrial towns and cities, tracking them down could be an exhausting process. Winding through reel after reel of microfilm, examining every name on every page, hoping against hope that you would stumble upon the family you were looking for was, for family historians of a certain vintage, a necessity and a way of life!

Online access to the National Archives' entire collection of census returns, fully indexed by name and other key pieces of information such as age, place of birth and residence, has changed all that. In recent years, the number of websites offering access to the census returns for England and Wales has increased rapidly and you no longer need to visit an archive to carry out your research. Now, in theory at least, tracking down anyone who was living in the country at the time of one of the censuses should be a fairly straightforward process. And it doesn't matter where they were living. Provided that you have enough information about your ancestor to make a positive identification, you should be able to find them – even if they were visiting relatives on the other side of the country! You simply enter their names, click on the search button and, within a matter of seconds, their details should appear on the screen in front of you.

Well that's the theory – and sometimes it works. But more often than not you'll find that you come up against one of two problems: either your search turns up too many results or it offers you none at all. That is why before you even begin a search in the census you need to ask yourself an important question: do you have enough information about the individual or family that you're hoping to find, to carry out an effective search? In other words, if you're presented with a list of names, will you be able to pick out your ancestor?

Census returns are a gateway into the nineteenth century but they're not necessarily the best starting point for your research. Before you set off on your journey, you should aim to arm yourself with as much information as possible about your ancestor: their name and an approximate date of birth are essential and some idea of their place of birth and parentage is also desirable. Without this sort of information your search is likely to be fruitless.

The census shouldn't be used in isolation. It's just one of many tools available to you to use in the course of your research: the information that you get from other sources such as birth, marriage and death certificates, parish registers, wills, gravestones and contemporary newspapers will, to a large degree, shape your investigations into the census and provide you with a structured research strategy.

There are two further points to make about census access. One is that although we now take 24 hours a day, 7 days a week, worldwide access to these records for granted, this is a relatively recent phenomenon. Family historians and other researchers have been using the records for over a hundred years and the research techniques which have been developed over time are just as valid today as they have always been.

Also, there's a very real danger that, by providing us with these instant results and dropping us straight on to the single page containing our ancestors' details, the websites may actually be doing us a disservice. In any type of historical research, context is crucial. When you're viewing a census page on your computer screen it's important to look beyond that single entry. Look at the neighbours; look at the size of the families; consider the social aspects – are there servants living in the households? What sort of trades or industries are the occupants involved in? Are they living in a rural or an urban district? The census can tell us so much more about our ancestors and the way they lived than the basic facts of age, occupation and birthplace.

How the census began

To fully understand the census, it helps to know a bit about its origins. Over the years, a number of excellent books have been written outlining the background to the UK censuses, most notably *Making Sense of the Census Revisited* by Edward Higgs. Higgs's book provides a definitive guide to the legislation that led to the taking of the censuses and to the political, social and economic issues that shaped the questions asked on the schedules. Even more detail, including the full text of the relevant Acts of Parliament and examples of the various forms used by the General Register Office, the census enumerators and the individual householders, can be found on the Histpop website: **www.histpop.org.uk**. Here you can also read essays about particular aspects of the returns, as well as a series of pen portraits of the major players behind the taking of the census.

The date 22 June 1753 was a momentous one for family historians – or rather, it nearly was. This was the date scheduled for the House of Commons to meet, to pass Thomas Potter's Bill for 'taking and registering an annual account of the total number of people, and of the total number of marriages, births, and deaths, and also of the total number of the poor receiving alms from every Parish and Extra-parochial Place in Great Britain'. The Bill had already passed through both Houses of Parliament (admittedly, not without some forthright objections from certain parties) but the House of Commons rose before the session could take place and the Bill lapsed.

That, as far as proposals for a national census were concerned, was that – at least for another fifty years or so. Family historians are left to salivate at the thought of what might have been.

Nevertheless, population – and the thorny issue of whether it was growing or shrinking – became one of the hot topics of debate in the late eighteenth century. Thomas Malthus, Britain's first professor in Political Economy, developed his controversial 'Principle of Population', which was originally published as *An Essay on the Principle of Population* in 1798. Malthus believed that increases in wages led to a growth in population which could not be matched by the required increase in levels of food production and, therefore, ultimately led to subsistence living for most labourers. His views were heavily criticized by social reformists such as William Godwin and Robert Owen, and have now been largely discredited; but at the time he gained influential support – most notably from the Prime Minister, William Pitt the Younger.

The idea of 'counting the people' was hardly a new one, and the practice was well established in other countries long before the United Kingdom embarked on its first census. In fact Britain lagged far behind many other European states. The Netherlands (1795), Denmark (1769), Spain (1768), Sweden (1749), Prussia (1719) and Iceland (1703) can all claim an earlier start date. And across the Atlantic the Americans beat us to it – the first US census being taken in 1790.

Another name worthy of mention alongside Thomas Malthus as a prime mover in the campaign for a national census in the UK is that of John Rickman. Rickman was a staunch opponent of Malthus, but the two agreed on one point: the need to have an accurate count of the British population and, most importantly, whether it was rising or falling. Rickman set out twelve reasons why taking a census would benefit the nation, ranging from military matters to concerns about food supply, but at the forefront of his philosophy was his statement that 'the intimate knowledge of any country must form the rational basis of legislation and diplomacy'. His idea was to hold a national census every ten years, and ultimately he got his way: in 1800 it was John Rickman who was responsible for drafting the first Census Act (also known as the Population Act), which resulted in the taking of the first national census of England, Wales and Scotland on 10 March 1801.

Unfortunately for the vast ranks of family historians around the world with British ancestry, the legislation behind this first census and the three that followed it didn't require the recording of any names. The pre-1841 censuses were no more than headcounts: of huge interest to local and social historians, providing exactly the sort of information that the government had hoped for, but of little or no direct use to people searching for their ancestors.

Nevertheless, under the direction of Rickman, the 1801 census was a masterpiece of planning and execution and a fine example of what Georgian Britain could achieve when it set its collective mind to it. At a time when central government had little day-to-day impact on our ancestors' lives, Rickman employed the services of an unlikely alliance of parish officials, town clerks, overseers of the poor, clergymen and householders to carry out the various tasks required by the Act.

By the standards of modern censuses the questions asked in 1801 were very simple and undemanding, but viewed from an early nineteenth-century perspective they were ambitious enough.

The census was divided into two parts, the first of which consisted of just three questions which were designed to fulfil the primary aim of the Act – namely to 'take an Account of the total Number of Persons within the kingdom of *Great Britain*.':

- the number of houses (inhabited and uninhabited)
- the number of persons (separate counts of males and females)
- the number of persons 'chiefly employed' in three categories
  - agriculture
  - trade, manufactures or handicraft
  - everything else

In England and Wales, this part of the census was to be taken by the local overseer of the poor – in Scotland the role was undertaken by a local schoolteacher. The legislation allowed for a 'substantial householder' to undertake the task if there was no available overseer and the appointed person was allowed to ask for the assistance of one of a number of church officials.

The second schedule, which was to be completed by the 'Rector, Vicar, Curate, or other Officiating Minister' of each parish, would help John Rickman to build up a picture of what he described in the Act as 'the progressive Increase or Diminution [of the population]'.

The task for the clergymen was to complete two tables (questions four and five respectively) showing firstly the numbers of baptisms and burials (separate totals for males and females) recorded in their registers for specific years in the eighteenth century; and secondly, the total number of marriages recorded each year from 1754 to 1800.

The next two censuses (in 1811 and 1821) were conducted on almost exactly the same lines. There were some changes to the layout and some minor alterations to the way the questions were formed, but the information requested was essentially the same. The only significant advance came in 1821, when the overseers were instructed to provide a breakdown of the 'ages of all persons enumerated'.

The 1831 census was a far more ambitious venture: the range of occupation categories was greatly enlarged, a question was asked about servants, and the clergymen were asked to provide data on illegitimate births occurring in their parish. The first small steps towards a truly modern census had been taken.

It's clear from the legislation that the overseers were expected to keep records showing how they had arrived at the totals for their parish, but there was no prescribed method for undertaking the work. The overseer's task was simply to 'inform themselves of the several Particulars relating to the Matters specified in the Three First Questions in the said Schedule, by proceeding together or separately from House to House, or otherwise, as they shall judge expedient for the better Execution of this Act'. The legislation required that the records should be 'safely kept and preserved by the churchwardens' and eventually sent to the Home Office where they would be 'digested and reduced into order'.

What is also clear is that certain efficient and dedicated overseers decided, for one reason or another, to compile lists of the names and other details of the people they were supposed simply to be counting. According to Gibson and Medlycott in *Local Census Listings: 1522–1930* over 750 such lists have been identified but many of them record only the householders' names and perhaps as few as 80 can be counted as full censuses.

Nevertheless the discovery of one of these pre-1841 name lists for your ancestors' parish can be a major boost to your research. The surviving records have generally ended up in County Record Offices amongst the miscellaneous parish material. It's important to note that they are not held by the National Archives (although there are a few transcripts available in the Open Reading Room at Kew).

These early censuses have been extensively researched and listed both by Gibson and Medlycott and by Colin Chapman in *Pre-1841 Censuses and Population Listings in the British Isles*. Both books are essential reading and include excellent introductions to the topic of pre-1841 censuses as well as comprehensive lists of those that are known to have survived, together with their present whereabouts.

The twentieth-century censuses

No book on the census should resist a glimpse forward to the returns that family historians will have access to in the future. The 1920 Census Act allowed for a census to be taken every ten years without needing to pass an individual Act each time and, with the exception of 1941 when our minds were on other more pressing matters, this is exactly what has happened ever since – the most recent census having been taken in 2001.

The story of the last hundred years of the census is a long and complex one; but since the details are not yet open to public inspection, and the returns are therefore only of passing interest to family historians, this is not the place to tell that story. Unfortunately, for future family historians the problems which the absence of a 1941 census will no doubt cause are exacerbated by the accidental destruction of the returns from 1931 resulting in a gap of thirty years between the 1921 and 1951 censuses.

The changing nature of the questions asked in the twentieth-century censuses reflects the particular concerns of the government of the time. Whereas the nineteenth-century censuses had focused on health, poverty and mobility, now the emphasis, beginning in 1911, shifted towards two main themes: fertility and social class. The analysis of occupations broadened and although the 1931 census (which was taken at a time of economic decline) saw a significant reduction in the number of questions asked, the trend in the post-war years was very much one of expansion, which reached a peak in 1971.

The 1981 census included just 21 questions and, remarkably, nearly half of them were identical or directly equivalent to the questions asked one hundred years earlier in 1881.

The process by which the census is taken has remained essentially the same since the first detailed enumeration was made nearly 170 years ago, and many of the same issues crop up year after year: acts of civil disobedience and attempts to disrupt the census are not recent developments. The 1991 census was certainly affected by protests about the Poll Tax, but in a similar way the 1911 census was targeted by the Suffragette movement. And of course the 2001 census has its very own urban myth: encouraged by an internet campaign, the idea grew that if enough people entered their religion as 'Jedi Knight' this would somehow force the government to recognize it as an 'official' religion. As a result, some 390,000 people (roughly 0.7 per cent of the population) are recorded as following the Jedi religion – it would be interesting to know quite what the descendants of those people will make of that!

1

THE VICTORIAN CENSUSES (1841–1901)

The 1841 census

The 1841 census was the first to be taken under the auspices of the recently formed General Register Office (GRO). It was also the first census of England, Wales and Scotland to record the names of every inhabitant. The 1841 Census Act required that 'every Enumerator, under the Direction of the Registrar of the District, shall visit every House within his District … and shall take an Account in Writing of the Name, Sex, Age, and Occupation of every living Person who abode therein'.

The hierarchy of Registration Districts and sub-Districts which had been established by the GRO for the purposes of registering births, marriages and deaths provided an ideal framework to use for the taking of the census. Each sub-District was further divided into Enumeration Districts and thousands of enumerators were appointed, each one responsible for collecting the returns for a particular district.

The Act was passed in August 1840 but just two months before the census was due to be taken, an amendment was rushed through Parliament which changed three crucial aspects. The untimely death of John Rickman had left the responsibility for taking the census in the hands of the recently appointed Registrar General Thomas Lister, and it appears that Lister was keen to introduce some of his own ideas at the earliest possible opportunity.

Firstly, the date of the census was brought forward from 30 June (a Wednesday) to 6 June (a Sunday). Secondly, precise ages of people aged over 15 would not be required. Instead 'every Person aged Fifteen Years and not aged Twenty Years may be set down as Fifteen Years, and every Person aged Twenty Years and not aged Twenty-five Years may be set down as aged Twenty Years; and in like Manner the Age of every

Person may be set down as that Multiple of Five Years which either expresses his or her real Age, or is next below his or her real Age.'

The third change brought about by the Census Amendment Act of 1841 introduced a new idea which completely changed the process by which the census was to be taken: the schedules were now to be completed not by the enumerator but rather by the householders themselves.

The basic process of delivering forms to the householders in the week leading up to census night and collecting them during the following week has stood the test of time and indeed was still in place for the last national census taken in 2001.

Each enumerator had been issued with the required number of blank householders' schedules, as well as a summary book and a memorandum book – the latter was to be used to make any notes which the enumerator felt might assist the registrar and the Census Office.

Having collected the completed householders' schedules, the enumerator's next task was the not inconsiderable one of copying the details into a book, known as the enumerator's schedule (or summary) book. This system was used for all censuses 1841 to 1901.

The original householders' schedules were destroyed many years ago (along with the memorandum books) but the enumerators' books were kept and it's these that we refer to when we talk about the census returns today. Each summary book had a number of nominal pages with space for a set number of entries. The enumerator copied the details from each schedule into the book and then drew a line to indicate the end of the returns for each household and the start of the next one. The precise manner in which this was to be done changed from year to year but in most censuses you should look out for the small angled double lines to the left of the individuals' names.

The result of this process is that each nominal page contains the returns for several households and also that the returns for a particular household may begin at the bottom of one nominal page and continue at the top of the next.

In addition to the nominal pages, the summary books also contain a number of forms and tables which had to be completed by the enumerator, recording such information as a description of the Enumeration District, the administrative hierarchy, and abstracts and summaries of the statistical data.

These pages provide essential background information about the district that our ancestors were living in. They also frequently include additional comments by the enumerators and if you're very lucky, you may come across a hand-drawn map showing the Enumeration District boundary.

Large institutions such as prisons, hospitals and workhouses were issued with special schedules that closely resembled the enumerators' books. The main differences were that the individual pages did not include an address column and the information was written directly into the books. The master of the institution was designated as enumerator, and was responsible for sending the completed books to the Superintendent Registrar.

Lister insisted that the abstraction of statistics should be done centrally, in the interests of uniformity, so a central office was needed to administer this, as well as the distribution of the forms and instructions to the enumerators, and their collection. The new General Register Office occupied part of Somerset House, but there was no space for the additional clerks needed for the census, so Lister secured temporary accommodation for them in nearby Adelphi Terrace.

The 1841 census records the following information about each individual:

- name (forename and surname)
- age (rounded down to the nearest five for those aged over 15)
- gender
- occupation
- whether they were born in the county in which they were living at the time of the census
- whether they were born in Scotland, Ireland or 'Foreign Parts'.

It also provided a count of the number of houses inhabited, or being built, or uninhabited.

Although this is clearly far more informative than the headcounts of the previous years, it still leaves something to be desired, and the usefulness of the 1841 census to family historians suffers in comparison with the later Victorian censuses.

There are a number of important points to consider when using the 1841 census.

Although every individual is named, the enumerators were asked to enter just their first forename and the surname. This instruction wasn't always strictly observed but it's fair to say that finding middle names recorded in 1841 is the exception rather than the rule.

There wasn't a great deal of space allowed for names on the schedule so forenames are frequently abbreviated. The most common abbreviations to look out for are:

Jno. = John
Wm. = William
Rbt. or Robt. = Robert
Eliz. or Elizth. = Elizabeth
Jas. = James
Thos. = Thomas
Chas. = Charles

This tendency of the enumerators to abbreviate forenames should not be confused with the use of 'pet' names such as 'Bessy' for Elizabeth or 'Fanny' for Frances. The abbreviation of forenames (and indeed the use of initials) also occur in later censuses but it is a particular problem with the 1841 census and therefore worth highlighting here.

One feature of the censuses which occurs throughout the years is the use of ditto marks or the abbreviation 'Do.' – particularly with surnames, occupations and birthplaces.

To get the best out of the 1841 census it is absolutely vital that you understand the practice of rounding down the ages of those aged 15 or over. Someone whose age is given as 40 would actually be aged between 40 and 44, someone entered as 65 would be aged between 65 and 69 and so on. In Chapter 3 we'll look at some general problems surrounding ages in the census, but the situation in 1841 is made that bit more troublesome by the absence of exact ages.

An individual's gender is not explicitly stated in any of the censuses but instead is indicated by the presence of their age either in the 'Male' or 'Female' column.

Occupations can cause problems here, again because of the frequent use of abbreviations. In addition to the ubiquitous Ag Lab (short for Agricultural Labourer and used throughout all the censuses) there are a few other abbreviations commonly used in 1841:

F.S. = Female Servant
M.S. = Male Servant
Ind. = Independent (i.e. of Independent Means)
M. = Maker (e.g. Shoe M. = Shoe Maker)
F.W.K. = Frame Work Knitter (common in Nottinghamshire and

surrounding counties)
Straw Pl. = Straw Plaiter (common in Hertfordshire and Bedfordshire)

The wording in the heading of the occupation column reads 'Profession, Trade, Employment or of Independent Means' – the term 'occupation' isn't actually used at all. The aim was to categorize the type of work undertaken by the chief wage earner in each household – usually the senior adult male – but the census takers also wanted to know about numbers of servants and about people who had private incomes so we regularly see 'F.S.', 'M.S.' and 'Ind.' in this column.

Perhaps the biggest disappointment for family historians using the 1841 census for the first time is the lack of detail regarding birthplace. The 'Where Born' section is divided into two columns: one for people born in England or Wales and the other for everyone else. A 'Y' or an 'N' in the first column indicates whether or not that person was 'born in the same county' – i.e. the county in which they are currently living. An 'S', an 'I' or an 'F' in the second column indicates that a person was born in Scotland, Ireland or 'Foreign Parts'.

Another frustration here is the absence of a precise address. In rural areas it's not at all uncommon to find just the name of the village or hamlet given, and even in the more built up areas, where street names are usually shown, it's rare to find house numbers in the returns.

The 1841 census is best thought of as work in progress. Huge steps had been taken and enormous advances had been made in the process of gathering information – the establishment of the General Register Office with its well defined structure of Registration Districts and sub-Districts was perfectly suited for taking the Victorian censuses. And by using the same administrative units that were being used to register births, marriages and deaths, statisticians could for the first time obtain meaningful data to help them understand and investigate population trends both nationally and from a local perspective.

Having taken the 1841 census using the administrative framework of Registration Districts and sub-Districts, the books were then rearranged into the old format of hundreds, wapentakes, lathes and other ancient local divisions. It took the census clerks two years to carry out this task, but it meant that the information gathered could be directly compared with that from the earlier censuses. This arrangement of the 1841 census books survives today.

The 1851 census

The first few years of Queen Victoria's reign can be seen as a golden era for family historians. Two of the most important events on the family history calendar – the start of civil registration and the taking of the first genuinely useful national census – occurred within four years of each other. Thomas Lister's work in setting up the General Register Office and in overseeing the 1841 census had proved a huge success but sadly Lister didn't live long enough to see the effects of all his efforts: he died in 1842 at the age of just 42. However, this second untimely death in the story of the census ushered in the era of arguably the most influential and successful Registrar General, George Graham (plate 1).

Graham served as the head of the GRO for the next 38 years, continuing to build on and develop the work started by Rickman and Lister. He was to be in charge of the preparations for the next four censuses and it was under his leadership that the design of the census form settled down into the classic layout that is so familiar to family historians today. Graham was assisted in this by Dr William Farr, who had joined the statistical branch of the GRO in 1839. He later became Deputy Registrar General, a post that he held until he retired in 1880, shortly after Graham's own retirement. The two men made a formidable team, each complementing the skills and qualities of the other. Farr was a doctor of medicine (although he never practised as a physician) and a founder of the Statistical Society of London, the forerunner of the Royal Statistical Society. Statisticians like Farr could see the potential of the information that could be gathered in a census, and wanted to add more questions. Graham, the administrator, had to balance this with the realities of the level of funding he could obtain from the Treasury, and the practical limitations of tabulating census data manually.

The premises at Adelphi Terrace used for the 1841 census had not proved satisfactory, and for 1851 the Census Office was established at Craig's Court, near Trafalgar Square, where it remained until the 1881 census. The premises consisted of three adjoining houses, each divided into several rooms. Clerks were employed on temporary contracts, since there was no permanent Census Office until the Census Act of 1920, and new staff had to be recruited each time. A number of experienced staff would be seconded from regular duties at Somerset House, including William Farr who was in charge of the Census Office. The great majority were employed only for the preparation of the census, and then for the time it took to process and analyse the results. A list had been kept of the temporary staff employed in 1841, and a number of them were re-engaged for the 1851 census.

As well as clerical staff, an office keeper, Edward Wells, was appointed to live on the premises, at £80 per annum, and the Treasury agreed to employ charwomen 'as necessary' at 12 shillings per week, and labourers at 23 shillings per week, to carry coals and deliver messages. The clerks were to be paid between 5 and 8 shillings, dependent on the standard of their work. In keeping with the practice of the time in the GRO itself, as much work as possible was to be conducted as 'taskwork'. This is what we would now call piecework, and was a system greatly favoured by George Graham, particularly when dealing with temporary staff.

> 'If temporary clerks and writers and boys are on day pay, they may be placed at desks; but no amount of supervision can obtain from all of them a good day's work. They know that the more work they execute in a day, the sooner their temporary employment will cease and they will be again turned adrift; therefore it is their interest to do as little work as possible.'

Adelphi Terrace must have been very unsatisfactory indeed, if Craig's Court was an improvement. The rooms were cramped and ill ventilated, and many of the staff complained of headaches from the fumes of the gaslights; they were burning for much of the working day, which could be as long as ten hours. In spite of this, every census from 1851 to 1881 was administered from there. It must have been difficult to find suitable office accommodation within a short distance of Somerset House, which was only required for a couple of years before and after each census, and at a reasonable cost.

Obtaining funds from the Treasury was no mean feat, as Graham had already discovered when he suggested in 1846 that a set of maps would be very useful in planning the 1851 census. There was at that time no published set of maps showing parish boundaries, so Graham suggested that the new maps being drawn up by the Tithe Commissioners would be ideal and an extra set could be produced for relatively low cost. The Treasury were not quick to respond, and Graham's patience was evidently growing thin by 1848 when they offered him an alternative that he felt was not up to standard:

> 'Nicely designed as they are and well executed as I have no doubt they will be by Mr Saunders, I cannot but consider them as merely pretty toys, when compared with the practically useful and much required maps to the formation of which under the Tithe Commissioners I have so frequently, not I hope pertinaceously and obstrusively, ventured to solicit the attention of the Lords Commissioners of H M Treasury.'

The Treasury finally agreed to pay for a set of the Tithe Commissioners' maps in September 1850, four years after they had first been asked for. With that problem out of the way, George Graham next had to make the final decision on the questions to be included in the 1851 census schedules, in order to assess the amount of work involved and the optimum size for the Enumeration Districts. There were representations from various interested parties, including Farr and the Statistical Society, to include details about education, amount of taxes paid, the size, construction and ownership of dwellings and more. These were all rejected, so as not to overburden the enumerators and keep the costs to a realistic level when the final set of questions was eventually decided on for the layout of the schedules. Some of this information was available from other sources, and other elements, such as the number of rooms occupied by each family, were introduced in later census years.

The layout finally arrived at for 1851 hardly changed over the six censuses from 1851 to 1901; in fact the core questions asked about address, name, age/gender, relationship, marital status, occupation and birthplace are identical throughout this period.

When you look at the details recorded about our ancestors on these mid to late Victorian censuses, it is difficult to imagine that they weren't taken with family historians in mind. There they are – neatly arranged in conveniently packaged family groups showing their relationships, ages and places of birth – what more could we possibly ask for?

The full list of column headings on the 1851 census schedules is as follows:

1. No. of Householder's Schedule
2. Name of Street, Place, or Road, and Name or No. of House
3. Name and Surname of each Person who abode in the House, on the Night of the 30th March 1851

4. Relation to Head of Family
5. Condition
6. Age of Males/Age of Females
7. Rank, Profession or Occupation
8. Where Born
9. Whether Blind or Deaf-and-Dumb

The addition of a number on the schedule given out to the householders provided the enumerators with an easy method of checking that they had collected in all the forms they had given out.

From 1851, addresses start to become more detailed and precise. House numbers are increasingly given in large towns and cities but often you'll just get the name of the street or road – be careful not to interpret the schedule number as a house number!

Names are usually given in full (the enumerators were instructed to do so), and middle names are sometimes included, but more often they're shown in abbreviated form, as initials or omitted altogether. Occasionally even the first names are given as initials, and its not uncommon to find the names of the inhabitants of institutions entered solely as initials. This is important to bear in mind when it comes to searching for your more elusive ancestors.

Columns four and five are the first two of the significant improvements introduced by George Graham and William Farr. The relationship to the head of the family (usually the oldest adult male in the household) and the condition (i.e. marital condition) are crucial elements for family historians as they enable us to reconstruct family groups – in the 1841 census this task involves much guesswork.

The ages are now exact ages and the occupations tend to be fuller and more descriptive. It was important that the various 'ranks, professions or occupations' could later be categorized for statistical purposes and the enumerators were issued with extensive instructions on how they should complete this section to ensure a consistent approach. This was part of a three-stage process: first the householder wrote down his occupation as he would describe it, then the enumerator entered it in his summary book in a standard form, and finally the clerks at the Census Office in London assigned it to one of several hundred predefined categories.

The system worked well and was retained throughout this period, the only significant change being an increase in the number and variety of categories used by the census clerks. These categories were set out in a list known as the 'Instructions to the Clerks', copies of which are available in the open reading room at the National Archives and online at the Histpop website <**www.histpop.org.uk/**>. This is an extremely useful (but underused) reference source which can be used to identify obscure or obsolete occupations.

The eighth column on the 1851 census – the birthplace – represents perhaps the most significant improvement for family historians from the information given in 1841. Now, for the first time, we have the full place of birth – county and parish for those born in England and Wales and the country of birth for everyone else. The purpose behind asking for this information was to answer one of the crucial questions of the time – the rate and intensity of migration from rural to urban areas.

When the results of the 1851 census were published, they confirmed that there had indeed been a significant shift from the countryside to the towns; for the first time it could be demonstrated that more of the population lived in towns and cities than in rural areas. Overall the population of the United Kingdom rose steadily throughout the Victorian period from under 28 million in 1841 to more than 41 million in 1901. This of course included Ireland, which suffered a dramatic decrease in population, by contrast with England, Wales and Scotland. If the Irish figures are removed from the total, the rise is even more dramatic, with the population doubling over the same period from just over 18 million to almost 37 million.

The questions of religion and education were addressed in separate religious and education 'censuses' in 1851. These were not carried out under the auspices of the 1850 Census Act, and participation was not compulsory, but the response rate was high and the results were included in the Census Reports for that year. The returns for the Ecclesiastical Census of 1851 can be seen on microfilm at the National Archives (TNA), in series HO 129. They include some returns from the Educational Census. However, it's important to note that these 'censuses' do not include the names of individuals, only statistical information.

At this time the Registrar General was responsible for the administration of the census for the whole of Great Britain, the Channel Islands and the Isle of Man. Scotland had its own General Register Office from 1855, which organized the Scottish census from 1861 onwards, but the returns of the earlier Scottish censuses remained in London for several decades to come. The Registrar General for England and Wales retained responsibility for censuses in the Channel Islands and the Isle of Man, so that the returns for these places are held by the National Archives together with those for England and Wales.

Another key refinement in the 1851 census was the introduction of special schedules for vessels in home ports or within British territorial waters, for which there had been no provision in 1841, although there had been head counts. The arrangements for recording the floating population were complex, and clearly not understood by most of the people involved. The schedules from merchant vessels were collected by Customs officers from vessels in port on Monday 31 March, the morning after census night, and forwarded directly to the Census Office. However, it is very difficult to establish exactly what happened to the schedules for either merchant or Royal Navy vessels in that year.

The 1861 and 1871 censuses

Having arrived at a satisfactory layout for the census in 1851, the ever-practical George Graham saw no reason to depart from this tried and tested formula in subsequent census years, although there were inevitably requests from many quarters that he should do so. There was a suggestion that religious affiliation should be included in 1861, but there were many objections to this, and in practice it is unlikely that it would have been seriously considered. Another request was from the British Temperance League, as to the legality of including 'teetotaller', to which George Graham had no objection, since it would be ignored anyway! He also received requests for the inclusion of extra questions specific to particular localities, but these too were rejected on the grounds of cost. Every extra question added to the expense of taking the census, and would delay the production of the final reports, so it is quite understandable that none were added in 1861. All the same, every family historian must wish that a way had been found to include the religious question.

The format of the 1861 census meant that for the first time the results of a detailed census could be compared with its predecessor, which had not been the position with 1851 and the rather hybrid census of 1841. With one successful census under his belt, George Graham could now approach his dealings with the government with added confidence. When it came to hiring the temporary staff, he told them:

> 'After the experience I have had in this matter I venture to impress upon Secretary Sir George Lewis the necessity for my being armed, as I was in 1851, with considerable authority and for special powers being entrusted to me, if I am to keep in proper order 80 or 90 or perhaps even 100 of these clerks.' (HO 45/7098 General correspondence and notes on the 1861 census)

Although some of the temporary clerks had been employed in the Census Office before – it was the fourth time for William Tattershall – most were unused to the public service and came from a variety of different work backgrounds. They needed a great deal of training and supervision, and 106 of them were employed in total. Despite the difficulties, when the office was finally wound up in 1863, George Graham was pleased with his workforce, some of whom had worked for over ten hours a day. He was also pleased to report to the Treasury that the whole census had been conducted at a cost of £4 15s 8d per head of population, compared with £5 4s in 1851, just the sort of thing he knew they would like to hear.

An attempt had been made in 1851 to deal with the perennial problem of temporary mobility. If a significant number of 'settled' inhabitants were temporarily absent, or if others were temporarily present, the enumerator was supposed to record the estimated numbers in his summary book. The exercise was not a great success, but nevertheless, another attempt was made in 1861 – this time with clearer instructions to the enumerators. The returns for Gedney in Lincolnshire include, under the heading 'Persons temporarily absent', an entry reading '1 - absconded' (RG 9/2328, folio 58, page iv). Turning to the nominal pages we come across an entry for a family consisting of a married woman (Hannah Miller) and her three children. No head of the household is entered but instead the enumerator has written the words 'Husband Absconded'. This only tells a small part of the fascinating story of the Miller family – in fact Hannah's husband George had emigrated to America in time to catch the tail-end of the Californian Gold Rush (RG 9/2328, folio 62, page 6).

The questions were repeated in the next two censuses and then abandoned.

The 1861 census was the first where an explicit promise of confidentiality was made, and the GRO published a 'Memorandum on Some of the Objects and Uses of the Census of 1861', which extols the benefits of the census and reassures the populace that they have nothing to fear by way of taxation, conscription or any such evils. This 'memorandum' was effectively a press release, and parts of it were indeed reproduced in the newspapers. George Graham recognized the value of good public relations, even if he would not have recognized the term. This may have been a circular from a government department and conveyed factual information, but its literary style is unexpectedly lyrical, including a quote from Oliver Goldsmith and statements such as:

> 'The *number of Souls*, in the expressive language of the old writers, will then be known, and will remind the nation of the extent of the institutions for the advancement of religion, education and justice, required to keep pace with its numbers.' (Memorandum on Some of the Objects and Uses of the Census of 1861 in RG 27/3 Forms and instructions issued for taking the census)

Even when giving straightforward advice on people who subtract a few years from their age, it still tends towards the whimsical: 'Should the ages of cooks, or of others, be found by any fatality standing still, or even retrograding, it should be corrected by their masters who fill in the return.'

The returns for 1861 at last include large numbers of schedules for vessels, so for the first time many family historians will be able to identify their ancestor's own handwriting on a census schedule. Previously this would only happen if your ancestor was an enumerator, or appears in one of the few household schedules to survive. There is a collection of household schedules for part of an Enumeration District in Newcastle upon Tyne St Andrew in 1851 (HO 107/2405 f276 to 325; plates 2 and 3). Normally the household schedules were kept while the statistical abstracting from the enumeration books was completed, so that they could be referred to in case of any queries. These ones may have been kept because part of the enumeration book was damaged or destroyed; there are other examples dotted throughout this and other census years.

Once the results were published in the form of the Census Reports, the press was always keen to publish interesting snippets, often referred to as 'Curiosities'. Following the publication in 1863 of the report on the 1861 census, *The Times* noted that the breakdown of occupations showed that there were ten solicitors enumerated as inmates of workhouses, 32 in prison for debt and 60 in lunatic asylums. It was also noted that the population of the parish of Aldrington in Sussex had doubled between 1851 and 1861 – from one inhabitant to two! The only building within its boundaries was a toll-keeper's cottage, which in 1851 was occupied by a single man, and by a married couple ten years later.

There were no significant changes in the 1871 census, and the layout is identical to that of 1861, but the instructions to the householders now asked them to include in the occupation column not only their trade or calling, but whether or not they were currently employed or unemployed. This was repeated in 1881, but then dropped again for subsequent censuses.

The 1881 and 1891 censuses

George Graham retired in 1880, so his successor, Sir Brydges Powell Henniker, only had to oversee the conduct of the 1881 census using the by now well-oiled machinery. He is not generally regarded as a great success as Registrar General, but George Graham was a hard act to follow, and Henniker encountered a set of problems that his predecessor did not have to face. Once the 1881 census was completed early in his period of office, there were now returns from five complete census years, each bigger than the last, stored in various government buildings. These of course still included the Scottish censuses of 1841 and 1851.

Brydges Henniker was not happy with the quality of the temporary staff recruited for the 1881 census. Part of the problem was that they were recruited by the Treasury, and not directly by the General Register Office. Henniker tried to persuade the Treasury to hand the job over to the Civil Service Commission, but with no more success than Graham when he complained about the same thing in 1861 and 1871. Of the 98 appointments made by the Treasury, Henniker claimed that four were unfit for work of any kind and two had actually died! More than half of the remainder he considered 'indifferent', 'bad' or 'very bad'. He wrote:

> 'In consequence of the physical, mental and moral inadequacy of a large proportion of the clerks employed, the Census of 1881 not only cost much more money, and took a much longer time in its compilation than was necessary, but also when completed was very much less trustworthy than it should have been.' (RG 29/3 Treasury Letter Book 1886-1907)

Of course he may have been exaggerating, bearing in mind that this was his first census and he was very inexperienced. Ten years later the

Treasury finally agreed to allow the expenditure for more of the census work to be done by experienced GRO staff, with only the less-skilled tasks entrusted to temporary workers. He managed to bring in the 1891 census at a lower cost than 1881.

The temporary Census Office was finally relocated from Craig's Court to a set of temporary buildings erected in Charles Street. These buildings were also used for the 1901 and 1911 censuses, but not in the same location – they were dismantled and re-erected in Millbank in 1899. Another innovation was that a telephone link was installed between the new buildings in Charles Street and Somerset House, which must have made life much easier for all concerned.

The only significant change in the 1881 and 1891 censuses related to questions regarding languages spoken (see Case study 6).

The 1901 census

Brydges Henniker was succeeded by Sir Reginald McLeod in 1900. He oversaw the 1901 census, organized from the relocated buildings in Millbank, now equipped with sprinklers in the event of fire. Women now formed a significant part of the workforce, and for the first time women clerks were employed to work on the 1901 census. A lady superintendent was seconded from the Post Office to be in charge of them. Some of these female clerks went on to become some of the first women to be employed permanently by the General Register Office. The War Office suggested that priority should be given to disabled ex-servicemen from the Boer War for temporary census work, although despite extensive publicity only two such men applied.

The 1901 census took the same form as that of 1891, but there had been many boundary changes during the decade, which made the administration of the census more complicated. Fortunately Ordnance Survey maps had been provided for census purposes since 1870, presumably to the great relief of George Graham in particular. A new set was provided for the planning of the 1901 census to cope with the boundary changes. The collection of maps used for census purposes dated 1870 to 1921 is held by the National Archives in record series RG 18.

The enumerator's lot

At the same time as the various Registrars General were struggling to get the resources they needed to collate, analyse and report on the results of the censuses, locally the census officials were facing an entirely different set of problems. And the most persistent difficulty was in recruiting efficient and reliable enumerators.

The lot of the nineteenth-century census enumerator was not always a happy one: some had genuine concerns about the perils of entering certain buildings. Anyone who's read the fictional works of Charles Dickens (think of Fagin's den) or the real-life accounts of poverty recorded by Henry Mayhew in his monumental study of *London Labour and the London Poor* will be only too familiar with the depredation and squalor of certain types of dwelling – the rookeries, 'backs' and cellars of industrial Victorian Britain. It's hardly surprising that some enumerators were less than happy at the prospect not just of having to enter the buildings, but of having to encourage the occupants to complete their census forms – particularly when we consider the general distrust of authority and the appallingly low standards of literacy of the times.

A letter dated 25 May 1841 from Registrar General Thomas Lister suggests that some districts were even requesting police assistance to enumerators (HO 45/146).

From time to time we come across comments and complaints written by the enumerators amongst the census records. The summary books offered the perfect forum for unhappy enumerators to voice their concerns: the enumerators could be fairly certain that their complaints would be seen by the registrars themselves. Their comments are by no means widespread, but they now form part of the official records of the census and provide us with a fascinating insight into the life of a Victorian enumerator.

By far the most regularly heard complaint was about the rate of pay. The Home Office and the Registrar General's correspondence files, and the Treasury Letter Books, include a number of letters written by dissatisfied enumerators. In 1851, as a test case, John Cohen, an enumerator from Whitechapel in east London, sued the Home Secretary Sir George Grey for the sum of 10d which he believed was owed to him. In the event, the judge found in favour of the Home Office but there was evidence of widespread dissatisfaction with the verdict (HO 45/3579).

An article in *The Times* of 20 May 1871 reported that 'the enumerators employed in taking the late Census, especially those in the more thickly-populated districts, are loud in their expression of dissatisfaction at the small amount of remuneration which has been fixed by the Government for their services, and within the last few days several meetings have been held ... with the view of taking measures to induce the Government to make some addition to the proposed rate of payment.' Feelings at the meetings seem to have run high: 'It was stated that the work which had been performed was not only difficult in many cases, but not altogether free from danger, an enumerator present having caught smallpox while discharging his duties.'

The problem of pay clearly wasn't going to go away – as late as 1931 a letter was written to *The Times* suggesting that 'the remuneration should be appreciably higher'.

These concerns come through loud and clear in some of the comments made by enumerators in the census returns themselves. Foremost amongst the ranks of belligerent enumerators was a man called Edward Henry Blade. In 1851 Blade was appointed to the post of enumerator for the parish of Allhallows, Barking, near the Tower of London. It was undeniably a larger than average Enumeration District – more than 2,000 people were crowded into the relatively small parish and Blade was expected to count and record them all single-handedly. He filled up his 84-page summary book and then started a second, completing 16 pages before launching into an astonishing diatribe:

> 'The enumeration of this district was undertaken by me in the belief that I should be fairly paid for my services. I was not aware that all the particulars were to be entered by the enumerator in a book, the work without that, being ample for the sum paid, nor had I any idea of the unreasonable amount of labour imposed. The distribution, collection etc. of the schedules together with the copying of the same, occupied between two and three hours for every 60 persons enumerated, and for this – the equivalent is – ONE SHILLING!!! ' (HO 107/1531, folio 193, page 18; plate 12).

Edward Blade certainly wasn't alone in holding feelings like this. The wonderfully named Myler Falla was employed as an enumerator for the 1871 census of Mortlake in Surrey. He used the description page of his summary book to record the following comment: 'Very badly paid.

I think if Government Officials had to do it, they would be paid treble the Amount' (RG 10/870, folio 25, page i; plate 10).

In 1861 James Haliwell, the enumerator of part of Skirkoat in Yorkshire, made a weary-sounding complaint on the last page of his summary book. After writing 'End of the Enumeration District' across the middle of page 27, he added the words: 'No more at this price' (RG 9/3285, folio 39, page 27).

George James Hall, the enumerator for part of the hamlet of Peckham, in 1861, had another large district to cover, containing nearly 300 households. He doesn't appear to have complained at all, but when he came to collect the schedule from 6 Arthur Terrace it seems that he was greeted with a less than welcoming smile by the single female inhabitant. He was able to get a name (Ann Hill) and her age (42) but no place of birth or marital status. In the occupation column he noted: 'Eccentric Lady' (RG 9/385, folio 82, page 21).

There's also no evidence that William Walker, the enumerator for part of Manchester's London Road sub-District, openly expressed any dissatisfaction about his experience, but it's clear from some of the entries in his summary book that his task was anything but straightforward. When he came to the returns for 'Pump Street Entry' he found some obstacles in his way. He listed the inhabitants of number 1 Pump Street Entry simply as a woman and her three sons; no names, no birthplaces and only approximate ages. He then went on to use the occupation column to make the following comment: 'No further information could be obtained, except that they slept in this cottage on Sunday night, April 7 1861. The cottage is 'To Let' and is left unlocked.'

Walker was able to get full details from the inhabitants of number 2 but he wasn't too convinced by their occupations. John Mulhal, the head of the household, gave his occupation as 'Top Stripper in a Card Room in a Cotton Factory', which the enumerator prefixed with the word 'Says…'. Mary Kane, the family's 20-year-old boarder, fared even worse than her landlord. For her occupation, Walker wrote: 'Says Tenter of Dyer's Frame in a Card Room (Cotton Factory). The neighbours say she is a Prostitute. She does not work' (RG 9/2944, folio 94, page 54).

But it wasn't all gloom and despondency: some enumerators actually seemed to enjoy the task that they had been asked to carry out and even took pride in what they were doing.

On 11 April 1861, *The Times* published a letter written by an enumerator who had also worked on the 1851 census. His district consisted mainly of 'tradespeople of the better class, but principally of the decent poor and the labouring class' and he remarked that his work had been made much easier by a 'great improvement in intelligence ... in the poorer neighbourhood since 1851'.

> 'In most families ... there was, if not a grown-up person, a boy or girl who had had sufficient schooling to enable them to fill up the schedule, and, failing this, it was taken to the baker's, or the publican's, or the chandler's shop, or to the rent collector ... there was an eager desire manifested to get the return of each family completed before the visit of the enumerator ... But when I came to the "upper ten thousand" of my district – those persons whom I expected would have given me the least trouble – there was hardly one in three ready for me; I was to call again, and again, and again, or to wait, so that had my district been composed entirely of this class, and of the same extent, I should have required three days instead of one to complete the enumeration.'

Ten years later, on 14 April 1871, an article in *The Cambrian* (the first English-language newspaper to be published in Wales) gave another largely positive enumerator's account. Despite expressing concerns about the accuracy of information supplied by certain groups in his community ('It is the ladies, – God bless them! of course – and the would be gentilities who have bothered me most') he concluded that:

> 'The two extremes of society performed their part towards the Census Office cheerfully and satisfactorily, and the short-comings (which have, after all, been very inconsiderable) all arose among those who were uncertain as to their social position, and feared writing themselves down in the world.'

Despite the conflicting views expressed here, when taken as a whole the above comments provide a remarkably clear picture of the major issues involved in the day-to-day operation of the census. As well as suggesting a number of ways in which the actions and opinions of some enumerators might have contributed to a degree of under-enumeration, the comments provide evidence of a genuine desire to get the job done – enough evidence, I would assert, to allow us to feel confident that the census is as complete as it could possibly have been.

A new role for the census

On 7 March 1891 Mr W. H. Primrose of the Ministry of Works wrote to the Home Office asking for permission to destroy the enumeration books from the 1861 census contained in 128 boxes stored in the roof space of the Houses of Parliament: 'As it is necessary that these papers should be removed as soon as possible I am to inquire whether they may be destroyed' (HO 45/10147/B19513; plate 13).

He wrote again in June, arguing that the enumeration books were neither necessary nor useful for research purposes: 'to attempt to verify any particular fact, or to extract further information by a reference to the Enumeration Books, would be a work of labour beyond the powers of any single individual'.

It transpired that the documents he referred to included the 1851 census as well as 1861. There seems to have been some confusion as to which government department had the power to authorize their destruction, the Local Government Board, the General Register Office or the Home Office, and the delay that this caused may have been the saving of them. The matter was referred to Brydges Henniker, and, whatever his shortcomings might have been as Registrar General, it is to his great credit that he recognized the historic importance of these records and argued strongly that they should be kept. He wrote to the Home Office on 17 June 1891:

> 'in my humble opinion it would be very unwise to destroy National records, the value of which will probably be hereafter very great to those persons who wish to investigate the condition of this country in past times. It is doubtlessly true that these documents have not been hitherto consulted. Not only, however, is it within my knowledge that they would already have been examined, had not the difficulty of access to them been so great as to be practically insuperable to a private enquirer, but I would point out that the value and utility of such records depends to a great extent upon their antiquity, and that documents which are as yet only forty years old have not yet reached their stage of full utility' (HO 45/10147/B19513; plate 14).

The documents were eventually moved to the Public Record Office, when it had space to accommodate them in its new building in

Chancery Lane. They were not opened to researchers until some decades later, but these crucial records were at least saved for posterity. It could have turned out so differently!

Not everyone shared Mr Primrose's opinion that it would be impossible to verify any fact from the enumeration books. In 1895 a man called William Paul wrote from his home in France to request a search in the 1841 census returns for proof that his mother had been born in Britain. He was born in France of British parents and had proof of his father's birth, but needed to prove that his mother was not French, so that he would not be conscripted into the French army. This was followed over the next few years by further requests for searches in early census returns, usually for legal purposes.

The first decade of the twentieth century saw the first requests for searches in old census returns, which only increased with the passing of the Old Age Pensions Act of 1908. For some elderly applicants who could provide neither birth, baptismal nor marriage certificates, entries in the census returns were accepted as proof of age. At first, the General Register Office was reluctant to provide this service, contending that this was not the purpose for which the census had been taken, and that there were great practical difficulties in searching these early enumeration books. Ultimately, though, special forms were provided for applications for searches in the census. In 1909 the enumerators books for the 1841 and 1851 Scottish censuses were transferred to Edinburgh at the request of the Scottish Registrar General. As there was no such post until 1855, these earlier Scottish censuses had been organized from London. It is perhaps a measure of his exasperation with the business of allowing searches that the then Registrar General, William Cospatrick Dunbar, told his Scottish counterpart: 'I advise you not to attempt to walk on such hazardous ice as these old censuses!'

The 1901 census was not quite the last of Victorian times (Her Majesty died on 22 January 1901, just a few weeks short of Census night), but it was very much of that era. For one thing, almost everyone in it was born in or lived through Victoria's reign. But it was also the last to be organized along the pattern established in 1841. The 1911 census was significantly different and was to usher in a completely new era of census taking in Britain.

Census returns – Scotland

The first six censuses of Scotland were administered from London. There were some slight differences in the method used to collect the information – principally the use of schoolmasters instead of Poor Law officials to distribute and collect the schedules – but for our purposes the differences are insignificant. Scotland didn't have its own Registrar General until 1855 and the 1861 census was the first to be set up under a specific census Act – the Census (Scotland) Act, 1860. Similar Acts were passed for the taking of the 1871, 1881 and 1891 censuses in Scotland but the 1901 and 1911 censuses of Scotland were taken under the terms of the Census (Great Britain) Acts of 1900 and 1910 respectively.

The passing of separate Acts made no difference to the substance of the censuses, and the questions asked and the layout of the forms in Scotland and in England and Wales remained essentially the same throughout the nineteenth century. This allowed the results to be compared both with the earlier censuses and with the returns for other parts of Great Britain.

The 1881 census saw the introduction of a question which is extremely useful for family historians. Householders were asked to write the word 'Gaelic' next to the birthplace of every individual who 'habitually' spoke Gaelic. The question seems to have been a bit of an afterthought and wasn't included on the original householders' schedules, but by 1891 it had become an intrinsic part of the census and had become more refined. This time householders were asked to give the language spoken as 'Gaelic' or 'G & E' – i.e. Gaelic & English – and the same question was repeated in 1901. A further refinement in 1911 offered three options: English only, Gaelic only or both English and Gaelic.

In all other respects, there was no significant difference between the Scottish census and its English and Welsh counterpart throughout the Victorian and Edwardian periods. The 1841 and 1851 census returns were eventually transferred to the General Register Office for Scotland (GROS) and along with the returns for the later years have remained there ever since. The GRO Scotland references to census returns are very straightforward, consisting of just three parts: the Registration District number (often including a suffix), the Enumeration District number and the page number.

Case study 1 – The Evetts

Our first case study illustrates how using the census returns can be a fairly straightforward process, utilizing the information you find in one census year to move back in time, identifying earlier generations as you go.

Our starting point is a woman named Dora Winifred Evett. She married William Fone in Aston, Warwickshire, in 1913, but our story starts with her appearance in the 1901 census as a 14-year-old girl, living in Whitmore Road in the Bordesley district of Aston (RG 13/2861 f.151 p.26). Also in the house on the night of the census were her father, Walter (a bank manager), her mother, Sarah, and her older sister, Ethel, aged 21.

A quick glance at the census page gives us an idea of the sort of neighbourhood in which the Evetts were living. Their immediate neighbours were a draper and a commercial clerk and there was a gun repairer (a distinctive West Midlands trade), a plumber and a cab driver all living nearby. Apart from the draper, everyone on the page was described as a 'worker' – i.e. employed by someone else. None of the households included a servant, but all of them were inhabited by single families. There were no boarders or lodgers and none of the families were occupying fewer than five rooms: a perfect picture of comfortable lower-middle-class life.

Dora's place of birth is given in the 1901 census as Birmingham, as is her sister's, while both of her parents were born in Shropshire. Finding the family ten years earlier in the 1891 census shouldn't prove too difficult and indeed a simple search for a Dora Evett (there's only one person of that name listed in the whole country) quickly turns up the relevant entry (RG 12/2411 f.78 p.25).

The family were living at 54 Golden Hillock Road (very close to Whitmore Road) and it's interesting to note how little has changed over ten years. William was already a bank manager in 1891 and, apart from a discrepancy over Sarah's age (she was 30 in 1891 and 44 in 1901) and a different place of birth for Ethel (Harborne, Staffordshire), the details match precisely. There's an addition to the household in 1891 – or rather, since we're working backwards here, we should probably think of it as a disappearance since that date! In 1891 the Evett family had a servant girl called Jane Hayfield living with them. Rather than suggesting that the family were in any way better off than in 1901, this probably has more to do with Sarah's need for help in looking after her four-year-old daughter, Dora.

We now move back another ten years, when we should expect to find Walter and Sarah with Ethel as a very young child. Sure enough we come across the Evetts in the 1881 census living in Harborne at 3 Regent Villas, Regent Road, with Ethel just one year old (RG 11/2958 f.73 p.34). Walter's occupation is given as 'Commercial Clerk (Banking)' and through the presence of Sarah's two unmarried sisters (Lucy and Martha) we get the added bonus of learning her maiden surname: Houlston. Sarah's age is given as 23, suggesting that the 1891 entry is probably the least reliable of the three that we now have.

Walter was entirely consistent in giving his birthplace in the 1881, 1891 and 1901 censuses as Shifnal in Shropshire. His given age was also consistent and points to a birth date of 1857 or 1858. These facts, combined with his distinctive name, allow us to search for him in earlier censuses with the confidence of being able to make a positive identification.

We find him in 1871 living at an address in Horse Fair, Shifnal, with his parents, James and Catherine (RG 10/2748 f.119 p.44). James Evett is described as a 'Surgeon not practicing' and Walter is the youngest of four children living in the house. Also in the house are two domestic servants – a housemaid and a cook – suggesting that James, despite not actively pursuing his profession, was clearly doing quite well for himself.

The 1861 census goes some way towards explaining this apparent life of leisure (RG 9/1854 f.90 p.40). The family are still (already!) living at Horse Fair in Shifnal and James's 'occupation' is given as 'Interest of Money' – he evidently had an income of some sort. There are now six children (including our Walter aged three years) and the household is again supplemented by two servants: a cook and a nurse.

The research has now reached a stage where we could head off in a number of different directions. We know that James was born in Wellington, Shropshire, so we could look for him there in earlier censuses. And if we're doing our homework properly, we would discover that there is a surviving 1821 census of Wellington held by Shropshire Archives (3129/5/5 00263): James Evett is listed there as a seven-year-old boy living with his parents and two siblings. His father was also called James Evett and he also was a surgeon.

We could also search forward in time for James and we would discover that he lived to a ripe old age and was still around for the 1901 census. He died later the same year in Yardley, Worcestershire, aged 87. We could look for Walter's siblings and find out where they went to, who they married and what children they had or we could work further back in time using the evidence from the earlier censuses to delve into the eighteenth century and beyond.

Of course, before claiming James Evett the surgeon as our ancestor, we would want to back up the details we found in the censuses with information from birth, marriage and death certificates, wills, parish registers and other nineteenth-century sources. However, you can see from the research outlined above that it's quite possible to work back through the nineteenth-century censuses, and in a matter of just a few hours trace a family back over a hundred years starting with relatively little information.

Researching a family history is not simply a lateral process. Once you start looking at a family in the census, ever-expanding avenues of research open up before you, offering virtually unlimited possibilities.

Case study 2 – The Asks

It is almost inevitable that in the course of your research you will come across at least one family where nothing about them quite seems to add up. You get to a particular event, a birth, a marriage or a census entry, and then ... nothing. The Ask family of Portsmouth – also known as the Pragnell family of Portsmouth! – provide a perfect illustration of the classic family history brick wall.

On 16 April 1892, Charles Edward Denham married Ada Ask in Portsmouth. Ada stated that her father was George Ask, a bricklayer, and gave her age as 19. At the time of the 1901 census, Charles and Ada were living at 153 Wingfield Street, Portsmouth, with two young sons, Charles and George. Ada's age was given as 27 and her place of birth as Portsmouth; from this information it wasn't too difficult to find her in the 1891 census.

She was working as a domestic servant to the Bayne family in Eaton Road, Margate, aged 17. Her surname is entered as Aske rather than Ask, but since all the other details are entirely consistent with the information from the 1901 census, we can be confident that this is the right person.

Unfortunately, this is where the trail (initially) runs cold. There's no sign of Ada in the 1881 census (when she should be aged seven) and there's no trace of a birth registration for her anywhere in the Portsmouth area – or indeed elsewhere. Perhaps more worryingly, there's no sign of George Ask (her supposed father) in any of the censuses or in the GRO's birth, marriage and death indexes.

It would be easy in a situation like this to conclude that Ada had simply been missed in the 1881 census, but that would leave a lot of other questions unanswered. And although the problem might seem unsolvable, this is exactly the sort of case where the ability to carry out searches using sophisticated online search techniques really pays dividends.

The name Ask is not particularly common – there are only seventeen 'Ask' events registered in the Portsea Island registration district during the nineteenth century. The only George Ask on the hit list is the birth of a boy called George Pragnell Ask in 1865 – clearly much too young to be Ada's father, but interesting nonetheless.

A search of the birth indexes for anyone called Ada born in Portsmouth (Portsea Island registration district) between 1873 and 1874 throws up a number of results. However, it's the entry in 1873 for a girl called Ada Pragnell that really jumps off the page and demands to be investigated further.

The 1881 census provides the first hint that this is in fact 'our' Ada. The Pragnell family (entered in the returns as Prangell) are living at 86 Lower Charlotte Street, Portsmouth, as boarders with the Pond family. Ada is there (aged nine) together with three sisters; Rosinna, Clara and Sarah. Their parents are listed as George and Pollie, although 'Pollie' turns out to be a pet name: she was usually known as Rosina (RG 11/1139 f.44 p.4; plate 16).

Ten years earlier, the Pragnell family were living at 4 George Place, Portsmouth: George and Rosina, with four children – Catherine, George, Rosaline and Clara. The births of Rosaline and Clara, as well as those of Ada and Sarah, were registered as Pragnell; however, those of the older children are in the GRO indexes under the surname Ask. So what's going on here? It appears all very confusing but, using the censuses in tandem with records of births, marriages and deaths, it's possible to put together the following story.

In 1855, Rosina Leary married a man called William Ask. William had previously been married to Julia Cox, who died in 1854, and with Rosina he had at least two children (William born in 1856 and Catherine in 1857) before he himself died in 1857.

Two years later, Rosina had an illegitimate daughter named Alice and then, sometime in the early 1860s, she met George Pragnell. There's no evidence that George and Rosina ever got married despite the fact that the 1871 and 1881 censuses both describe Rosina as George's wife. The registration of their son as George Pragnell Ask in 1865 suggests that they were together but not legally married at that stage.

George's birth was followed by the arrival of Rosaline (in 1867), Clara (1870), Ada (1873) and Sarah (1875) – all registered as Pragnell. Ada's birth certificate describes her mother as Rosina Pragnell, late Ask, formerly Leary. George Pragnell died in 1885, and at the time of the 1891 census Rosina is in the Portsea Island Union Workhouse, listed as a widow and a pauper (RG 12/860 f.91 p.4; plate 17). Her name is given as Rosina Ask. At some stage, the whole family seem to have reverted to the name Ask, even those who were actually George Pragnell's biological children. When Ada gave her father's name as George Ask, this was in fact an amalgam of her mother's two partners – William Ask and George Pragnell.

Rosina certainly seems to have had a hard life. She had at least eight children by two (possibly three) men and ended up in the workhouse.

She was born on the Isle of Wight (although the 1881 census is the only one to indicate this) and the 1841 and 1851 censuses both find her living there. In 1841, aged just eight years, Rosina was in the Isle of Wight 'House of Industry' in Newport. Ten years later she was still there, now described as a prostitute (HO 107/1663 f.394 p.8; plate 15). She eventually left the workhouse to marry into a life of poverty across the Solent in Portsmouth – for Rosina, this almost certainly represented a step up in the world.

2

THE 1911 CENSUS

The 1911 census may not have been the first census of the new century, but it was certainly the first of a new age of information gathering. Every census from 1861 to 1901 had been very similar to its predecessor, with only small variations and additions. In 1911, however, a completely new approach was taken by the General Register Office as it embarked on a much more ambitious project.

The need for national information

There had always been pressure from the Statistical Branch of the GRO and elsewhere for more questions to be added to each successive census. There were even proposals for a census to be taken every five years instead of ten, but the Treasury would not sanction the expenditure. Furthermore the manual methods of processing the collected data had reached their limits by 1901. There was now even more demand for information about the state of the nation's health, and there were serious concerns at the decline in the birth rate during the last decade of the nineteenth century. Combined with the scale of emigration, there were fears that Britain would fall behind the rising economies of countries such as Germany and the USA. A modern industrial nation with an empire to run needed a large and a healthy workforce. There was also the matter of the armed forces: many of the men who volunteered for the army in the Boer War of 1899–1902 had been rejected as physically unfit. Surveys such as those conducted by Booth in London and Rowntree in York, combined with the GRO's own statistics, confirmed that the health and living conditions of the poorer classes in Britain were very bad indeed. Despite the many improvements in public health, housing and education during the latter half of the nineteenth century, the health of poor children was not significantly better than it had been in the 1840s, and infant mortality was still very high. There was now wider acceptance of the idea that government should intervene to improve the lives of the working classes, and the first step to solving a problem is to find out the nature and extent of it, so there was an increasingly urgent need for more and more detailed information.

The climate of opinion in the country was beginning to move in favour of state intervention, eventually leading to the modern Welfare State. For example, charitable organizations like the Salvation Army, and some local school boards, began to provide meals for needy children, and in 1906 a Liberal government was elected which was committed to reform. Health checks on schoolchildren were introduced, and at the other end of the age scale Old Age Pensions were introduced in 1908. This particular measure greatly increased the number of requests for searches in the Victorian census returns – an episode which appears to have exasperated the Registrar General, William Dunbar. The work involved in searching in these old census returns was considerable, and the GRO was understandably reluctant to carry them out, claiming that this was not the purpose for which the census had been taken. However, census evidence was essential to provide proof of age for some of the pension applicants, many of whom were too old to have birth certificates. Baptism certificates were acceptable, but many people did not know the exact place of their birth or baptism, which could be supplied from what their parents had put down in the census when they were children. In other cases there was no baptism record, and the census itself was the only documentary evidence of age. In the end the GRO had not only to conduct the searches but also to provide application forms for the purpose.

The census was the ideal method to gather the detailed information that was now required by the government. However, William Dunbar was the first Registrar General who did not have to oversee the administration of a census, being replaced by Sir Bernard Mallet in 1909.

Boundary changes

The preparations for the 1911 census had been started in 1908, and the Census Office reopened at Millbank in 1909. One of the problems identified early on was that of the many boundary changes that had taken place since 1901. In fact there had always been boundary changes between census years, but there had never been a thorough review, only piecemeal changes. This was partly caused by the fact that the census was administered through the Registration Service of the GRO, whose own districts and sub-Districts had never been subject to any comprehensive revision, but were altered at odd intervals, usually to coincide with the resignation or retirement of individual registrars. This in turn was because the registrars were not salaried, but paid according to the number of events registered and certificates issued. Therefore the reduction in size of a district would directly affect a registrar's income, so it was much easier to split a district that had grown too large into more manageable units when he or she left office. This was compounded by the instructions that had previously been circulated to registrars regarding the 'Plans of Division' to divide their sub-Districts into census Enumeration Districts. Up to 1891, they had always advised registrars to 'retain as far as possible same Enumeration Districts as used at the previous census'. This was dropped from the instructions in 1901, but, owing to the limited time available for preparation, few substantial revisions were actually made. Lack of preparation time was a recurring problem with every census, since a separate Act of Parliament had to be passed each time until the Census Act of 1920 finally established a permanent Census Office. By 1911 the situation was even worse, according to a lengthy memorandum on the improvement and revision of census methods:

> 'At present a limited number of Enumeration Districts contain parts of two or more
> Administrative Counties
> Civil Parishes
> Urban Districts
> Wards of Urban Districts
> Rural Districts
>
> In all such cases the Enumeration Districts should where possible, be rearranged so that in future no Enumeration Districts should comprise parts of two or more Administrative Areas of a like kind.' (RG 19/45)

Machine tabulation

The same document, dated 1908–1909, recommended that the practice of filling out enumeration books should be retained, despite its disadvantages compared with that of machine tabulation directly from the household schedules. So it was at a late stage in the planning that the decision was taken to dispense with them after all. The new Registrar General, Sir Bernard Mallet, took a keen interest in the statistical functions of the department, and was also President of the Royal Statistical Society. He was in favour of using tabulation machines, which had already been used for processing census information in other countries. Sir Bernard and his Superintendent of Statistics, Thomas Stevenson, travelled to Washington, DC, where machines had been used in tabulating census data for some years, to see them in action. As a result of their visit they decided to use 'Hollerith' machines made by the British Tabulating Machine Company (plate 18).

Using a completely new system to process the information from the census schedules was not without its problems, and there were many 'teething problems', but the results were worth the extra effort and expense. The advantages were considerable. First of all, the errors and ambiguities that could result from the enumerators' copying were eliminated at a stroke. Secondly, tabulating by machine meant that more questions could be included in the schedule, and the data could also be cross-referenced and sorted in a number of ways. As a result, the household schedules for 1911 could record up to 19 separate pieces of information for each individual. Some of these were simply extra levels of detail, such as in the data on occupations; people were now asked to give the kind of trade or industry they worked in, as well as their actual occupation. Much more accurate figures could now be obtained, because a bookkeeper, for example, who worked in a cotton mill, could now be listed under both categories, depending on the particular information that was being sought.

Administering the census

Lengthy and detailed instructions were produced for all the groups of people involved in the administration of the census. These included registrars, enumerators, masters of vessels and institutions, and the police, who between them were responsible for distributing and collecting the information from individuals; the police were involved because they had to collect details as best they could on anyone found in 'a barn, shed, kiln etc, or under a railway arch, on stairs accessible to the public, or wandering without a shelter'. This category would include any suffragettes who appeared to be carrying out their threatened boycott of the census.

The instructions to the householders were of course printed on the schedules themselves, but the GRO did not rely on these alone to convey information about the census to the population at large. Perhaps in view of the increasing complexity of the questions, they made extensive use of other means of publicity. Circulars were sent to editors of provincial newspapers enclosing copies of the detailed memoranda sent to enumerators appealing for 'accurate completion of the occupation column on census schedules' relating to the predominant industries in their areas. These memoranda and other material were also sent to schoolteachers for them to use in the classroom, explaining to the children how the census was to be carried out and why it was important that it should be taken accurately. The explanatory notes suggested 'that the instructions given therein should, as far as possible, be expounded with special reference to the prevailing trades or industries of the district'.

In addition to the usual schedules printed in Welsh, in 1911 the GRO for the first time produced special householders' schedules translated into German and Yiddish. Registrars 'in certain quarters of the East End of London, and in some towns where there are considerable numbers of Jewish aliens', were encouraged to select enumerators with some knowledge of Yiddish and copies of the translated schedules were forwarded to the registrars in the relevant districts. The schedules were to be presented to any householder who had a difficulty with the English language, along with a copy of the schedule in English. A letter from the Census Office dated March 1911 emphasized that 'it must be clearly understood that the English schedule must be filled up and not the translated copies'. The enumerators were also expected to offer assurance that the census was 'not for the purpose of taxation, not for enforcing military service, and not on account of religion'.

Despite all the detailed instructions, preliminary examination of the collected returns revealed many mistakes and omissions. On 30 June

1911 Bernard Mallet wrote to the Treasury: 'I have therefore reluctantly come to the conclusion that it will be necessary to examine the whole of the returns, and correct them where necessary.' He went on to ask for funds to employ ten extra female checkers, since in his judgement the work would be better performed by them than by male clerks. Moreover, he added, they could eventually be discharged on a week's notice.

As in previous census years institutions such as workhouses and industrial schools were enumerated separately using special institutional schedules. The questions asked on these schedules were in essence the same as those on the standard householders' schedules. The significant difference from the process with householders is that people's details were entered into enumeration books by the relevant official (as in previous years) and although there are associated enumerators' summary books (ESBs), these only record the basic statistical details.

The enumeration of people on board vessels both in the Merchant Navy and the Royal Navy was carried out in the same way as in previous census years.

Once collected, the schedules were sent to the Census Office in Millbank where a whole army of coders, clerks and punchers all played their part in processing and tabulating the data. Although the stage of copying into enumeration books had been eliminated, a whole new operation had to be included, that of coding information into numbers in preparation for punching onto cards (plate 19). This was a skilled job, carried out by experienced clerks, who wrote the numbers that appear on the schedules in pencil. By contrast, the punch card operators were recruited from girls leaving elementary schools in the area around Millbank at Easter 1911. The instructions to the coding clerks occupied several pages, while those for the 'girl punchers' comprised a single sheet. This single page, however, included the important instruction that the same code should be used for suffragettes and vagrants.

'Fertility in marriage'?

Despite the increase in the number of questions asked in 1911, much of the basic information remained the same as it had been throughout the Victorian period. The greatest innovation, however, was the addition of questions on fertility in marriage. Married women were asked to state how long they had been married, the number of children born of the current marriage, the number of those children who were still alive and the number who had died.

These questions had been a feature of the American census since 1890, and may have been directly inspired by Mallet and Stephenson's visit to Washington. This was not merely a new area of enquiry, but would be the first time that the census both recorded a moment in time, and asked people about their behaviour in the past. Using this data, we should now be able to trace marriage records more easily, assuming of course that the information is accurate. It should also be easy to work out whether a man's wife was also the mother of any or all of his children, which would not be obvious from the rest of the information in the census schedule.

This is well illustrated by an entry in the 1911 census showing David Bridges and his wife Laura living at 2 Church Road, Gillingham, Kent. David was aged 60 and employed as a dockyard labourer, while Laura was 54. The entry indicates that she had been married to David for only six years and that there were no children from the marriage. But David had two young grandchildren in the household and if the schedule hadn't included the information indicating a relatively recent marriage, it would be all too easy to assume that the couple had been married much longer and that Laura was also grandmother to the two young grandchildren. A search of the 1901 census finds David as a lodger without any other family members present, but describes him as a married man, which does nothing to contradict this assumption. Of course, the information in the census may not always be accurate, but the detail in 1911 about the marriage and children suggests that further investigation is necessary (RG 14/3937/213).

Another entry in the 1911 census reinforces how useful the information about marriages is going to be to family historians. The Coomber family of Chiddingstone, Kent, is headed by Ellen, a widow, aged 101. Her son Ira is 62, but has only been married to his wife Caroline for 4 years 7 months – the census only asks for whole years but the Coombers obligingly give more detail, and a search in the GRO's marriage indexes shows that this is indeed accurate, at least with regard to the date, but the correct spelling of the family name appears to be Camber, not Coomber. Ira Camber appears in the 1901 census with his widowed mother and his first wife, Eliza, but since the enumerator has (very clearly) copied his forename as 'Tar' he could prove difficult to find by means of a name search, so once again the 1911 census alerts the researcher to a late second marriage that might otherwise be missed (RG 14/4034/118).

Occupational data

Another innovation in the 1911 census was the request for additional information about each individual's occupation. If all we had been given was the 'Trade or Industry' in which our ancestors were employed, this would have been useful enough, but it appears that a significant number of householders misinterpreted this question as a request for the name of their employers.

So William Bailey of 24 Duncombe Street, Moston near Manchester, not only gives his occupation in great detail (Water Softening Plant Attendant) but also tells us that he worked for the Lancashire & Yorkshire Railway Company (RG 14/24246/142; plate 20).

Arthur Owen of 79 Inniskillin Road, Plaistow, and his boarder William Duffin both gave their occupations as 'General Labourer' but they then went on to very helpfully inform us that they actually worked for the Gas, Light & Coke Company (RG 14/9445/301).

Arthur's near neighbour, Harry Holmes of 100 Olive Road, Plaistow, was similarly obliging in stating that he carried out his trade of a stonemason with the Port of London Authority (RG 14/9448/105).

Again, it is almost certain that many more examples of this will crop up as we delve deeper into the 1911 census, offering unexpected additional information about some of our ancestors.

The records

For family historians the biggest change between this and previous censuses is that what we're looking at in the 1911 census are the actual forms that our ancestors completed, in their own handwriting and with their own errors and, occasionally, their own, unasked-for additional comments. For the first time the census has become a primary, and not a secondary, source for the researcher.

The 1911 census returns actually comprise two sets of documents: the bound volumes of householders' schedules and an associated series of enumerators' summary books (ESBs). The good news is that the two sets of records have a one-to-one relationship; each ESB has a corresponding set of schedules.

The link between the two sets of documents is through a unique three-part reference number which is made up of the following items:

- Registration Ristrict number
- Registration sub-District number
- Enumeration District number

The enumerators' summary books include all the information which, in earlier censuses, was contained in the first section of the summary books, i.e. a description of the Enumeration District, listing local subdivisions, the boundary of the Enumeration District and a list of the streets covered by it. This was followed by a set of instructions to the enumerator and a number of examples of how to complete the book.

The main section of the ESBs contains the summary pages, comprising a list of the properties included in the Enumeration District. All properties are listed whether or not a census schedule was completed. Schedule numbers are given, as well as the address of each household, the type of property (i.e. domestic, shop, office, etc.), the surname of the head of the household, the title of the head (Mr, Mrs, Miss, Dr, etc.) and a summary of the number of males and females in each household.

At the back of the ESBs are the enumerator's abstract pages, which were used to add up the totals from the summary pages in order to produce the final figures for the district. The last page contains the Statutory Declaration which was signed and dated by the enumerator and the registrar.

The householders' schedules were bound into volumes, arranged by Enumeration Districts, each bound volume of schedules corresponding to an ESB as outlined above. The instructions on how to complete the form were quite clear, but it's obvious that they weren't always strictly adhered to and the quality of the information supplied varies greatly from one schedule to the next – as does the neatness and legibility of the handwriting.

As we saw in the previous chapter, householders had been completing their own census schedules since 1841 and it's certain that their forms would have contained additional unsolicited comments as well as a whole range of errors and inaccuracies. But whereas in previous census years many of these errors (and almost all of the extraneous comments) would have been 'edited out' by the diligent army of enumerators, in 1911 they have largely survived – warts and all! Some attempt seems to have been made (whether by the enumerator, the registrar or the clerks at the Census Office is not clear) to score through the incorrect entries but mostly the original data is still perfectly legible.

So when, for example, a widow erroneously enters the details of the duration of her marriage and the number of children born to it, we can still make use of this information even if it shouldn't have been given and has been partly obscured.

Jane Scully of 10 West Bank Street, Salford, provides a good example of how this works in practice. As a widow, she shouldn't have entered the number of children she had borne – 12, 11 of them living – but it is fortunate that she did, because only seven of them are present in the household, and they were all born in Ireland, so she has helpfully told us that she had four other children somewhere that we might otherwise not have known about (RG 14/24046/96).

The National Archives' reference for the 1911 census schedules consists of three parts: the series number (RG 14), the piece number, and the schedule number. The ESBs are in a separate record series (RG 78).

Civil disobedience

Throughout the first decade of the twentieth century there was increasing political activity from trades unions and other radical groups. The Labour Party was formed in 1900 and, three years later, the Women's Social and Political Union was founded, with the aim of campaigning for women's suffrage. Although the Suffragettes are remembered for their militant activities during this period, it is perhaps less well known that it wasn't until after the First World War that all adult males finally got the vote and there was continuing agitation from this direction too. It was the Suffragettes, however, who had the idea of boycotting the 1911 census as part of their campaign. The boycott was probably not as successful as they might have hoped, but it certainly earned them a great deal of publicity. The idea may have come from Emmeline Pankhurst, a registrar of births and deaths from 1898 to 1907, and had therefore been involved in the administration of the 1901 census.

To what degree Suffragettes and their supporters were actually successful in avoiding the census is not clear, but a number of instances of civil disobedience have already been discovered by seemingly ordinary householders. In one such case, a householder from Edmonton refused to complete his form as he felt that it was wrong for the women in his house to be asked to provide personal information when they were not allowed to vote. His refusal resulted in some frenzied correspondence between the enumerator, the registrar and the Census Office. The householder declared that he had no disagreement with the enumerator or the registrar but that he had no intention of completing the form: if the registrar had to press charges he would be quite happy to face the consequences. Eventually, the Census Office instructed the registrar to obtain as much information as he could about the family. As the local registrar of births and deaths, he was able to get accurate information about the children in the family but some of the details about the older members of the household are pure guesswork. The result of all this is that there are two schedules in the records; firstly, the original 'spoilt' by the householder and, secondly, the registrar's effort.

The benefits of the 1911 census

A significant feature of the 1911 census is the fact that it can be used in conjunction with another major record source of around the same date, namely, the Valuation Office Survey, also known as 'Lloyd George's Domesday'. As the name suggests, this was a survey to establish the value of property throughout England and Wales for Estate Duty purposes, carried out following the 1910 Finance Act, when David Lloyd George was Chancellor of the Exchequer. Since the survey was done at around the same time as the census, it should be possible to find out a great deal about the actual buildings that your ancestors inhabited, once you've found their address in the census. Conversely, local and house historians using the Valuation Office records can use the 1911 census to find out more about people and communities. The records for England and Wales are held at the National Archives, and enquiries about the records of the survey in Scotland and Ireland should be referred to the National Archives of Scotland and the Public Record Office of Northern Ireland respectively.

Another benefit of this census relates to the fact that just three and a half years after the 1911 census was taken, war broke out in Europe. This was the 'war to end all wars' and despite the common assertion that it would be 'over by Christmas', as we know, it actually raged on for another four years, by which time nearly a million Britons had lost their lives. The vast majority of these men will be listed in the 1911 census, providing us with a poignant glimpse of Britain's lost generation.

And it's not just the hundreds of thousands of volunteers and conscripts who signed up for the duration of the war that we'll be able to trace. The 1911 census has one final treat in store for us. While previous censuses had done no more than provide a headcount of the officers and men of the British Army, the 1911 census saw a hugely significant development. For the first time, a full enumeration of the British Army serving Queen and country overseas, in such places as India, South Africa, the West Indies and Ireland, was carried out. Names, ages, marital status, birthplaces: all the usual information is recorded in 23 volumes of schedules, as are the details of the wives and families who had accompanied the men on the often perilous journeys to the far flung corners of the earth.

National Archives census references 1841–1901

Throughout this book you will see mention of census 'references.' In fact, each page of the census records has a unique reference, which reflects how the documents are organized. A typical census reference might look something like: RG 9/566, folio 74, page 3 (or perhaps condensed into RG 9/566/74/3). What does this mean?

- Each census reference starts with a **series code**, which applies to all census records for that year. The 1841 and 1851 censuses share the code HO 107, the 1861 census has RG 9, the 1871 has RG 10 etc.
- The enumeration books for a census year are collected into a number of 'pieces,' each covering a particular area, and each with a unique **piece number**. This forms the second part of the reference.
- Within the piece, each sheet of paper has a unique **folio number** stamped on it – this number is on the top of the right-hand page, but also applies to the page on the back of that sheet. Folio numbers run sequentially through an entire piece.
- Within each Enumeration District, each page has a unique **page number**.

More information about census references will be found on p. 252.

Case study 3 – The Peters

The nineteenth century was a period of huge social change and the census returns provide an excellent illustration of one aspect of this. Between 1801 and 1901 the population of Great Britain nearly quadrupled, but it's not just the overall increase that is significant here. At the start of the nineteenth century, nearly three-quarters of the population lived in rural areas. By the end of it, however, a dramatic shift had taken place: the 1901 census revealed that 74 per cent of people now lived in towns and cities.

There are a number of factors behind this change. The development of the railways, improvements in communications and some quite spectacular advances in the world of science and technology combined to transform Britain from a predominantly rural society into the most urbanized nation in the world – all in the space of just one hundred years.

The Peters family had lived in Gloucestershire for hundreds of years, making their homes in a number of small parishes in and around the Tewkesbury/Newent area. On 18 January 1801, just a few short months before the first UK census was taken, a boy named Richard Peters was baptized at St Michael's church in the parish of Tirley. The population of Tirley, as recorded in the 1801 census, was just 405, increasing to 550 by the time of the 1841 census. This was very much a rural area and the census shows that a significant proportion of the inhabitants were employed either in agriculture or, thanks to Tirley's location on the River Severn, as fishermen or watermen.

Richard Peters married Elizabeth Geers in the adjacent parish of Deerhurst in 1820, and the following year their son John was born. The 1841 census finds Richard and Elizabeth living back in Tirley with four children (HO 107/354/28 f. 10 p. 13). Richard was a shoemaker by trade, but the majority of his immediate neighbours were agricultural labourers. He continued to live in Tirley until his death in 1862, but his older brother James was more adventurous.

James Peters married Martha Gannaway in Tewkesbury in 1818, but in the late 1830s he moved to London, settling in the Paddington area. His son Peter was a shoemaker, like his father and uncle before him, and although he stayed in the London area, he moved away from the city to the slightly more rural surroundings of Staines, Middlesex.

Richard's son John meanwhile had also left Tirley, and in April 1841 he married Amelia Cox in Harborne, Staffordshire. Two months later the young couple were living in Oldbury (HO 107/908/11 f. 24. p. 7), which was then in Shropshire (it was transferred to Worcestershire in 1844 but continued to form part of the West Bromwich registration district which was in Staffordshire!). By the time of the 1851 census John and Amelia had settled in Rowley Regis, Staffordshire (HO 107/2028 f. 38 p. 15). They had seemingly developed an unusual taste in boys' names: their first three children rejoiced in the names Theophilus, John Eliphaz and Zenas!

John Peters had kept up the family tradition of shoemaking, but the 1861 census shows that two of his sons were employed in the local iron works. He lived the rest of his life in Rowley Regis, dying in 1903 at the age of 81.

His sons John Eliphaz and Zenas moved to Spennymoor in County Durham. It was almost certainly the prospect of work in the rapidly expanding Tudhoe Iron Works that prompted these two young men to make the journey to the Northeast. They were not alone: the census tells us that the population of the parish of Tudhoe (which included Spennymoor) increased from just 400 in 1861 to over 5,000 twenty years later.

In the 1871 census the Peters brothers are recorded as boarders living with the Perry family – fellow exiles from Staffordshire – in the Mount Pleasant area of Tudho (RG 10/4964 f. 78 p. 5). Tragically, John Elpihaz died in 1872, aged only 28, and soon after Zenas seems to have moved back to Staffordshire. On 5 May 1873 he married Margaret Parkin at St Giles' church in the parish of Rowley Regis. Margaret was originally from Tudhoe, and we can only speculate as to why the couple married in Staffordshire and not in Margaret's native Durham. There's also an intriguing suggestion that Margaret may previously have been married to John Eliphaz Peters, but this is one problem that the census returns can't answer. It's important to remember that a lot can happen to a family over a ten-year period. The census is simply a snapshot, recording the population on a single day.

Zenas and Margaret remained in Staffordshire for a few years (their first two children, Flora and Thomas, were born there). However, they soon moved back north and the 1881 census finds them living with Margaret's parents in Tudhoe (RG 11/4921 f. 70 p. 64). Another tragedy was soon to strike the Peters family as Margaret died later that year, aged only 29.

Zenas moved back to Rowley Regis once more, where he had a further four children with his second wife, Caroline Deeley.

Our final subject here is Flora Peters – Zenas and Margaret's oldest child, who was living with her parents in Tudhoe in 1881. Ten years later Flora was working as a domestic servant to the Major family in Handsworth, Staffordshire (RG 12/226/ f.64 p. 18). In 1894 she married Albert Holmes, a widower from Birmingham and a bookbinder by trade; by the time of the 1901 census he was employed as a foreman bookbinder. The family – Albert, Flora and their first four children, Mabel, Hilda, Irene and Cyril – were living in Walsall (RG 13/2704 f. 98 p. 13), but they were soon on the move again. Their youngest daughter, Dorothy Flora Holmes, was born in Birkenhead, Cheshire, in 1907.

The 1911 census finds the Holmes family living at 11 Frodsham Street, Tranmere (RG 14/22008/189). Albert was away from home at the time and until the census is fully indexed, we won't know exactly where he was.

Starting with Dorothy Flora Holmes and her mother Flora Peters, we have now traced the family back over 100 years. Over that period we found the family living in seven counties: Gloucestershire, Shropshire, Worcestershire, Staffordshire, Durham, Cheshire and Middlesex. We also saw them move from the village of Tirley in rural Gloucestershire to the 'dark satanic mills' of the West Midlands and then to the booming industrial Northeast. The story of the Peters family may be exceptional, but it serves well to illustrate the transformation that took place in nineteenth-century Britain.

Case Study 4 – The Jewish East End

Many Jewish families migrated into the East End of London during the nineteenth century and the first decade of the twentieth century. By 1911 there were so many recent Jewish immigrants from Eastern Europe that census schedules were translated into German and Yiddish to help with the enumeration of this community (RG 27/8; plate 21). These schedules were not for the actual enumeration, which was always carried out using the English version, but to help explain to these newly arrived immigrants what was required of them. In fact since 1891 the census authorities had been assisted by Jewish organizations with the translation and distribution of information circulars and schedules into Yiddish, Hebrew and German. Many of the recent arrivals were refugees from oppression, and it was feared that they might be reluctant to fill in the papers, particularly with details of their foreign birthplaces. However, as a result of the co-operation of the Chief Rabbi, the Board of Guardians of British Jews and others, the GRO was confident that accurate returns were obtained from the Jewish parts of the East End of London (RG 27/6 and RG 19/11).

In 1911 Abraham Lazarus Shedletsky and his family lived at 37 Lolsworth Buildings, 79 Commercial Street (RG 14/1459/30; plate 22). The ages and birthplaces of his children show that they must have arrived in England in the late 1890s. Abraham was a kosher butcher aged 42, and his wife Deborah, who was a year younger, helped him in his business. They and their 16-year-old son Lewis had been born in 'Russia (Poland)', but their other children were born in Whitechapel: David, 12; Deborah, 10; Samuel, 6; and Fanny, 5. As a married woman, Deborah was asked for the duration of her current marriage and the number of children, living and dead, of that marriage. She had been married 22 years, and in addition to the five children present in the census she had given birth to two others who had since died. The family seems to have been doing well in their adopted homeland because Abraham was in business on his own account and they could afford for their eldest son to be a student of theology and not earning a wage at the age of 16. They also had a servant, Annie Nehmann, who was born in 'Russia (Lithuania)'. The birthplace information is interesting because Russia is often used to indicate the whole Russian Empire, extending well beyond the borders of Russia itself. In this case more specific information is supplied, but it is worth remembering that a birthplace given as Russia might be Lithuania, Latvia, Poland, Ukraine or one of a number of other places.

The 1901 census shows that the Shedletsky family was at the same address in Commercial Street (RG 13/298 f. 30 p. 4). Abraham was already well established in his business, since he is described as an employer, and they have a servant. The names are recorded a little differently from 1911, although this is undoubtedly the same family. Abraham and his son Lewis appear in exactly the same way, but his wife Deborah appears as Dorah, his son David as Davis, and his three-month-old daughter Deborah as 'Berby'. When comparing any other two census years, we might suspect that the man had married twice, first to Dorah and then to Deborah, but the information collected in 1911 about the length of the marriage means we can be sure this is the same woman.

The birthplaces are simply given as 'Russia' in 1901, the Shedletsky family being described as Russian subjects, but in 1911 they describe themselves as naturalized British subjects. Such claims often turn out to be untrue, but in this case they have included the date of naturalization, 1903, which gives a ring of truth. Sure enough, a search in the National Archives' online catalogue reveals that Certificate of Naturalization 13938 was issued to Abraham Shedletsky on 23 November 1903 (HO 144/718/110322).

A number of other immigrants who had become British subjects added the year of naturalization to their 1911 census schedules. Another such example was Esther Cohen, a widow and provisions dealer at 25 Wentworth Street, Spitalfields (RG 14/1466/24). She was born in Russia, but all of her five children – Rachel, Augusta, Blumah, Solomon and Jessie, ranging in age from 14 down to 5 years old – had been born in Spitalfields. As a widow, she was not asked for the duration of her current marriage, or the number of children she had borne. However, she misunderstood the question and gave the information anyway, and her confusion is our gain. She had married 15 years previously, and as well as the five children present in 1911 there had been another child who died. Like the Shedletsky family, the Cohens had occupied the same address since 1901, when Esther's husband Joseph was still alive. Joseph had been a little older than Esther, 30 years old to her 27, and both described themselves as Russian subjects who had been born in Russia (RG 13/299 f.127 p.17). In 1911 Esther gave 1904 as her year of naturalization, which is the year when Joseph was naturalized.

These two families were not typical of Jewish migrant families in London; more prosperous than most, they also went to the trouble and expense of becoming naturalized. However, the extra details gathered in 1911 are particularly helpful with regard to all migrant families because foreign nationals were asked, for the first time, whether they were resident in this country or only visiting. There was a tendency to give more detail than was asked for, perhaps because the schedules were more complicated. Perhaps people took the view that when in doubt, it was better to give too much information than too little. Whatever the reason, it makes the release of the 1911 census very exciting for researchers.

3

WHY CAN'T I FIND MY ANCESTOR?

One of the most frequent comments we hear in the reading rooms at the National Archives is something along the lines of 'Oh, my ancestors weren't on the 1891 census'. The aim of this section of the book is to convince you that if they were living in the country at the time of the census, then they were almost certainly recorded and, unless you are particularly unlucky, you should be able to find them. The odds are very firmly stacked in your favour.

Civil disobedience

It is an undeniable fact that some individuals were genuinely missed out of the returns and we'll start by taking a brief look at some of the reasons why and how this might have happened, beginning with the associated issues of active avoidance of the census and an individual's refusal to give the required information to the enumerator.

The first of these would have been relatively hard to achieve: even in the early years of the census, the system was fairly watertight. The registrars recruited local people to be enumerators – people with an intimate knowledge of their areas, who were expected to be familiar with the whereabouts of every house, however large or small.

Refusing to give information to the census takers was an offence: the legislation was quite clear on this point. Clause XXIV of the 1851 Census Act stated that 'every Person refusing to answer or wilfully giving a false Answer to such Questions or any of them shall for every such Refusal or wilfully false Answer forfeit a Sum not exceeding Five Pounds nor less than Twenty Shillings'.

Every now and then an example crops up in the census returns themselves. The enumerator for the parish of St Swithin's in the City of

London in 1841 entered the following note on page 6 of his summary book regarding one of the inhabitants of St Swithin's Lane: 'John Travers will not give any information respecting the persons who abode in his house on the night of June 6th only that the number was 12 (males) 5 (females).' A later note added by the registrar on the same page states: 'Mr Travers fined Five Pounds at the Mansion House by Sir Peter Laurie. June 23-1841. Alfred Nelson Wickes, Registrar' (HO 107/723/12, folio 6, page 6; plate 23).

The Registrar General at the time of the 1851 census (George Graham) appears to have adopted a more relaxed view than his predecessor: 'I treat these cases of obstinacy as more or less connected with insanity; and being isolated cases not very frequently met with, I do not think it necessary to prosecute the recusants.'

Nevertheless, from time to time we do come across instances of civil disobedience in the records. In 1861 the enumerator of Highgate in north London evidently had some problems when he came to call for the census forms at the house of a coal merchant called Thomas Lea. Thomas had provided the required information about himself, his wife, their twelve children, a visitor and three servants but a fourth servant, Elizabeth Green, was (initially) less forthcoming. The enumerator made a note at the foot of the page stating: 'Elizabeth Green refuses to state her age or place of birth.' This was later crossed through and the words 'afterwards gave particulars' were entered together with the missing details (RG 9/792, folio 146, page 44; plate 24).

The number of people in this category remained low and all the evidence suggests that the chances of your ancestors having avoided the census are slim.

Under-enumeration?

Of course not all the enumerators employed to undertake the task were as efficient as we might hope. It's inevitable that the system *did* break down from time to time and that some properties and certain individuals living at a particular address may have been missed out altogether. As we saw in Chapter 1, there were some enumerators who were less than happy about having to enter certain buildings to deliver and collect their schedules.

One group of people who were particularly vulnerable to omission from the census were lodgers and boarders – more correctly, these are in fact two distinct groups and the instructions for enumerating them were quite clear: lodgers were supposed to be issued with their own schedules, whereas boarders should be included on the householder's schedule. But it's not too difficult to see how a householder could omit to include such people who were not strictly part of the household.

In the spring of 1851, Charles Darwin's beloved daughter Annie fell seriously ill with a stomach complaint. On 28 March, Darwin took Annie, together with her younger sister Henrietta (Ettie) and their nurse Jessie Brodie, by train from London's Euston Station to Worcester, from where they travelled on to the spa town of Great Malvern. The idea behind the trip was for Annie to spend a month in Malvern, taking the waters under the supervision of Doctor James Gully, a specialist in this developing area of medicine. After getting the girls settled in lodgings at Montreal House, on the Worcester Road, Charles returned to London, intending to stay for a few weeks with his brother, Erasmus.

The landlady of the lodging house was called Eliza Partington and we know from a letter which Ettie wrote to her mother the following week that there were 'a great many ladies' in the house at the time.

The girls arrived in Malvern on Thursday afternoon – just three days before the 1851 census was due to be taken. The schedules had almost certainly been distributed to the householders by then and it may be that the ultra-efficient landlady immediately completed her form, listing all the people then living in her lodging house. Perhaps Annie, Ettie and nurse Brodie arrived after the form had been filled in – their names certainly do not appear in the census for Montreal House. We know, beyond reasonable doubt, that they were staying there on the night of the census, but the only people listed in the returns for the lodging house are Eliza Partington (described as a Lodging House Keeper) and her two servants, along with four female visitors (presumably the 'ladies' mentioned in Ettie's letter) and one of their servants.

A sad postscript is that Annie's treatment was not successful. She died on 23 April, without returning home from Malvern.

This is as close as you can get to incontrovertible evidence of under-enumeration in the census, but it's only possible to prove that the girls and their nurse were omitted thanks to the existence of contemporary sources such as the letter written by Ettie and Darwin's own diaries. Proving that your own ancestors were missed in this way might be rather more troublesome.

My personal feeling is that this sort of instance was rare. Of course, the system was run by fallible human beings, but the General Register Office was a model of Victorian efficiency managed by a succession of gifted and dedicated men. The very idea of a significant number of people being allowed to slip through the net would have felt like failure to men like George Graham and Brydges Henniker. (It's interesting to note here that statisticians have often argued that any shortfall in the population count caused by these deficiencies in the system would almost certainly be balanced out by the number of people who were recorded twice!)

Beyond the seas?

Failure to find a family in the census can inspire researchers to come up with all kinds of elaborate 'solutions'. One that is frequently suggested is that they may have been temporarily absent from the country – and for a certain class of person this is a distinct possibility. As a possible explanation for why an agricultural labourer from Wiltshire is missing, however, it lacks a certain credibility!

Members of the upper classes (and increasingly through the nineteenth century, the middle classes) may have had cause to travel overseas – either for pleasure or for business. Of course, soldiers in the British Army, sailors and fishermen, by the very nature of their work, would have spent some time out of the country and there was a small body of 'unsuccessful emigrants' who left to start a new life and later returned to the United Kingdom. But by and large, the vast majority of the population would never have set foot on any foreign shore.

Occasionally you might get a clue from a later census to suggest that a family had indeed been out of the country for a while. Joseph Rhodes, an engine fitter from Alfreton in Derbyshire, married Ann Simpson in the spring of 1849. The couple went on to have a succession of children, born in the small Derbyshire town of Ripley, before moving to Greenwich where their son George was born in 1859. There is no sign whatsoever of this family in the 1861 census which, as it turns out, is hardly surprising: the 1871 census provides the answer, through the listing in the returns of a 10-year-old daughter, Emma, who had been born in Spain. Joseph had evidently taken a short-term job on the Continent, meaning that the family were out of the country at the time of the 1861 census.

But although this type of situation is always a possibility, you need to think very carefully about its likelihood before considering it as an explanation in your own particular case.

Name unknown

The final category of ancestors who might genuinely be missing from the returns is also one of the trickiest to spot – and in certain respects the people in this group are only partially 'missing'. This is where the enumerator was unable to get the required information but still managed to provide some sort of headcount.

It's difficult to say what the story might be behind the somewhat deficient returns for 70 Landells Road, Camberwell, in the 1891 census. Judging by the occupants in the neighbouring houses (a civil servant, a silver polisher, an insurance agent and a painter and grainer), this was a fairly respectable lower-middle-class area – the families didn't have servants but all the houses were single occupancies. These neighbouring families are all fully enumerated, but all we know about the family at number 70 is that it comprised a man (aged about 40), his 32-year-old wife and a succession of children aged twelve, ten, seven, six, four and two years. No places of birth are given but intriguingly we have an occupation for the head of the household: 'Supposed Serjt. Major in Army'. How could the enumerator have known this while being unable to obtain the rest of the information? (RG 12/471, folio 84, page 32; plate 25)

Another entry which leaves us with more questions than answers is to be found amongst the 1861 census returns for West Street, Stepney. The enumerator had evidently returned to number 21 to collect the lodger's returns only to find that not only had the lodger departed but he had taken the schedule with him. The enumerator made the following note in his summary book: 'Lodger left Saturday and took schedule with him – gone to Woolwich' (RG 9/298, folio 60, page 5).

It would be interesting to know whether the enumerator in Woolwich managed to 'capture' the lodger.

The census aimed to provide a true and accurate count of the population, but it was always recognized that there were groups of people who lived either on the edge of, or entirely outside, 'normal' society and that these people would be very difficult, if not impossible, to fully enumerate.

The various groups of people that the census legislators described as vagrants, tramps or gypsies form the majority of the unknowns. In most cases there was a genuine effort to count the numbers of these 'itinerant travellers', but if your ancestor is described in the census as an unknown 45-year-old living in a caravan on the common this will be scant consolation to you as, without a name, you will have no way of identifying him or her.

You'll often find these people listed at the end of an enumeration book and sometimes you are fortunate enough to get their names. No fewer than 162 travelling showmen, toy dealers and stallholders living in tents and caravans were recorded in the 1861 census returns for the parish of St Paul's, Deptford.

The enumerator had found it 'impossible to deliver' any schedules to work from and according to a note at the top of page 28 of his summary book had copied the details from his memorandum book: 'The following persons slept at an intended casual Fair on the night of the 7th April 1861 in a field adjoining the Boundary of the St Paul Deptford, but no information could be obtained respecting the place of birth.' (RG9/396, folios 135–138; plate 27)

At the end of the list of names, on page 34, the enumerator expands on his previous note:

> Sir, I forward to you a List of those persons who slept at the intended Fair on the night of the 7th instant. The enclosed was as correct as could be ascertained there being a great deal of difficulty to gain any information – especially the place of Birth – I had to forego that enquiry for the more important information respecting names & ages which was given with much reluctance, not being willing to be disturbed.

The distrust of the authorities is quite obvious here and we can only admire the commitment of the enumerator in getting as much information as he did. Other enumerators weren't quite as successful.

The 1881 census for the Berkshire village of Shottesbrook includes entries for five people (in two separate groups) who were living in sheds. The first group consisted of a man (an Edge Tool Grinder), a woman and a child. It's tempting to assume that this is a family group, but other than the occupation and some intelligent guesswork regarding their ages no details are recorded about them. In the second shed we find two men whose ages are given as 48 and 35. This time we get a name for the one of them – William Neal – and an occupation of sorts; the enumerator has written: 'None (too idle)'!

In 1871 the enumerator for Balcomb in Sussex included five 'tramps' and one named individual at the end of his summary book. William James's residence was given as 'Edmunds Barn': he was described as a 50 year old, unmarried Ag. Lab. – birthplace unknown. Underneath the entry for William James, the enumerator had initially written 'Tramps Names N. K. Man, Woman & 3 children', but this was scored out and an attempt of sorts was made to come up with some approximate ages – these were presumably no more than guesses (RG 10/1060, folio 126, page 18).

There are hundreds, probably even thousands, of people recorded in the censuses in this sort of way. Some of them are our ancestors and it's just possible that the family in Balcomb or the edge tool grinder living in the Berkshire shed are the very people that you're looking for. But the chances of ever being able to prove anything are remote.

Missing censuses

The number of people who fell into any of the categories we've looked at so far is relatively small and (with the possible exception of people serving in the British Army or at sea) these 'solutions' are unlikely to explain the apparent absence of your ancestors. Of greater concern to us are the large sections of the census that are known to be missing.

Our census records have had a somewhat chequered and confusing history. The original householders' schedules were destroyed and it perhaps says something about the lack of importance attached to the records in general that the enumerators' summary books have not been well looked after for much of their existence. At various periods in the nineteenth and early twentieth centuries the whereabouts of some of the records was unclear – indeed for a while the whole of the 1851 census was thought to be lost!

Initially, of course, these were working records: clerks at the Census Office spent months going through them, checking them for accuracy and then annotating them and extracting data from them for statistical purposes. As a result, some of the books suffered a significant amount of wear and tear. In the 1861 returns there are numerous instances, particularly in the London districts, where the front and back pages of the books or other single pages have been lost.

As a researcher, it can be particularly frustrating to find that the returns for the family you're looking for have only partly survived, offering only a tantalizing glimpse of what might have been. For many years, the Swale family lived at 3 Leicester Place, Saffron Hill, in Holborn, London. They were listed at that address in the 1851 census and were evidently still there at the time of the 1861 census. However, we only have the details of the head of the house. William Swale is listed at the bottom of page 80 but pages 81 and 82, which would have included the returns for the rest of the Swale family, are unfortunately missing (RG 9/187, folio 85, page 80).

But it's not just the odd page here and there that's missing. Some whole sub-districts and in one case an entire registration district have, over the years, been misplaced, destroyed or possibly even stolen! The most significant gaps in the collection are:

1841	the whole of the parish of Paddington, a few parishes in Kent, Northamptonshire and significant parts of North Wales, particularly in Denbigh and Flint
1851	parts of the Newmarket district and the whole of the Dunmow (Essex) district
1861	the whole of the Belgravia (Westminster) and Woolwich Arsenal sub-districts, a small number of parishes in Wales
1871	part of Leicester, a few places in Wales
1901	the whole of Deal (Kent)

1881, 1891 and 1911 have no significant gaps

The Findmypast website has a comprehensive list of known missing pieces of the census at: <**www.findmypast.com:80/helpadvice/knowledge-base/census**>.

No one has ever been able to explain what happened to these documents and no one knows when they disappeared. Perhaps some of them were 'borrowed' by interested parties – the fact that the 1841 and 1861 censuses were stored for a while in an attic at the Houses of Parliament (apparently in a haphazard and disorganized manner) made them particularly vulnerable to this sort of pilfering. It's possible that in the fullness of time some of them will turn up amongst collections of private papers. As recently as the 1970s, an 1841 enumerator's summary book for part of Wrexham was discovered in a second-hand bookshop, so hope is not fully extinguished. It goes without saying that the surviving records are secured for posterity and that there is no danger of any further losses occurring.

Clearly, if your ancestors were living in any of these 'missing' areas at the time of the census, you're not going to find them; but even if we add the total in this category to the unfortunate few on the missing pages and then include those not enumerated in the first place, we're still looking at a very small percentage of the total population.

It's important to understand this point: our ancestors were almost certainly 'captured' by the census enumerator. If you've failed to find them, then the reason is unlikely to be that they are not recorded: the much more likely explanation is that one or more of the pieces of information that you're using to carry out your search is, in some crucial way, 'wrong'? I've used inverted commas here to highlight the fact that this simple word can hide a multitude of meanings.

We'll now go on to look at the many reasons why your ancestors may not appear in the census as you would expect to find them.

Is the census wrong?

It's very easy to fall into the trap of thinking that, since the census returns were created by a highly efficient nineteenth-century government department, they will necessarily be totally accurate and comprehensive. We have to remember that the primary purpose of the census was to provide the government of the day with workable and meaningful statistical data – and with this in mind it was undeniably fit for purpose. The question we have to ask is whether, as a source of family history data, it can be relied upon in the same way.

We've already looked at the various problems that the enumerator might have faced in delivering and collecting the householders' schedules. Now we need to follow him home and consider the conditions in which he carried out the task of copying the details into his summary book. The enumerators were not salaried General Register Office employees; they were local people who, in most cases, had another, full-time job and who, therefore, had to complete this work at home in the evenings, with no separate office, no electric lighting and, quite possibly, a large family around them, providing ample distractions. If we're looking for reasons why information recorded in the census returns might be inaccurate, here's a prime candidate. Even the most diligent and conscientious enumerator, working in conditions like this, is capable of making a mistake or two with crucial details like names, ages or places of birth.

And as we've seen from some of the complaints made by the enumerators, there was little incentive for them to create a quality product. The enumerators were supposed to get the job done quickly and their payment wasn't based on any measure of quality: they were simply paid a fixed amount for each completed schedule. Edward Blade (the 1851 enumerator from Allhallows, Barking; see p. 26) made a crucial point when he asked the question, 'How then can a correct return of the population be expected?' Yes, the quality of their work was checked, by the local registrar and later by the Superintendent Registrar, but with the best will in the world these can only have been superficial checks.

And this is just one of the stages at which errors can be introduced into the records. From the family historian's point of view, it doesn't really matter whether the mistake was made by the householder, the enumerator or by a modern transcriber. Any mistake in the records is liable to cause us problems when attempting to locate our ancestors in the returns, but it's important nonetheless to consider the various possibilities so that we can gain a better understanding of how we can overcome these problems.

Reading the writing

The summary books are, as we have seen, the census records that we use in our research today and it's from these books that the online indexes have been created. There can be no question that these indexes have improved, beyond all recognition, our ability to find individuals in the census, but it's true to say that they have also created some new problems. Put in very simple terms, it's inevitable that a further transcription process will introduce a further set of errors.

However you look at it, there's no denying that some of the transcription on some of the census websites leaves a lot to be desired, but thanks to the power and flexibility of modern search engines this shouldn't prevent us from finding our ancestors – in Chapter 5 we'll take an in-depth look at how to search the various online indexes.

But let's not be too quick to criticize the modern census transcriptions. Anyone with experience of using the returns would no doubt confirm that the handwriting, possibly as a result of the poor working conditions and low morale amongst the enumerators mentioned above, can be extremely difficult to read. Any attempt to interpret and copy handwritten documents from an earlier era is naturally going to be fraught with difficulties. However much we may be familiar with the form of writing, it's the little nuances – the exceptions to the rule – that present us with the problems.

Ultimately, a researcher trying to interpret a particularly difficult piece of text needs to consider two points: first of all, what does it say? and, secondly, what did it mean to say? This is an important distinction and, to my mind, the transcriber's job is only to copy what it actually says and to leave the second part of the process in the hands of the researcher. No attempt should be made at this stage to editorialize or to second-guess what the enumerator meant.

Interpreting our ancestors' handwriting was clearly just as much of a challenge for the enumerators as deciphering the enumerators' handwriting was for the twenty-first century transcribers. And more than anything else, it's the personal names and the birthplaces which seem to have caused the enumerators the biggest problems.

Of course, the average nineteenth-century enumerator wouldn't have had access to a decent selection of atlases and gazetteers – the sort of research tools that modern researchers take for granted. So if they were unable to read or understand what the householder had written, the only option open to them other than going back to the householder to check (which, considering the need to get the job done quickly, was not usually a practical option) was to make an intelligent guess.

Over the years I've come across a number of instances where it seems that this is exactly what the enumerator did: the only problem is that the guess doesn't always seem to have been that intelligent! How else can you explain 'Essex, Coackerter', Henry Bullifant's place of birth as given in the 1881 census? It's clearly supposed to be Colchester (the 'shape' is practically identical) and the only logical conclusion must be that the Sheffield-based enumerator was unable to identify what Henry had written and simply transcribed what he thought it said, copying the shape of the letters. It does seem quite strange though that the enumerator had never heard of Britain's oldest recorded town (RG 11/4647, f. 113, p. 27; plate 28).

It's not obvious on first viewing what the 1851 Clerkenwell enumerator meant when he entered the birthplace of three members of the

Bennett family as 'Bucks., Jugford'. There is in reality no such place in Buckinghamshire, or indeed elsewhere in England and Wales. Further research on the family in later censuses reveals that they were born in Twyford. Leaving aside for a moment the additional complication that Twyford is in Berkshire, it's not hard to see how someone who didn't recognize the place name could come up with 'Jugford' as a possible interpretation, based entirely on the shape of the word (HO 107/1516, f. 5, p. 2 and RG 10/1288, f. 70, p. 16; plates 29 and 30).

It's surprising how often what initially appears to be a modern error turns out instead to be a faithful and accurate transcription of what's in the records. I clearly remember jumping to the wrong conclusion many years ago when I found an Annal family in the 1881 census indexed as Allan – only to check the original entry and find that the whole family were indeed listed as Allan and not Annal (RG 11/4539, f. 91, p. 27).

I suspect that this is another example of enumerator error, although it's difficult to say in cases like this whether the 'mistake' was initiated by the householder or introduced by the enumerator.

As family historians, we need to adopt an open and questioning mind when dealing with our ancestors and the information that they've left behind in the various documents that we use in our research. The challenge facing us is to work out which of the 'facts' about their lives are true and which are not.

This of course is easier said than done. The untruths we come up against comprise a wide range of eventualities: as well as the honest errors, there are the misunderstandings and misinterpretations, and lastly, and perhaps everyone's favourite, the downright lies. So how do we spot the mistakes, the lies and the half-truths? How do we separate the wheat from the chaff?

Ignorance, errors and lies

Any data source which is based on a series of questions and answers relies in the first place on the accuracy of the initial answers. It doesn't matter how efficient the administrative process behind producing the end product is: if the original data is flawed, we're going to have problems using and understanding it. This is certainly true of the census, which relies for its accuracy and detail on people who had an astonishing number of reasons to get things wrong – namely, our ancestors.

It has been estimated that as many as one in four birth, marriage and death certificates contains an error of one kind or another, and we know from bitter experience that the information that our ancestors gave to the census enumerators is similarly riddled with inaccuracies.

Spelling must surely come right near the top of the list of issues that regularly cause errors to crop up in the census. In Chapter 7 of Charles Dickens' *Great Expectations*, the following dialogue takes place between our hero, Pip, and his brother-in-law Joe Gargery:

> 'How do you spell Gargery, Joe?' I asked him, with a modest patronage.
> 'I don't spell it at all,' said Joe.
> 'But supposing you did?'
> 'It can't be supposed,' said Joe.

The point of this is that not only could many of our ancestors not read and write, but they actually had no concept of the 'correct' spelling of their names. The significance of this to family historians is, I hope, quite clear and the lesson is an obvious one; yet it never fails to surprise me how often we hear researchers comment, for example, that the William Browne they've found can't be theirs because their name has always been spelt without an 'e'.

This fixation with 'correct' spelling is a relatively modern one. It certainly wasn't shared by our Tudor and Stuart ancestors and even into the latter half of the nineteenth century inconsistencies in spellings of place names as well as personal names were commonplace. The situation began to change with the introduction of compulsory education in England and Wales. The Education Act of 1870 began the work by allowing school boards to be set up around the country, but it was the 1876 Elementary Education Act that really opened the doors to an era of virtually universal literacy. This landmark Act compelled parents to send their children to school to receive basic education in 'the three r's': reading, writing and arithmetic.

If the householders were unable to complete their census forms, the enumerators were supposed to help them, or even to write down the details themselves. And this is where regional accents, misunderstandings and misinterpretations come into play – all of which can account for a lot of questionable information ending up in the returns.

As family historians we naturally like to think the best of our ancestors. We imagine them as fine upstanding members of their local community, as people of honesty and integrity. It can come as a bit of a shock to us therefore to discover that many of them had a rather distressing habit of lying. And when it came to filling out their census form, they had any number of reasons why they might have chosen to be economical with the truth. They could never have envisaged that we would one day be able to untangle some of the webs that they wove with their lies. Thanks to the miracles of modern computer technology our ancestors' secrets are no longer safe.

Errors, however they originate, can of course occur right across the census form, but it's the names, ages and birthplaces which are likely to have the biggest impact on your search. Let's look at each area in turn, starting with the problems that might crop up in the 'name' field.

Names

When dealing with our ancestors' surnames, we mustn't fall into the trap of applying our modern prejudices about accuracy, detail and consistency. We need to allow for significant discrepancies in spelling occurring between one census and the next – there may be some perception of a 'usual' spelling of a name, but, as we have seen, there are many reasons why it may appear in the census in a different form.

Take the case of Henry Patterson (plate 31): he was recorded in the 1881 census, aged 40 and living in Stockton on Tees, County Durham, with his surname spelt exactly as we would expect. But you might struggle to find him ten years earlier because he's entered as Henry Pattison, as indeed he is in 1861. And when we go back to 1851, he's down as Henry Paddison. So what are we looking at here? Is this a positive decision by Henry (and/or his parents) to change the name – to adopt a different spelling? Personally, I doubt it. These were labouring folk, semi-literate at best, and they were to a large degree at the mercy of the enumerator. Of course, we cannot tell from the surviving records whether the different spellings of the name were the result of the family members completing their householders' schedules themselves or the product of a succession of enumerators' attempts at interpreting the details that the Patterson family gave them, hurriedly, on the doorstep. What is clear is that examples of this kind are commonplace.

Another situation which presents plenty of opportunity for error occurs when the details on a schedule were completed by the householder on behalf of a lodger or servant. If that person had only recently arrived at the house in question or perhaps if he or she was someone who kept themselves to themselves and only rarely associated with the family, it's easy to see how the householder could have been unaware of some important details.

And this is just one of the surname-related problems that the Critcher family of Langley Marish, in Buckinghamshire serve to illustrate. Edward was born in 1832, the son of William and Elizabeth Critcher, and the whole family are living at George Green, in Langley Marish, at the time of the 1841 census. Ten years later, the family are still at George Green but Edward, now aged 18, is living away from home. He's listed in the 1851 census at Hunton Bridge in the parish of Abbots Langley, Hertfordshire, where he was working as a ploughman: his surname is entered as Crutchet.

Moving on another ten years and Edward's father William is now an inmate in the Eton Union Workhouse, but his name has been entered by the Master of the Workhouse (or perhaps by a clerk) as Crutcher. Edward meanwhile is now married and living in the Buckinghamshire parish of Chenies, 'correctly' listed as Critcher, but in the 1871 census Edward and family are entered as Critchard. So within a period of 20 years we have the surname spelt in four different ways: Critcher, Crutcher, Crutchet and Critchard.

Sometimes we come across evidence that an enumerator made a genuine attempt to get more detailed information than was originally supplied by the householder. Balfour Annal was born in Gravesend in 1853. He never married and as a single working-class man seems to have spent much of his life living in lodging houses; at the time of the 1901 census he was living as a boarder in the parish of Milton. He was originally entered in the enumerator's summary book simply as Mr. Andon, but at some later stage the name 'Balford' was added.

Forenames tend to be less of a problem. Our ancestors worked from a relatively small palette of forenames and if we go back to the sixteenth and seventeenth centuries, we find that roughly half of the male population was represented by just three names; John, William and Thomas. Although there was a slightly larger pool of female names to choose from, the top five (Jane, Margaret, Ann, Elizabeth and Mary) were used by over 40 per cent of women.

So it's highly likely that your ancestors' forenames will have been correctly recorded. As mentioned in Chapter 1, abbreviations were frequently used in the census, but in most cases this shouldn't present too many obstacles to your research.

The problem that we have here is more to do with the annoying habit that some people seem to have had of changing their forenames from one census to the next, often by adopting their middle name as their preferred first name.

The Swale family of Holborn (mentioned on p. 61) provide a good example of this. Ellen Jane Swale was born in 1839 and married William Hayes in October 1864. She is listed in the 1841 census as Ellen Swale but in 1851 she appears as Jane. Unfortunately, as we saw earlier, she is genuinely missing from the 1861 census but we pick her up again, by now married to William Hayes, in 1871 and 1881: in both cases her forename is once more given as Jane.

In this case, it seems likely that Ellen Jane simply chose to be known by her middle name, but sometimes our ancestors appear in the census with different forenames for no apparent reason. The case of the Foyle family of Clapham, Surrey, illustrates this quite well. Richard Foyle married Elizabeth Weatherley at Battersea in 1834 and five children were born in Clapham over the next sixteen years. It's fairly easy to find the family in the 1841 and 1851 censuses living in Clifton Street but when we come to the 1861 census, although we can find the same family, still living in Clifton Street, the parents are entered not as Richard and Elizabeth but as William and Eliza.

Where the 1861 census enumerator got these names from we'll never know. All we can say for certain is that someone, somewhere along the line, got their wires crossed and the wrong names ended up in the census.

Ages

Ages on census returns are notoriously inaccurate and it's actually not at all uncommon to find someone's age increasing by slightly more or, perhaps more often, slightly less than ten years between censuses. A Registrar General's report from 1896 stated that 'the one column in the householders' schedule which gives the most trouble to occupiers … and is most liable to the suspicion of inaccuracy when filled up, is the Age Column'.

Birthdays weren't celebrated in the same way that they are today, and in the era before the state began to record every detail of our lives, these matters didn't always hold as great importance as we attach to them today.

Whether the problem with ages is more to do with ignorance or deception is neither here nor there, but it's certainly an area that presents us with more than its fair share of difficulties and we would do well to learn to take the ages we see in the census with a large pinch of salt. Take the example of my great-great-grandfather, James Annal, and his sister Betsy. James was born in 1837, a year after Betsy, but by the time of the 1871 census James had overtaken Betsy, and was shown as being two years older than her! It wasn't until the 1901 census that Betsy regained the missing years and admitted to her true age.

Henry Grover was born in Rickmansworth, Hertfordshire, in 1830. His age in five successive censuses is recorded as follows: 1851 – 20; 1861 – 25; 1871 – 39; 1881 – 42; 1891 – 60. Henry was listed as a lodger in 1861 and a boarder in 1871, which may have contributed to the discrepancies highlighted here but cannot explain the age given in 1881, when Henry was the head of his own household and therefore responsible for completing his own schedule. Again, examples are not hard to find but it's all too easy to forget this when carrying out a search.

Don't forget that in the 1841 census the ages of people aged 15 or over were supposed to be rounded down to the nearest five. Another important point to remember is that, from 1851 to 1911, the census was always taken either at the end of March or the beginning of April.

It's easy to fall into the trap of assuming that someone who was aged two years at the time of the 1901 census was necessarily born in 1899. In fact (providing that the age was given accurately in the first place) they would have been born between April 1898 and April 1899 – with 1898 being the more likely year of birth.

Birthplaces

The age column may well be, as the Registrar General's report of 1896 stated, 'the most liable to the suspicion of inaccuracy', but it's our ancestors' inconsistency when referring to their birthplaces which causes family historians the greatest headaches.

Unfortunately, many of them simply didn't know where they were born. Orphans, adoptees or people who were brought up a long way from where they were born may have been unaware of the identity of their native parish, so it's not at all uncommon to find the words 'Not Known' (often abbreviated to 'NK') where you would expect to find a place of birth.

Of course, the vast majority of the population knew where they were born – the problem, however, is that they may have had a variety of ways of describing that place. At one extreme there are the (admittedly rare) cases where a precise address of birth is given – at the other, the all-too-common instances of 'NK'.

When William Barker completed his census schedule in 1881, he gave rather more information regarding his children's places of birth than he was required to:

Lucy A Barker	1 Robert St., Grosvenor Sqre.
William J Barker	4 Brunswick Yd., Marylebone
Frederick J Barker	25 Randolph Mews, Maida Vale

A single page from the 1891 census (RG 12/39, folio 170, page 10) illustrates the huge range of possibilities that the place of birth column can throw up.

Of the 30 names on the page, only 16 gave their birthplaces in the usual 'County, Parish' format. Of the other 14, four gave the name of the county without identifying the parish, while four more were born in Scotland and one in Jersey. A further four were born overseas, two in Jamaica and two in the USA (one in New York, one in New Jersey), leaving one person, Sarah Christmas, whose place of birth was given as 'London, Jermyn St.'.

And it's this unpredictability which can make our searches so hard to structure. Henry Ralph Bleeze was born in London, but as a young man he moved out of the capital first to Hitchin in Hertfordshire and then to Bedfordshire.

His birthplace as given over successive censuses makes interesting reading:

1851	London
1861	London, Holborn
1871	Middlesex, Fetter Lane, Holborn
1881	London, Middlesex
1891	London, Fetter Lane, Holborn
1901	London, St Andrew

None of these is in any way 'wrong' – they all refer to the same place, but with varying degrees of precision.

While some were unsure of their birthplaces, others may have had cause to be less than truthful with the information they supplied. The Poor Law played a huge part in the lives of the Victorian working classes and the fear of being removed from their homes back to their parish of legal settlement (usually the parish they were born in) seems to have led many of our ancestors to claim a false birthplace in the census. The assurance of confidentiality given by the census administrators evidently wasn't enough to convince everyone.

County boundaries can also throw up a variety of issues. The Henry Grover mentioned above was born in Hertfordshire but the 1891 census records his place of birth as 'Middlesex, West Hyde'. The hamlet of West Hyde is part of the parish of Rickmansworth which is, and always has been, in Hertfordshire, but it is so close to the Middlesex border that it's easy to see how confusion could creep in.

Alfred Genner grew up around the turn of the twentieth century in the North Yorkshire village of Tollerton but, according to the 1901 census, he had been born many miles away in Ludlow, Shropshire. However, the 1891 census gives his place of birth as Hereford. So we have a problem here which is only partly explained by the tendency people have to be less precise when describing their birthplace the further they are away from it. A Shropshire man like Alfred's father might well give a Yorkshire census enumerator the name of the market town nearest to the village where his son was born instead of the name of the village itself. But in this case we have an extra difficulty which has as much to do with our country's often confusing geographical and administrative borders.

When we dig a bit deeper we discover that Ludlow is only a few miles from the Shropshire/Herefordshire border – indeed the Ludlow registration district includes several parishes which are actually situated in Herefordshire. And it turns out that Alfred was actually born in one of these parishes – a small village called Ludford. An 1871 directory of Shropshire summarizes the geographical difficulties rather neatly: 'Ludford is a parish joining Ludlow ... and only separated from the town by the River Teme. The village and church of Ludford is in the county of Hereford, and the townships are in Salop (i.e. Shropshire).'

So we have two different places of birth for Alfred in two censuses and neither of them are, strictly speaking, 'correct'. At least, in this case, and in the case of Henry Bleeze, it's fairly easy to explain what was going on but the next example throws up more questions than it provides answers.

Charles Lewington (plate 34) was born in 1839 in Eversley in Hampshire. He grew up in a number of different parishes on the Hampshire/Berkshire border as his agricultural labourer father moved around in search of work. In the 1851 census he was living with his family in Hartley Wintney and his place of birth was then correctly given as Hampshire, Eversley. By the time of the 1871 census (there's no trace of him in 1861 when he was almost certainly serving overseas with the army) Charles was married and living in the parish of Wrockwardine in Shropshire. The other details in the census (his name, age and occupation) tie in precisely with what we know about him – all of which makes it very difficult to explain why his birthplace was entered as 'Warwickshire'.

But it gets even stranger: ten years later, by which time the Lewington family have moved to Liverpool, Charles gives his place of birth as 'Shropshire, Walton'. In 1891 he reverts to the correct 'Hampshire, Eversley', but he has one more trick up his sleeve: the 1901 census records his birthplace as 'London'!

This remarkable variety of birthplaces is by no means commonplace – you'd be unlucky to come across something as extreme as this in your research, but it serves to drive home a crucial point. Namely, that there is really no telling what you might find in the census returns, and that you sometimes just have to make the most of what you do find and try to work your way around the obstacles that are placed in your way.

You need to find your ancestors in each of the censuses so that you can start to see the patterns in the data and, hopefully, identify the 'rogue' entries.

The examples outlined above are merely representative of the errors and inconsistencies that you might encounter: it would be impossible to cover every eventuality. Once you accept the fact that the census returns are *not* the model of accuracy that we'd like them to be, and train yourself to look at every piece of information they throw up with a critical eye, you'll find that the problems you had in tracking down those elusive ancestors start to fade away.

Case study 5 – The Darwins

Traditionally, family historians carry out their research backwards. We start from the present and work into the past: from the known to the unknown. However, census returns can also be used by biographers and historians to tell their stories in a chronological timeframe, working forward in time.

The family of Charles Darwin (plate 32), the scientist and evolutionary biologist, provides a good example of how this can be put into practice to tell the story of your own ancestors.

Charles Robert Darwin was born in the parish of St Chad's, Shrewsbury, in 1809. He attended the local grammar school before studying medicine at Edinburgh University and graduating from Christ's College, Cambridge, in 1831. In the same year Darwin accepted an invitation to join the HMS *Beagle* on its expedition to chart the coast of South America. The voyage lasted nearly five years and the events experienced by the young naturalist in the course of the expedition were to fundamentally change the way we look at the world around us.

A few years after his return to England, Darwin married his cousin Emma Wedgwood and the young couple moved into a house in London.

But all of this took place before our story begins on Sunday 6 June 1841, the night of the 1841 census. Charles and Emma's second child, Annie, had been born three months earlier and in May the whole family had travelled to the Wedgwood family home at Maer in Staffordshire for Annie's christening. So at the time of the 1841 census, rather than being listed at home in Upper Gower Street in London, the Darwins were living with the in-laws at Maer Houses (HO 107/989/3 f. 3 p. 1).

The Darwin/Wedgwood family tree is remarkably involved – complicated as it is by a succession of first and second cousin marriages. Staying at Maer House that night were five Wedgwood cousins, the four members of the Darwin family (Charles, Emma and the children William and Annie) and a whole host of servants including Darwin's butler, Joseph Parslow, and a young female servant named Elizabeth Harding. The head of the house (although not actually specified in the 1841 census) was Josiah Wedgwood, Emma's father and the son of the famous potter.

The following year the Darwins moved to Down House in Kent, which was to be the family home for the rest of their lives.

The story of Annie and Henrietta Darwin's absence from the 1851 census is told in Chapter 3. The rest of the family were properly recorded but are split between three different locations.

After settling Annie and Etty into their lodgings in Great Malvern, Charles returned to London and is listed in the census (as C.R. Darwin) at the house of his brother, Erasmus, in Park Street, Mayfair (HO 107/1476 f.240 p.12; plate 33). Emma, meanwhile, was at Down House together with the four youngest children, George, Elizabeth, Francis and Leonard, and a number of servants, including Parslow the butler, Elizabeth Harding (now described as a 'House Maid') and a young kitchen maid named Margaret Evans (HO 107/1606 f.247 p.5). Finally, the Darwin's oldest child, William, was at a boarding school in Mitcham, Surrey, preparing for his Public School entrance examinations (HO 107/1602 f.115 p.11).

The situation in 1861 was much less complex. Charles, Emma and their seven surviving children were all living at Down House together with the usual bevy of servants (RG 9/462 f.74 p.10). Joseph Parslow and Margaret Evans are both listed, the latter having risen in station to become the family's cook. Also among the servants is Parslow's daughter Ann.

In 1871, Charles was once more staying with his brother in London, but this time he was accompanied by Emma and four of the children: Henrietta, Elizabeth, Francis and Horace (RG 10/157 f.81 p.16). Ann Parslow had travelled with the Darwins as Emma's lady's maid, while Ann's father, with the assistance of Margaret Evans (now the housekeeper) and four other servants, was left in charge of Down House (RG 10/875 f.34 p.2).

The three remaining boys were by now making their own way in the world, each following their chosen profession. William was already in business as a banker in Southampton (RG 10/1201 f.65 p.11), while George (a law student) was living in lodgings in London (RG 10/100 f.57 p.4). Leonard had joined the army and was at the School of Military Engineering in Gillingham, where he is listed as a Lieutenant in the Royal Engineers (RG 10/913 f.25 p.6).

The 1881 census finds the Darwins once more back at the family home, where no fewer than 21 people are listed. The household comprised Charles and Emma, five of their children, a daughter-in-law, a grandson, a cousin, a niece (actually Emma's niece) and her husband (described as a visitor), eight servants and, finally, another visitor, described as a 'Ladies Maid' (RG 11/855 f.83 p.1).

The youngest daughter Elizabeth, who never married and was a permanent inhabitant of Down House, is listed immediately after her parents, followed by the oldest son William and his American wife Sara. Next comes George, now a fully qualified barrister, and the recently widowed Francis with his young son Bernard (who was later to become the golf correspondent for *The Times* newspaper). Rose Frank was the daughter of Emma's brother Francis Wedgwood and just happened to be visiting the Darwins at the time of the 1881 census with her husband Herman.

The next inhabitant in the household was Charles Wood Fox, a cousin on the Darwin side. He was followed by the servants, including, once more, Margaret Evans, now aged 49 and with at least thirty years' service with the family. Joseph Parslow, Darwin's butler, friend and confidant, retired in 1875 but stayed close to the family and, in 1881, is living in the village of Downe (RG 11/855 f.85 p.6).

Harriet Wells is listed as a visitor, but her occupation is given as 'Ladies Maid' – she was in fact in the employ of William and Sara Darwin. The final name listed in the household is, somewhat surprisingly, that of Leonard Darwin, Charles and Emma's fourth son. It's impossible to say for certain why he was listed here at the foot of the schedule and not with the other family members – it may be that he had turned up at Down House unexpectedly, sometime after the form had been completed, and his details were simply added at the foot of the schedule.

Horace Darwin, the youngest surviving son, was visiting his uncle Erasmus together with his wife Emma (RG 11/140 f.47 p.1). Henrietta was also in London, living nearby in Marylebone with her husband, Richard Litchfield (RG 11/146 f.24 p.41).

Charles died the following year at Down House, aged 73, but the Darwin connection with the old family home continued for sometime afterwards. Charles and Emma's second son, George, moved in with his young family and is listed at Down in the 1891 census (RG 12/631 f.38 p.18).

The remaining members of the Darwin family dispersed to various parts of the country. The stories of their families can be told using the later Victorian and Edwardian censuses.

Case study 6 – The Welsh question

Between 1841 and 1881 the layout of the schedules issued to householders in Wales was identical to that of the forms used in England. However, from 1851 a version of the schedule printed in Welsh was available for enumerators to give to those who were unable to understand English. From 1871 the enumerators were asked to indicate which schedules had been completed in Welsh by writing a 'W' underneath the schedule number in the summary book. They were also asked to enter the total number of forms completed in Welsh on page iv of the book.

The questions asked on the census returns had always been about social demography and medical health, so the addition of a question on the Scottish census in 1881 about the use of the Gaelic language, and an equivalent question about the Welsh language in 1891, can be seen as significant departures. Both questions were introduced as the result of lobbying by special interest groups, within and outside Parliament.

The 'Welsh' question was only asked in Wales and Monmouthshire, but was supposed to be answered by all inhabitants of those areas. The wording of the question ('If only English, write "English"; if only Welsh, write "Welsh"; if English and Welsh, write "Both"') left plenty of room for misunderstanding, and the accuracy and reliability of many of the answers should be questioned. Take, for example, the Davies family from the village of Castell in Llanbedr-y-Cennin, Caernarvonshire: according to their entry in the 1891 census, the head of the household, Evan Davies, spoke Welsh while his Liverpool-born wife Jane spoke English (RG 12/4671 f. 52 p.3; plate 35). It may well be that Evan 'habitually' spoke Welsh while Jane was more fluent in English, but the correct entry for Evan (if not for Jane) must surely have been 'Both' – which indeed was the case for all of their children. In the 1901 census, the same information is given: 'Welsh' for Evan and 'English' for Jane, but this time their daughter Eveline is also shown as speaking Welsh only (RG 13/5287 f. 22 p. 2).

It is clear that many householders did not understand how to answer the new question and the authorities were well aware of the problems facing them in interpreting and using the data that was gathered. The official 1891 census report stated that 'abundant evidence was received by us that it was either misunderstood or set at naught by a large number of those Welshmen who could speak both languages, and that the word "Welsh" was very often returned, when the proper entry would have been "Both"; on the ground, it may be presumed that Welsh was the language spoken habitually or preferentially'. The report went on to suggest that the figures may even have been deliberately falsified by some householders in order to 'add to the number of monoglot Welshmen'. Brydges Henniker, the Registrar General, was later forced to issue an apology, retracting this allegation (Census of England and Wales, 1891, General Report, vol. IV, 1891, p. 81).

There was also, perhaps understandably, a concern about the number of Welsh children who were entered as speaking Welsh only, when English was compulsorily taught at schools.

The language question was repeated (with some refinement) in the 1901 and 1911 censuses – the 1901 Census Act clarified the point that the data should only be gathered for those aged three years or upwards. Despite the concerns about the 'quality' of the answers, there is no doubt that this is a useful piece of additional information for those of us with Welsh ancestry, and it will be interesting to be able to compare the details for our ancestors over three successive censuses.

John Richards, a coal miner from Pembrokeshire, was living in Merthyr Tydfil in 1911 with his wife Margaret Jane (née Lewis) and their six children. The census tells us that they had been married for 15 years (confirmed by an entry in the GRO's marriage index for the September quarter of 1895) and that the marriage had produced nine children, three of whom had died. We also learn that John and the children spoke English while Margaret could speak both Welsh and English (RG 14/32439 schedule 89). This information is confirmed in the 1901 census where we also discover one of the three children who sadly didn't survive infancy: a one-month-old boy called Martin Luther Richards.

According to the 1891 census, Margaret Jane's parents were, like her, able to speak both languages and perhaps her children grew up to speak some Welsh but the trend towards the dominance of the English language seemed unstoppable at the time.

It would be difficult to argue that the inclusion of the language question in the census returns played a significant role in the battle for the survival of Welsh as a living language, but it certainly helped to draw attention to the very real fear that the Welsh language might go the same way as its Cornish cousin and disappear altogether. The contemporary statistics certainly support the idea that this was a genuine possibility: while still questioning the reliability of the data, the official 1901 census report suggested that the number of people speaking Welsh only had fallen from 30 per cent in 1891 to 15 per cent in just ten years.

Thankfully the threat has long since passed and Welsh is now once more a thriving, living language.

4

THE CENSUS ONLINE

In April 2006, within a few days of each other, ScotlandsPeople and Ancestry announced that they had placed the 1841 census (for Scotland, and England and Wales, respectively) online. This meant that, for the first time, all the released censuses for England, Wales and Scotland were available in digital form to anyone with an internet connection.

Since the advent of personal computers, family historians had dreamt of having the censuses in digital form to be easily searched. As early as 1982 the Berkshire Family History Society had a project for transcribing the 1851 census using the BBC Model B computer.[1]

In fact the country's first census digitization project was the 2 per cent sample of the 1851 census, created in the 1970s. But this was part of a research project based in the Sociology Department at the University of Edinburgh, which aimed to 'explore various salient aspects of the nineteenth century social and economic structure' and was not aimed at family historians. It was made available for download in about 1995, without the permission of the owner, and this was the first time it was publicly available.[2] (It is now available on CD-ROM and at Ancestry UK.)

Family history societies initially created census indexes to provide look-up services for their members, but with the advent of CD-ROM they started to publish these indexes commercially. The most impressive result of this development was the 1881 Census Index, created in a massive volunteer project of the Genealogical Society of Utah and the Federation of Family History Societies (FFHS), which led to the first publication, on microfiche and then on CD, of a national census dataset. (A history of the project will be found at <**www.familyhistoryonline.net/database/1881history.shtml**>.)

By the second half of the 1990s, record offices and family history societies were starting to have a presence on the web. Official census datasets started to appear online in 2001. In April, the National

Archives (or Public Record Office, as it then was) launched an index and images for the 1891 census of Norfolk as a pilot for the subsequent 1901 census. In August, Scots Origins, launched in 1998 for the Scottish civil registration data, added the 1891 census for Scotland to its datasets.

The biggest event in the development of online census services was the launch of the 1901 census in January 2002. Unfortunately, it was not, initially at least, a great success. The census was digitized in a partnership between the National Archives (Public Record Office) and the defence contractor QinetiQ. There had always been scepticism from the genealogical community about the likely quality of the indexing, and these misgivings turned out to be well-founded – the indexes contained a host of very obvious and entirely avoidable errors.[3] But the very size and novelty of the resulting dataset lay at the root of the main problem: the unprecedented level of demand had not been adequately planned for and the service had to be withdrawn within five days. It was November before the service was fully up and running.

It is now strange to remember that the PRO came in for a lot of criticism at the time for prioritizing online availability, now accepted as the norm. However, the overwhelming demand for the 1901 census proved beyond doubt the huge market for online census data, and September 2002 saw the first commercial subscription service when Ancestry launched its UK data service at <**www.ancestry.co.uk**> with the 1891 census for England and Wales. Since then we have seen an increasing number of commercial sites offering census indexes and images. A few have also changed hands, the 1901 census being bought up by GenesReunited as the basis of a new data service, and Stepping Stones census images were acquired by S&N for TheGenealogist. The most recent takeover was the purchase of Findmypast by Scotland Online (now Brightsolid), who run ScotlandsPeople.

It wasn't until 2003 that any significant amount of free census data was available on the web, when the 1881 Census Index was finally added to the LDS Church's family history site FamilySearch at <**www.familysearch.org**>. The same year saw the launch of data for the 1891 census by FreeCEN, a project started in 1998 to harness the efforts of volunteer transcribers to provide a free census index.

Until now, there has been a clear separation between the commercial sites and those hosting free data, but a significant development took place in July 2008. FamilySearch's pilot for its new Record Search site at <**pilot.familysearch.org**> (see p. 115) started to offer free of charge the 1841 and 1861 census indexes from Origins and Findmypast with links to the images at Findmypast. In due course, all Findmypast's census indexes are due to be added to FamilySearch.[4]

	1995	2 per cent sample of 1851 census available (possibly illegally) for download by FTP
April	2001	TNA's 1891 census pilot goes live
August	2001	Scots Origins launches first Scottish census data
January	2002	1901 census launched and almost immediately closed down
September	2002	Ancestry.co.uk launched with 1891 census
November	2002	1901 census finally fully operational
January	2003	Launch of FamilyHistoryOnline, with census indexes from family history societies
February	2003	1881 Census Index added to FamilySearch
July	2003	Launch of FreeCEN search engine with 1891 census transcriptions
November	2003	National Audit Office report on 1901 census
December	2004	The National Archives and Ancestry.co.uk launch the 1881 and 1891 census under the Licensed Internet Associateship initiative
February	2005	1837online (now Findmypast) launches 1861 census index and images
March	2005	1841 census launched on British Origins
August	2005	QinetQ sells 1901 census service to Genes Reunited
December	2005	Agreement between the National Archives of Ireland and Library and Archives Canada to digitize Irish census records for 1901 and 1911
April	2006	ScotlandsPeople release the 1841 census index and images for Scotland. Ancestry release the 1841 census index for England and Wales All censuses for England, Wales and Scotland are now available online
December	2006	In response to a Freedom of Information ruling, the National Archives announce that the 1911 census will be available online from 2009 rather than 2012
March	2007	An online petition to reduce the classified period for census data from 100 years to 70 years closes with 23,602 signatories

December	2007	Irish 1911 census for Dublin goes online
July	2008	GROS reveals that Scottish data will no longer be exclusive to ScotlandsPeople FamilySearch, Findmypast and Origins announce a joint project to make UK census indexes available on FamilySearch and at Family History Centers

Table 4-1 Timeline: the census online (based on British Isles Genealogy on the Internet: timeline at <**homepages.gold.ac.uk/genuki/timeline/**>).

What's online

The websites offering census data can be classified in two ways: is the data free or charged? Is the coverage local or national?

FREE

There are three free sites with national data:

- FamilySearch at <**www.familysearch.org**> has the 1881 Census Index for England and Wales. Its pilot record search site at <**pilot.familysearch.org**> has limited indexes for the 1841 and 1861 censuses with links to commercially available images on Findmypast.
- FreeCEN at <**www.freecen.org.uk**> has indexes to all censuses for England and Wales in progress, except for 1881.
- Library and Archives Canada is digitizing the Irish 1901 and 1911 census for the National Archives of Ireland.

There are many sites maintained by individuals or volunteer groups with local data, some with scope as small as a single village. The only major site with a range of individual local datasets is FHS Online, which has free census indexes from individual family history societies.

The free sites are covered in Chapter 6, apart from those for Ireland, which are described in Chapter 15.

CHARGED

There are currently six main commercial providers of national census datasets. These are as follows:

- Ancestry at <**www.ancestry.co.uk**> – see Chapter 7
- Findmypast at <**www.findmypast.com**> – see Chapter 8
- S&N Genealogy Supplies who have two sites, TheGenealogist at <**www.thegenealogist.co.uk**> and RootsUK at <**www.rootsuk.com**> – see Chapter 9
- Genes Reunited at <**www.genesreunited.co.uk**> incorporates the data from the original 1901 census digitization, which still has a separate site at <**www.1901censusonline.com**> – see Chapter 10
- Origins at <**www.origins.net**> – see Chapter 11
- ScotlandsPeople at <**www.scotlandspeople.gov.uk**> – see Chapter 12.

In addition:

- By autumn 2008, FamilyRelatives at <**www.familyrelatives.org**> expects to have images of census records online, with indexes to follow.
- The 1911 census for England and Wales will be coming online early in 2009 – see Chapter 13.

There is currently no commercial data service with only local census data. Until recently, this niche was occupied by the Federation of Family History Societies' data service FamilyHistoryOnline at <**www.familyhistoryonline.net**>. Although the site is still up and running as this book goes to press, the FFHS has reached agreement for much of the data to be migrated to Findmypast, and FamilyHistoryOnline itself will close by the end of 2008. When that happens, many of the small county-based census indexes on the site will cease to be available online, and will probably only be available on CD-ROM from the family history societies which created them (see Chapter 16). However, county indexes for the 1851 census are being incorporated in a new national 1851 index at Findmypast, which is discussed in more detail in Chapter 8, p. 149–50.

How it's done

The original census records are held by the National Archives, the General Register Office for Scotland (GROS) and the National Archives of Ireland. For all the censuses up to 1901, these bodies have microform copies of the enumeration books, and these have formed the basis of all previous digitizations.

The National Archives (TNA) has taken three different approaches to the digitization of census records. The 1901 census was, and the 1911 is being, digitized through a partnership with a commercial company, QinetiQ in the case of the 1901 census and Brightsolid (formerly Scotland Online) in the case of the 1911 census. The result is a website run by the company on behalf of TNA. TNA also offers what it calls 'Licensed Internet Associateships' (LIA), where a commercial data service carries out the digitization and places the data on its own site, but the material is 'co-branded' and the company is assisted and promoted by TNA. For example, the census page on TNA's web site at <**www.nationalarchives.gov.uk/census/**> has links to the census data at Ancestry (see Chapter 7), which is so far the only company to have an LIA for census records. TNA gets free access at Kew for its users. (You can see details of other records which have been licensed under this scheme at <**www.nationalarchives.gov.uk/business/popular_records.htm**>.) Finally, companies can purchase copies of the microfilms and a licence to digitize them.

In Scotland, the situation has until very recently been quite different. GROS has had an exclusive arrangement with a commercial provider for its data, making Scottish census records available on only one site, initially Scots Origins and then ScotlandsPeople (see Chapter 12). In fact the Scottish government has kept tight control over this service, and even minor changes to the way the service operates, such as how long pay-per-view credits remain valid, have to receive government approval via a Statutory Instrument.[5]

However, in July 2008 it was reported in the press that GROS would be granting licences to other commercial data services to provide indexes and images for the Scottish census.[6] No firm details were available as this book goes to press, but a spokesman for the Scottish government confirmed to us that 'GROS anticipates that two possibilities will exist: a licence to enable a company to use digital images and indexes already created by GROS; and a licence that would enable a company to make digital images and indexes of the original records (most likely from microfilm)'. Parliamentary approval is not needed for this new move, but the new licensing arrangements won't be made public until the legal details have been sorted out, presumably by the end of 2008. There is no information about this so far on the GROS website at <**www.gro-scotland.gov.uk**>, but clearly there will be in due course.

In fact Ancestry has already provided indexes to the Scottish censuses, apparently without GROS approval, but has been unable to negotiate the right to digitize the images. However, this will presumably change once the new licensing arrangements come into force.

In Ireland, again the situation is quite different: there has been no commercial digitization at all, apart from a few small census extracts, but the National Archives of Ireland's own website has recently started hosting an index and images free of charge (see Chapter 15).

Access

The majority of family historians will have home internet access. If you haven't got your own computer or internet connection, there is still no reason why you shouldn't have access to these online resources.

First, the National Archives in Kew offers free access to the 1901 census at 1901censusonline (Chapter 10) and to Ancestry's census data not including 1901.

If you are a member of the Society of Genealogists, the Society's computer suite offers access to a range of data services.

You should be able to access the free sites from any public access computer with an internet connection. But some of the commercial services may not be accessible in this way. The reason for this is that some of them require a specific browser plug-in which you are not likely to find installed on such computers, and whoever is providing the computer will certainly not let you install a new plug-in.

Several of the data services offer a 'Library Subscription', which allows public libraries to make their service available, free of charge to the individual user, from computers in the library. If you do not have your own internet connection, or if you simply want cheaper, though less convenient, access, it is worth asking at your public library. The information may well be on the library's web page, which will be part of your local authority website. For example, the website for the Leeds public libraries indicates that the central library and some community libraries have access to both Ancestry and Origins. (Follow the link to 'Libraries – information services' from <**www.leeds.gov.uk/Community_and_living/Libraries.aspx**>.) GROS has a programme for encouraging the availability of access to ScotlandsPeople from Scotland's public libraries.

1 Major George Graham (Registrar General 1842–1879) was responsible for the planning and execution of every census from 1851 to 1871.

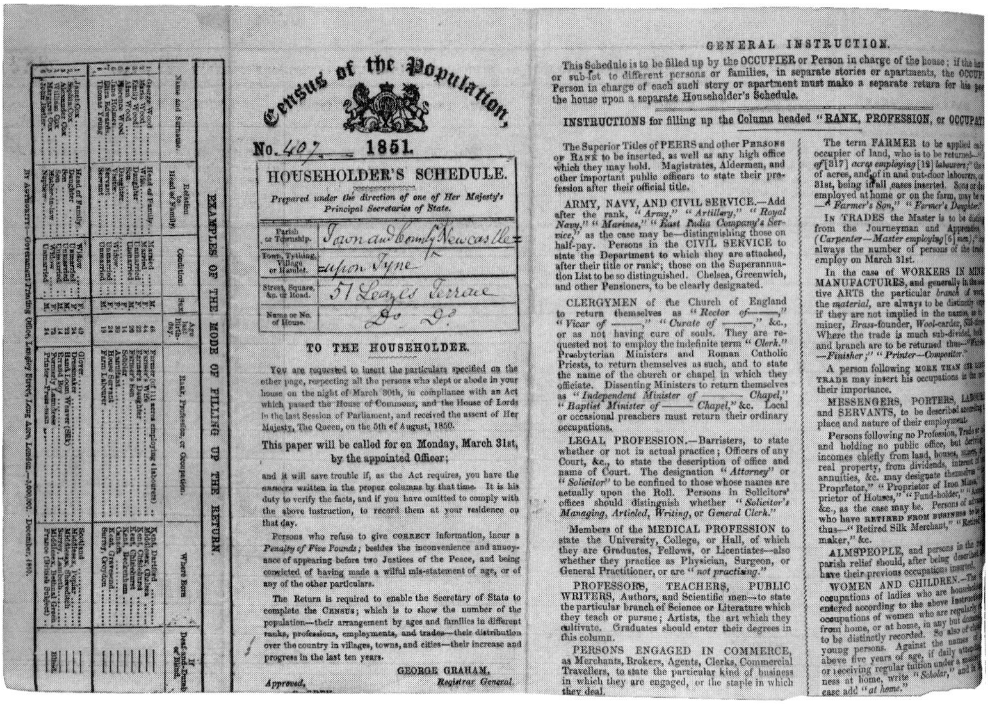

Census of the Population,

No. 407 1851.

HOUSEHOLDER'S SCHEDULE.

Prepared under the direction of one of Her Majesty's Principal Secretaries of State.

Parish or Township.	Town and County Newcastle
Town, Tything, Village or Hamlet.	upon Tyne
Street, Square, &c. or Road.	51 Leazes Terrace
Name or No. of House.	Do Do

TO THE HOUSEHOLDER.

You are requested to insert the particulars specified on the other page, respecting all the persons who slept or abode in your house on the night of March 30th, in compliance with an Act which passed the House of Commons, and the House of Lords in the last Session of Parliament, and received the assent of Her Majesty, The Queen, on the 5th of August, 1850.

This paper will be called for on Monday, March 31st, by the appointed Officer;

and it will save trouble if, as the Act requires, you have the answers written in the proper columns by that time. It is his duty to verify the facts, and if you have omitted to comply with the above instruction, to record them at your residence on that day.

Persons who refuse to give correct information, incur a *Penalty of Five Pounds*; besides the inconvenience and annoyance of appearing before two Justices of the Peace, and being convicted of having made a wilful mis-statement of age, or of any of the other particulars.

The Return is required to enable the Secretary of State to complete the Census; which is to show the number of the population—their arrangement by ages and families in different ranks, professions, employments, and trades—their distribution over the country in villages, towns, and cities—their increase and progress in the last ten years.

GEORGE GRAHAM, *Registrar General.*

Approved,

GENERAL INSTRUCTION.

This Schedule is to be filled up by the OCCUPIER or Person in charge of the house; if the house is let or sub-let to different persons or families, in separate stories or apartments, the OCCUPIER or Person in charge of each such story or apartment must make a separate return for his portion of the house upon a separate Householder's Schedule.

INSTRUCTIONS for filling up the Column headed "RANK, PROFESSION, or OCCUPATION."

The Superior Titles of PEERS and other PERSONS OF RANK to be inserted, as well as any high office which they may hold. Magistrates, Aldermen, and other important public officers to state their profession after their official title.

ARMY, NAVY, AND CIVIL SERVICE.—Add after the rank, "*Army*," "*Artillery*," "*Royal Navy*," "*Marines*," "*East India Company's Service*," as the case may be—distinguishing those on half-pay. Persons in the CIVIL SERVICE to state the Department to which they are attached, after their title or rank; those on the Superannuation List to be so distinguished. Chelsea, Greenwich, and other Pensioners, to be clearly designated.

CLERGYMEN of the Church of England to return themselves as "*Rector of* ———," "*Vicar of* ———," "*Curate of* ———," &c., or as not having cure of souls. They are requested not to employ the indefinite term "*Clerk*." Presbyterian Ministers and Roman Catholic Priests, to return themselves as such, and to state the name of the church or chapel in which they officiate. Dissenting Ministers to return themselves as "*Independent Minister of* ——— *Chapel*," "*Baptist Minister of* ——— *Chapel*," &c. Local or occasional preachers must return their ordinary occupations.

LEGAL PROFESSION.—Barristers, to state whether or not in actual practice; Officers of any Court, &c., to state the description of office and name of Court. The designation "*Attorney*" or "*Solicitor*" to be confined to those whose names are actually upon the Roll. Persons in Solicitors' offices should distinguish whether "*Solicitor's Managing, Articled, Writing*, or *General Clerk*."

Members of the MEDICAL PROFESSION to state the University, College, or Hall, of which they are Graduates, Fellows, or Licentiates—also whether they practice as Physician, Surgeon, or General Practitioner, or are "*not practising*."

PROFESSORS, TEACHERS, PUBLIC WRITERS, Authors, and Scientific men—to state the particular branch of Science or Literature which they teach or pursue; Artists, the art which they cultivate. Graduates should enter their degrees in this column.

PERSONS ENGAGED IN COMMERCE, as Merchants, Brokers, Agents, Clerks, Commercial Travellers, to state the particular kind of business in which they are engaged, or the staple in which they deal.

2 A rare example of a household schedule from the 1851 census for 51 Leazes Terrace, Newcastle upon Tyne, showing the instructions to the householder for filling it in.
(HO 107/2405)

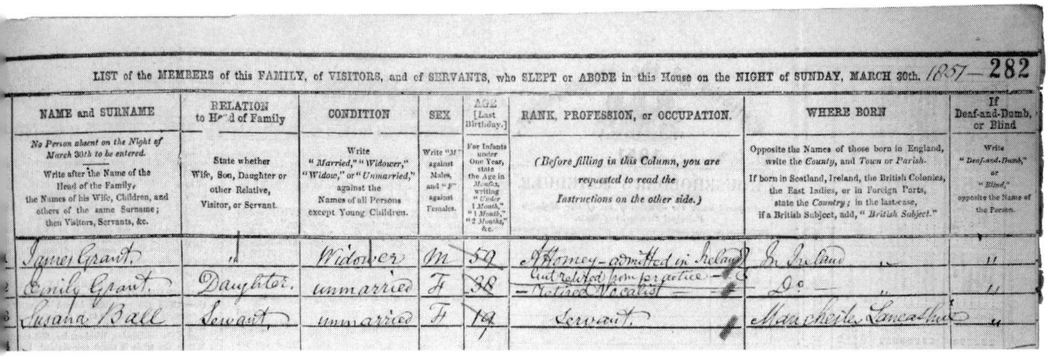

LIST of the MEMBERS of this FAMILY, of VISITORS, and of SERVANTS, who SLEPT or ABODE in this House on the NIGHT of SUNDAY, MARCH 30th, 1851 — 282

NAME and SURNAME	RELATION to Head of Family	CONDITION	SEX	AGE [Last Birthday.]	RANK, PROFESSION, or OCCUPATION.	WHERE BORN	If Deaf-and-Dumb, or Blind
No Person absent on the Night of March 30th to be entered. Write after the Name of the Head of the Family, the Names of his Wife, Children, and others of the same Surname; then Visitors, Servants, &c.	State whether Wife, Son, Daughter or other Relative, Visitor, or Servant.	Write "*Married*," "*Widower*," "*Widow*," or "*Unmarried*," against the Names of all Persons except Young Children.	Write "M" against Males, and "F" against Females.	For Infants under One Year, state the Age in Months, writing "Under 1 Month," "1 Month," "2 Months," &c.	(*Before filling in this Column, you are requested to read the Instructions on the other side.*)	Opposite the Names of those born in England, write the *County*, and *Town or Parish*. If born in Scotland, Ireland, the British Colonies, the East Indies, or in Foreign Parts, state the *Country*; in the last case, if a British Subject, add, "*British Subject*."	Write "*Deaf-and-Dumb*," or "*Blind*," opposite the Name of the Person.
James Grant	1	Widower	M	59	Attorney-admitted in Ireland but retired from practice	In Ireland	
Emily Grant	Daughter	unmarried	F	38	Retired Vocalist	Do	
Susana Ball	Servant	unmarried	F	19	Servant	Manchester Lancashire	

3 Household schedule showing attorney James Grant, 'admitted in Ireland but retired from practice', his daughter Emily, a 'retired vocalist', and their servant Susana Ball.
(HO 107/2405)

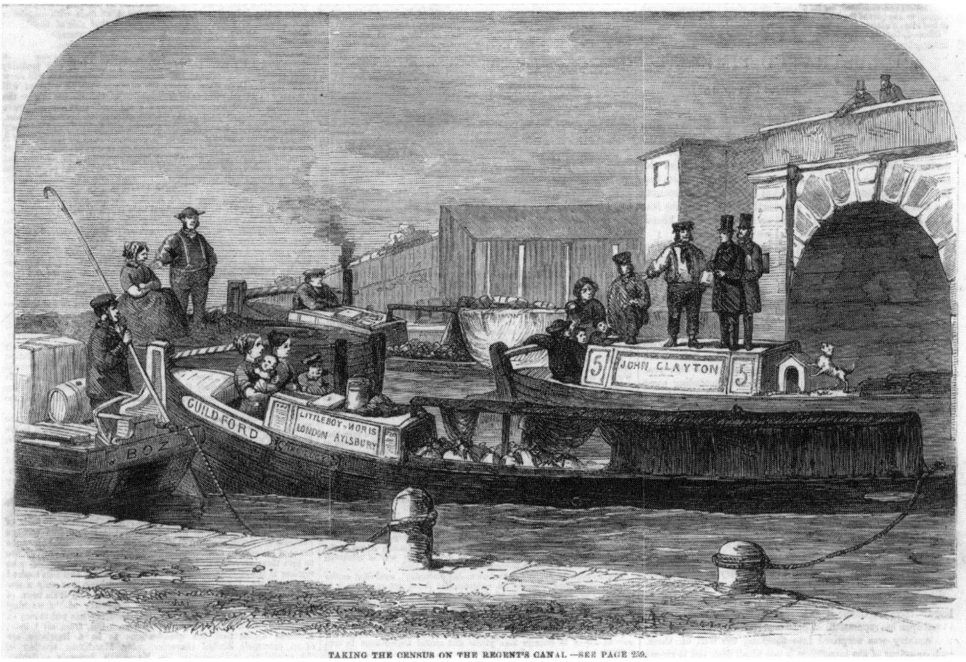

TAKING THE CENSUS ON THE REGENT'S CANAL.—SEE PAGE 259.

4 *Above:* The enumerator gathering information from the occupants of a barge on the Regents Canal in 1861.

5 *Below:* 'Memorandum respecting the Enumeration of Persons in Boats, Barges &c.' from the Census Office 1861. (RG 27/3)

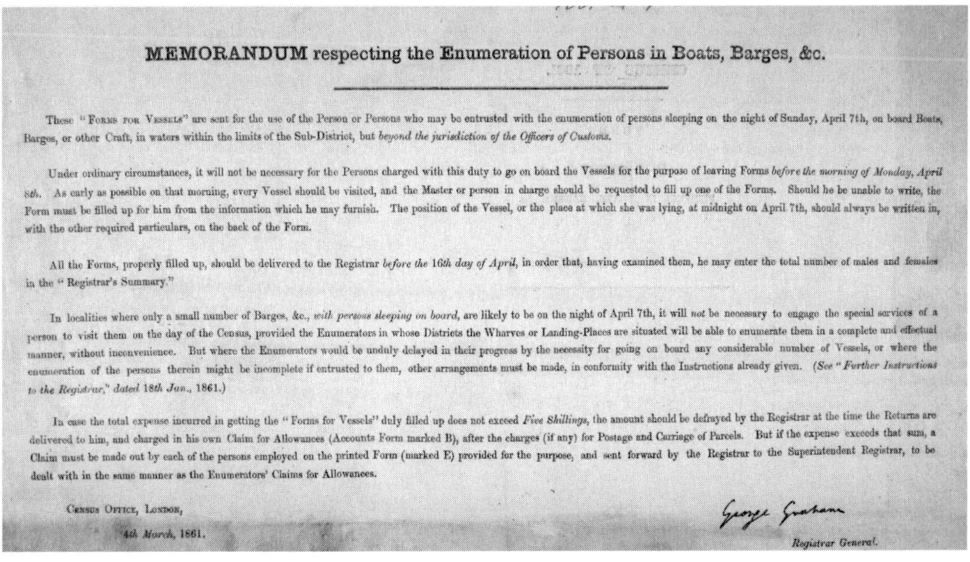

MEMORANDUM respecting the Enumeration of Persons in Boats, Barges, &c.

These "FORMS FOR VESSELS" are sent for the use of the Person or Persons who may be entrusted with the enumeration of persons sleeping on the night of Sunday, April 7th, on board Boats, Barges, or other Craft, in waters within the limits of the Sub-District, but *beyond the jurisdiction of the Officers of Customs.*

Under ordinary circumstances, it will not be necessary for the Persons charged with this duty to go on board the Vessels for the purpose of leaving Forms *before the morning of Monday, April 8th.* As early as possible on that morning, every Vessel should be visited, and the Master or person in charge should be requested to fill up one of the Forms. Should he be unable to write, the Form must be filled up for him from the information which he may furnish. The position of the Vessel, or the place at which she was lying, at midnight on April 7th, should always be written in, with the other required particulars, on the back of the Form.

All the Forms, properly filled up, should be delivered to the Registrar *before the 16th day of April*, in order that, having examined them, he may enter the total number of males and females in the "Registrar's Summary."

In localities where only a small number of Barges, &c., *with persons sleeping on board*, are likely to be on the night of April 7th, it will *not* be necessary to engage the special services of a person to visit them on the day of the Census, provided the Enumerators in whose Districts the Wharves or Landing-Places are situated will be able to enumerate them in a complete and effectual manner, without inconvenience. But where the Enumerators would be unduly delayed in their progress by the necessity for going on board any considerable number of Vessels, or where the enumeration of the persons therein might be incomplete if entrusted to them, other arrangements must be made, in conformity with the Instructions already given. *(See "Further Instructions to the Registrar," dated 18th Jan.*, 1861.)

In case the total expense incurred in getting the "Forms for Vessels" duly filled up does not exceed *Five Shillings*, the amount should be defrayed by the Registrar at the time the Returns are delivered to him, and charged in his own Claim for Allowances (Accounts Form marked B), after the charges (if any) for Postage and Carriage of Parcels. But if the expense exceeds that sum, a Claim must be made out by each of the persons employed on the printed Form (marked E) provided for the purpose, and sent forward by the Registrar to the Superintendent Registrar, to be dealt with in the same manner as the Enumerators' Claims for Allowances.

CENSUS OFFICE, LONDON,
4th March, 1861.

George Graham
Registrar General.

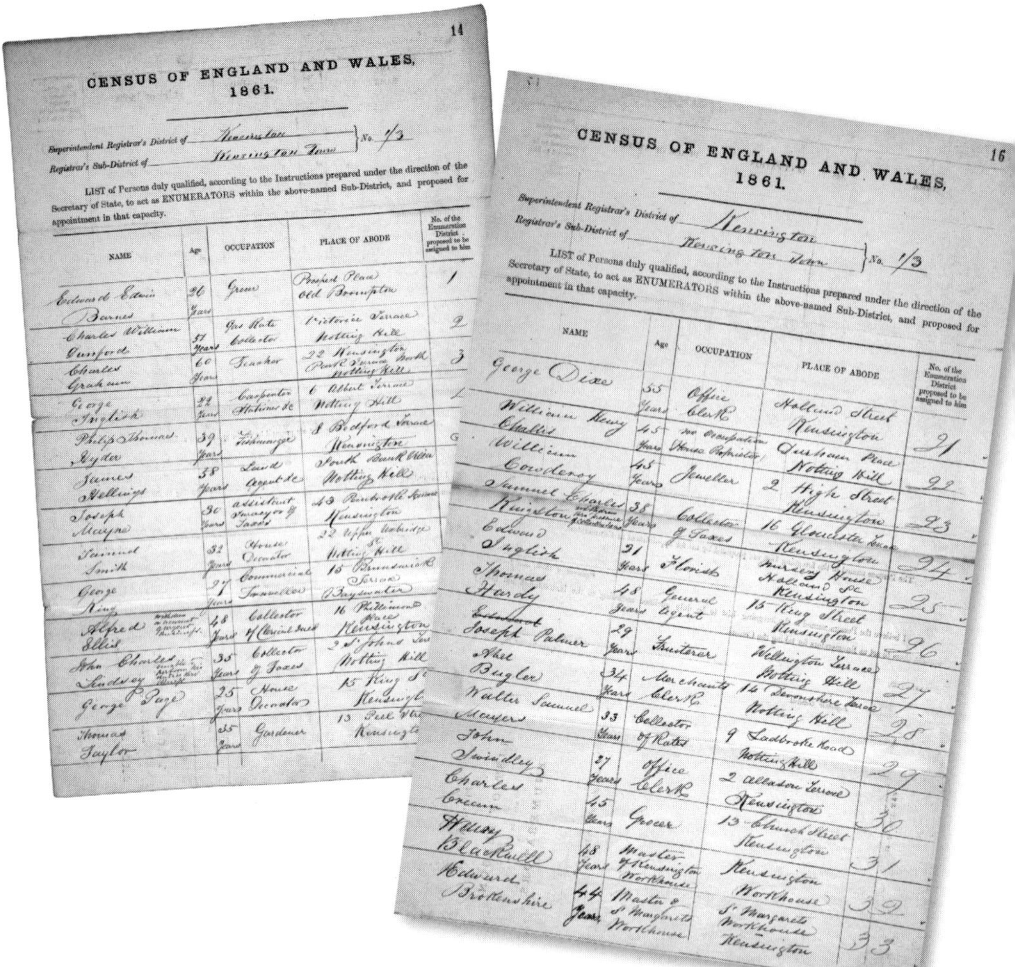

14

CENSUS OF ENGLAND AND WALES, 1861.

Superintendent Registrar's District of Kensington } No. 1/3
Registrar's Sub-District of Kensington Town

LIST of Persons duly qualified, according to the Instructions prepared under the direction of the Secretary of State, to act as ENUMERATORS within the above-named Sub-District, and proposed for appointment in that capacity.

NAME	Age	OCCUPATION	PLACE OF ABODE	No. of the Enumeration District proposed to be assigned to him
Edward Edwin Barnes	26 Years	Grocer	Prospect Place Old Brompton	1
Charles William Dunford	51 Years	Gas Rate Collector	Victoria Terrace Notting Hill	2
Charles Graham	60 Years	Teacher	22 Kensington Park Terrace North Notting Hill	3
George Inglish	22 Years	Carpenter Stationer &c	6 Albert Terrace Notting Hill	4
Philip Thomas Ryder	39 Years	Fishmonger	8 Bedford Terrace Kensington	
James Hellings	38 Years	Land Agent &c	South Bank Villa Notting Hill	
Joseph Mayne	30 Years	Assistant Surveyor of Taxes	43 Pembroke Square Kensington	
Samuel Smith	32 Years	House Decorator	22 Upper Uxbridge St Notting Hill	
George King	27 Years	Commercial Traveller	15 Brunswick Terrace Bayswater	
Alfred Ellis	48 Years	Collector of Church Rates	16 Phillimore Place Kensington	
John Charles Lindsey	35 Years	Collector of Taxes	2 St Johns Terrace Notting Hill	
George Page	25 Years	House Decorator	15 King St Kensington	
Thomas Taylor	35 Years	Gardener	13 Peel St Kensington	

16

CENSUS OF ENGLAND AND WALES, 1861.

Superintendent Registrar's District of Kensington
Registrar's Sub-District of Kensington Town } No. 1/3

LIST of Persons duly qualified, according to the Instructions prepared under the direction of the Secretary of State, to act as ENUMERATORS within the above-named Sub-District, and proposed for appointment in that capacity.

NAME	Age	OCCUPATION	PLACE OF ABODE	No. of the Enumeration District proposed to be assigned to him
George Dixe	55 Years	Office Clerk	Holland Street Kensington	21
William Henry Challis	45 Years	No Occupation House Proprietor	Durham Place Notting Hill	22
William Cowderoy	45 Years	Jeweller	2 High Street Kensington	23
Samuel Charles Kingston	38 Years	Collector of Taxes	16 Gloucester Terrace Kensington	24
Edward Inglish	21 Years	Florist	Nursery House Holland St Kensington	25
Thomas Hardy	48 Years	General Agent	15 King Street Kensington	26
~~Edmund~~ Joseph Palmer	29 Years	Upholsterer	Wellington Terrace Notting Hill	27
Abel Bugler	34 Years	Merchants Clerk	14 Devonshire Terrace Notting Hill	28
Walter Samuel Meyer	33 Years	Collector of Rates	9 Ladbroke Road Notting Hill	29
John Swindley	27 Years	Office Clerk	2 Allason Terrace Kensington	30
Charles Green	45 Years	Grocer	13 Church Street Kensington	31
Henry Blackall	48 Years	Master of Kensington Workhouse	Kensington Workhouse	32
Edward Brokenshire	44 Years	Master of St Margarets Workhouse	St Margarets Workhouse Kensington	33

6 and 7 *Above:* List of enumerators for Kensington, showing ages, addresses and occupations. These and a few other pages from 1861 are the only examples of such lists that have survived from any census year. (RG 9/4543)

8 *Right:* The enumerator's lot was not always a happy one!

THE ENUMERATOR ENDURES SOME CHAFF.

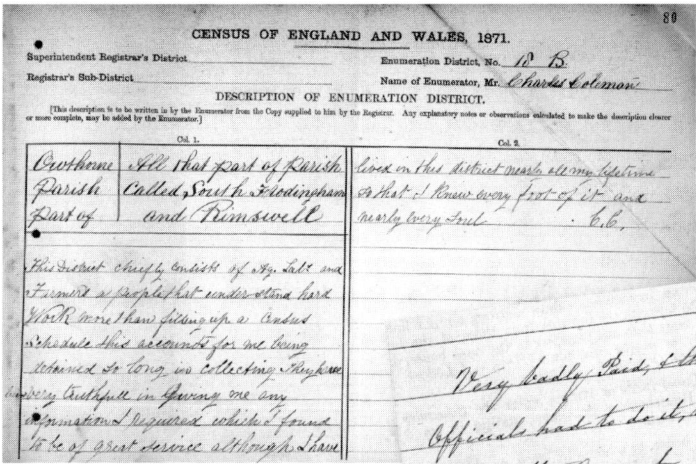
CENSUS OF ENGLAND AND WALES, 1871. 80

Superintendent Registrar's District

Registrar's Sub-District

Enumeration District, No. 18 B.

Name of Enumerator, Mr. Charles Coleman

DESCRIPTION OF ENUMERATION DISTRICT.

[This description is to be written in by the Enumerator from the Copy supplied to him by the Registrar. Any explanatory notes or observations calculated to make the description clearer or more complete, may be added by the Enumerator.]

Col. 1.		Col. 2.
Owthorne Parish Part of	All that part of Parish Called South Frodingham and Rimswell	lived in this district nearly all my lifetime so that I knew every foot of it and nearly every Soul. C.C.

This District chiefly Consists of Ag. Lab. and Farmers a people that under stand hard Work more than filling up a Census Schedule this accounts for me being detained so long in collecting They have been very truthfull in Giving me any information I required which I found to be of great service although I have

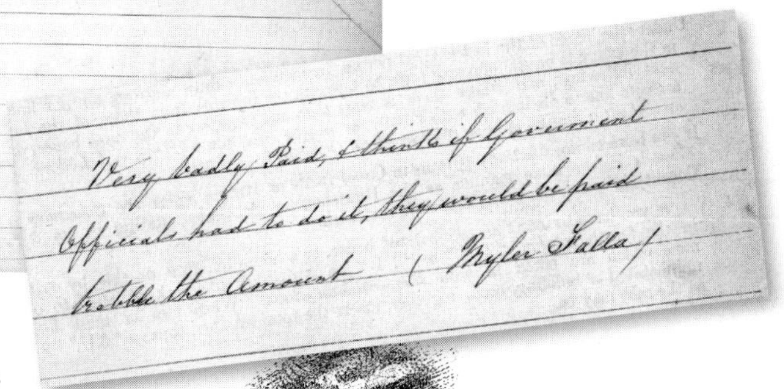
Very badly Paid, & think if Government Officials had to do it, they would be paid treble the Amount (Myler Falla)

9 *Above left:* Some enumerators were unusually conscientious, such as Charles Coleman in the East Riding of Yorkshire in 1871. (RG 10/4799)

10 *Above right:* Myler Falla was unhappy with his rate of pay as an enumerator for Mortlake, Surrey in 1871. (RG 10/870)

11 *Right:* Not all householders treated the census schedule with respect.

12 *Below:* Edward Henry Blade demonstrated his displeasure at the small sum paid for a lot of work in a very crowded part of the East End of London in 1851. (HO 107/1531)

THE MAN WHO LIGHTS HIS PIPE WITH THE SCHEDULE.

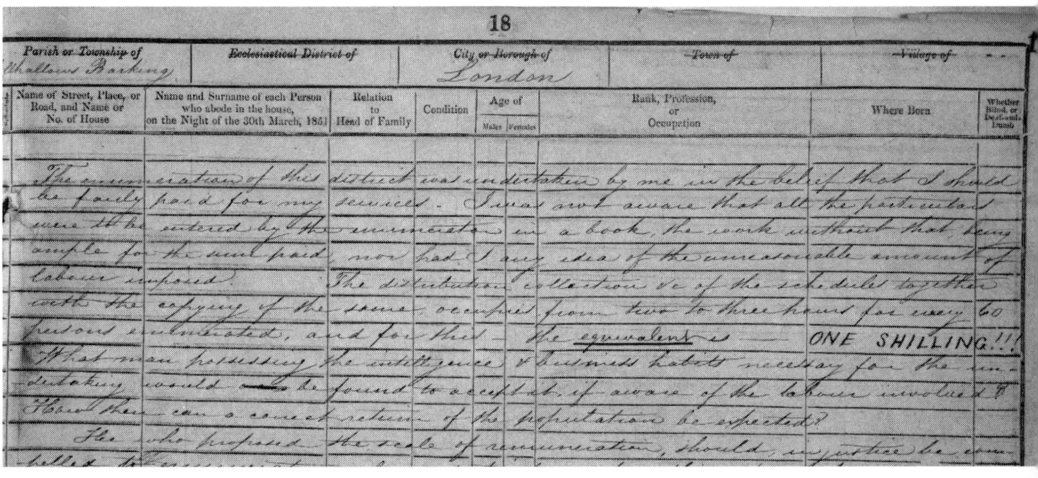
18

Parish or Township of Allhallows Barking	Ecclesiastical District of	City or Borough of London	Town of	Village of

Name of Street, Place, or Road, and Name or No. of House	Name and Surname of each Person who abode in the house, on the Night of the 30th March, 1851	Relation to Head of Family	Condition	Age of Males	Age of Females	Rank, Profession, or Occupation	Where Born	Whether Blind, or Deaf-and-Dumb

The enumeration of this district was undertaken by me in the belief that I should be fairly paid for my services. I was not aware that all the particulars were to be entered by the enumerator in a book, the work without that being ample for the sum paid, nor had I any idea of the unreasonable amount of labour imposed. The distribution, collection &c of the schedules together with the copying of the same occupies from two to three hours for every 60 persons enumerated, and for this the equivalent is ONE SHILLING!!! What man possessing the intelligence & business habits necessary for the undertaking would be found to accept it, if aware of the labour involved? How then can a correct return of the population be expected? He who proposed the scale of remuneration, should, in justice be compelled to

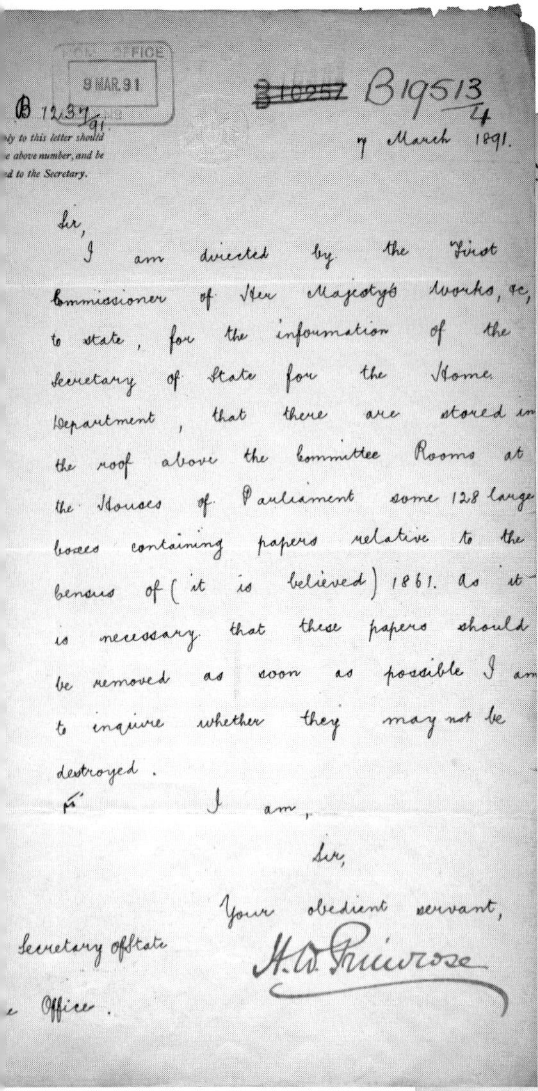
HOME OFFICE 9 MAR.91

B 1237/91

~~B10257~~ B19513/4

...ply to this letter should ...e above number, and be ...d to the Secretary.

7 March 1891.

Sir,

I am directed by the First Commissioner of Her Majesty's Works, &c, to state, for the information of the Secretary of State for the Home Department, that there are stored in the roof above the Committee Rooms at the Houses of Parliament some 128 large boxes containing papers relative to the Census of (it is believed) 1861. As it is necessary that these papers should be removed as soon as possible I am to inquire whether they may not be destroyed.

I am,

Sir,

Your obedient servant,

H.W. Primrose

Secretary of State

...e Office.

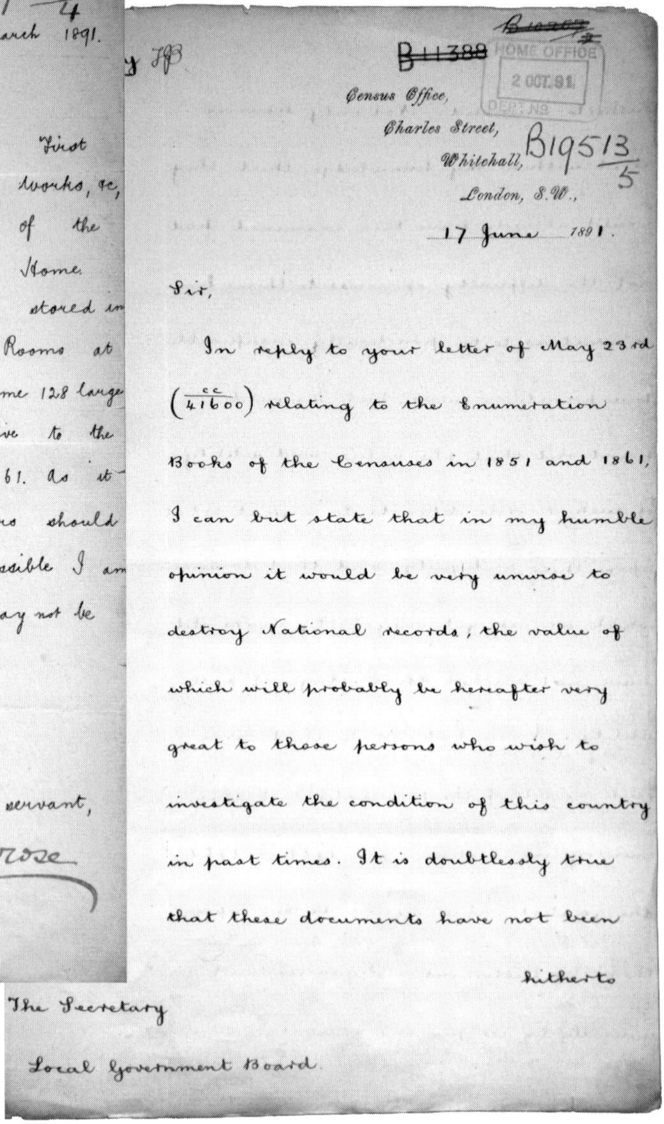
~~B10257~~ ~~B11388~~ HOME OFFICE 2 OCT.91

Census Office,
Charles Street,
Whitehall,
London, S.W.,

B19513/5

17 June 1891.

Sir,

In reply to your letter of May 23rd (cc/41600) relating to the Enumeration Books of the Censuses in 1851 and 1861, I can but state that in my humble opinion it would be very unwise to destroy National records, the value of which will probably be hereafter very great to those persons who wish to investigate the condition of this country in past times. It is doubtlessly true that these documents have not been hitherto

The Secretary
Local Government Board

13 *Left:* In 1891 Mr Primrose was very keen to dispose of the Enumeration Books for 1851 and 1861. (HO 45/10147)

14 *Right:* Fortunately for posterity, Registrar General Brydges Henniker took the opposite view. (HO 45/10147)

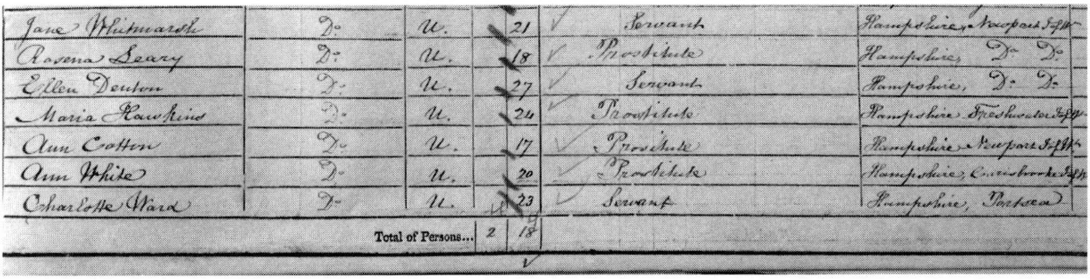

Jane Whitmarsh	Do	U.	21	Servant	Hampshire, Newport I of W
Rosena Leary	Do	U.	18	Prostitute	Hampshire, Do Do
Ellen Denton	Do	U.	27	Servant	Hampshire, Do Do
Maria Hawkins	Do	U.	24	Prostitute	Hampshire, Freshwater I of W
Ann Cotton	Do	U.	17	Prostitute	Hampshire, Newport I of W
Ann White	Do	U.	20	Prostitute	Hampshire, Carisbrooke I of W
Charlotte Ward	Do	U.	23	Servant	Hampshire, Portsea
Total of Persons...		2	18		

15 18-year-old Rosina Leary in the Isle of Wight 'House of Industry' in 1851, described as a prostitute. She bore at least eight children by William Ask and George Pragnell. (HO 107/1663)

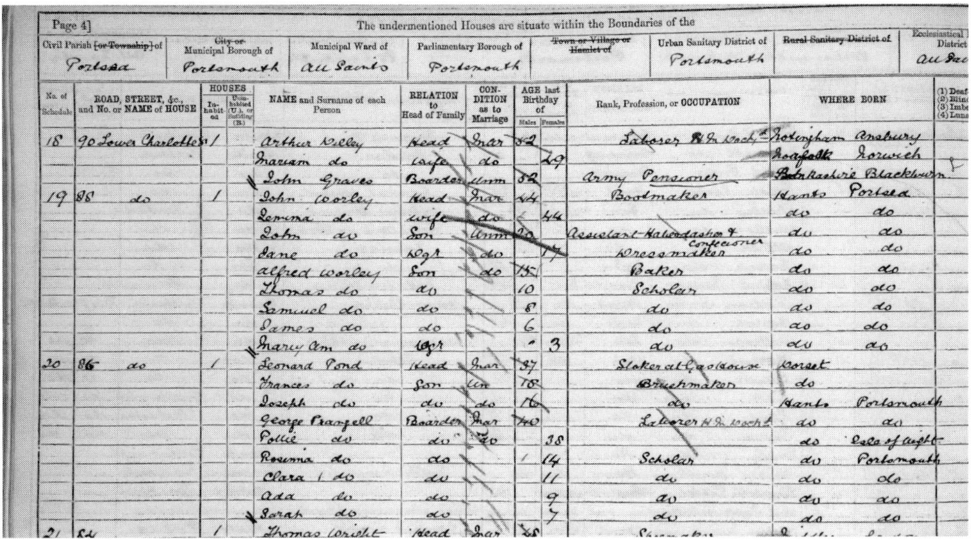

Page 4] The undermentioned Houses are situate within the Boundaries of the

Civil Parish [or Township] of Portsea | City or Municipal Borough of Portsmouth | Municipal Ward of All Saints | Parliamentary Borough of Portsmouth | Town or Village or Hamlet of | Urban Sanitary District of Portsmouth | Rural Sanitary District of | Ecclesiastical District All Sa[illegible]

No. of Schedule	ROAD, STREET, &c., and No. or NAME of HOUSE	Inhabited	Uninhabited	NAME and Surname of each Person	RELATION to Head of Family	CONDITION as to Marriage	Age Males	Age Females	Rank, Profession, or OCCUPATION	WHERE BORN
18	90 Lower Charlotte St	1		Arthur Willey	Head	Mar	52		Laborer H M Dock Yd	Nottingham Ansbury
				Mariam do	Wife	do		29		Norfolk Norwich
				John Graves	Boarder	Unm	52		Army Pensioner	Lancashire Blackburn
19	88 do	1		John Worley	Head	Mar	44		Bootmaker	Hants Portsea
				Lemina do	Wife	do		44		do do
				John do	Son	Unm	20		Assistant Haberdasher & Confectioner	do do
				Jane do	Dau	do		17	Dressmaker	do do
				Alfred Worley	Son	do	15		Baker	do do
				Thomas do	do		10		Scholar	do do
				Samuel do	do		8		do	do do
				James do	do		6		do	do do
				Mary Ann do	Dau			3	do	do do
20	86 do	1		Leonard Pond	Head	Mar	37		Stoker at Gas House	Dorset
				Frances do	Son	Un	18		Brickmaker	do
				Joseph do	do	do	16		do	Hants Portsmouth
				George Prangell	Boarder	Mar	40		Laborer H M Dock Yd	do do
				Pollie do	do	do		38		do Isle of Wight
				Rosina do	do			14	Scholar	do Portsmouth
				Clara do	do			11	do	do do
				Ada do	do			9	do	do do
				Sarah do	do			7	do	do do
21	84	1		Thomas Wright	Head	Mar	58		[illegible]	[illegible]

16 The Pragnell family (entered as 'Prangell') boarding with the Pond family in Portsmouth in 1881. The whole family later reverted back to the name Ask. (RG 11/1139)

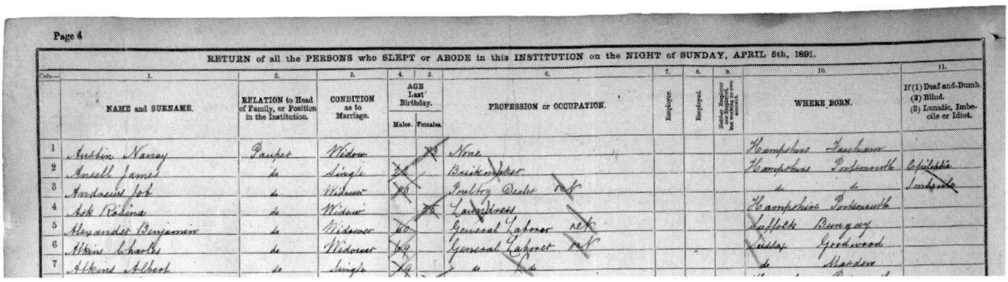

Page 4

RETURN of all the PERSONS who SLEPT or ABODE in this INSTITUTION on the NIGHT of SUNDAY, APRIL 5th, 1891.

	NAME and SURNAME	RELATION to Head of Family, or Position in the Institution	CONDITION as to Marriage	AGE Last Birthday Males	Females	PROFESSION or OCCUPATION	Employer	Employed	Neither Employer nor Employed	WHERE BORN	If (1) Deaf-and-Dumb (2) Blind (3) Lunatic, Imbecile or Idiot
1	Austin Nancy	Pauper	Widow		[illegible]	None				Hampshire Fareham	
2	Ansell James	do	Single	[illegible]		Brickmaker				Hampshire Portsmouth	Epileptic
3	Andrews Job	do	Widower	[illegible]		Poultry Dealer				do do	Imbecile
4	Ask Rosina	do	Widow		[illegible]	Laundress				Hampshire Portsmouth	
5	Alexander Benjamin	do	Widower	60		General Laborer				Suffolk Bungay	
6	Akins Charles	do	Widower	69		General Laborer				Sussex Goodwood	
7	Atkins Albert	do	Single	[illegible]		do				do Marden	

17 The widowed Rosina Ask, laundress, in the Union Workhouse, Portsea Island, in 1891. (RG 12/860)

18 *Left:* A Hollerith punch-card machine as supplied to the GRO by the British Tabulating Machine Company.

19 *Centre:* An example of one of the punch-cards used to tabulate the results of the 1911 census. (T 1/11243)

20 *Below:* The 1911 census asked for information about occupations. William Bailey supplied much more detail than was actually required. (RG 14/24246/142)

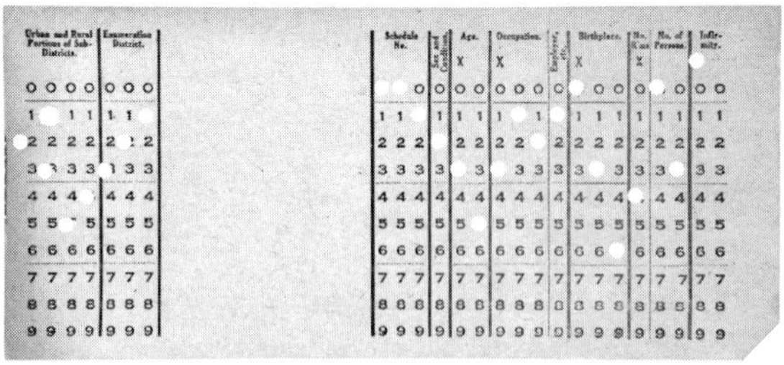

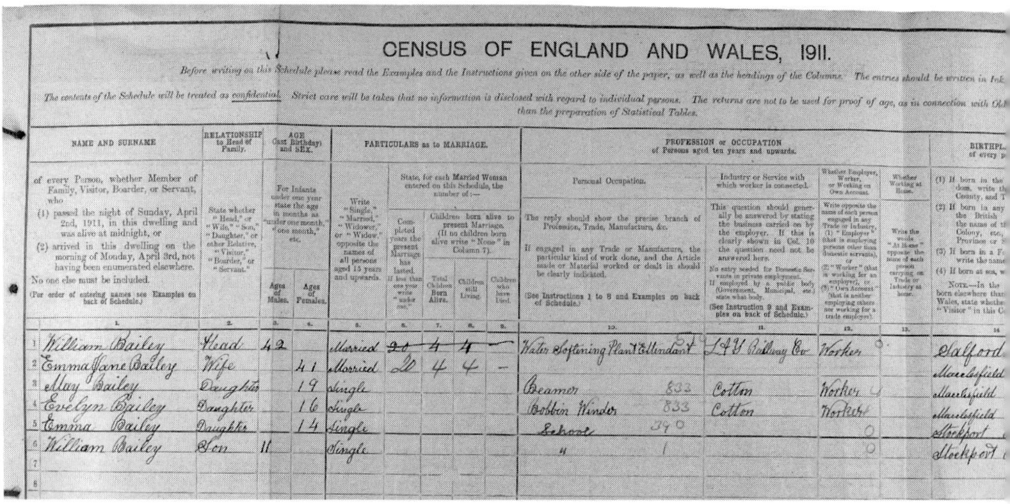

CENSUS OF ENGLAND AND WALES, 1911.

Before writing on this Schedule please read the Examples and the Instructions given on the other side of the paper, as well as the headings of the Columns. The entries should be written in Ink

The contents of the Schedule will be treated as confidential. Strict care will be taken that no information is disclosed with regard to individual persons. The returns are not to be used for proof of age, as in connection with Old … than the preparation of Statistical Tables.

	NAME AND SURNAME	RELATIONSHIP to Head of Family	Ages of Males	Ages of Females	PARTICULARS as to MARRIAGE	Completed years the present Marriage has lasted	Total Children Born Alive	Children still Living	Children who have Died	Personal Occupation	Industry or Service with which worker is connected	Whether Employer, Worker, or Working on Own Account	Whether Working at Home	BIRTHPLACE
1	William Bailey	Head	42		Married	~~20~~	~~4~~	~~4~~	~~—~~	Water Softening Plant Attendant	L & Y Railway Co	Worker		Salford
2	Emma Jane Bailey	Wife		41	Married	20	4	4	—					Macclesfield
3	May Bailey	Daughter		19	Single					Beamer 833	Cotton	Worker		Macclesfield
4	Evelyn Bailey	Daughter		16	Single					Bobbin Winder 833	Cotton	Worker		Macclesfield
5	Emma Bailey	Daughter		14	Single					School 340				Stockport
6	William Bailey	Son	11		Single					" 1				Stockport
7														
8														

When the 1901 census was first released, there was a great deal of concern about the fact that the index was only going to be available online, and at a cost. The general tenor was, 'These are public records – why should we pay to have access to them?' Although there is now much more general acceptance of online delivery of information and online payment, one still hears grumbles in this vein.

Disregarding the fact that family historians have always had to pay for access to birth, marriage and death certificates and census at GROS, there are two answers.

First, you don't have to pay to access them. The National Archives provides free access to online indexes for every census year; and, as just mentioned, many public libraries have access to one or more genealogical data services, normally free of charge. Alternatively, the microfilms for the nineteenth century censuses are widely accessible – the LDS Church's Family History Centers have complete sets for the British Isles and these can be viewed free of charge. Central libraries, local studies centres and county records offices often have the microfilms for their own catchment area.

But of course, you have to pay for your travel to Kew or a Family History Center, and you have to take the extra time out of your schedule to do so. In fact, it makes little sense to complain about paying for online access but be happy to pay the same amount for petrol and parking, or to transport companies. At least with online access, the money goes to organizations making genealogical data available, with licence fees to the archives holding the original records.

Creating an online census is a massive and expensive undertaking. The 1881 Census Index took 9,000 volunteers (admittedly not working full time) six and a half years to create, and that was without scanning the images and linking each image to all the matching index entries. FreeCEN has been running since 1998 and has almost 13 million records, but that's equivalent to just half a nineteenth century census. In half that time, commercial data services have digitized all the available censuses for England, Wales and Scotland.

For many people in fact, regardless of the expense, the availability of genealogical data on the web from home at any time of day or night is the only thing that makes progress with their family tree possible at all. And for anyone with reduced mobility or vision, getting to a repository and trying to read microfilm were never comfortable experiences.

Technical requirements

While the volunteer-based indexes do not require any particular software or computer set-up, all the commercial census sites have some technical requirements, and it is as well to be aware of these before you start to use them for serious genealogical research.

First, like all commercial websites, they require cookies to be enabled. A cookie is a small text file that is stored on your computer to keep information about your connection to a website. Some people prefer, as a security measure, to set their browser to block cookies. But there is no good reason to block cookies from reputable genealogy companies and blocking them will make it impossible to use the commercial census data services. If you are worried about this, you can always switch cookies on while you use such a site and then turn them off again afterwards.

It is a simple matter to check whether you have cookies enabled or not. If you are using Internet Explorer:

1. Tools → Internet Options → Privacy → Advanced
2. The slider under 'Setting' should be set to 'Medium' or 'Medium High'.

If you want a fuller explanation of what these settings mean, see the article on Cookies in the Microsoft Knowledge Base at <**support.microsoft.com/kb/283185**>.

In Firefox:

1. Tools → Options → Privacy
2. Make sure that 'Accept cookies from sites' is ticked.

On any other browser look for an Options menu item or use the online help.

It is clear from some of the online discussion forums that people sometimes have problems which turn out to be caused by their firewall or anti-virus software. It is very difficult to give general instructions for identifying and dealing with such problems – the symptoms will vary according to the operating system, browser, anti-virus software, and the website being accessed. If you are having trouble with a specific online service, it will be worth checking their help pages. If that does not provide the answer, contact the site's technical support. Even though the problem is unlikely to be caused by their system, they're likely to be aware of common causes of problems among their users and how to solve them.

Web browsers come with built-in facilities to view certain types of digital image, but have very limited facilities for anything other than viewing, saving or printing an image. In particular, a zoom function (which you may need to examine a census image closely to try and decipher some problematic detail) is not provided by your browser.

For this reason, the data services do not provide unadorned images in these standard formats; they either use special formats or offer enhanced image viewing facilities via some sort of image viewer. Both of these options mean that you will almost certainly have to install some sort of browser plug-in before you can view the images.

One of the commonest plug-ins, and one required for many other websites, is the Adobe Acrobat reader for displaying documents in PDF format. If you have not already got the Adobe Reader installed on your computer, you will need to download it from <**www.adobe.com/products/acrobat/readstep2.html**> and install it on your computer. It will normally install automatically in your browser, so that your browser will automatically use the reader to display any PDF file you encounter.

Limitations

The problems inherent in the census records themselves have already been highlighted in Chapter 3, but if you are consulting digitized census records there are additional issues to consider. How these affect the actual practice of searching for ancestors in the census will be discussed in the following chapter, but the main issues are reviewed here to draw attention to some important limitations in online census material.

One preliminary matter, which is often overlooked, is the distinction between a transcription and an index. A transcription is an exact representation of the text of the original document; an index is a finding aid. The job of a transcription is to be accurate; the job of an index is to be helpful, to point you to the correct place in a transcription, or to the right image. If an index has to 'correct' a transcription in order to do its job, that is perfectly acceptable. Any correction of a transcription, however, makes it less of a transcription.

You can see the difference between a transcription and an index if you imagine that we are looking for Charles Smith, born in Surrey. His census entry might well be 'Chas Smith, birthplace Surry'. If we have to search for Chas and Surry to find him, then we are searching a transcription, if we can find him looking for Charles Smith, Surrey, we are searching an index. In principle, there is no reason why one could not have just an index, but a transcription without a separate index will bring significant difficulties.

The reason for belabouring this point is that the commercial data sites, in particular, aren't always clear on the distinction. Indeed, to be pedantic, no site gives a 100 per cent accurate transcription of any entry for one simple reason: in the original record, the gender of an individual is not represented by a word or mark, but is indicated by the column in which the age is placed. For very sound reasons, no commercial site attempts to reproduce this way of indicating gender.

MISTRANSCRIPTION

All transcriptions of historical records are prone to error, and expecting a census index of 30 million or so records to be error-free is completely unrealistic. With datasets of this size, even a very low error rate still means lots of individual errors: 0.1 per cent would be a very demanding target, but still means 30,000 potentially unfindable people in 30 million records. Although it is certainly possible for the currently available transcriptions to be better than they are, having transcriptions done by better qualified people and instituting higher levels of quality control would add to the cost of digitization. Would you pay twice as much to consult data that was 1 per cent or 2 per cent more accurate? Probably not. If you would, then you can effectively do so by using more than one census index. Of course, some identical errors may be found in two different census indexes, but they will tend to be the ones where the original document is problematic anyway.

INDECIPHERABLE TEXT

Often, an 'error' is not really the fault of the transcriber – there are plenty of pages in the enumeration books where, with the best will in the world, a letter or a word is impossible to decipher with any certainty.

The problem is how to deal with these problematic entries. The proper course is that taken in the professional editing of historical documents: to indicate the position of the indecipherable letters, with suggested readings consigned to notes. With a clear distinction between transcription and index, an index can then contain entries for several possible readings of a problematic name.

The problem is that the online censuses all offer a poor substitute: the 'best guess'. Given that this is the best guess of someone with almost certainly no palaeographic training and probably little familiarity with the surnames and place names common in a particular area of the country, there is no reason to put any faith in such guesses. (The exception would be the 1881 Census Index, where the records were transcribed by volunteers from local family history societies. To be fair, however, we are not aware of any study that actually demonstrates the superiority of this index in the indexing of, for example, birthplaces.) Of course, given the potential costs of better solutions, this approach is understandable. But that doesn't make it satisfactory.

LACK OF VALIDATION

One of the key techniques for ensuring the accuracy of items of data in a database is 'validation'. This means making sure that a piece of information in an index is, if not demonstrably correct, at least plausible. With types of information that can be looked up, this is easily done: there are only so many counties in the British Isles at any one time, and we know what they are. It is therefore trivial to check that text entered in a 'County' field is the correctly spelled name of a valid county. Of course, the original document may indeed include an invalid county or a misspelling of the name, which in a transcription one would want to preserve. But identifying the oddity would be a sign to check whether the error was in the original or arose in the transcription process. It's more problematic with the town and village names given in the birthplace field, but again we have gazetteers against which these can be checked, with unrecognized entries at least flagged, if not manually corrected. For example, in several of the indexes we have noticed people born in 'Parkmouth, Hampshire'. It doesn't take long to establish that there is no such place, and so far we have not come across a single one which is not, as you might expect, a misreading of 'Portsmouth'. Some of these are indeed hard to read and one can appreciate the reason for the initial error. But the fact that there was a potential error here could easily have been spotted by validation against a gazetteer.

When the 1901 census for England and Wales was digitized, there was no adequate validation in place for the age column. The result was a census index which initially had dozens of people who appeared to be over 120 years old, in some cases even over 200 years old. It is slightly puzzling that the data entry staff didn't notice this themselves without any prompting, but even so it should not take users to point out this sort of error, which can be found (if not corrected) by an automated process.

Of course, misspellings of names can be very problematic to spot – there's no definitive list against which any spelling can be checked. But is it too much to expect digitizers to check that all their Willaims really are recorded as Willaim, all their Jhons aren't in reality Johns?

Sometimes it's not that a single field is self-evidently wrong, but that a particular combination is implausible, suggesting that one field is wrong, and that both need checking. For example, all the censuses seem to have a lot of girls called John. This would be a fascinating insight into nineteenth-century naming patterns, if it weren't manifest nonsense. Of course, we can't be sure there were no girls called John in nineteenth-century Britain, but clearly most such instances will be transcription errors, and the potential inconsistency should prompt manual checking. And of course, it almost always turns out that the gender has been got wrong or the name has been mistranscribed (it's usually Jane); often it seems the transcriber has confused data from two different lines on the enumeration form, or misunderstood a correction made by the enumerator. In fact, it would be a trivial matter to check a database, even a very large one, for the ten commonest male and female forenames. Even if one does not then check every apparent oddity, such entries could be flagged as potentially inconsistent.

Ancestry's census index for 1901 claims to find 3,098 individuals aged ten or under who are heads of household. However, before you shed too many tears for poor little Louisa M Jefferies, aged but two years, sole member of her own household in Islington, you should realize that she is in fact a *seventy*-two-year-old widow living on her own means (RG 13/198, f. 40, p. 17).

IMAGE QUALITY

One of the most significant limitations of the online census services is that you will often come across cases where the digital image is unclear. There are two main reasons for this: all digital image formats have a limited resolution, so there may be fine detail on the page which you cannot see. Of course, photographic film also has a limit to its resolution, the grain size of the emulsion, but at something like 75,000 dots per inch photographic film shows over 300 times more detail than a typical digital scan of the same 35mm frame.

The second problem is that all census indexes have been made from monochrome photographic film, which shows the original documents in shades of grey rather than the original colour. The reason this is a problem is that when the enumeration books were evaluated, the clerks made marks on the original pages in a different coloured ink. This is easy to see when you look at the originals, but in a monochrome film the subsequent marks often obliterate original details. This is particularly irritating when an age has been ticked off in such a way as to become unreadable (see Figure 4-1). Occupations, which were often subsequently annotated during analysis of the census, are another victim of this process.

Unfortunately, the chance of the 1841–1901 census records being redigitized, in colour, from the original enumeration books is very remote – it would be an expensive and time-consuming project that could not possibly recoup its costs. (And most of us would probably prefer the effort to be put into scanning new records rather than improving existing scans.) However, the 1911 census has been digitally photographed in colour direct from the original documents, and so does not suffer from this problem.

The final issue is the image format chosen by the data services. The ideal, given that we are starting from monochrome film, would be a greyscale image with the highest possible resolution. But there are practical limitations to consider. An entire census might contain one and a half million images, and the higher the resolution the more space they will take up on the data service's servers, and the more time they will require to download. In practice, 256 shades of grey is the standard for greyscale image – this is called 8-bit greyscale. There might occasionally be some benefit in scanning the census microfilms with more shades of grey, but any gains would be quite marginal and there

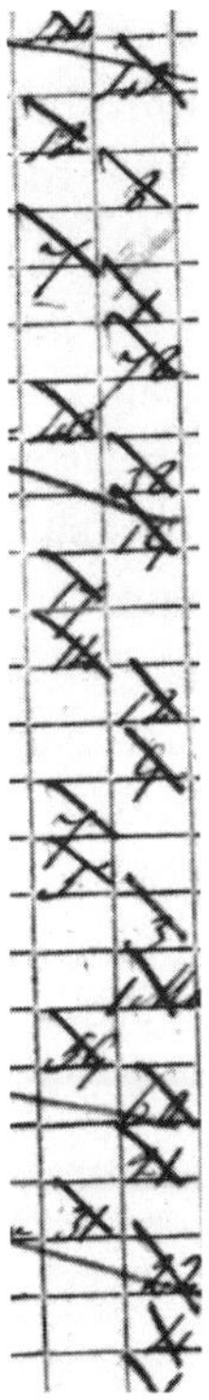

Figure 4-1 Check-marks obscuring ages (RG 9/426, f. 103 p. 14)

would be the problem that much computer graphics software could not cope with such images.

However, the problem is made worse where the digitizer decides to scan the shades of grey in the origin film as pure black and white, i.e. every mark on the pages is either black or white, nothing in between. Black and white scans, particularly at good resolution, can be very readable, but they are a bad choice where the original itself has poor legibility. This issue is discussed in more detail in Chapter 14, but the point here is that this is yet another factor making the digital scans harder to interpret, which in turn means that it increases the potential for errors in any transcription or index.

Of course, all these compromises in image quality have some justification. When the first digital census images were created, almost no home computer users had broadband connections. This meant that a high quality image would have taken a considerable time to download at the modem speeds that were then available. Some of the data services have recognized the need to improve image quality to keep up with the times and have been replacing black and white images with greyscale. But that doesn't do anything to help correct the errors that arose by creating indexes from poor quality originals.

Terms and conditions

One question that is often raised is what limits there are on what you can do with the data and images you download from a census site. While we are hardly qualified to offer legal advice, there are a number of issues to be aware of.

The census records are the property of the various national archives which hold them. These repositories also hold the copyright on the microfilms which are used as the basis for digital images. The individual data services purchase copies of the microfilms and a licence to digitize them. Even if there is an argument that copyright claims relating to photographs of out-of-copyright historical documents have no foundation (as is the case in the USA, for example), when you use a commercial data service you sign up to its terms and conditions. These are usually quite specific about what you can and can't do with the images and will set strict limits. Here, for example, are the relevant terms from Findmypast (<**www.findmypast.com/terms/**>):

> 4.2 You must not download, copy, reuse, resell, or republish online or in print or in any other format any part of the Material, except in the context of an individual family history.
> 4.3 You must not make any of the Material available to anyone online, but you may publish your personal family research online even where this incorporates information extracted from the Material.
> 4.4 You must not resell any of the Material or any information obtained through the findmypast.com Service, but you may sell a personal family history you have created even where this incorporates information extracted from the Material.

Copyright restrictions only apply to original materials, so you can make and publish your own transcriptions from the online census images, and of course this should include information on the source. What you can't do is simply copy and paste, say, all the census entries for a particular surname on a website to republish on your own website.

All the services either explicitly (as in the case of TheGenealogist, <**www.thegenealogist.co.uk/terms.php**>) or implicitly (Findmypast) forbid you to use the site to offer a look-up service. You will find plenty of messages in discussion forums where someone requests a look-up in census records. If you occasionally respond to such requests, you are not likely to be in any trouble, but you would be very unwise to post a message to a mailing list announcing a look-up service.

In fact, given that all the censuses are available both by subscription and on a pay-per-view basis (not to mention the free trials), and that the censuses are an essential genealogical source, it's difficult to find any good reason for a family historian to request a look-up at someone else's expense.

Useful census sites

Chapters 5 to 15 concentrate on sites offering census data, but there are many other sites with material relating to the censuses which may be of use.

The most comprehensive general resource for online census information is Cyndi's List, which has a Census Worldwide page at <**www.cyndislist.com/census2.htm**> and a UK and Ireland Census page at

< **www.cyndislist.com/census-uk.htm**>. This has around 400 links, including many to individual small-scale transcriptions.

The Histpop site at <**www.histpop.org**> has digitized copies of an enormous number of official documents relating to the censuses, including the population abstracts, documents relating to the planning of each census, and the final census reports. For those with an interest in local history, an essential site is A Vision of Britain Through Time at <**www.visionofbritain.org.uk**>, which uses the census reports for the history of individual places, with graphs showing the population change between 1801 and 2001.

Genuki has a gazetteer for the places in the 1891 census at <**www.genuki.org.uk/big/census_place.html**>. This gives the county, district, sub-district and TNA piece number for any place in England, Wales and the Isle of Man.

Jeff Knaggs has two very useful pages for the 1901 census of England and Wales, with lists of institutions and naval vessels included in the census, giving the piece and folio number of the entry. If you are using a commercial site which has the facility for a reference search, then the information on these pages will save you a lot of time in locating the entries for orphanages, schools, prisons, and the like.

There are a number of discussion forums devoted to using the online censuses. RootsWeb has seven mailing lists for discussion of UK census records, though in fact most of these are for volunteer transcribers. The only general ones are UK-1901-CENSUS, UK-1911-CENSUS and the somewhat premature UK-1921-CENSUS. Links to all three will be found at <**lists.rootsweb.com/index/other/Census-UK/**>. British-Genealogy has a British Census forum at <**www.british-genealogy.com/forums/**>. TalkingScot at <**www.talkingscot.com**> has a forum devoted to the Scottish censuses. The online censuses are a regular topic of discussion on the main mailing list for British genealogy, GENBRIT. Details will be found at <**lists.rootsweb.com/index/intl/UK/GENBRIT.html**> with a link to the searchable archives of past messages. As this mailing list is also a newsgroup, current and past messages can be seen at Google Groups, <**groups.google.com/group/soc.genealogy.britain/**>. You will often see requests for help with census records on this list.

NOTES

1 C. Bingley, 'Data Entry for Census Transcription', in *Computers in Genealogy*, Vol. 1, No. 3 (March 1983) pp. 60–63.

2 A formal description of the project will be found on the UK Data Archive website at <**www.data-archive.ac.uk/findingData/snDescription.asp?sn=1316**>. Rosemary Lockie's article 'The 2% 1851 Census Sample', in *Computers in Genealogy*, Vol. 5, No. 3 (September 1994), pp. 109–22, is probably the earliest published description of this material from a genealogist's point of view.

3 For example, Jeanne Bunting discovered 39 people with the surname Ditto, including Ada Ditto, born in Ditto Ditto — see <**listsearches.rootsweb.com/th/read/SOG-UK/2002-01/1010018139**>. The list archives for the UK-1901-CENSUS mailing list at <**archiver.rootsweb.ancestry.com/th/index/UK-1901-CENSUS/**> provide a record of initial reactions to the 1901 census.

4 More information can be found in the 21 July 2008 press release — from the FamilySearch home page at <**www.familysearch.org**> follow the 'Press Room' link at the foot of the page.

5 You will find a description of the process in the minutes of the ScotlandsPeople User Group at <**www.scotlandspeople.gov.uk/content/images/1st%20UG%20Meeting%20Minutes.pdf**>.

6 'Licence sale may mean money doesn't grow on family trees', *Sunday Herald*, 6 July 2008, most easily found by searching the paper's website at <**www.sundayherald.com**>.

5

ONLINE SEARCH TECHNIQUES

Although there are many differences between the various online census databases, the techniques for searching them have much in common, and there are certain general principles for successful searching that apply no matter which site you are using. The search facilities of the major census sites are described in detail in the eight following chapters and are summarized in Table 14-3. The purpose of this chapter is to offer some general advice on using the most common search field and facilities, and to highlight the benefits and shortcomings of the various options. (Some of the recommendations here apply only to the large national datasets, which tend to have the most comprehensive and sophisticated search options.)

There are three basic reasons for any problems you may have in locating people in census records:

- the records themselves are incomplete and flawed in various ways discussed in Chapter 3
- you start your census search on the basis of information you already have about your ancestors, but it is quite possible for that information to be wrong or incomplete
- the electronic indexes contain errors resulting from the transcription process, as discussed in Chapter 4.

Together, these mean that you shouldn't be surprised if an initial search does not turn up the person you are looking for.

There is a basic dilemma when searching for ancestors in the online census indexes. The more search terms you enter, the more likely you are to enter something that does not match your ancestor's record. Result: a failed search.

The fewer search terms you enter, the larger the number of matching entries you will find. Result: too many entries to check.

In fact, it will in some cases need a process of trial and error to work out which information in which fields on the search form will locate the right person. You can either start with minimal information – just a forename, surname and county perhaps – and add fields when your initial search is too broad. Alternatively, you can fill in all the fields you have information for and experiment with cutting them out to find the best combination. If a forename or surname is quite unusual, then the first strategy is recommended; for common names the second. But which of these suits you will depend in part on what sort of site you are using. If you are using a free site or a subscription service, you can do as many searches as you like. If you are using a pay-per-view site, you may be paying to look at the search results each time, so you will clearly want to minimize the number of searches where you look at the full results. Just looking at the number of hits may tell you whether you have narrowed down your search sufficiently.

Names

One of the hardest problems to solve in searching the census records is when there seems to be no correct entry for the surname you are looking for. Some names are inherently unstable, patronymic pairs like Richard and Richards particularly. Perhaps an enumerator, encountering a speaker with an unfamiliar accent, may not take down a name the way you'd expect. Or modern data entry staff have had trouble reading Victorian handwriting. Personal names are the most difficult textual data on the census form to validate. If a transcriber can't read key letters in a name, it may be impossible to make a sensible guess.

This means you need to be open-minded about surname spellings. But looking for each possible variant in turn would be a very tedious process, so the data services offer a range of options for finding variants with a single search.

Because of the level of variation, you will find that many sites offer loose matching as the default type of name search and you have to select an 'exact match' option if you want to find only the spelling you have entered. But of course the looser the match, the more entries you will have to check.

WILDCARDS

One of the most useful options in any search field is the 'wildcard', a special character that can stand for any letter or letters, including no letter at all. The commonest wildcard character is the asterisk (*).

At its simplest this lets you search for common surname variants that differ in their last letter: Brook, Brooke, Brooks and Brookes can be searched for simultaneously with Brook*, though of course the results will include Brooker, Brookbank, Brookshaw, etc. Another obvious use is where there are forms of a name with a different vowel. Blackw*ll finds both Blackwall and Blackwell.

Wildcards are particularly useful for coping with transcription errors, since they allow you to ignore the letters which have been got wrong. The disadvantage is that you may miss odder variants or misspellings – it relies on your knowledge of, or at least ability to imagine, variants.

One limitation with wildcards as implemented in the online indexes is that they are normally not permitted at the beginning of a field (the Irish census site and ScotlandsPeople are the only exceptions). This is unfortunate, because it is precisely the sometimes florid Victorian initials which give rise to many transcription errors. Also you will usually have to enter at least three characters before the wildcard. So, although you can use Alcr*ft to find Alcraft and Alcroft, you would need separate searches to find Aldcroft and Allcroft, not to mention Oldcraft, Oldcroft and Ouldcroft.

Although wildcards are most often thought as a tool for names, they can also be useful for place-name variants when searching for locations, particularly birthplaces.

SOUNDEX

Soundex is a surname matching technique originally invented for the US census to try to get round the spelling variations, and some sites with census data make it available as a search option.

Soundex gives each surname an alpha-numerical code based on the first letter and the remaining consonants, with similar codes for similar sounding consonants. The code for Radcliffe, for example is R324, and a Soundex search for Radcliffe will look for all names which are coded as R324. These will include variants like Ratcliffe, Radcliff, Ratcliff, Reddcliff, as well many others that are less likely to be misspellings or genuine variants, such as Ridgewell, Rudkin, Rattigan, and even

Rothschild. So a Soundex search will always give you a lot more names, and therefore a lot more individuals, than you really want.

Soundex is designed to ignore double consonants, and ignores vowels entirely except at the beginning of a word. So Wilman and Wellman have the same code (W455). Its advantage over wildcards is that only the first letter has to be specified.

On the other hand, some very obvious surname variants have different codes and won't turn up as matches. For example, Wood has code W400, while Woods is W420. Again, it has the problem that it cannot cope with different initial letters.

Because of its limitations, Soundex is not now widely used on commercial sites, though you will often encounter it elsewhere. Ancestry will be phasing out its Soundex option with the introduction of its new search form (see Chapter 7, p. 125) and the only major census site to offer a Soundex search will then be ScotlandsPeople (Chapter 12). You can find out more about Soundex and how it works at <**www.archives.gov/genealogy/census/soundex.html**>, and there are many Soundex calculators on the web.

NAMEX

Soundex is a very crude tool and there have been a number of attempts to improve or replace it. While Ancestry has an unnamed matching algorithm of its own, the system that is used by Origins, Findmypast and GenesReunited is NameX. This is, incidentally, a proprietary system requiring a licence so the exact details of how it works have not been published and you will not find it on non-commercial sites.

Soundex works by giving every name a code and then claiming all those with the same code as matches. NameX works by taking the name you are starting with and giving every other name a score based on how closely it matches. This allows you, in principle, to look at only close matches or to include more distant ones (though only Origins actually offers you this choice).

Table 5-1 shows the NameX scores (out of 100) for the surname Darwin. You can see that it would be impossible to search for this group of names with wildcards or Soundex. And while some of the forms are hardly plausible variants of Darwin, there are many you would not have thought to try and which might be mistranscriptions of the name. You can try NameX out on the website of Image Partners, who originally developed the system, at <**www.namethesaurus.com/**

Thesaurus/>. This will show you for comparison the much less satisfactory lists produced by Soundex and the Soundex-like Metaphone algorithm.

Origins has background information about NameX at <**www.originsnetwork.com/namex/aboutnamex.html**>, which is also well worth reading for its explanation of the problems of identifying surname variants in historical records.

Surname	Match Score	Surname	Match Score
Darwine	99	Dorwing	80
Dearwin	99	Durwint	80
Darwina	97	Darwaine	80
Daarwin	97	Dawin	80
Derwin	96	Dawrin	80
Dirwin	96	Daurin	79
Dorwin	96	Darwit	79
Durwin	96	Darwan	79
Darwins	95	Darwen	79
Darwyn	93	Darrin	79
Dirwine	93	Darein	79
Derwine	93	Darine	79
Darwyne	90	Darwon	79
Dariwin	89	Darvin	77
Daruwin	89	Dearin	77
Derwina	89	Dawine	76
Dorrwin	89	Dawins	76
Darwind	88	Darwinkel	76
Darwint	88	Darini	76
Darwing	88	Darino	76
Derwins	87	Darins	76
Dirwyn	85	Darina	76
Derwyn	85	Doorwin	76
Durwyn	85	Derewin	76
Darwinge	84	Derwain	76
Darwain	84	Durwim	76
Darin	83	Dorwain	76
Darwis	82	Dewrin	75
Dariyn	81	Dearwis	75
Drwin	81	Darwick	75
Derwoin	81	Darwigi	75
Derwint	80	Darwitt	75
Derwing	80	Darwitz	75

Table 5-1 NameX matches for Darwin, from <**www.namethesaurus.com/Thesaurus/**>

FORENAMES

Forenames also have their problems. There are three main reasons why the forename you search on may not find who you are looking for:

- the person actually uses a middle name and this is what is recorded on the form
- the form shows a nickname rather than the formal name – for example, there are five Bill Smiths and a Billy Smith in the Origins 1871 index
- the name has been abbreviated – William Smith could easily be recorded as 'Wm', or even plain 'W'.

The data services recognize this problem and have ways of dealing with it, but they don't all deal with it in the same way so it's well worth checking any help they offer on forename searching. Most sites automatically catch a wide range of forename variants, some offering this as the default, which you can override by selecting an exact match. On Ancestry, even searching for an exact match will actually find some variants.

When you look at your initial search results, always look at the forename column to see what variants have been captured. Does a search for Charles have some entries for Chas?

You can, of course, use a wildcard – Will* will find quite a few variants of William. But this will not identify very short forms like Wm, or nicknames like Billy which start with a different letter. It certainly won't help with pairs as different as Margaret and Peggy.

NameX (see above) can also be used for forenames, though only Origins offers this at present. The NameX site has a separate forename thesaurus at <**www.namethesaurus.com/Thesaurus/Forenames.aspx**>, which will tell you what variants are likely to be found by NameX.

ScotlandsPeople has a very useful page on Scots forename variants at <**www.scotlandspeople.gov.uk/content/help/index.aspx?r=551&561**>.

Age

The problems with the legibility of the ages on the census forms have already been mentioned in Chapter 4 (see Figure 4-1). But there is a separate problem that is entirely down to the modern data services.

Ages in the censuses after 1841 are the age last birthday. Quite apart from the issue of people being ignorant of their correct age (see Chapter 3, p. 69), many of the census sites invite you to search not on age but on year of birth. There are good reasons for this. It is something you might already have information on, perhaps from a later census. Also it's less of a challenge than leaving you to do the mental arithmetic required to subtract the birth date from the census date to give an accurate age. However, the problem is that this switch is implemented with a fatal flaw, with the result that almost three-quarters of birth years in the census indexes are wrong!

For anyone whose birthday falls earlier in the year than the date of the census, subtracting the age from the census year will give the correct birth year. For everyone else, the calculated birth year will be one year later than the correct birth year. For example, a child aged ten years in the 1861 census could have been born on any date between the 7th April 1850 and the 7th April 1851. Statistically, a child who is ten on the night of the 7th April 1861 is almost three times as likely to have been born in 1850 as in 1851, yet the year of birth calculated by the census indexes all agree such a child was born in 1851.

Of the major census sites, the following use only a calculated age: Ancestry, Findmypast, Genes Reunited/1901censusonline, and the 1881 Census Index. Admittedly Findmypast shows both calculated birth year and age in its search results, and Ancestry is honest enough to prefix these birth years with 'abt', but even so this field needs to be approached with caution. RootsUK, incidentally, offers neither option in its basic search but both in the advanced search, which has an interesting option to exclude 'records with no age or ambiguous age'.

This means that if you use a search field which expects a birth year, give the right year only where an ancestor's birthday falls later in the year than census night. Otherwise, do not give the right year *and* request an exact match. Instead, give a year range or add one to the correct year.

In general, given the likelihood of an ancestor being mistaken about their age, it is always best, initially at least, to avoid giving a single birth year and selecting an exact match. Specify a range of years to start with.

Geography

There are three groups of geographical information for each person recorded on an enumeration schedule:

- the administrative units under which a household falls, at the top of the form
- the street address, in the left-hand column
- the birthplace, to the right.

The most reliable by far is the first of these. The enumerator will have started out with this information, not gathered it from a resident; since it will be identical for a whole group of pages, there's every reason to expect the digitization process to capture this information accurately. Some sites offer a very precise set of fields for searching this information – see for example the options offered at Findmypast shown in Figure 8-3 – but the problem with using this information to search is less the accuracy of indexing than your own geographical knowledge. You need to put exactly the right information in exactly the right fields in order for the search to work.

In general these fields can be useful for searching if it is at a high level (county, town), but unless you are a local historian or you have an authoritative source (e.g. a birth certificate of similar date), it is probably best to avoid fields like civil parish, municipal borough, ward, etc. You are almost certainly better off using a general-purpose Location field, into which you can type any place names without worrying about the exact type of place each one is.

The address information in the first column on the form is in fact not always searchable in a person search in the online census indexes, but if you have a street name which you think is reliable it can be worth trying it out in a general Location field. If your interest is local rather than genealogical, you may find the separate address search offered by some sites useful (see Table 14-3). It is also a good potential standby if name searches fail but you have some idea where your ancestor lived.

Depending on who you are searching for, the birthplace field may be essential or useless. If you are tracing backwards, this may be the one piece of information you are using the census to try to discover. But it will be useful if you have already found an ancestor in an earlier or later census. And if you are tracing your family tree forwards, looking for other descendants of an ancestor, this may be the only field which offers definitive proof that a person living in a major city or at the other end of the country is actually the offspring of an ancestor who lived elsewhere. If you are dealing with a common name, it may be the only way of distinguishing between several families. But of course, as was pointed out in Chapter 3, this is one of the most problematic fields on the original forms and is made more so by the levels of error in the online indexes. Here, too, the distinction between a transcription and an index discussed in the previous chapter becomes important.

Let's say you are looking for family members born in Guildford, Surrey. What you cannot tell without testing is whether a particular index has normalized the spellings of town and county. If it has, then a search for the standard spelling will be sufficient. If not, you may need to do three more searches to cope with the most common alternative spellings: Guildford, Surry; Guilford, Surrey; and Guilford, Surrey. Findmypast, for example, in the 1891 census has 13,750 people born in 'Guildford' and 51 in 'Guilford'. True, those missing 51 are only a small fraction, but they will be ancestors to someone. And, of course, there is even one, Letticia M. Jones, born in 'Gilford, Surrey'.

County spellings are usually normalized, but you can still be caught out. Findmypast's 1891 census index rather surprisingly finds that there were only 124 people claiming to be born in Dorset, which sounds like a horrific error. But in fact the index is quite correct: the people apparently missing are in fact listed on the original forms as born in Dorsetshire. The 124 'Dorset' people are those who claim to have been born, rather bizarrely one might think, in 'Dorset, Dorsetshire'.

One thing to look for is a drop-down list, such as the County and City/Town fields in the search form for the 1881 Census Index (Figure 6-2). By definition, these give you only valid options and will only be offered where the index has normalized the spellings. But drop-down lists can also be your enemy. By restricting what you can select, they may be effectively useless. If you are looking for someone living in Guildford in the 1881 Census Index, your only options once you have selected Surrey as the county are: Guildford Bowling Green, Guildford Friary, Guildford Holy Trinity, Guildford St Mary, and Guildford St Nicholas. If you don't know the place and your ancestor's location within it well enough to select the right one, there is no fallback option to select just Guildford.

Gender

A gender field is probably one of the least useful fields on a search form. For a start, most forenames in the census were gender-specific in the Victorian era, so selecting a gender doesn't really narrow down your search at all; it's just something else which can stop you finding an ancestor by being wrongly transcribed. As pointed out in Chapter 4, there are thousands of entries in the census indexes which have a mismatch between gender and forename. If you search for 'John, male' you will miss all the entries for 'John, female'. Of course many of these will be for people who were really called Jane, but some will be for Johns given the wrong gender by the modern transcriber. If you know the forename, don't bother with gender.

The real use of the gender field is to narrow down your search results when you either don't know a forename or have failed to find a match when using the forename you believe to be correct.

Occupation

Another search field that is less useful than you might think is that for occupation, which some sites offer. Even supposing you know exactly what your ancestor did for a living in the census year, there can be many different ways to express the same occupation. Also, because on the original records they have often been partially overwritten with annotations or strokes of the pen, occupations are particularly liable to be mistranscribed. Save the occupation field as a last resort when other approaches fail. Alternatively, with a common name, it may be worth entering an occupation in your initial search, but it should be one of the first fields you abandon if that initial search fails.

Family members

One of the most useful options which is starting to appear on the commercial sites is a set of fields to enter the forenames (or sometimes full names) of other family members. Table 14-3 shows which sites offer this facility.

Even if the names themselves are quite common, a particular combination of forenames for father, mother and a couple of children may help identify a family whose surname has been horribly mangled for whatever reason. See p. 159 and Figure 9-9 for an example.

References

There are circumstances in which it can be useful to search by TNA reference (see p. 48). For example, none of the free census sites has digital images of the census returns, so in order to check an entry you have found in the free index, you will need to use one of the commercial data services and locate the matching image. In the case of the free census indexes on the FamilySearch pilot record search site (see Chapter 6, p. 115), the link to the commercially available image is in fact provided in the search results. But in other cases you will need to sign in to a commercial site and do a search for the right record. This is much easier if you can give the precise reference and go straight to the right image.

General advice

In addition to specific recommendations about how you formulate your search, there are some very general things to bear in mind.

- Don't be too attached to any one piece of information. Even if you haven't got it wrong (or rather, even if your source hasn't), there can be no guarantee that the enumeration schedule has the correct information and it has been correctly transcribed in the online index.
- Be flexible and imaginative with names. The name matching systems available on the online censuses can do a lot to find variants, but none of them can cope with errors in the initial letters, and few sites allow wildcards at the beginning of a name. Unfortunately, there are also some spectacular mistranscriptions of names in the indexes, so be prepared sometimes to think about how to find someone without using the surname.
- Ultimately, be prepared to use more than one online index. You may baulk at the expense of this, but if the site you normally use cannot turn up your ancestor, then an alternative may be your only chance. If you choose a pay-per-view option, you may not need to pay more than £5 or £6 to find an otherwise unfindable ancestor. Before you do this though, check the relevant chapter in this book to make sure that your second site does not use the same index as the first.

6

FREE CENSUS INDEXES ONLINE

Later chapters are devoted to the commercial sites offering census data on either a subscription or a pay-per-view basis. However, many sites offer census data, mostly for individual towns or counties.

The limited amount of Irish census data that is online is mostly accessible free of charge, but the Irish censuses have peculiarities of their own, so it is covered in a separate chapter.

Because these sites are free of charge, they are accessible from any public internet terminal. If you have not got your own internet connection at home, you can access them from the networked computers available in many public libraries.

1881 Census Index

The largest collection of free online census data is the 1881 Census Index. This index was created by volunteers from family history societies and the LDS Church in a mammoth project run jointly by the Federation of Family History Societies and the Genealogical Society of Utah. It was initially published on microfiche, and then on CD-ROM (see p. 246). It was put online free of charge at FamilySearch in February 2003, though the online index does not include data for Scotland, which remains, however, available on CD-ROM. Like all LDS genealogical data, it is accessible from the computers at any Family History Center. A history of this project will be found at <**www.familyhistoryonline.net/database/1881history.shtml**>.

In general, the material for 1881 available on the commercial sites covered in the following chapters is taken from this index and for that reason is usually offered free of charge. (Commercial sites do charge for access to images of the 1881 census, as these have to be licensed on microfilm directly from the National Archives and each commercial service has created its own digital images from the microfilm.) Since you will need to check index entries against the original documents anyway, there is no particular reason to use FamilySearch for the 1881 Census Index if you have already signed up with one of the commercial data services which include it.

To access the 1881 Census Index at FamilySearch:

1. Direct your browser to <**www.familysearch.org**>.
2. Click on the Search tab at the top of the home page.
3. Select Census from the list in the left-hand column.
4. From the drop-down list marked census, choose 1881 British Census.

The initial search screen is shown in Figure 6-1. Once you get to this page, it is a good idea to bookmark it so that you can go straight to it next time.

By default, FamilySearch uses its own surname-matching database to offer variants for any surname or forename entered. Unlike other sites, it does *not* use an algorithm for calculating variants, but instead relies on a list that was created manually and is almost certainly not comprehensive. It is therefore much more inconsistent than the surname matching procedures used by the commercial data services, though the forename matching is much more reliable. If you want to

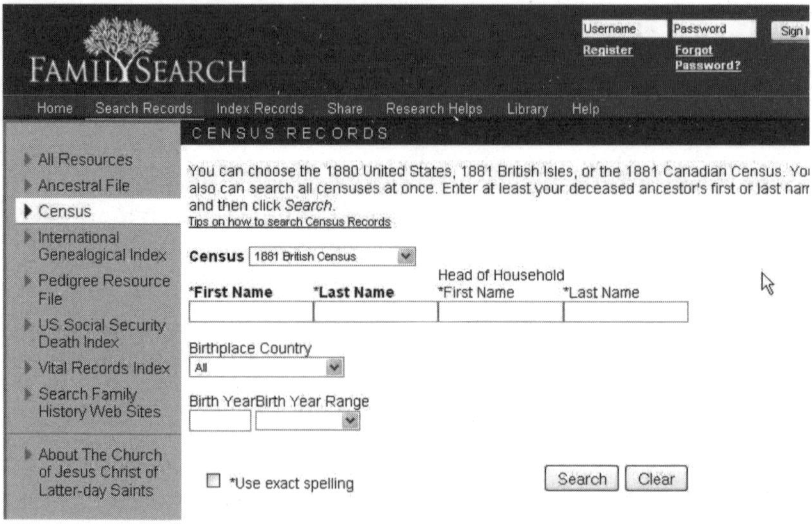

Figure 6-1 1881 Census Index search form

switch this off and search only for exact matches, you can select 'Use exact spelling' at the bottom of the screen – but note that this applies to both surname and forename, and you cannot search for an exact surname with a fuzzy forename or vice versa. You can in fact enter just a forename or just a surname.

On the form as it initially appears, it may seem that you can only select a country for Birthplace and Census place, but in fact once you select a census 'country' (England, Wales, Channel Islands, Isle of Man), a new drop-down list appears with the names of the counties in the country. If you wish, you can then select an individual town or city. (See Figure 6-2.)

London does not appear in the list of available counties for England (the London County Council did not come into existence until 1889), but is listed as a city/town in Middlesex. However, the parts of Middlesex later incorporated into the LCC metropolitan boroughs in 1889 (such as Shoreditch, Hammersmith or Islington) are not listed among the places in Middlesex and are all included in London. The Kent, Surrey and Essex places which became metropolitan boroughs (e.g. Greenwich, Lambeth, West Ham respectively) *are* listed under their pre-LCC counties, as you'd expect. This means that if your ancestors lived in one of the Middlesex parts of London, it can be quite difficult to tell where in London they lived, unless you recognize the street names. However, this is a limitation in the search facilities on

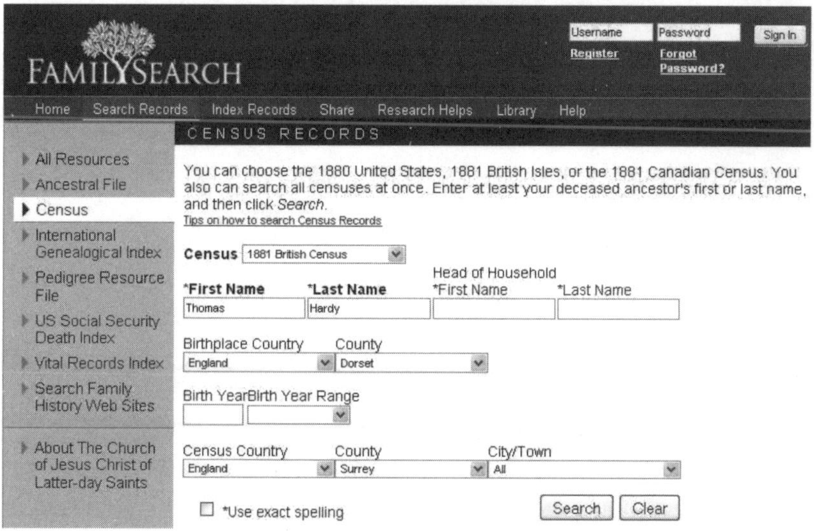

Figure 6-2 1881 census search form with county and town fields

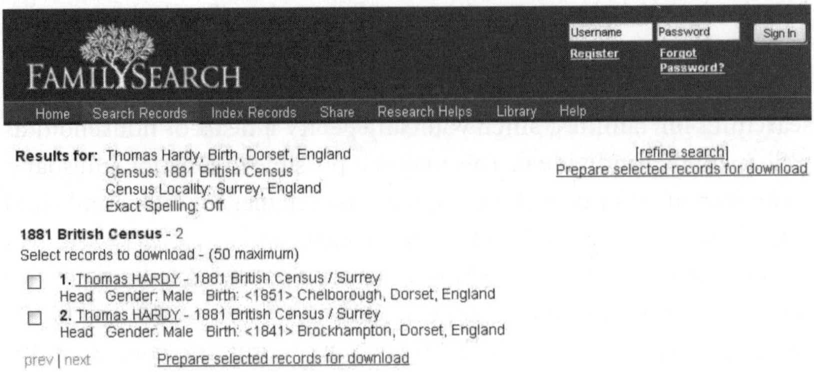

Figure 6-3 1881 census search results

FamilySearch, and more precise location data is searchable in the 1881 Census Index offered on the commercial sites.

The Isle of Wight is listed separately from Hampshire, but rather oddly is accompanied by a drop-down list of all the Hampshire towns. The island's towns are all listed under Hampshire.

The census 'countries' also include an entry labelled 'British Isles-Misc.' This covers all those listed as inmates of institutions or on board vessels.

For the birthplace location, if you choose a country within the

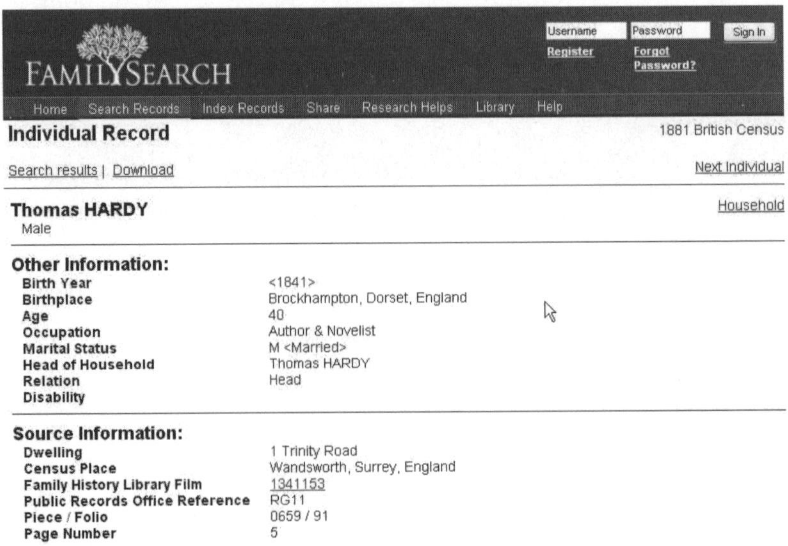

Figure 6-4 1881 census individual record

British Isles (including Ireland), you will again be offered a list of counties. This time, London *is* included in its own right.

You can from the search form see that the site offers some help with searching for families, since you can specify a head of household as well as another individual. This makes it possible to look for a husband and wife pair or a particular combination of names for father and child (or, of course, a widowed mother and child).

The search results (see Figure 6-3) list each matching individual with their position in the family, gender, calculated year of birth and birthplace. Unfortunately, for the address it gives only the county, and it doesn't indicate the occupation. This means that it won't always be clear which person in a listing is the one you are looking for. If you have too many results to manage, you can use the 'Refine search' to go back and look for ways of narrowing things down. Another limitation of the results is that it does not give an accurate total unless it is under 200. If it is more than 200, it just says '200+'. The results are listed 200 to a screen, and there is no way of telling how many screenfuls there are. However, if you get more than 200 results, it is probably better to think about refining your search rather than trying to check them all visually.

Clicking on the name takes you to the Individual record page (see Figure 6-4), which additionally provides the occupation and marital status, as well as the full address and TNA reference. A useful point to note is that it also gives the Family History Library Film reference. If you go to a Family History Center, this number will enable you quickly

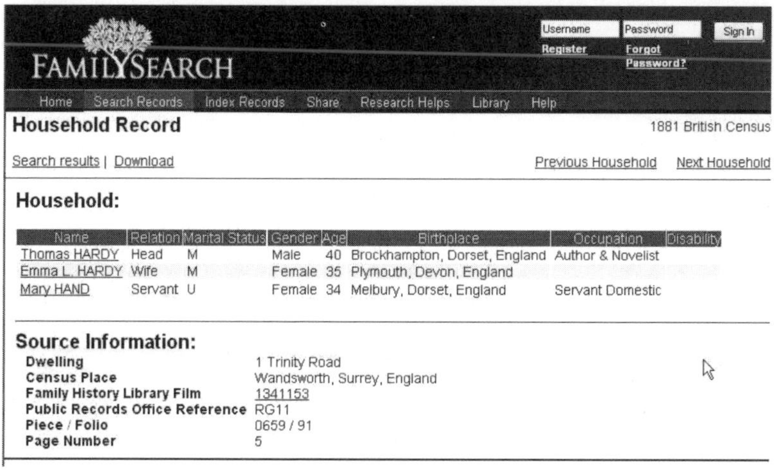

Figure 6-5 1881 census household record

to identify which microfilm the original record is on, so that you can check the index against the original entry. From the Individual record, there is also an option to view the whole household. From here you can go to the next or previous household (Figure 6-5, see p. 113), an option which is probably not much use to a genealogist but is very useful for the local historian who wants to scroll through a whole street or entire enumeration district.

The flowchart in Figure 6-6 shows the search process for the 1881 Census Index.

An unusual option, not offered on the commercial sites, is to select and download the results. If you do this on the search results screen, you first have to select which individuals to download. On the Individual record page, obviously enough, it downloads the details of the individual, and on the Household records page all household members. The data is downloaded into a GEDCOM file, which you could import into your family tree software. If you do this by selecting

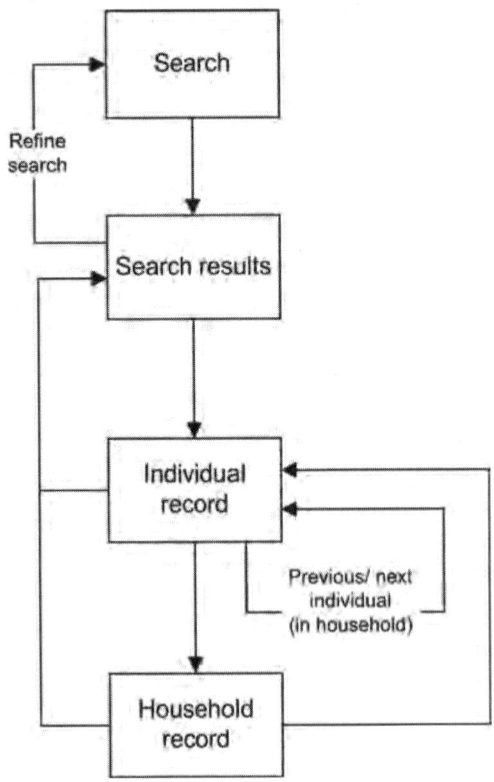

Figure 6-6 1881 Census Index flowchart

individuals from the search results page, you can gradually build up a file of all the people you are interested in and then download all their details in a single file by clicking on the 'prepare selected records for download' link at the bottom of the page. This is very useful for anyone doing a one-name study, though there is no way to select automatically everyone listed on a page – you have to select each one manually.

The 1881 Census Index, unlike most online census indexes, is a finished product and is not being improved by the acceptance of corrections. Since it does not link to images of the original records, it would be an immense task to check any submitted corrections before modifying the data, effort which can hardly be justified for a free resource. The full National Archives reference given on the Household and Individual records pages should make it straightforward to check the index entry against the microfilm.

The Family History Library has a page with detailed guidance on using this index. Unfortunately the web address is 174 characters long, impossible to type without making a mistake, and it seems to be impossible to navigate to it on FamilySearch, so the best way to find it is actually to enter the phrase '1881 British Census Indexes Resource Guide' in a search engine. If the right page is not the only result, it will certainly be the first one listed.

FamilySearch record search

While the 1881 Census Index has been available online for many years, FamilySearch has been piloting a new record search facility. This is currently located at <**pilot.familysearch.org**>, but presumably all the data will eventually be integrated into the main FamilySearch site once the pilot is complete.

Among the datasets currently available in the record search pilot are indexes to the 1841 and 1861 censuses. These are not new indexes but are the ones created by Origins and Findmypast respectively, and available on those two sites. FamilySearch does not provide the digital images, but instead there is a link from the search results to the images at Findmypast. However, the images are not free – you need to be a Findmypast subscriber or purchase pay-per-view credits in order to view them. If you are accessing FamilySearch from a computer in a Family History Center, though, access to the images is free. The remaining census indexes available at Findmypast are to be added to FamilySearch in due course.

To use these indexes, select the link '1841 England and Wales Census' or '1861 England and Wales Census' from the Record Search home page at <**pilot.familysearch.org**>. The search form, shown in Figure 6-7, is a general-purpose Record Search form and is not designed specifically for census records. Hence the slightly odd 'Life event' list, which includes birth/christening, marriage and death/burial. You can click on 'More' to see further search fields, but these cannot be used in searching census records.

The search form currently (July 2008) offers quite limited options. The Place field uses a look-up table to specify the exact place, so if you enter the name of a town or village, it will offer you the various possibilities to complete the full details, including county and country. However, testing suggests that this field can only be used for the birthplace, not for the place of residence. Even so, it does not seem to be possible to use the Birth/Christening option to specify a calculated birth year: Figure 6-8 shows the error message when entering the details for Thomas Hardy in the 1861 census, using details taken from the original index at Findmypast.

If, however, you run this search without entering a year, you will get much better results, just Thomas Hardy and his father. Clicking on one of the entries brings up more details and a link to the image at Findmypast (Figure 6-9).

A useful feature, if you get more results than this, is that you are offered a series of options at the top of the screen to narrow down the

Figure 6-7 FamilySearch search form

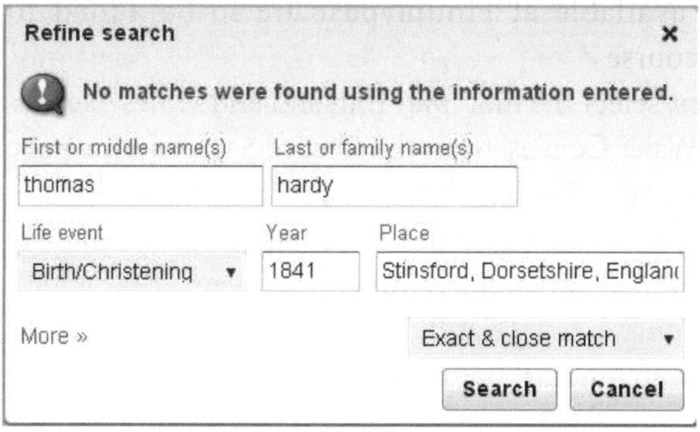

Figure 6-8 FamilySearch failed search with birth year

search by various criteria. This way, you could search on just a name initially and then gradually whittle down the full list of results until you find the right person.

As it stands, the site offers quite limited options compared with even the basic search on Findmypast (Figure 8-2), never mind the advanced search (Figure 8-3). However, the service is explicitly offered as a pilot, and our tests were carried out only three days after the site was launched. The press release which accompanied the launch in fact promised that additional data fields would be added in the future.

There will still be the limitation that if you are accessing the site from home, you will need to sign up with Findmypast in order to view the images. But the value of this site is not so much to the user with his or her own internet connection at home. Its real value lies in the fact that

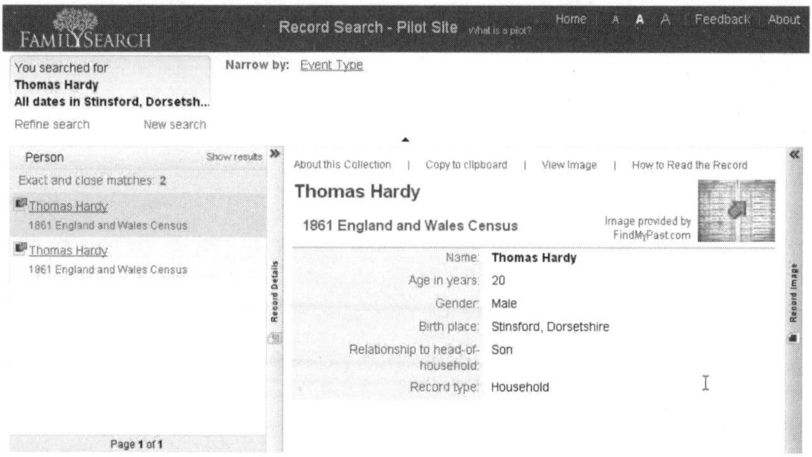

Figure 6-9 FamilySearch search result and individual record

it gives free access to census indexes and images to those using Family History Centers. Certainly if you are on a very tight budget and want to do a lot of census searching, this makes a Family History Center a useful alternative to finding a public library with free access to census data.

FreeCEN

FreeCEN at <**www.freecen.org.uk**> is a volunteer-based project based on the better known FreeBMD (<**www.freebmd.org.uk**>). It aims to provide a free online searchable database of the nineteenth-century century UK census returns for England, Wales and Scotland. There is some coverage for the Channel Islands, but none for the Isle of Man or Ireland. The main focus is initially on the 1891 census, but there is also some work being undertaken on the earlier censuses. As of June 2008, it had transcribed around 13 million census entries, with about one-third of these relating to the 1891 census. Because this is only a fraction of the total 150 million records or so for the period covered, it is worth checking the coverage before you start using it. Since the 1881 census already has a free index online (see above), there is almost no data for this on FreeCEN; there is no data for 1901.

The statistics page at <**www.freecen.org.uk/statistics.html**> shows

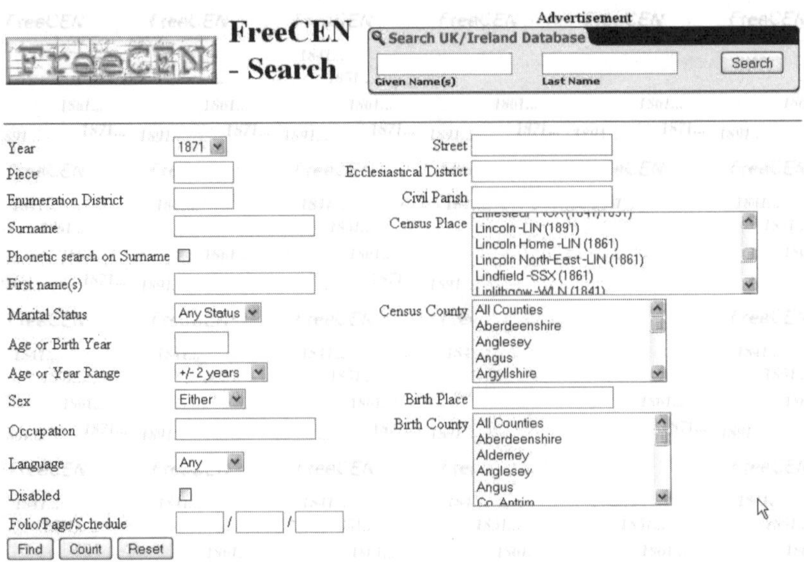

Figure 6-10 FreeCEN search form

what percentage of records have been transcribed for each county in each census year. In some cases there is 100 per cent coverage (mostly Scottish counties in fact), but for most there is considerably less, in some cases nothing at all. One English county, Cornwall, has 100 per cent coverage or near it for all censuses.

The search form (see Figure 6-10) allows you to search on any field on the enumeration schedule, including the language and disability fields.

If you wish to assist with the project, whether in transcribing or checking, there are contact details for each county sub-project at <**www.freecen.org.uk/project.htm**>.

FHS Online

S & N Genealogy Supplies, who run TheGenealogist and RootsUK (Chapter 9), also have a site called FHS Online at <**www.fhs-online.co.uk**> designed to allow family history societies to publish their datasets. The site should not be confused with FamilyHistoryOnline at <**www.familyhistoryonline.net**>, which is the data service run by the FFHS for a similar purpose and which is in the process of closing down.

Although some of the data is available only on a commercial basis, it currently has almost 50 county census indexes for individual years covering 29 different counties in England and Wales. Registration is required before you can search the indexes, but this does not involve payment.

The indexes, which can be searched on name and age, usually give the TNA piece and folio number, though some give only the piece number. Figure 6-11 (see p. 120) shows a typical page of search results. All the census indexes are marked as partial, so you cannot be sure to find someone even if you are certain of their location on census night.

There is also a master search available from the home page, which searches all the databases.

Local projects

Alongside these two national projects, there are many local (sometimes *very* local) indexes made by local organizations or individual volunteers. Here are just a few examples:

- Dumfries and Galloway Council has an 1851 census database at <**www.dumgal.gov.uk/HistoricalIndexes/census.aspx**> covering all the parishes of Dumfriesshire, Kirkcudbrightshire and Wigtownshire.
- The 1841 census for the Channel Islands has been transcribed by Lorna Pratt at <**members.shaw.ca/Jerseymaid/**>.
- The Wirksworth Parish Records site includes a full transition of the 1841–1901 census for 33 enumeration districts in the Wirksworth area at <**www.wirksworth.org.uk/CENSUS.htm**>.
- There is a partial list of names with TNA references for the 1851 census of Cumbria at <**www.btinternet.com/~grigg/1851Consolidated16042006.pdf**>.
- Durham Records Online at <**www.durhamrecordsonline.com**> provides a free name index for County Durham, complete for the 1841 census and covering a large part of the county for 1851 to 1891. The site operates a pay-per-view system for access to the full individual records, though this is quite expensive at over £1 per record.
- The Sheffield Indexers have an index for the 1841 census in Sheffield at <**sheff-indexers.thewholeshebang.org/1841Census_Index.html**>.
- The Froyle Censuses 1841-1901 at <**www.froyle.com/census.htm**> has transcripts for all the censuses for the parish of Froyle in Hampshire.

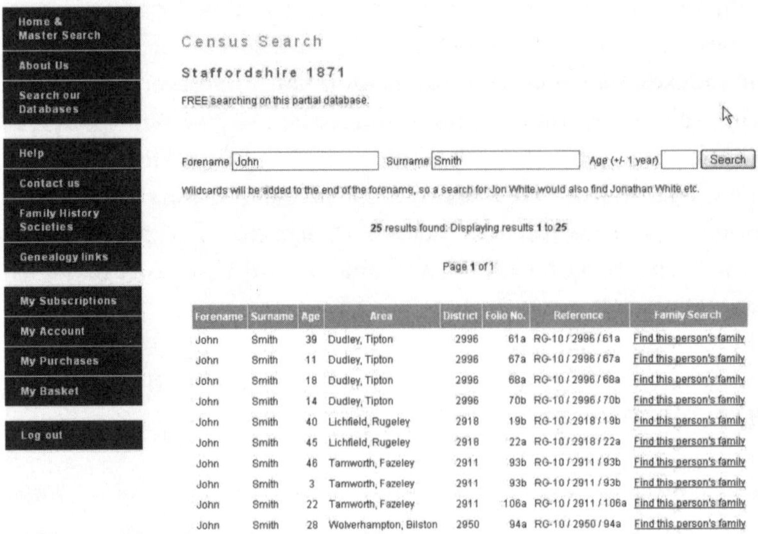

Forename	Surname	Age	Area	District	Folio No.	Reference	Family Search
John	Smith	39	Dudley, Tipton	2996	61a	RG-10 / 2996 / 61a	Find this person's family
John	Smith	11	Dudley, Tipton	2996	67a	RG-10 / 2996 / 67a	Find this person's family
John	Smith	18	Dudley, Tipton	2996	68a	RG-10 / 2996 / 68a	Find this person's family
John	Smith	14	Dudley, Tipton	2996	70b	RG-10 / 2996 / 70b	Find this person's family
John	Smith	40	Lichfield, Rugeley	2918	19b	RG-10 / 2918 / 19b	Find this person's family
John	Smith	45	Lichfield, Rugeley	2918	22a	RG-10 / 2918 / 22a	Find this person's family
John	Smith	46	Tamworth, Fazeley	2911	93b	RG-10 / 2911 / 93b	Find this person's family
John	Smith	3	Tamworth, Fazeley	2911	93b	RG-10 / 2911 / 93b	Find this person's family
John	Smith	22	Tamworth, Fazeley	2911	106a	RG-10 / 2911 / 106a	Find this person's family
John	Smith	28	Wolverhampton, Bilston	2950	94a	RG-10 / 2950 / 94a	Find this person's family

Figure 6-11 FHS Online search results

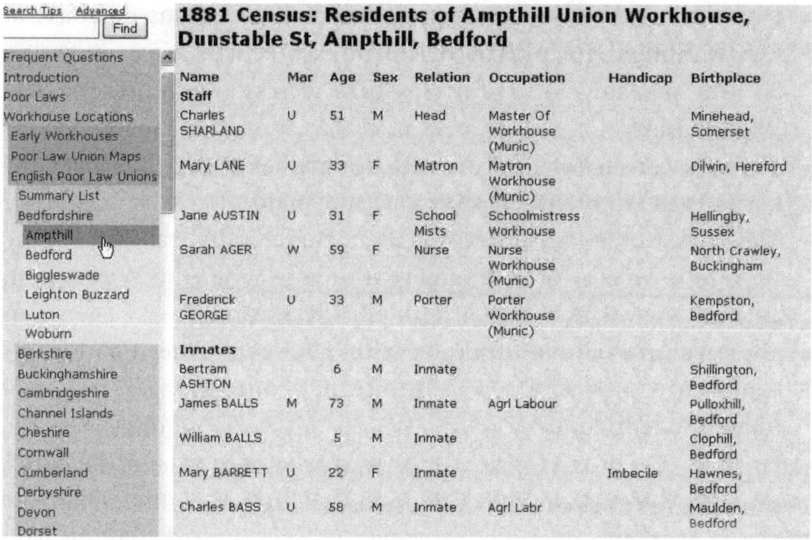

1881 Census: Residents of Ampthill Union Workhouse, Dunstable St, Ampthill, Bedford

Name	Mar	Age	Sex	Relation	Occupation	Handicap	Birthplace
Staff							
Charles SHARLAND	U	51	M	Head	Master Of Workhouse (Munic)		Minehead, Somerset
Mary LANE	U	33	F	Matron	Matron Workhouse (Munic)		Dilwin, Hereford
Jane AUSTIN	U	31	F	School Mists	Schoolmistress Workhouse		Hellingby, Sussex
Sarah AGER	W	59	F	Nurse	Nurse Workhouse (Munic)		North Crawley, Buckingham
Frederick GEORGE	U	33	M	Porter	Porter Workhouse (Munic)		Kempston, Bedford
Inmates							
Bertram ASHTON		6	M	Inmate			Shillington, Bedford
James BALLS	M	73	M	Inmate	Agrl Labour		Pulloxhill, Bedford
William BALLS		5	M	Inmate			Clophill, Bedford
Mary BARRETT	U	22	F	Inmate		Imbecile	Hawnes, Bedford
Charles BASS	U	58	M	Inmate	Agrl Labr		Maulden, Bedford

Figure 6-12 Workhouse census transcription

- Census data for Amlwch on the Isle of Anglesey is searchable at <**www.amlwchhistory.co.uk/data/searchsurname2.htm**>. This includes names, addresses and occupations from the 1801 census, as well as the 1841–1891 censuses.

Some sites with national coverage offer census indexes by individual locations.

A special-purpose set of transcriptions is provided by the Workhouses site at <**www.workhouses.org.uk**>, with 1881 census records for many workhouses in the British Isles. There is no central listing; each is linked from the individual page from the relevant workhouse – from the home page, select 'Workhouse locations', then the Poor Law Unions for the country you want, then the county, then the individual town. At the bottom of the page you will find a link to the census data (see Figure 6-12).

You can also enter a name in the search box at the top left of the home page to look for individuals across the whole site. If you include forename and surname, you will need to put them between inverted commas.

Local census indexes for Ireland are covered in Chapter 15.

Finding free census data

Many of these local indexes are on small sites which may not be easy to find using a search engine unless you know what places and years they cover, but it is always worth using a search engine to look for the word 'census' along with a county and a census year.

But there are several good places which provide listings of online census indexes. It is probably worth checking these first before you spend time on the rather more laborious business of using a search engine.

Cyndi's List has a very substantial page devoted to online census material for the UK and Ireland at <**www.cyndislist.com/census-uk.htm**>. This page also has links to the related pages for the censuses of the United States and Canada, and there is a Census Worldwide page at <**www.cyndislist.com/census2.htm**>.

Census Online at <**www.census-online.com**> has links to census sites for the British Isles (separate pages for England, Wales, Scotland and Ireland), the United States and Canada. There are over 600 links for the British Isles, with a page for each county.

Census Finder has a very comprehensive collection of links to both commercial and free census indexes at <**www.censusfinder.com**>.

Finally, Genuki's county pages are also good places to look for censuses indexes relating to individual counties.

7

ANCESTRY

Ancestry is a long-established US genealogical data service, launched in 1995 and now part of the Generations Network, which has a dozen genealogy sites. The UK version of Ancestry at <**www.ancestry.co.uk**> was launched in September 2002 with the 1891 census. It now provides indexes to all the released censuses for England and Wales 1841–1901 along with images of the original records.

Ancestry is also so far the only site to provide indexes to the Scottish censuses in competition with ScotlandsPeople (Chapter 12), having its own indexes for all seven of the released censuses for Scotland. As of summer 2008, these indexes do not include images of the original records, because the company was unable to negotiate the right to digitize them from GROS. However, with the imminent changes to GROS's licensing regime (Chapter 4, p. 85), it is probable that the images will be added in due course, though at the time of writing there was no official confirmation of this from Ancestry.

The 1881 data for England and Wales is taken from the 1881 Census Index created by the volunteer project discussed in Chapter 6, and also available on FamilySearch at <**www.familysearch.org**>. But Ancestry have created their own index for the 1881 census of Scotland.

Charges

Ancestry is essentially a subscription site. There are two subscriptions relevant to UK family historians: UK Deluxe, which includes access to all records relating to the UK and Ireland, and World Deluxe, which covers the entire body of data on the site. UK membership is £9.95 per month or £79.95 for a year; World membership is £24.95 per month or £199.95 for a year.

If you live in the US, Australia or Canada, Ancestry has sites at **<www.ancestry.com>**, **<www.ancestry.com.au>** and **<www.ancestry.ca>** with subscriptions for access to local records as well as the World subscription. It can be worth checking current exchange rates before subscribing – the Canadian World Deluxe subscription is C$299, which at the exchange rate current at the time of writing is equivalent to £150 rather than £199.95, though you have to allow for VAT to be added to any sterling subscription price. If you are taking out a World Deluxe membership, it does not matter which national site you use to subscribe (your username and password work on all Ancestry sites), but of course you can subscribe to the UK site only from **<www.ancestry.co.uk>**. The Australian site offers a UK Heritage Package, which includes both the UK/Irish records and Australian records for a similar price to the UK Deluxe membership, so if you are also interested in tracing Australian branches of your family it would make sense to sign up for the UK Heritage Package. There is no equivalent on the Canadian site, so if you have British Isles and Canadian ancestry, you would need to go for the World Deluxe membership.

Although Ancestry is known as a subscription site, when it introduced the 1901 census, it introduced a pay-per-view option, which gives you 12 record views for 14 days for £6.95. 'Records' here means 'images of records', not just the transcriptions, which are not charged. However, while this is not necessarily bad value, it hardly compares with the unlimited access provided by the 14-day free trial, discussed below, and the monthly £9.95 subscription.

A relatively new payment option is the pre-paid voucher. The page at **<www.ancestry.co.uk/voucher/>** lists about twenty places where you can buy vouchers, including the National Archives' shop and a number of public libraries. This is ideal for anyone who does not want to use a credit/debit card online, or for giving access to Ancestry as a gift.

Some features of Ancestry do not require any form of subscription or payment, but you are still required to register and receive a Registered Guest account. In the case of the census records, this means you can search all the indexes for 1881 apart from that for Scotland. Obviously, this does not give you access to the images.

Ancestry provides a 14-day free trial. To register for this you have to give credit/debit card details and if you do not cancel the trial before it expires, the cost of a full annual subscription is charged to your card. In the past this system has come in for a lot of criticism, and given rise to accusations that cards were being debited without authorization, though in fact when you sign up for the trial you are effectively taking out a subscription, but with a 14-day cooling-off period. Part of the problem was that when the UK site was first launched the only way to cancel was via a US phone number; one could not cancel via the site or by email. However, Ancestry have responded to UK subscribers' concerns by setting up a UK freephone number and an online form for cancellation, so there is no need to be wary of the free trial.

The key thing if you do not want your trial to turn into a subscription is to ensure that you do not leave cancellation until the last minute. In particular, if your trial runs out on a Sunday, make sure you do not leave any cancellation until the Sunday itself, as it will not be processed until the following day. Ancestry provides detailed information on cancellation – click on the 'Help' link at the top right of any page and view the article 'How to cancel a subscription'.

Access to Ancestry is widely available free of charge in public libraries, as well as at the National Archives at Kew and at the Society of Genealogists, so there is plenty of opportunity to try the site out without signing up for the trial. This also means you can use Ancestry's census indexes even if you have not got your own internet connection.

Searching

In July 2008, Ancestry introduced a new search interface, which is initially available alongside the old one. However, since the old search will probably be removed during the autumn of 2008, we have described only the new search in this chapter. A flowchart of the search process is shown in Figure 7-1 (see p. 126).

When you log in to Ancestry, the Search home page offers a form covering all the datasets included in your subscription, but below that are links to the individual censuses for England, Wales and Scotland for each census year. Note the separate links for Wales – most data services combine England and Wales. There are also separate indexes for the Channel Islands and the Isle of Man. These are not directly linked from the initial search page, but you need to click on the link to 'UK Census Collection' (under 'More Collections') or go directly to **<www.ancestry.co.uk/search/rectype/census/uk/>**.

Once you have selected which census you want to search, you will see the search form (Figure 7-2). The 'Advanced' button at the top right allows you to toggle between this basic form and the advanced search form (Figure 7-3). The forms for the 1841 census do not have the fields for Family Members.

The essential difference between the two forms is the availability of exact matches in the advanced search. The basic form provides only a ranked search on the whole name. That is, the search results include many records which don't match all fields of your search form, but those which match closest come nearer the top. This is also the default on the advanced form, but you can choose any field for an exact match, or all the fields.

The site does not use any of the standard name-matching systems (Chapter 5, p. 99), but has its own method of identifying variants. There is some information on the help pages: 'A Ranked Search automatically returns alternate spellings and abbreviations for name(s) of your ancestor. For example, a search for Bill Smith might return William Smith, Wm Smith, Bill Smyth or B. Smith.' You will also notice in any ranked search results that they include individuals where a middle initial might indicate the forename you have specified – in this example, John W. Smith, perhaps.

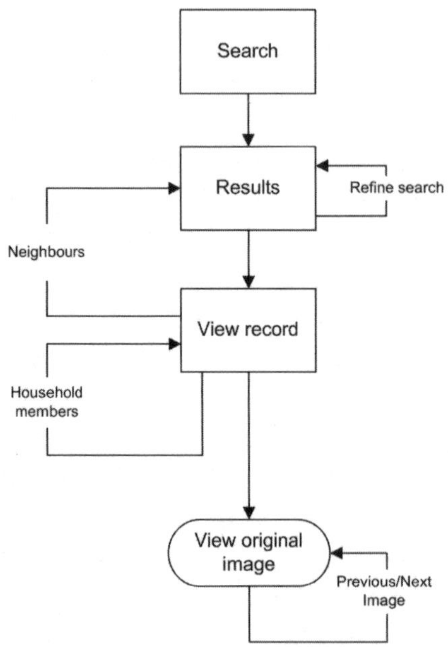

Figure 7-1 Ancestry search process

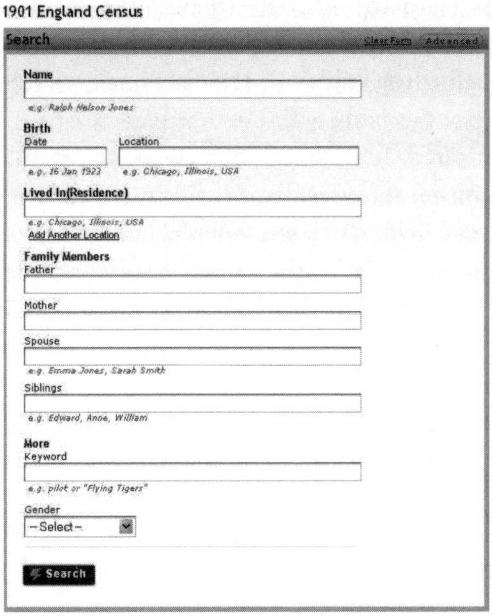

Figure 7-2 Ancestry basic search form

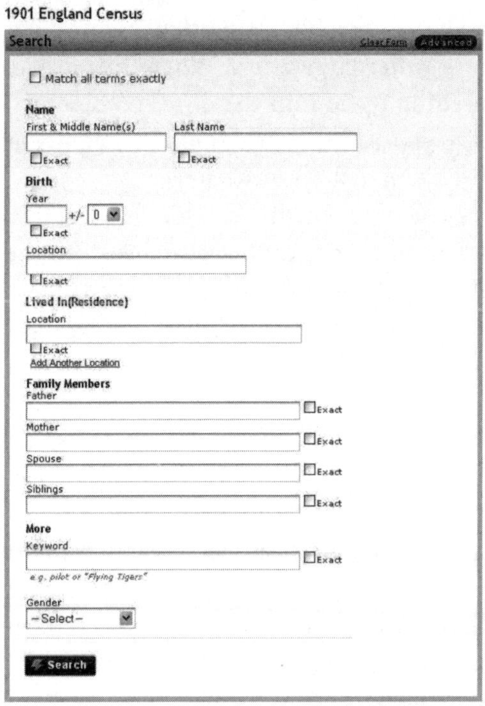

Figure 7-3 Ancestry Advanced search form

Ancestry allows wildcards, with the asterisk (*) standing for 0-5 characters and the question mark (?) for a single character. You must give at least three characters before the wildcard. The old search offered a Soundex option, but this is not available with the new search form.

In fact even the basic form offers some quite sophisticated options, with the ability to search for other families, the possibility of adding more locations, and the Keyword field which lets you add text for other fields not listed on the form:

- Ecclesiastical parish
- ED, institution, or vessel
- Relation
- Age
- Registration district
- Sub-registration district
- Household schedule number.

Some of these duplicate possibilities for the Location field.

An interesting feature of the search forms is the 'Add Another Location' option to allow more detail for a place – particularly useful if you are searching in London or other large cities. Where this differs from the advanced place searching option on the other commercial sites is that it does not require you to know whether the name you enter is that of a parish, a registration district or whatever.

On the whole, the advanced form seems preferable, as it makes switching between exact and ranked results easy. It also gives you the essential option of a birth date range. The only advantage of the basic form is that it spares you the embarrassing possibility of getting forename and surname the wrong way round.

Clicking on the 'Search' button brings up the search results. What you get here will depend on whether you have chosen to do an advanced search with exact matching or not, and how many fields you have completed on the search form. Records are always sorted by relevance and you cannot do anything to modify this. Each search result is given a number of stars from 5 down to ½ depending on the closeness of the match. But even an exact match will not necessarily get 5 stars: if you only enter a name, an exact match gets 3 stars; whereas with name, residence and year of birth you will get a 4-star match.

However, the ranking system is not exactly transparent and you should be cautious about putting too much reliance on it. In a search for Thomas Hardy as the head of a family in the 1901 census for England, the search results include 23,604 matches. The exact matches received 3 stars, but the same number of stars were assigned to 'Thomas Hardy, lodger', 'Thomas Hardy, Grandson' and, bizarrely, 'Thomas Hardy, Grandmother', while 'Thos Hardy, Head', which you would have thought would count as a closer match, received only 2½ stars. However, if you give a lot of information, this should not worry you – close matches will certainly be at the top of the list. Conversely, the top matches will genuinely be close to your search terms, but there might be other near misses that are further down the listing and lower ranked than some obvious non-matches. The ranking offers general guidance but should not be treated as authoritative.

If you do an advanced search with exact match you will get only the exact matches. You can see the difference in Figure 7-4, which shows exact matches, and Figure 7-5 (see p. 130) which shows all matches.

To the left of the search results, you can see the 'Refine search' box. This allows you to change any of your original search criteria without going back to the original search form. In particular, it allows you to switch easily between exact matches and all matches.

You can select between 10, 20 and 50 entries on each page of the results. But in fact there is also a simple trick for getting many more: when you are viewing a list of search results, your browser's location bar will have a web address for the page you are viewing. It will actually be over 200 characters long, so we're not going to quote an example here, but somewhere in it will be the characters '&hc=' followed by

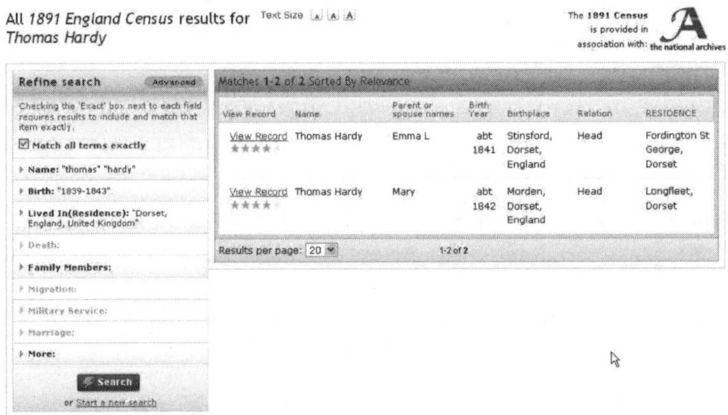

Figure 7-4 Ancestry search results (exact match)

Figure 7-5 Ancestry search results (any match)

a number. The number after '&hc=' is the number of results on the page. (If you cannot see this, just select an option from the Results per page box at the foot of the page and it will be added to the URL.) If you edit this number in the location field and then press the return/enter key, you will get a listing with that number of results per page. Once you have done this, the site will remember the setting until you override it.

One reason for doing this is that there is no way to save the results of the search to your computer other than copying the content of the page and pasting it into a text editor or word processor, something you will very likely want to do for a one-name study. If you have several thousand results, you will probably prefer not to have to do this repeatedly at 50 entries per page, when you could do it at 1,000 per page. Of course, the larger the number you enter, the longer the results page will take to display.

From the list of search results, the next step is to view the record for an individual (Figure 7-6). This shows most of the information on the original census form except for the fields where it says 'View Image'. The full TNA reference is below the 'Save This Record' box.

From this page, you have three main options:

- the 'View Image' or 'View original image' links take you to the image viewer (see below)
- you can click on the name of any other household member to see the full record for that person

- under 'Neighbors', the 'View others on page' link brings up a results-style listing with the names of all the other people listed on the same page of the enumeration book.

At the top left of this page is a box with 'Page Tools' (Figure 7-7). These are discussed below.

Ancestry does not offer a separate census address search, and there is no simple way to find who is living at a particular address. But there are two facilities for finding particular places. On the main search form, you can in fact leave the name field blank and enter a place in the Location field. Once you have typed an initial word, the form should offer you a list of options, from which you should select the one you want. You can use the Add Another Location field to enter additional place elements. The Keyword field will also accept registration district and parish names. However, while this is good for finding places, it seems only occasionally possible to find a street this way – we

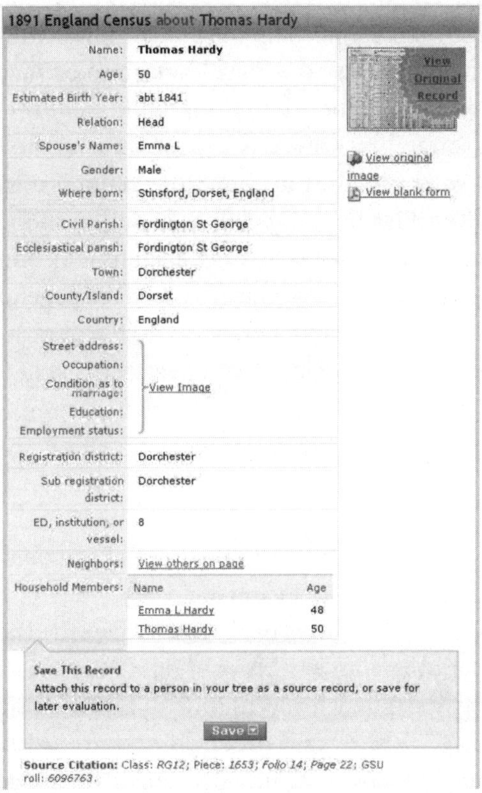

Figure 7-6 Ancestry individual record

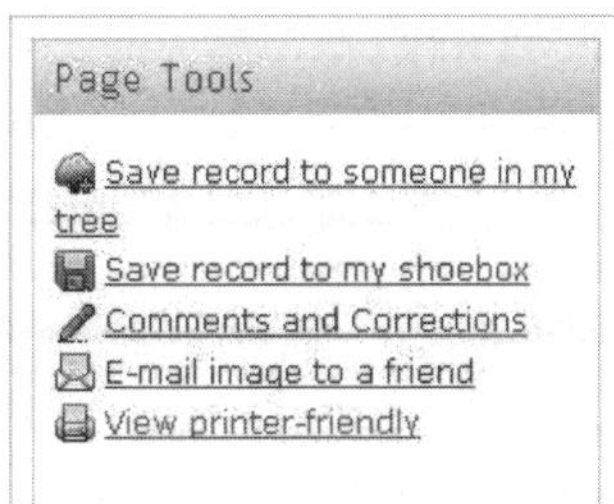

Figure 7-7 Ancestry Page Tools

tried entering street names in the Keyword field and had few successes (to be fair, the form does not mention street name as a candidate for this field).

An alternative is the browse option which is available for all the indexes except those for Scotland. This is quite time-consuming if you are just looking for a specific address, but will certainly be of interest to anyone using the census for local history. It can also be a last resort if you are pretty sure where an ancestor lived but have completely failed to find him or her in the search.

At the bottom of the page with the search form is a list of counties. This links to a list of each county's civil parishes, and then a list of enumeration districts (EDs) within the parish. For urban areas, there is a level of sub-registration districts before you get to the individual EDs. The districts are listed just by number so you need to read the accompanying description to see precisely what area the district covers. Unfortunately, urban areas tend to have large numbers of enumeration districts, and finding the right one for a particular street can be a long process. Clicking on the link to the ED opens up the image viewer with the first page of entries. You can then use the 'Next' button to browse through the pages.

Another use of the browse facility, which is not obvious at first glance, is to look for Royal Navy vessels. For the 1861–1881 and 1901 census indexes for England, 'Royal Navy' is listed alphabetically among the counties and the link takes you to a list of vessels, each of which in turn links to the image of the description page and to the first page of crew members.

Ancestry does not offer any facility to search for a page reference.

Images

Ancestry's census images are greyscale and seem mostly to have been scanned at around 200dpi. They are in JPEG format.

The site offers two different image viewers, basic and enhanced. The basic viewer will work automatically with any browser on a PC or Mac, while the enhanced viewer is designed for Windows systems using Internet Explorer or Firefox. (The site warns that: 'If you are using Internet Explorer 7 and having difficulty installing the Enhanced Image Viewer it may be necessary to turn off your phishing filter. The phishing

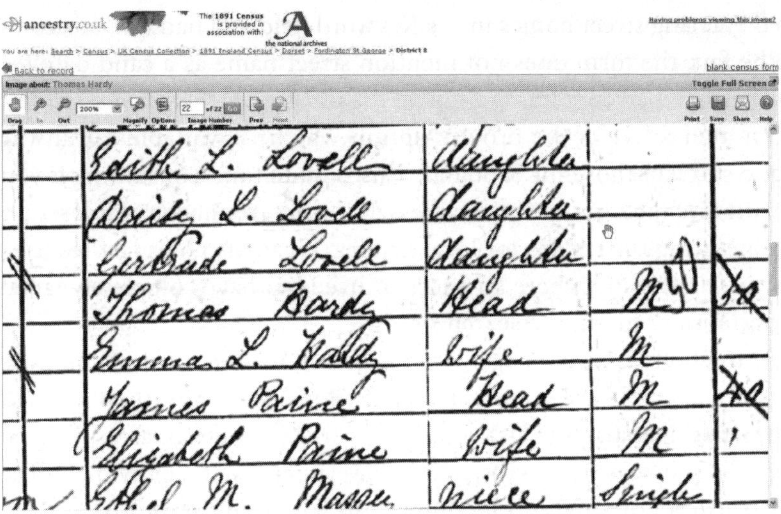

Figure 7-8 Ancestry enhanced image viewer

filter settings are located under the tools menu of Internet Explorer 7.') Where the enhanced viewer is available, you will see a message above any image inviting you to switch to it if you are not already using it.

The benefits of the enhanced viewer include a wider range of functions and, in particular, access to higher quality images, so there is no reason not to use it. If you have a slow internet connection, the enhanced image viewer still allows you to switch back to lower quality images to reduce the download time if you wish to. The enhanced viewer is shown in Figure 7-8, with the zoom level set to 200 per cent. In addition to the Zoom options there is also a Magnify function which allows you to see a small portion of the image at even higher magnification. The Options button offers a range of image quality and display options.

Whereas the basic viewer only allows you to save the image to your computer (and then only by a tedious process making use of the browser's built-in image saving function), the enhanced viewer provides three options:

- attach to someone in my tree
- save to my 'shoebox'
- save to your computer.

The first two of these are discussed below under 'Other resources'. The

Save option automatically saves as a JPEG image.

The Share button allows you to share the image with someone else. It sends an email containing a link to the image, which does not require a subscription to view it. The email says 'Hurry ... the above link will expire soon, click it now to see the image', but in fact the link seems to remain active for a few weeks at least. This facility can be very useful for those accessing Ancestry on a public computer in a library or elsewhere. Instead of saving the image to the computer, which you may not be permitted to do, you can simply email the link to yourself.

Help and feedback

Help for Ancestry will be found using the 'Help' link at the top right of most pages. This leads to a set of pages with a comprehensive body of answers to the most common questions. You can either browse through the list or use the search facility to find a relevant topic. The commonest questions are those relating to subscriptions and image viewing. Certainly if you have any problem using the enhanced image viewer, you should be able to find the answer here. There is also an option to send an email to Ancestry Support.

There is specific help with reading the handwriting in the original documents: to the right of every search form is an oddly phrased link to 'View a sampling of handwriting examples'. This brings a pop-up window with an image which can also be viewed separately at <**c.ancestry.com/i/content/handwriting.gif**>.

The help option in the image viewer gives help only with the images and the viewer itself.

For reporting errors, there is a 'Comments and Corrections' link on the Page Tools box (Figure 7-7). This brings up a page with three options: one for reporting errors in the transcription of personal names; another for simply adding a comment to the record 'to assist other researchers or explain or correct confusing information' – this is not for corrections; and a third for reporting images problems. There is no facility for reporting indexing errors in fields other than the two name fields, though this is mentioned as a potential improvement.

In response to error reports, the original record is not in fact modified. What happens is that a cross-reference is created in the index. For example, a search for Thomas Christian in the 1901 census includes a

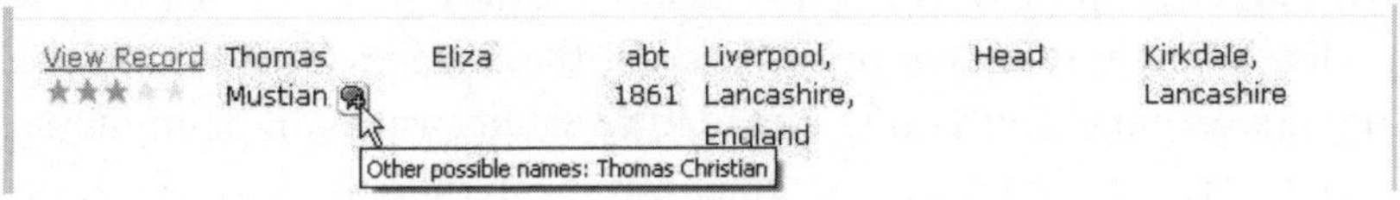

Figure 7-9 Ancestry name corrections in the search results

3-star match for a Thomas Mustian living in Kirkdale, Lancs. There is an icon beside it which pops up the message 'Other possible names: Thomas Christian' (see Figure 7-9). When you then view the full record and click on an identical icon beside the name, this brings up the original submission made on the name correction form, explaining why another user thinks 'Mustian' is wrong. Note that this entry is still going to turn up if you do a search for Thomas Mustian, so even if the correction is mistaken, the original data is not affected.

In some cases, it is quite clear that an undisputed error has been made in transcription, something that is not a matter of debate about hard-to-read letters. Typically this involves things such as a single surname being given to a whole household, even though some members actually have different surnames. In this case the corrected name comes first, with the original name second, followed by a yellow triangle both in the search results and in the individual record.

The image viewer also has a facility for reporting image problems. There is a link at the top right of the image viewer, 'Having problems with this image?', which brings up a pop-up window for reporting image problems.

Other resources

Ancestry has easily the largest collection of genealogical datasets for the UK. As of July 2008, there are almost 800 databases for the UK, and the most important are listed at the bottom of the initial search page at <**search.ancestry.co.uk/search/**>. If you follow the 'Go to the Card Catalog' link, this takes you to a searchable master list at <**search.ancestry.co.uk/search/CardCatalog.aspx**>. The easiest way to find the UK databases in this listing is to use the 'Filter by Location' option in the sidebar.

Since there are now many places where one can search UK genealogical records, Ancestry has been trying to maintain its position in the market not just by adding new datasets, but also by making the site useful for more than just record searching. There are two main areas: making contacts and family trees. The contacts area can be found by clicking on the 'Community' button at the top of most Ancestry pages and has links to message boards for individual surnames and for each county in the British Isles, and for finding other Ancestry subscribers with similar surname interests.

The other useful feature is the ability to keep family trees on the site. You can make this tree public so that anyone can see it, or you can just restrict it to individuals you have invited. For anyone using the census records, though, the key feature is that you can link census records to individuals in your tree.

To create a tree on Ancestry, you need to go to the My Ancestry area and either create a family tree by entering individuals or upload a GEDCOM file. Once your tree is in place, when you view the record for an individual (Figure 7-6), you can click on the 'Save record to someone in my tree' link to copy data across – it will add a new 'Residence' field, giving the census year and the place. And if you have no birth details for the person, you can choose to copy an approximate birth year and place of birth from the census record (see Figure 7-10). When you then view the individual in your tree, a link to 'Historical Records' will bring up the census record.

Sometimes you will come across a census record you may feel is relevant to your tree but you are not certain enough to link it to a

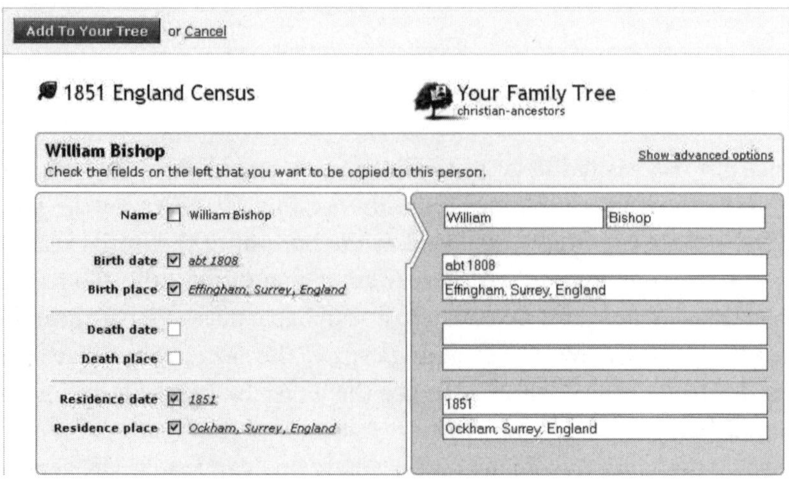

Figure 7-10 Ancestry adding census records to a family tree

particular individual. Alternatively, you may choose not to have a tree on Ancestry but nonetheless want to keep a record of what you have viewed. In both cases, Ancestry's 'shoebox' feature is useful. This can be accessed from the Page Tools box (Figure 7-7): clicking on the 'Save record to my shoebox' link will save the record. You can also save to the shoebox from the image viewer. When you view the My Ancestry page, it lists all the individual entries saved to the shoebox with a link to the original record.

Future developments

Ancestry's census collection is complete in terms of indexes, so the only developments are likely to be corrections, annotations and enhancements. Some potential enhancements for the search facility are listed at <**search.ancestry.co.uk/search/preview.aspx**>.

As mentioned at the start of this chapter, the site lacks images for the Scottish censuses, but it seems likely that these will be added once GROS has announced licensing arrangements.

8

FINDMYPAST

Findmypast at <**www.findmypast.com**> started life in April 2003 under the name 1837online, providing images of the GRO indexes, the first site to do so. It launched its first census data in early 2005, and in 2006 the site changed to its present name. In 2008, the company was purchased by Scotland Online (now called Brightsolid), who run ScotlandsPeople.

Findmypast currently offers indexes and images for the censuses of England and Wales in 1841, and 1861, 1871, 1891 and 1901, though the 1901 census is still in progress at the time of writing. The 1841 and 1871 censuses are licensed from Origins (see Chapter 11), and Findmypast's 1861 census data is licensed to Origins, so these three indexes are identical on the two sites. The 1881 data is taken from the 1881 Census Index created by the volunteer project discussed in Chapter 6 (also available on FamilySearch at<**www.familysearch.org**>), and has no associated images.

An index for the 1851 census is currently in preparation and Findmypast is likely to be one of the first sites to offer the 1911 census after the National Archives starts to offer licences (see pp. 149 and 211).

As mentioned in Chapter 4, Findmypast's census indexes are starting to be available free of charge on the FamilySearch pilot record Search site (described on pp. 115–8), though you must still pay to view the images unless you are accessing FamilySearch from a Family History Center.

Charges

Findmypast offers both subscription and pay-per-view access to its data collections. Its Explorer subscription plan gives access to all the datasets on the site and costs £89.95 for 12 months or £54.95 for six months. There are plans to introduce a monthly subscription, though details were not yet available when this book went to press. The site also offers a Voyager subscription, but this covers only the passenger list data and does not include the censuses. There is currently a 20 per cent loyalty discount for renewing subscribers.

The pay-per-view service offers 60 units for £6.95, valid for 90 days, or 280 units for £24.95, valid for a year. Census household transcriptions and census images are both charged at 3 units each, i.e. just under 35p. You can see the cost in units for other records on the site at <**www.findmypast.com/paymentOptions/payperview.jsp**>. If you purchase more units before the expiry of the 90 days, your remaining units will be carried forward to your new 90-day expiry date.

The site does not offer a free trial, but the 60-unit pay-per-view option gives you three months to try out the site at a minimal cost and enough units to view 20 household transcriptions or images. Alternatively, if you take out a subscription, you have a cooling-off period of 14 days. If you cancel your subscription within those 14 days, you get a full refund, less the cost of units you have actually used.

The normal method of payment is online with a credit or debit card. For those unwilling to use their cards in online transactions, there is a voucher scheme, which is described at <**www.findmypast.com/paymentOptions/vouchers/**>. Vouchers give you 50 units valid for 90 days (£5) or one year's access to civil registration and census records (£90). Vouchers can be purchased in person or by mail order from the National Archives, and are available at many public libraries. There are also stockists in Australia and New Zealand. A list of stockists will be found by following the 'find the nearest stockist to you' link on the Vouchers page.

Although, in principle, the subscription affords unlimited usage, the terms and conditions allow a subscription to be suspended if usage seems unreasonably high However, this is mainly intended to prevent people using their subscription to offer look-up services and in practice you are not likely to be affected by this limit. See <**www.findmypast.com/terms/**> for an explanation of what counts as unreasonable.

Searching

The site offers three types of search: a person search (with basic and advanced options), an address search (again, basic and advanced), and a census reference search. You access all three by clicking on the 'Census' tab at the top of the home page, and are then offered a list of all the census years with links to person and address search. There is a single link to the census reference search before the boxes for the individual years.

The flowchart for the person search is shown in Figure 8-1, and the basic person search form is shown in Figure 8-2. The 'counties' you can select from the County drop-down list include the Isle of Man, Guernsey & Adjacent Islands, and Jersey. For some years, you can also select the ridings of Yorkshire individually as well as the whole county.

The exact spellings will be searched for in the First name and Last

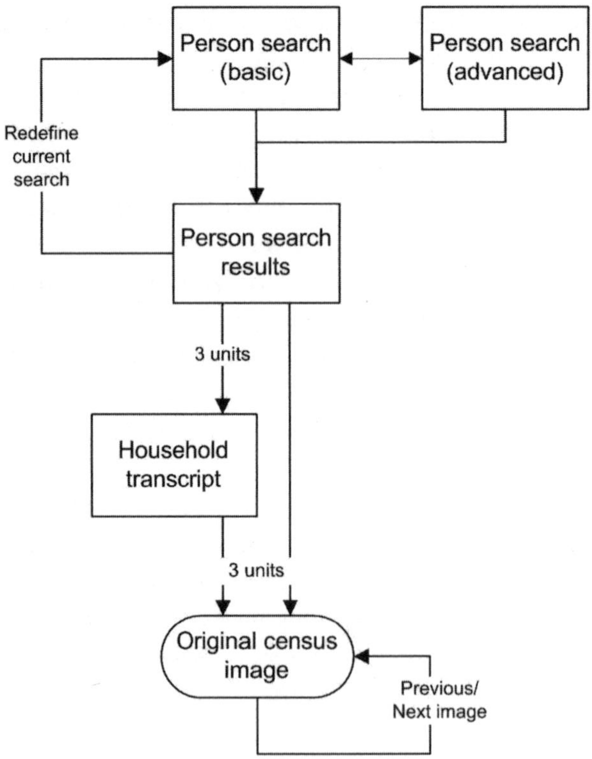

Figure 8-1 Findmypast person search flowchart. (The unit costs apply only to pay-per-view access.)

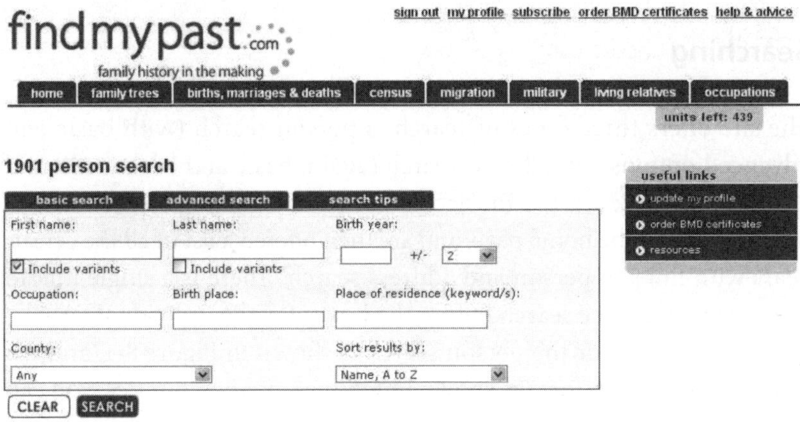

Figure 8-2 Findmypast person search flowchart. (The unit costs apply only to pay-per-view access.)

name fields, unless you tick either or both of the Include variants boxes, in which case the site uses NameX (see Chapter 5, p. 101) to generate the variants.

The advanced person search (shown in Figure 8-3, see p. 142) offers many more options. Some of these are of only occasional usefulness (the sex and marriage condition, perhaps), while others are just what you need if searching for a common name or a particularly elusive ancestor. The ability to specify the relationship to the head of the household and look for another name within the household is a very useful combination: you may be able to locate a family from the names of a parent and child or from two children's names. This form also lets you restrict your search to households, institutions or vessels. (You cannot, however, search for institutions or vessels by name.)

However, the wide range of geographical options is a real trap, unless you are very familiar with the administrative geography of the place where your ancestors lived. Do you really know that the name you are entering is that of a municipal borough, or was it a civil parish? You are very likely not to find the results you are looking for if you use these fields on the basis of guesswork – the all-purpose Place of residence field in the basic search is a much safer bet. On the other hand, if you do have accurate information about this, say from the previous or next census, it can be a very good way to narrow down searches for a common name.

Figure 8-4 (see p. 142) shows the results of a person search for

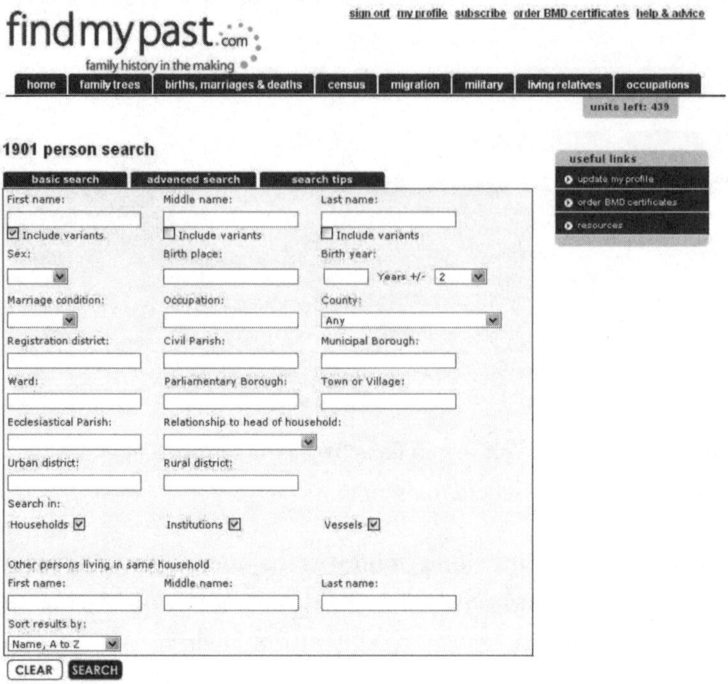

Figure 8-3 Findmypast advanced person search

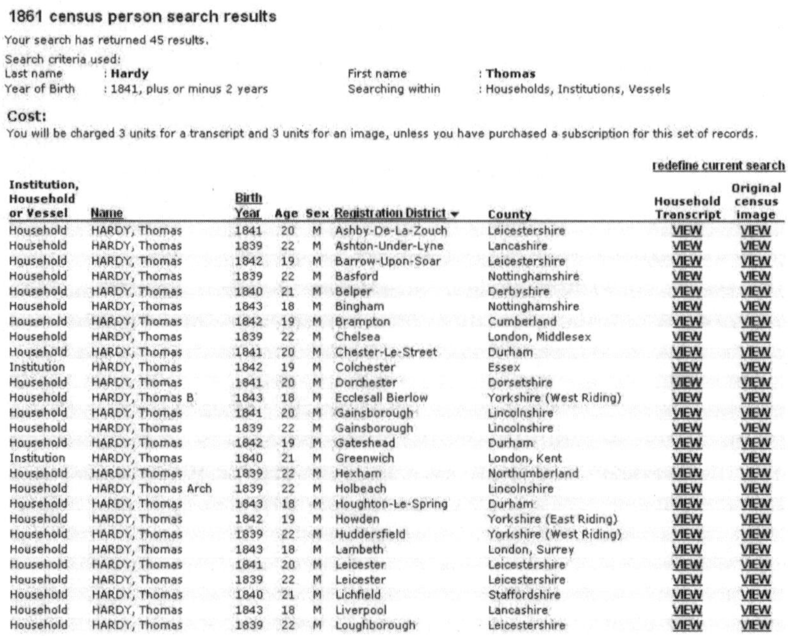

1861 census person search results

Your search has returned 45 results.

Search criteria used:

Last name : **Hardy** First name : **Thomas**

Year of Birth : 1841, plus or minus 2 years Searching within : Households, Institutions, Vessels

Cost:

You will be charged 3 units for a transcript and 3 units for an image, unless you have purchased a subscription for this set of records.

redefine current search

Institution, Household or Vessel	Name	Birth Year	Age	Sex	Registration District	County	Household Transcript	Original census image
Household	HARDY, Thomas	1841	20	M	Ashby-De-La-Zouch	Leicestershire	VIEW	VIEW
Household	HARDY, Thomas	1839	22	M	Ashton-Under-Lyne	Lancashire	VIEW	VIEW
Household	HARDY, Thomas	1842	19	M	Barrow-Upon-Soar	Leicestershire	VIEW	VIEW
Household	HARDY, Thomas	1839	22	M	Basford	Nottinghamshire	VIEW	VIEW
Household	HARDY, Thomas	1840	21	M	Belper	Derbyshire	VIEW	VIEW
Household	HARDY, Thomas	1843	18	M	Bingham	Nottinghamshire	VIEW	VIEW
Household	HARDY, Thomas	1842	19	M	Brampton	Cumberland	VIEW	VIEW
Household	HARDY, Thomas	1839	22	M	Chelsea	London, Middlesex	VIEW	VIEW
Household	HARDY, Thomas	1841	20	M	Chester-Le-Street	Durham	VIEW	VIEW
Institution	HARDY, Thomas	1842	19	M	Colchester	Essex	VIEW	VIEW
Household	HARDY, Thomas	1841	20	M	Dorchester	Dorsetshire	VIEW	VIEW
Household	HARDY, Thomas B	1843	18	M	Ecclesall Bierlow	Yorkshire (West Riding)	VIEW	VIEW
Household	HARDY, Thomas	1841	20	M	Gainsborough	Lincolnshire	VIEW	VIEW
Household	HARDY, Thomas	1839	22	M	Gainsborough	Lincolnshire	VIEW	VIEW
Household	HARDY, Thomas	1842	19	M	Gateshead	Durham	VIEW	VIEW
Institution	HARDY, Thomas	1840	21	M	Greenwich	London, Kent	VIEW	VIEW
Household	HARDY, Thomas	1839	22	M	Hexham	Northumberland	VIEW	VIEW
Household	HARDY, Thomas Arch	1839	22	M	Holbeach	Lincolnshire	VIEW	VIEW
Household	HARDY, Thomas	1843	18	M	Houghton-Le-Spring	Durham	VIEW	VIEW
Household	HARDY, Thomas	1842	19	M	Howden	Yorkshire (East Riding)	VIEW	VIEW
Household	HARDY, Thomas	1839	22	M	Huddersfield	Yorkshire (West Riding)	VIEW	VIEW
Household	HARDY, Thomas	1843	18	M	Lambeth	London, Surrey	VIEW	VIEW
Household	HARDY, Thomas	1841	20	M	Leicester	Leicestershire	VIEW	VIEW
Household	HARDY, Thomas	1839	22	M	Leicester	Leicestershire	VIEW	VIEW
Household	HARDY, Thomas	1840	21	M	Lichfield	Staffordshire	VIEW	VIEW
Household	HARDY, Thomas	1843	18	M	Liverpool	Lancashire	VIEW	VIEW
Household	HARDY, Thomas	1839	22	M	Loughborough	Leicestershire	VIEW	VIEW

Figure 8-4 Findmypast person search results

1861 census - household transcription

Person: HARDY, Thomas
Address: Bookhampton, Stinsford

Cost:
You will be charged 3 units for a transcript and 3 units for an image, unless you have purchased a subscription for this set of records.

REPORT TRANSCRIPTION CHANGE | PRINTER FRIENDLY VERSION

Name	Relation	Condition	Sex	Age	Birth Year	Occupation Disability	Where Born	Original census image
HARDY, Thomas	Head	Married	M	49	1812	Mason & Bricklayer Master Employing 6 Men	Stinsford Dorsetshire	VIEW
HARDY, Jemima	Wife	Married	F	47	1814		Melbury Osmond Dorsetshire	VIEW
HARDY, Thomas	Son	Unmarried	M	20	1841	Architects Clerk	Stinsford Dorsetshire	VIEW
HARDY, Henry	Son		M	9	1852	Scholar	Stinsford Dorsetshire	VIEW
HARDY, Catherine	Daughter		F	4	1857		Stinsford Dorsetshire	VIEW

RG number: RG09	**Piece:** 1354	**Folio:** 89	**Page:** 2
Registration District: Dorchester	**Sub District:** 1 Dorchester	**EnumerationDistrict:** 10	**Ecclesiastical Parish:**
Civil Parish: Stinsford	**Municipal Borough:**	**Address:** Bookhampton, Stinsford	**County:** Dorsetshire

Figure 8-5 Findmypast household transcription

Thomas Hardy in the 1861 census (specifying 1841 as his birth year). The results can be sorted on the three columns whose headings are underlined: Name, Birth Year and Registration District (which is the sort column in Figure 8-5). If you are using Firefox and want to return from this page to your search form to refine the search terms, use the 'redefine current search' link rather than the browser's 'Back' button – if you use the 'Back' button, the 'Search' button on the search form is unusable and just says 'Please wait'. This works properly in Internet Explorer.

If you know the age and address of a person, this may be enough to identify the correct record so you can go straight to viewing the image, but it makes sense to follow the Household Transcript link, which gives you all the information on the original census form and includes the National Archives reference (Figure 8-5).

If you are using Internet Explorer, there is one thing to note about the household transcription: using the browser's 'Back' button to return to the person search results will give an error ('Webpage has expired'); instead you need to click on the 'census search results' link at the bottom. This is not a problem with other browsers.

The basic address search is very simple, with fields for Street name, Residential place and County (Figure 8-6, see p. 144). If your street name is unique, it will take you straight to the Street details screen, which lists all the houses in the street. From here you can choose to look at the Address transcript (i.e. the list of inhabitants for a house), and then view the page image. If your street name is not unique, you

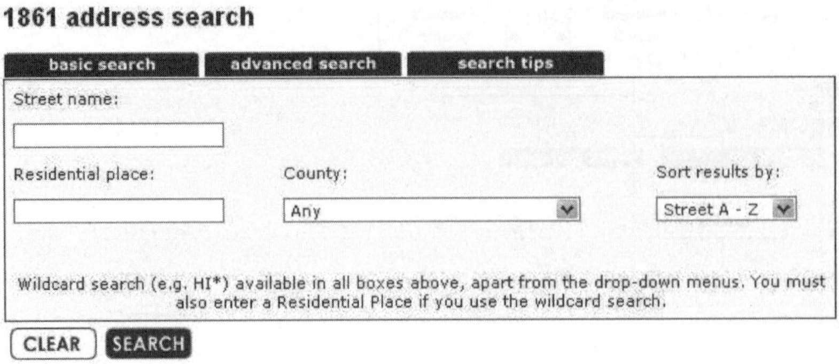

Figure 8-6 Findmypast address search

are first presented with the Address search results screen which lists all the matching streets (see Figure 8-7) – selecting one will take you to the Street details page.

You can use wildcards both in the Street name and Residential place fields. As long as you enter at least six characters before the wildcard, you can actually leave the Residential place field empty and leave the County set to 'any'. So in a search for streets with the name 'Waterloo', it rejects a search for 'Water*' without a place, but accepts 'Waterl*' (see Figure 8-7). Note that this was confirmed to us by Findmypast, and the text shown at the bottom of the address search form in Figure 8-6 is to be corrected.

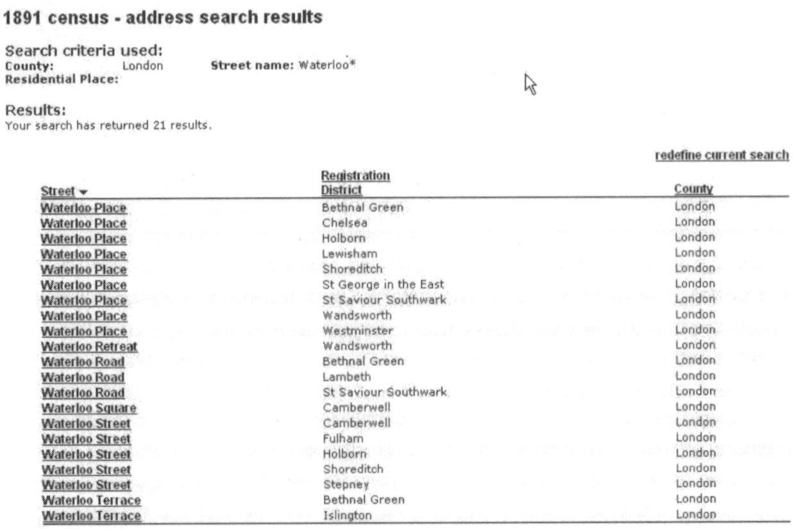

1891 census - address search results

Search criteria used:
County: London Street name: Waterloo*
Residential Place:

Results:
Your search has returned 21 results.

redefine current search

Street	Registration District	County
Waterloo Place	Bethnal Green	London
Waterloo Place	Chelsea	London
Waterloo Place	Holborn	London
Waterloo Place	Lewisham	London
Waterloo Place	Shoreditch	London
Waterloo Place	St George in the East	London
Waterloo Place	St Saviour Southwark	London
Waterloo Place	Wandsworth	London
Waterloo Place	Westminster	London
Waterloo Retreat	Wandsworth	London
Waterloo Road	Bethnal Green	London
Waterloo Road	Lambeth	London
Waterloo Road	St Saviour Southwark	London
Waterloo Square	Camberwell	London
Waterloo Street	Camberwell	London
Waterloo Street	Fulham	London
Waterloo Street	Holborn	London
Waterloo Street	Shoreditch	London
Waterloo Street	Stepney	London
Waterloo Terrace	Bethnal Green	London
Waterloo Terrace	Islington	London

Figure 8-7 Findmypast address search results

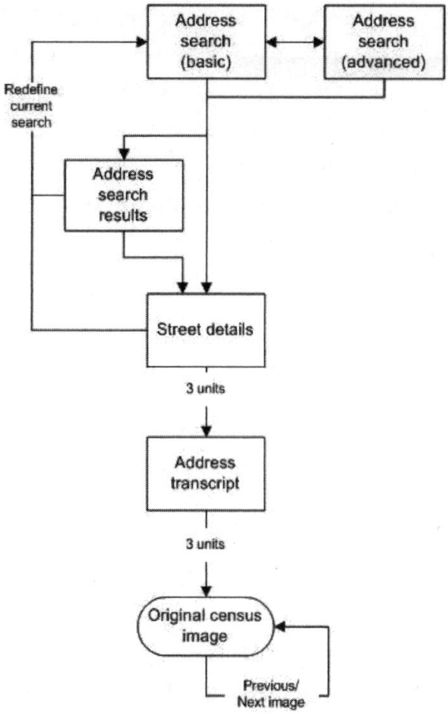

Figure 8-8 Findmypast address search flowchart. (The unit costs apply only to pay-per-view access.)

The advanced address search differs from the basic in offering all the extra administrative unit fields found in the advanced person search (see Figure 8-3). You can use wildcards in any field except the county, where you must select from the drop-down list.

Figure 8-8 shows a flowchart for the address search.

While the person and address searches use a separate form for each census year, there is only one census reference search form, from which you must select the census year and enter a piece and folio number. You can optionally enter a page number. The census reference search results page lists all the individuals on the matching folio or page.

Images

From the person search results and the household transcript, there is a link to the page image, which appears in a separate pop-up window.

All the images are greyscale, save for some of those for the 1871 census licensed from Origins. These will presumably be replaced with greyscale images in the near future, as Origins replaces them on its own site (see Chapter 11, p. 192). There is some variation in resolution, but all are at least 250dpi and many as high as 350dpi.

Findmypast offers two different image viewers. The enhanced image viewer, shown in Figure 8-9, uses an unusual graphics format, DjVu (pronounced like *déjà vu*). Your browser will not be able to display the images in this format without a special plug-in. If you do not have the DjVu plug-in installed (which you certainly won't the first time you view an image on the site), your browser will use the Adobe Flash player if it is available. This is a widely used plug-in, typically used to provide website animation, and you are quite likely to have this already installed on your computer.

Whether or not the Adobe Flash player is available, it makes sense to go for the enhanced viewer by clicking on the 'Download free enhanced viewer' link at the top of the page. If you are using Internet Explorer, the viewer will be installed from within your browser; with other browsers, the installation file will be downloaded to your hard disk and you will then have to start it by clicking on it; you should *not* close your browser while it installs, then when the installation is

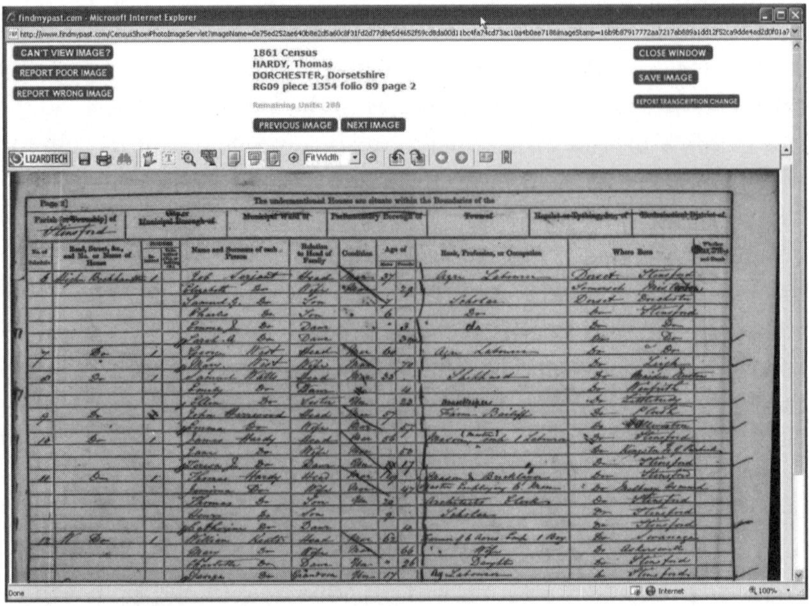

Figure 8-9 Findmypast enhanced image viewer

finished, click on the 'Continue' button rather than the 'Close Windows' button. There is a help page on the viewer at <**www.findmypast.com/helpadvice/faqs/djVu-viewer/**>.

The advantage of the DjVu viewer is that the images will display much more quickly. Another significant difference between the two viewers is the format in which images are saved. If you click on the 'Save Image' button, the Flash viewer will save in JPEG format, while the DjVu saves in DjVu format. The problem with the latter is that few graphics programs recognize the DjVu file format, so you may be unable to use your normal graphics software to display or manipulate the saved image – for example, you may want to enhance the contrast. There are two solutions. First, ignore the 'Save Image' button and instead right-click on the image, then select 'Export to File'. From the drop-down file type list, you will be able to select DjVu or BMP. BMP is the standard Windows Bitmap format, which any graphics program should be able to deal with. Unfortunately it is an uncompressed file format and the file may be as much as ten times larger than the original DjVu image, but once you have saved it, your graphics viewer will be able to convert it to a more compact format such as JPEG or GIF. The alternative solution is to find a graphics program which supports the DjVu image format (for example, if you use Windows, download the IrfanView graphics viewer and its DjVu plug-in free from **www.irfanview.com**). But even without this you will still be able to view the saved images – clicking on the file name in an Explorer window will load the image in a standalone version of the DjVu viewer.

When you save an image from the DjVu viewer, it is more convenient to use the big 'Save Image' button at the top right of the page than clicking on the floppy disk 'File Save' icon in the viewer toolbar. By default, using 'Save Image' gives the image a unique, sensible file name partly based on the National Archives reference. For example, the image of Thomas Hardy's household in Figure 8-9 would be automatically saved with a file name starting '1861Census-RG9...'. In contrast, the 'File Save' button gives every image the same default name 'census-GetImage.action.djvu'.

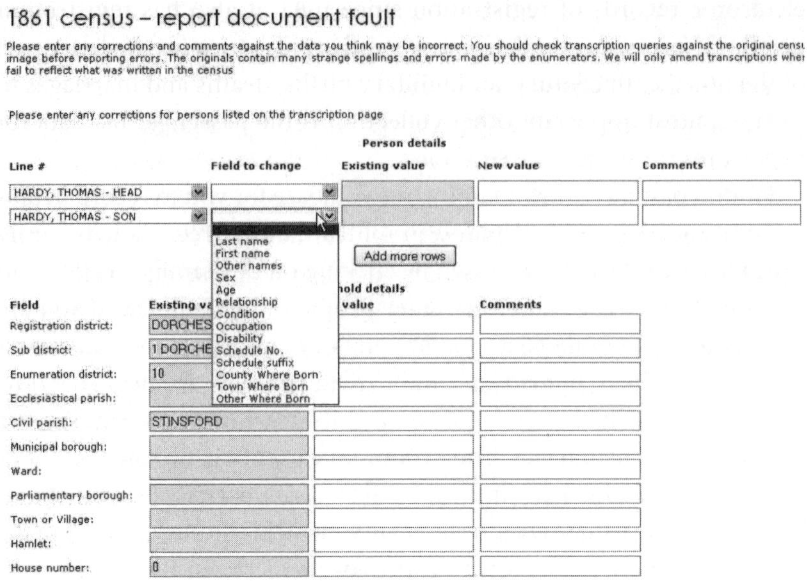

Figure 8-10 Findmypast transcription error report form

Help and feedback

The site's help pages can be found by clicking either on the 'Resources' link on the left of the home page or the 'help & advice' link at the top. There are two main pages in the help section which are relevant to using the census: a brief page of frequently asked questions about the census, and a very substantial article in the Knowledge Base section. One useful section on the latter page if you fail to find someone is a list of missing piece numbers in the 1841 and 1871 censuses.

Findmypast offers two places where you can report errors. On the household transcription page you can report transcription errors in any field of any entry in the household (see Figure 8-10). From the image viewer you can report transcription errors, a poor quality image or the fact that the wrong image has been displayed.

Other resources

The main focus of Findmypast before its introduction of census records was civil registration. Alongside images of the GRO indexes and the electronic records of registration since 1984, it also has registration details for overseas events from 1761 and events at sea for the latter part of the nineteenth century, and military births, deaths and marriages to 1994. Its most important other collection is the passenger list data for departures from the UK 1890–1960.

Findmypast has its own family tree database for you to record details of your ancestors and display a graphical family tree. Called Family Tree Explorer, it can be accessed by clicking on the 'family trees' tab on the home page. You can either enter people individually or, if you are already using a family tree program on your computer, you can export a GEDCOM file to upload to Family Tree Explorer – for details of how to do this for whichever family tree software you are using, see the program's own help pages. The maximum capacity is two trees of up to 25,000 individuals each. At present all trees are entirely private, but in future you will also be able to share with particular individuals or make a tree completely public. There is no linkage between the Family Tree Explorer and the census records, i.e. you cannot link an individual in your tree to a specific record or import the details from the census search results, though you can of course manually enter the information you have found. Information about Family Tree Explorer will be found at <**www.findmypast.com/family-tree-explorer.jsp**>.

Future developments

In May 2008 the 1901 data for Gloucestershire and Somerset were made available on the site. Cornwall, Durham, Glamorganshire, Norfolk, Northumberland, Middlesex and Yorkshire are due to follow next, and all the remaining counties should have been added by the end of 2009.

Findmypast and Origins are currently co-operating to provide an enhanced version of the 1871 census, with improved images and full transcription, and this should be available before the end of 2008.

Findmypast, as a subsidiary of Scotland Online, is heavily involved with the digitization of the 1911 census for England and Wales, and expects to offer its own index in due course (see Chapter 13, p. 211).

In September 2007, the Federation of Family History Societies announced that its own data service FamilyHistoryOnline (FHO) at <**www.familyhistoryonline.net**> would in the future be hosted at

Findmypast (see the press release at <**www.familyhistoryonline.net/general/press_release2007sep01.shtml**> and the FAQs about the transfer at **www.familyhistoryonline.net/general/fmpfaq.shtml**). Many of the datasets at FHO were county census indexes prepared by individual local family history societies. Since Findmypast has not yet indexed the 1851 census, it is currently working with the FFHS and individual societies to provide a complete index to 1851 at Findmypast.

Findmypast censuses have been selected for use by UK Data Archive (<**www.data-archive.ac.uk**> based at the University of Essex) in their academic study of the population over time. The Data Archive is working with Findmypast to enhance the data and ensure its accuracy.

The connection with ScotlandsPeople means that the Scottish census may well be available on Findmypast at some point in the future, thus giving subscription access to the Scottish data in addition to the pay-per-view service already provided by ScotlandsPeople. As this book goes to press, there are no firm details or schedule for this development.

9

THEGENEALOGIST AND ROOTSUK

TheGenealogist at <**www.thegenealogist.co.uk**> and RootsUK at <**www.rootsuk.com**> are two of the online data services run by Genealogy Supplies (Jersey) Ltd. The company is probably better known as S & N Genealogy Supplies, a long-established genealogy software retailer. It has a number of sites for genealogical data and a very comprehensive portfolio of censuses on CD-ROM (see Chapter 16).

TheGenealogist and RootsUK provide access to exactly the same indexes and images, which is why they are treated together in this chapter, but they differ in their charging mechanisms and search facilities. TheGenealogist offers more sophisticated facilities and its subscription options are designed for those who are going to do a significant amount of searching. RootsUK has much more basic search options, which together with its pay-per-view charging makes it better for the beginner. Alternatively, a seasoned family historian who is just trying to fill a few gaps may only need to make a small number of searches and for this sort of user RootsUK will probably be a cheaper option. On the other hand, if you are looking for a difficult to find family, the search facilities of TheGenealogist may be more successful.

At the time of writing, these two sites have full transcripts of the 1841–1871, 1891 and 1901 censuses. The site also has images for the 1881 census for London.

S & N have other census-related sites, such as <**www.londoncensus.co.uk**>, <**www.yorkshirecensus.co.uk**>, <**www.lancashire census.co.uk**>, and a whole series for individual census years at <**www.uk1841census.com**>, etc. These simply link to the company's main census sites and to information about their CD-ROM products.

S & N also run FHS Online at <**www.fhs-online.co.uk**> to host census and other data from family history societies. Since the census data on this site is accessible free of charge, it is discussed in Chapter 6 with the other sites offering free data.

As discussed on p. 170, it seems certain that S & N's nineteenth century census indexes have also been licensed to Genes Reunited.

Charges

TheGenealogist's charging model is quite complex, but there are three basic types of access:

- The 'All-inclusive' subscription provides credit-free unlimited access to all databases (not just the census transcriptions) for a year, with two rates: a 'Personal Premium' subscription at £68.95 per annum, or a 'Professional Premium' at £149.95 per annum. The latter is intended for professional researchers.
- The 'Personal Plus' subscription is in reality a halfway house between subscription and pay-per-view: you have access to all the datasets, but there is a limit (albeit a very high one) on how many searches you can carry out and how many images you can view. The annual subscription gives you 800 credits for £55.95, and there are two quarterly options: 175 credits for £24.95 or 75 credits for £14.95.
- There is also a 'Pay As You Go' option: in this you get access to a single county for a single census year with 150 searches and 50 image views.

The choice is therefore between credit-free access, credit-based access to all databases, and credit-based access to a single database. Full details are available from <**www.thegenealogist.co.uk/nameindex/products.php**>.

If you go for a credit-based option, any credits you don't use up are carried forward to the next charging. Also, if you use up your allowance, additional credits can be purchased: viewing credits cost 50 for £5.00 or 200 for £14.95; search credits cost 150 for £9.95 or 75 for £5.

The information on how many credits things cost is not easy to find on the site, but there is a table at <**www.thegenealogist.co.uk/help/credits.htm**>.

The Pay As You Go option seems quite expensive – you will need to sign up for several different census years to trace your ancestors, even if they all stayed in the same county. To get a complete run of years for a single county via this option will cost you twice the price of the All-inclusive subscription.

For a local historian this might make some sense, but for that purpose you would be better off purchasing the same material on CD-ROM, where you will have all the images and can carry out as many searches as you want. Also, of course, the other subscriptions allow you to view all the other datasets available on the site (see p. 168).

The best-value option is clearly, as you would expect, the All-inclusive subscription. However, the annual Personal Plus subscription is probably sufficient for many people: the 800 credits are enough to do 100 advanced searches, and view 100 transcriptions and 100 images. By contrast, the two quarterly subscriptions are more expensive and offer fewer units. On the other hand, if you've already done a lot of work on your nineteenth-century ancestors and just need to consult the online censuses to fill in gaps and check what you've already found by other means, the single-quarter £24.95 option will be the cheapest way to access the site, though in fact RootsUK's pay-per-view charges (described below) will probably work out cheaper.

The best way to evaluate the site is to take advantage of the free trial, details of which will be found at <**www.thegenealogist.co.uk/freesub/**>. This does not require you to give any credit card details, so it does not automatically turn into a fully fledged subscription, as is the case with Ancestry's free trial (see Chapter 7, p. 124). The trial gives you 30 days access to all databases, with 10 credits, enough to do a couple of searches and view two images. At the end of the trial, there is a special deal on a subsequent Personal Premium subscription.

Subscriptions can be purchased online by credit or debit card (though only a credit card is acceptable for the £14.95 quarterly Personal Plus subscription). If you prefer to pay by cheque, or do not want to give your card details online, you can print off the subscription form <**www.thegenealogist.co.uk/tg_subscription_form.pdf**> and submit it by post.

Once you have subscribed, your subscription will be automatically renewed and charged to your card, unless you cancel two weeks in advance of the renewal date.

Unlike TheGenealogist, RootsUK is a purely pay-per-view site and its charging structure is very simple. Credits cost £5 for 100 (i.e. 5p each) or £14.95 for 400 (about 3.75p each). Full details of how many credits everything on the site costs are given at <**www.rootsuk.com/help/credits.php**>, but for the census records there are three chargeable items and they are each charged at 5 credits (i.e. 25p):

- viewing the full details for an entry
- viewing the original image
- the advanced search and reveal details options.

Since you cannot view an image without going via the view details screen, the minimum cost for an image is effectively 10 units, which also gives you a transcription for the individual.

Searching: TheGenealogist

The site offers five types of search:

- Classic Master Name Search
- Keyword Master Search
- Family Forename Search
- House & Street Search
- Individual database search.

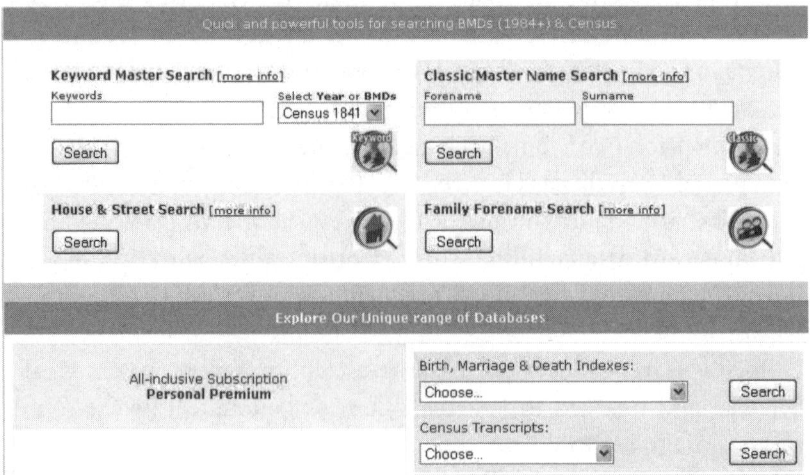

Figure 9-1 TheGenealogist search forms

Search Results

A full search will allow you to enter extra search criteria to increase or decrease the number of results.

You may also be able to find Thomas Hardy in our **other databases** (including census name indexes, pre-1984 BMD records, parish records, landowner records, directories).

Transcript	Number of possible matches					
	Exact: [Thomas Hardy]		Wildcard: [Tho* Hardy]		Surname Only: [Hardy]	
Births 1837-1983	Available	Full Search				
Births 1984-2005	204	Full Search	188	Full Search	11,349	Full Search
Marriages 1837-1983	Available	Full Search				
Marriages 1984-2005	57	Full Search	54	Full Search	10,210	Full Search
Deaths 1837-1983	Available	Full Search				
Deaths 1984-2005	150	Full Search	143	Full Search	8,763	Full Search
1841 Census Transcript	538	Full Search	540	Full Search	9,708	Full Search
1851 Census Transcript	545	Full Search	572	Full Search	10,786	Full Search
1861 Census Transcript	546	Full Search	583	Full Search	11,897	Full Search
1871 Census Transcript	552	Full Search	637	Full Search	14,314	Full Search
1891 Census Transcript	552	Full Search	666	Full Search	17,850	Full Search
1901 Census Transcript	587	Full Search	752	Full Search	21,375	Full Search

Figure 9-2 TheGenealogist search results

All are available from the page which comes up once you have logged in (see Figure 9-1).

The simplest of these is the Classic Master Name search. This works in a slightly unusual way as you first select a census year and then a county before you get any actual listing of records. You start by entering a forename and surname on the form shown in Figure 9-1 and you first get a list of how many matches there are in each of the censuses and in the six BMD databases (see Figure 9-2).

In the initial search box in Figure 9-1, you can leave the forename field blank, but you must enter a surname. If you enter a forename, it automatically includes results for the surname alone and for a wildcard search with the first three letters of the forename, as you can see in Figure 9-2.

From the list of dataset matches, if you click on the 'Full Search' button for one of the censuses you get a county-by-county breakdown of the number of matching records (Figure 9-3, see p. 156). A recently introduced feature is that from this listing you can narrow down your results by entering an occupation, birth county or approximate age.

Finally, clicking on the link by an individual county, you will get a transcript (as the site calls it) of all the matching records for the county and year you have chosen (Figure 9-4, see p. 156).

If you don't want to go through this step-by-step procedure and already know which year and county you want, then instead of going

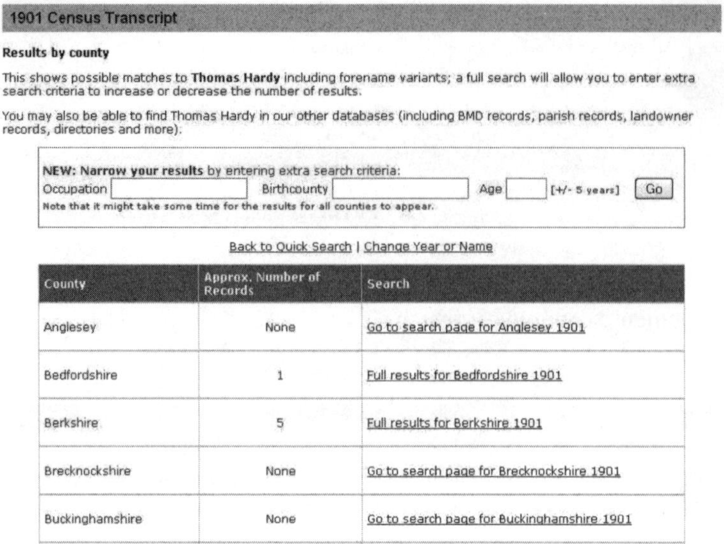

1901 Census Transcript

Results by county

This shows possible matches to **Thomas Hardy** including forename variants; a full search will allow you to enter extra search criteria to increase or decrease the number of results.

You may also be able to find Thomas Hardy in our other databases (including BMD records, parish records, landowner records, directories and more).

NEW: Narrow your results by entering extra search criteria:
Occupation Birthcounty Age [+/- 5 years] Go
Note that it might take some time for the results for all counties to appear.

Back to Quick Search | Change Year or Name

County	Approx. Number of Records	Search
Anglesey	None	Go to search page for Anglesey 1901
Bedfordshire	1	Full results for Bedfordshire 1901
Berkshire	5	Full results for Berkshire 1901
Brecknockshire	None	Go to search page for Brecknockshire 1901
Buckinghamshire	None	Go to search page for Buckinghamshire 1901

Figure 9-3 TheGenealogist search results by county

through the Classic Master Name Search to get a count of matching records, you can go straight to a search form for that year and county. To do this, select your year and county from the drop-down list under the heading Census Transcripts. There are two forms, for standard and advanced search (Figure 9-5 and Figure 9-6 respectively), and you can toggle between them.

In both forms there are options to include surname variants and

Results

Can't find the person you're looking for? See our Search Strategy

New! Click the occupation to search for a description of the occupation.

Key: View the census images for this record (if available) | Download the census image files for this record (if available) | Report a problem | Search for families grouped by surname on matching or adjacent folios [results appear in a new window] | Search for everyone in this household [results appear in a new window]

1 pages of 9 matching records found: displaying records 1 to 9
«« « [1] » »»

Use the arrows at the top of each column to order the results accordingly.
After viewing a household or family, close or minimise the window to see the search results window.

Research Log	Surname	Forename	Age	Relation	Occupation	Birth Place	Address	[illegible]	[illegible]
☐	Hardy	Thomas	68	Head	Retired Master Mariner Seas	Swanage, Dorset	Grosvenor Road, Swanage	RG13/1985/~F34	CD2 R_1985.pdf p.66
☐	Hardy	Thomas	13	Son		Swanage, Dorset	Mount Pleasant Lane, Swanage	RG13/1985/~F41	CD2 R_1985.pdf p.79
☐	Hardy	Thomas [Wife: Florence]	35	Head	House Painter	Weymouth, Dorset	7 Spring Lane, Weymouth	RG13/1995/~F26	CD2 R_1995.pdf p.50
☐	Hardy	Thomas	60	Head	Author	Stinsford, Dorset	Mexo House, Dorchester	RG13/2001/~F55	CD3 R_2001.pdf p.107
☐	Hardy	Thomas [Wife: Alice]	43	Head	Agricultural Labourer	Bere Regis, Dorset	Pond Houses, Puddletown	RG13/2003/~F40	CD3 R_2003.pdf p.77
☐	Hardy	Thomas [Wife: Phoebe Ann]	27	Head	Groom (Not Domestic)	Wynford Eagle, Dorset	Maiden Newton, Maiden Newton	RG13/2004/~F75	CD3 R_2004.pdf p.148
☐	Hardy	Thomas	30	Head	Farmer	Broadwinsor, Dorset	Sandpit, Netherbury	RG13/2010/~F45	CD3 R_2010.pdf p.88
☐	Hardy	Thomas H [Wife: Eliza]	28	Head	Labourer In Stone Quarry	Parbeck, Dorset	23 Straits, Portland	RG13/1997/~F34	CD2 R_1997.pdf p.65
☐	Hardy	Tom [Wife: Thersa E]	44	Head	Boot Maker	Carne, Dorset	Lower Tything, Carne	RG13/2005/~F51	CD3 R_2005.pdf p.99

TICK THE RELEVANT BOX(ES) and then click 'Save' to save individual records to your research log or TreeView exhibits

Save Record(s) to **Research Log** Save Record(s) to TreeView

Go to My Research Log | Go to My TreeView Exhibits | Go to Information about TreeView Exhibits

Figure 9-4 TheGenealogist search results

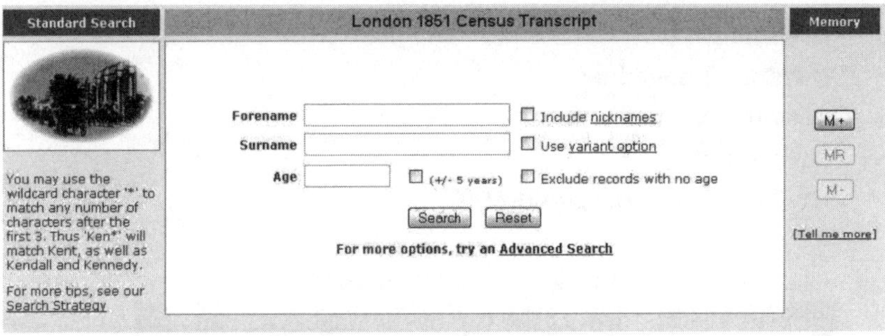

Figure 9-5 Standard county/year search

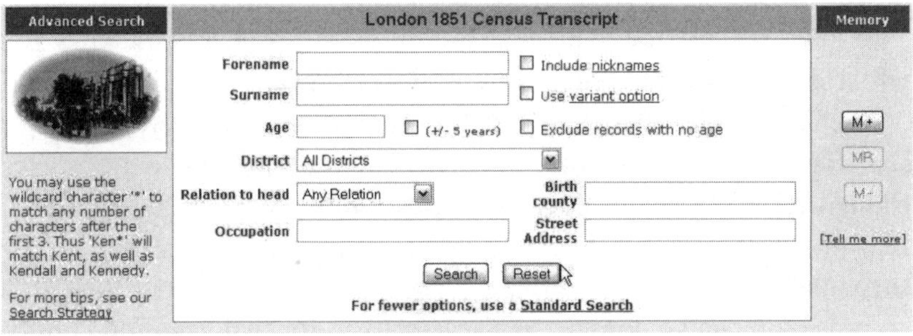

Figure 9-6 Advanced county/year search

nickname variants of forenames, and to select a range of five years either side of the age. (The site does not indicate which surname matching system it uses (see Chapter 5, p. 99). You can also use wildcards. The advanced search form gives you the opportunity of specifying information for a range of other fields.

Clicking on the 'Search' button brings up an identical listing to that shown in Figure 9-4. The search form is in fact shown above the listing, whichever route you have taken, and you can then modify the contents of the form to refine your search.

The transcript includes most of the fields from the original record, including occupation and birthplace. A useful feature is that for a male head of household the name of a wife is included. This helps to identify the right household without actually looking at the household transcript. However, the name of a husband is not included in the listing of females.

The transcript is initially unsorted, but you can sort on any column by clicking the two-chevron icon to the left of the column heading.

From here, the icons at the right of each individual entry provide five options, from left to right:

- View Image
- Download Image File
- Query index entry
- View Family
- View head with household.

Viewing and downloading images are discussed below.

From the search form at the top of the page, you can also go back to the county listing and select a different county.

A combined flowchart for the Custom Master Name Search and the Single-Database Search is shown in Figure 9-7.

While these are the main search options and probably the ones you will use most often, the others are well worth exploring.

The Keyword Master Search offers you, initially at least, only a single search field, into which you can enter names, places, occupations, etc., though from the results page you can subsequently select a county. It is probably best used if you have either very precise and accurate

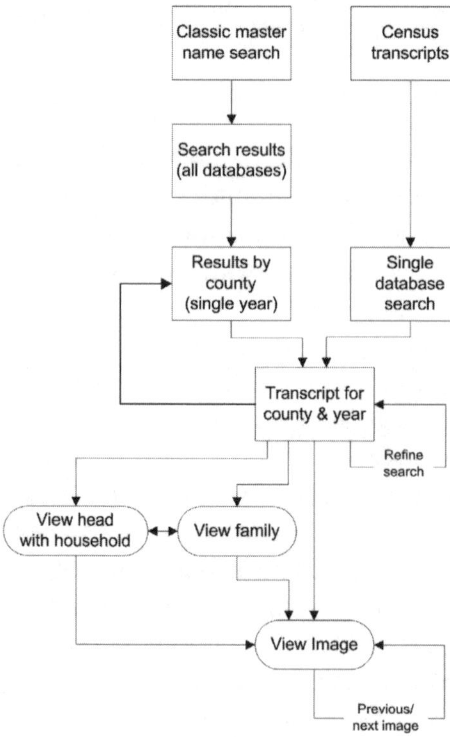

Figure 9-7 TheGenealogist main search process

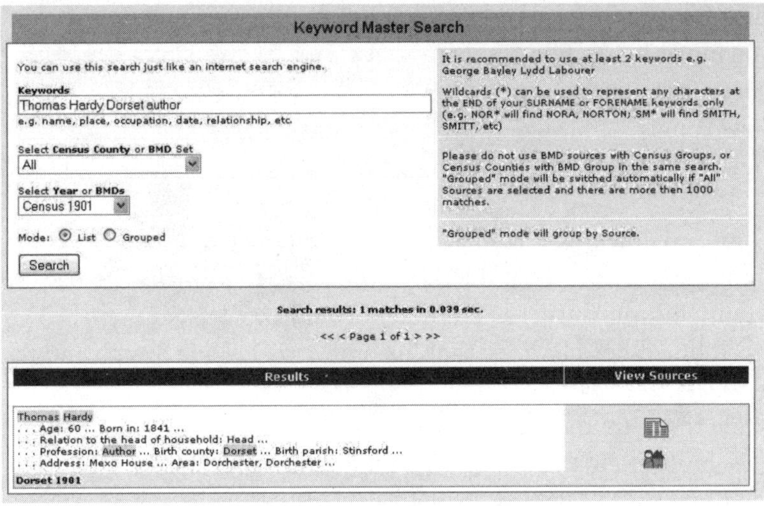

Figure 9-8 TheGenealogist keyword search results

information or a fairly unusual name, as the results are presented in a much less flexible manner and the scope for modifying the search is quite limited, with no options for surname variants, for example.

Figure 9-8 shows the single result found when selecting the 1901 census and entering 'Thomas Hardy Dorset author' as the keywords.

The Family Forename Search is an interesting addition to the standard search facilities. It allows you to enter a set of forenames and find all matching families. This has a number of uses. It is particularly useful if you are looking for ancestors with a common surname, but can also be used if you don't know the surname at all. For example, in the case of a widowed ancestor who has remarried, you may not know the new surname, but you know the names of the children from her first marriage. It may be the only way to find a family where the surname has been recorded or indexed incorrectly.

This search has its own separate search page, where you can enter up to six forenames, and you can also include the surname. Of course, you need to be cautious about the year of birth, not just because people did not always know how old they were, but also because strictly speaking you cannot derive a single year of birth from the age given in a census.

Figure 9-9 (see p. 160) shows the results of a search for a Lincolnshire Smith family in 1891, with names John, Sarah and William. The results give quite a lot of detail, certainly enough to identify the family you are looking for. Clicking on the 'View Source' button will display the original page.

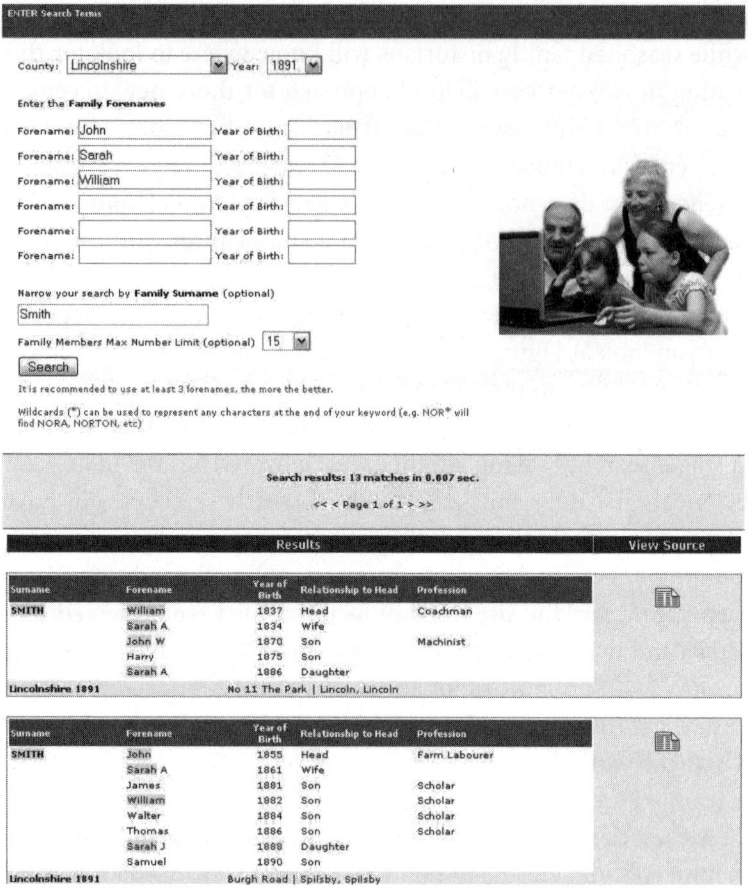

Figure 9-9 TheGenealogist Family Forename Search

The House and Street Search (still being trialled at the time of writing) allows you to enter a street name for a particular county and census year. The initial results list the matching streets together with their district and piece number. Each of these leads to a list of house numbers and you can either view a transcription of the household or the original page.

TheGenealogist does not have any facility for search by TNA reference and its support for TNA references is rather half-hearted. In many cases the transcript gives only the piece number, sometimes also the folio number, but never the page number. It's true that folio and page numbers should be visible on the images, but if you are a pay-per-view customer, you might not like the fact that you may have to pay to view the previous image to get the folio number (which is only printed on alternate pages). Also, these are not always easy to read in the images. And while seasoned family historians will know where to look for this information, it is not a very helpful approach for those new to census records, who may not realize that a piece number alone is not an adequate census reference.

TheGenealogist does not automatically keep a record of your viewed records or images, though if you are on a subscription you can view records and images as often as you want.

However, you can record your search terms so that you can repeat a search. If you look at Figure 9-5 and Figure 9-6 you will see calculator-style memory buttons to the right of the search form. You can use these to save, retrieve or clear a search from the memory. Note that this only saves a single search – saving another search overwrites the first.

TheGenealogist does not keep track of which searches you have carried out, so if you think you will want to refer to search results again and you are on a credit-based subscription, you will need to print or save them. However, the site has two facilities for keeping a record of individuals and these are discussed below under 'Other resources'.

Searching: RootsUK

RootsUK's search screen could hardly be simpler. If you want to search all the RootsUK databases, use the search form on the home page; otherwise, clicking on the census tab will take you to the Census transcript search shown in Figure 9-10 (see p. 162).

You need to select a census year and enter a name. You can in fact carry out a search with a surname only, but if it produces more than 50 results for an individual county you will not be able to view them. You can also tick the forename variants box if you want to find abbreviations or nicknames . The resulting page lists how many results there are for each county (similar to the page shown in Figure 9-3), and offers two options: to view the results for any individual county for which there are matches, or to carry out an advanced search on any one county. This latter option brings up the Advanced Search form. In addition to the fields on the initial search form, it automatically fills in the county you have selected and allows you to enter an occupation and either an estimated birth year or an age. You can also select to include surname variants. Note that you cannot conduct an advanced

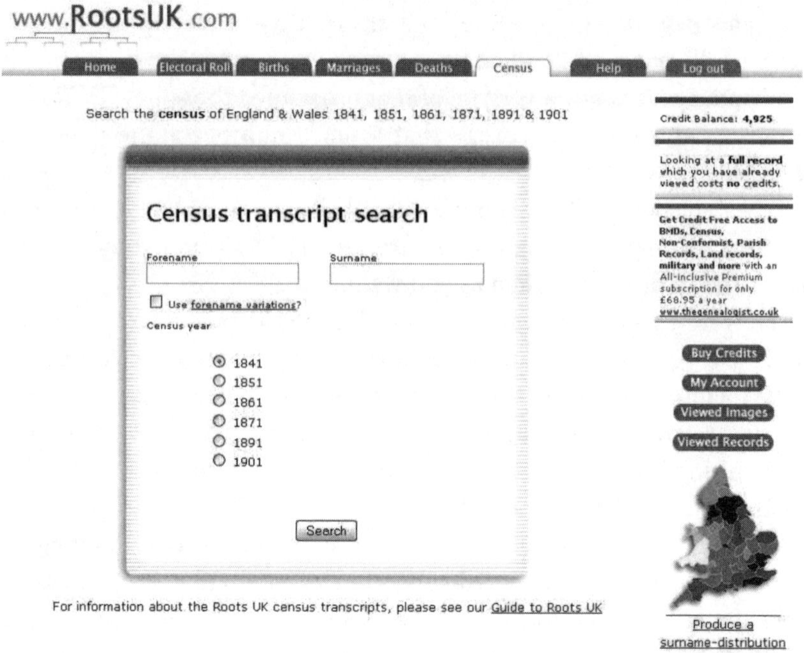

Figure 9-10 RootsUK Census transcript Search

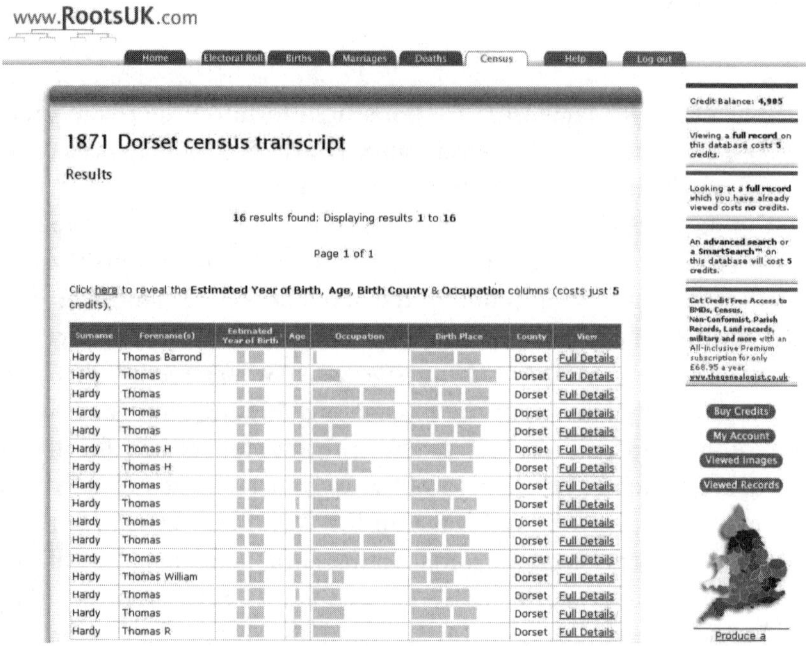

www.RootsUK.com
Home
Electoral Roll
Births
Marriages
Deaths
Census
Help
Log out
1871 Dorset census transcript
Results
16 results found: Displaying results 1 to 16
Page 1 of 1
Click here to reveal the Estimated Year of Birth, Age, Birth County & Occupation columns (costs just 5 credits).
Surname
Forename(s)
Estimated Year of Birth
Age
Occupation
Birth Place
County
View
Hardy Thomas Barrond Dorset Full Details
Hardy Thomas Dorset Full Details
Hardy Thomas Dorset Full Details
Hardy Thomas Dorset Full Details
Hardy Thomas Dorset Full Details
Hardy Thomas H Dorset Full Details
Hardy Thomas H Dorset Full Details
Hardy Thomas Dorset Full Details
Hardy Thomas Dorset Full Details
Hardy Thomas Dorset Full Details
Hardy Thomas Dorset Full Details
Hardy Thomas Dorset Full Details
Hardy Thomas William Dorset Full Details
Hardy Thomas Dorset Full Details
Hardy Thomas Dorset Full Details
Hardy Thomas R Dorset Full Details
Credit Balance: 4,985
Viewing a full record on this database costs 5 credits.
Looking at a full record which you have already viewed costs no credits.
An advanced search or a SmartSearch™ on this database will cost 5 credits.
Get Credit Free Access to BMDs, Census, Non-Conformist, Parish Records, Land records, military and more with an All-inclusive Premium subscription for only £68.95 a year www.thegenealogist.co.uk
Buy Credits
My Account
Viewed Images
Viewed Records
Produce a

Figure 9-11 RootsUK Initial transcript screen

www.RootsUK.com
Home
Electoral Roll
Births
Marriages
Deaths
Census
Help
Log out
1871 Dorset census transcript
Results
16 results found: Displaying results 1 to 16
Page 1 of 1
Back to Results by County | Standard Search | Advanced Search
Credit Balance: 4,900
Viewing a full record on this database costs 5 credits.
Looking at a full record which you have already viewed costs no credits.
An advanced search or a SmartSearch™ on this database will cost 5 credits.
Get Credit Free Access to BMDs, Census, Non-Conformist, Parish Records, Land records, military and more with an All-inclusive Premium subscription for only £68.95 a year
www.thegenealogist.co.uk
Buy Credits
My Account
Viewed Images
Viewed Records

Surname	Forename(s)	Estimated Year of Birth	Age	Occupation	Birth Place	County	View
Hardy	Thomas Barrond	c. 1871	4m	-	Broadwinsor Dorset	Dorset	Full Details
Hardy	Thomas	c. 1860	11	Scholar	Frome Vauchurch Dorset	Dorset	Full Details
Hardy	Thomas	c. 1830	41	Agricultural Labourer	Wynford Eagle Dorset	Dorset	Full Details
Hardy	Thomas	c. 1800	71	Agricultural Labourer	Wynford Eagle Dorset	Dorset	Full Details
Hardy	Thomas	c. 1857	14	Shoe Maker	Cerne Abbas Dorset	Dorset	Full Details
Hardy	Thomas H	c. 1812	59	Builder	Stinsford Dorset	Dorset	Full Details
Hardy	Thomas H	c. 1841	30	Architect Clerk	Stinsford Dorset	Dorset	Full Details
Hardy	Thomas	c. 1842	29	Model Maker	Morden Dorset	Dorset	Full Details
Hardy	Thomas	c. 1863	8	Scholar	Dorchester Dorset	Dorset	Full Details
Hardy	Thomas	c. 1866	5	Scholar	Swanage Dorset	Dorset	Full Details
Hardy	Thomas	c. 1822	49	Agricultural Labourer	Broadway Dorset	Dorset	Full Details
Hardy	Thomas	c. 1852	19	Agricultural Labourer	West Knighton Dorset	Dorset	Full Details
Hardy	Thomas William	c. 1856	15	Farm Boy	Bere Dorset	Dorset	Full Details
Hardy	Thomas	c. 1866	5	Scholar	Weymouth Dorset	Dorset	Full Details
Hardy	Thomas	c. 1812	59	Labourer	Piddletown Dorset	Dorset	Full Details
Hardy	Thomas R	c. 1830	41	Mariner	Weymouth Dorset	Dorset	Full Details

Figure 9-12 Transcript screen with details revealed

search on the whole of England and Wales – you must select an individual county.

If you choose to view the matches, you get a screen showing just the items you have already searched on, with the other fields greyed out (Figure 9-11). Although there is a link to the full details for each individual, this is an item which will cost you 5 credits, so unless you have a very small number of entries on this page and you are sure which one you are looking for, you will want to select the option to reveal the greyed-out data by clicking on the link marked 'here'. This will also cost you 5 credits, but it will give you much more information before you select the individual(s) for which you will look for full details (Figure 9-12).

When you click on the 'Full Details' link, you will get a page for the selected individual (Figure 9-3). Although the page is called 'Full details', it does not in fact indicate either the gender (which you probably know already!) or the marital status. Also, the TNA reference is incomplete.

From here, you can view an image of the original census record. The images are the same as those for TheGenealogist and the viewer for the PDF files is similar (see below).

From the Full details page, there is also a link to two 'Smart Search'

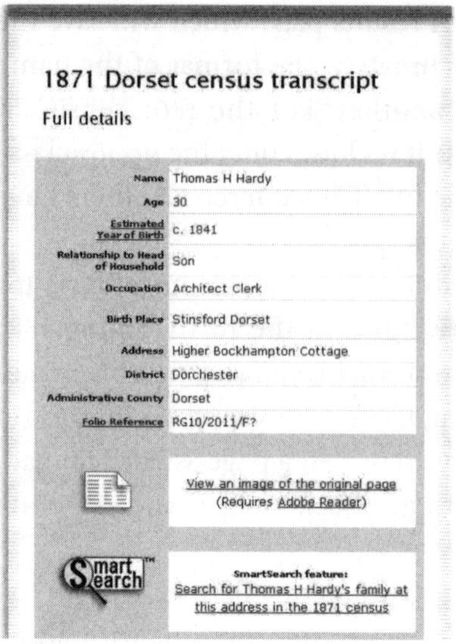

1871 Dorset census transcript
Full details
Name Thomas H Hardy
Age 30
Estimated Year of Birth c. 1841
Relationship to Head of Household Son
Occupation Architect Clerk
Birth Place Stinsford Dorset
Address Higher Bockhampton Cottage
District Dorchester
Administrative County Dorset
Folio Reference RG10/2011/F?
View an image of the original page
(Requires Adobe Reader)
SmartSearch
SmartSearch feature:
Search for Thomas H Hardy's family at this address in the 1871 census

Figure 9-13 RootsUK full details

options. One allows you to search the site's civil registration records for the birth of the individual, the other lists the family of the individual displayed. The point of this is to identify people who are in the same household but are not on the same page of the enumeration schedule – if you have searched for a child, the parents could be on a previous page; if you have searched for a head of household, the youngest children or some of the servants may be on the following page.

A flowchart for the RootsUK search process is shown in Figure 9-14.

Images

The images for both sites are provided in Adobe Acrobat (PDF) format (see Chapter 4, p. 89). On TheGenealogist, each image opens in an Acrobat window. The standard Acrobat toolbar provides options for printing, saving and zooming, while the toolbar at the top of the browser window allows you to go to the previous or following census page, or to report a problem with the image. If you have a credit-based subscription, it also shows you how many credits you have left.

While you can save the image from the Acrobat window, there's a good reason not to do this – your file will end up with a meaningless name, unless you call it something else. It's much better to use the

'Download image file' from the search results page which will save the file with a more helpful name. Unfortunately, the format of the name seems to vary from one census to another. For the 1861 census, it includes the folio number; for the 1851 it includes only the HO 107 classmark. Some of the images include the full TNA reference; others have only page or folio numbers on the actual pages.

The images have been scanned at different colour depths. Those for the 1841 census are greyscale, as are those in the forthcoming 1881 census. The remainder are generally monochrome (i.e. just black and white), but S & N have been replacing these with greyscale images on an ad hoc basis. Where customers have reported a page as hard to read, S & N have been replacing these with greyscale images and targeting them for retranscription.

It is difficult to establish the exact resolution of a PDF image, but the resolution of most images seems to be around 200dpi, with some higher and some lower. The greyscale images are quite satisfactory, but

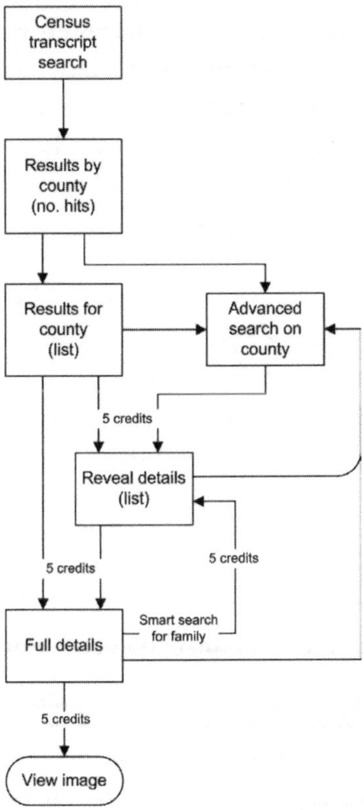

Figure 9-14 RootsUK search flowchart

at this resolution some of the poorer quality original documents are far from easy to read where they have been scanned in black and white.

While the site does not currently have an index to the 1881 census, it is starting to provide images for this census which can be used in conjunction with the free 1881 Census Index at FamilySearch, discussed in Chapter 6, p. 109. At the time of writing, only the images for London are available. You first need to search for an individual in the 1881 census at <**www.familysearch.org.uk**>. That will give you the TNA piece and folio numbers – you can see them in the penultimate line of text in Figure 6-4 on p. 112. Then click on the 'Search' button for London 1881 Image Index on the main search page, and enter the piece and folio numbers in the form.

On RootsUK, any image you have already paid for can be viewed again without further payment for a period of 30 days. However, it is much better to download any images you have paid for, even those that turn out not to contain the ancestor you were looking for – that way you don't have to worry about the 30-day limit. What is useful is that you can return to an image without charge to check the pages either side, though if you have not previously viewed them this will cost you an additional 5 credits each time. You can also revisit the full details for any individual you have paid for in the previous 30 days.

Help and feedback

TheGenealogist's main help page for searching will be found by following the 'Search Strategy' link on the main search form (Figure 9-5 and Figure 9-6). But there is also a Help Wizard accessible by following the 'Help/FAQs' link at the top of most pages. Most of the topics covered relate to subscribing, logging in and viewing images. The equivalent information on RootsUK will be found by clicking on the 'Help' tab.

TheGenealogist offers two places from which you can report a problem, the 'Query index entry' link on the transcript pages and the 'Report Image' link in the image viewer. Both of these lead to the same problem reporting form.

On RootsUK, the full details page for an individual has a link at the foot of the page 'Report a problem with this record', which can be used to report apparent errors or other problems with the data. There is no separate form for reporting errors with the image itself.

Other resources

In addition to its short-term memory feature (mentioned on p. 161), TheGenealogist provides two ways for you to save the results of your searches. The Research Log can store the full details of any individual records you are currently viewing. If you are viewing the household or family screen, you can save the entire household or family to the Research Log. You can also add annotation to the individual entries (see Figure 9-15). Note that you cannot go directly from the Research Log to the matching page image – you would need to carry out a search for the individual.

The other way of recording your ancestors is to save them individually, or by family, to the TreeView. It is not possible here to discuss TreeView in detail, since it is a fully fledged online pedigree database, to which you can add individuals by hand or by uploading a GEDCOM file. When you save an individual from the census to TreeView, the details of the census entry are added to what is called the 'Exhibit List' in

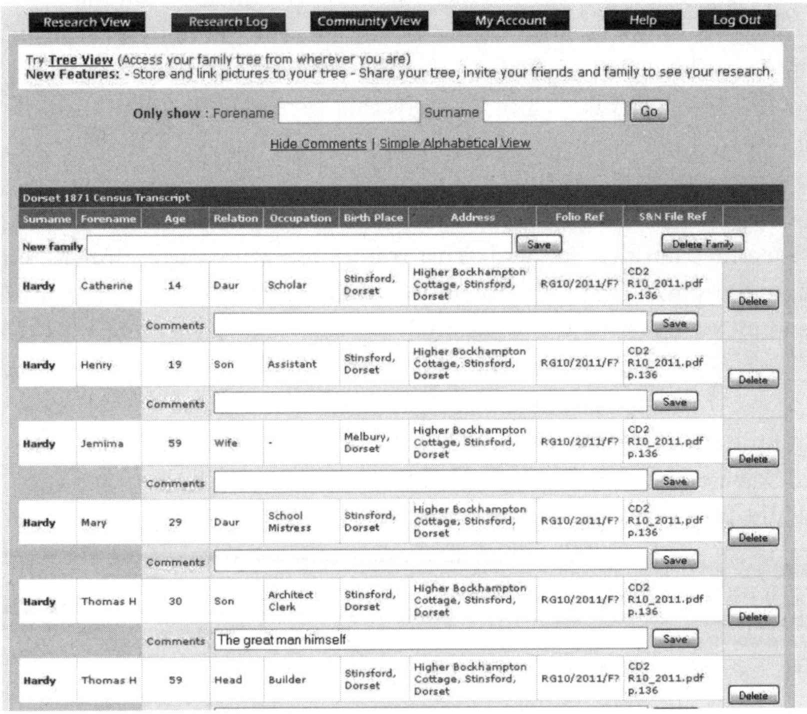

Surname	Forename	Age	Relation	Occupation	Birth Place	Address	Folio Ref	S&N File Ref
Hardy	Catherine	14	Daur	Scholar	Stinsford, Dorset	Higher Bockhampton Cottage, Stinsford, Dorset	RG10/2011/F?	CD2 R10_2011.pdf p.136
		Comments						
Hardy	Henry	19	Son	Assistant	Stinsford, Dorset	Higher Bockhampton Cottage, Stinsford, Dorset	RG10/2011/F?	CD2 R10_2011.pdf p.136
		Comments						
Hardy	Jemima	59	Wife	-	Melbury, Dorset	Higher Bockhampton Cottage, Stinsford, Dorset	RG10/2011/F?	CD2 R10_2011.pdf p.136
		Comments						
Hardy	Mary	29	Daur	School Mistress	Stinsford, Dorset	Higher Bockhampton Cottage, Stinsford, Dorset	RG10/2011/F?	CD2 R10_2011.pdf p.136
		Comments						
Hardy	Thomas H	30	Son	Architect Clerk	Stinsford, Dorset	Higher Bockhampton Cottage, Stinsford, Dorset	RG10/2011/F?	CD2 R10_2011.pdf p.136
		Comments	The great man himself					
Hardy	Thomas H	59	Head	Builder	Stinsford, Dorset	Higher Bockhampton Cottage, Stinsford, Dorset	RG10/2011/F?	CD2 R10_2011.pdf p.136

Figure 9-15 TheGenealogist Research Log

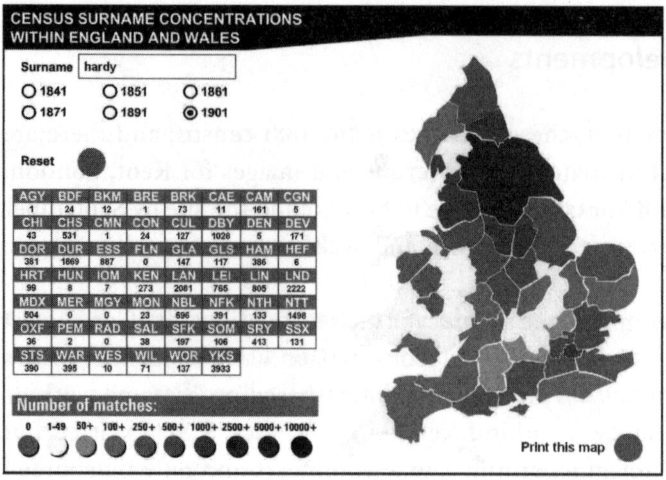

Figure 9-16 Distribution of the surname 'Hardy' in the 1901 census

TreeView. You can take any record in your general exhibit list and attach it to the exhibit list for a particular individual. This way, your family tree can include the census details of all your nineteenth-century ancestors.

A 'surname concentration maps' feature is accessible from the home page. This shows the distribution of any surname in a single census of your choice. Figure 9-16 shows the distribution of the surname Hardy in the 1901 census. Unfortunately this provides only an absolute number, so London, Yorkshire and Lancashire have a tendency to predominate in a way they would not if the distribution were proportional. You can get a more accurate idea of the relative frequency of a surname from the National Trust Names site at <**www.nationaltrustnames.org.uk**> (though statistics are available only for the 1881 census and 1998), which shows, for example, that the true 'Hardy' hotspots are Dorset, Derby and Notts, not London and Yorkshire. Each map costs 10 units if you are not on the all-inclusive subscription.

Both sites have more data than just the census returns. RootsUK has the civil registration indexes and the London electoral roll for 2005, while TheGenealogist has an extensive collection: BMD data, parish registers (both digital indexes and scans of printed volumes), directories, military records, and wills.

Future developments

The obvious gap on these two sites is the 1881 census, and there are plans to add this material. Transcripts and images for Kent, London, Lancashire and Yorkshire are due to be added to the site by September 2008, with the remaining English and Welsh counties to follow in due course.

In order to improve the accuracy of its transcriptions, TheGenealogist does not rely solely on ad hoc feedback from users to identify errors for correction but has an active volunteer-based programme, with its own website at <**www.ukindexer.co.uk**>. In fact, S & N started out their census indexing with in-house volunteers and only outsourced the work when the volume grew too great. Volunteers are rewarded with credits which can be used on the site, a model which suggests that the traditional volunteer culture of the genealogical community need not be in conflict with the commercialization of the records. Future correction efforts are being focused on those pages where black and white images are being replaced by more legible greyscale scans.

10

GENES REUNITED AND 1901CENSUSONLINE

When it was launched in January 2002, the 1901 census data was the first complete census for England and Wales to go online. With some 32 million records and 1.5 million images it was by far the largest genealogical dataset for the UK available on the web. It was initially available on a dedicated site run by QinetiQ at <**www.1901census.nationalarchives.gov.uk**>. Further details of the project are given on p. 81.

Genes Reunited was launched under the name Genes Connected in 2003 as a genealogical offshoot of the immensely popular Friends Reunited. Initially it concentrated on hosting user-submitted family trees as the basis for its contact service, and did not offer a data service. This changed in August 2005, when it purchased the digitized 1901 census from QinetiQ (for £3.3 million). Subsequently Genes Reunited has added the remaining censuses, apart from 1881.

There is no information on the site about the source of the indexes for earlier census years and we are unaware of any public announcement. However, comparing the errors in these indexes with those on TheGenealogist (see Tables 14-x to 14-y) shows conclusively that the two sites use identical data for 1841–1891. Given that TheGenealogist had been building up its collection of county census indexes since long before the earlier indexes appeared on the 1901 Census site, we conclude that Genes Reunited has licensed its nineteenth century indexes from that source.

Genes Reunited offers this data on two sites: the main Genes Reunited site at <**www.genesreunited.co.uk**> and a successor to the original 1901 Census site at <**www.1901censusonline.com**>. The data and images are identical. However, there is a minor difference in charging and some significant differences in features.

The initial 2002 web address for the 1901 Census is in fact still operational and can be used interchangeably with <**www.1901censusonline.com**> — both sites recognize your username and remaining credits.

Charges

Genes Reunited has maintained the pay-per-view charging system which it inherited from QinetQ for the 1901 census and extended it to other records. Confusingly, however, the way the units are calculated and the actual prices differ on the two websites.

If you access census records via the original 1901 Census site, you can buy 500 credits for £5, with transcripts for an individual or a household costing 50 units and images costing 75 (i.e. 50p and 75p respectively). If you access the data via Genes Reunited, you get 50 credits for £5, with all items costing 5 units (i.e. 50p). This means that images on Genes Reunited are 25p cheaper. On the 1901 Census site you can only buy £5 worth of units in any one transaction, which is inconvenient if you have a lot of searches to do.

Units on both sites are valid for seven days after purchase, from the time your card payment is accepted, to be precise.

When the 1901 Census site was first launched, many family historians were still fairly new to the internet. Indeed, for many, it would be the 1901 census that persuaded them to venture online for the first time. There were concerns that many people would be reluctant to make credit card purchases online, in view of the supposed dangers of online transactions. For this reason, alongside the ability to purchase credits online with a credit or debit card, The National Archives provided physical vouchers with an ID and password, which could be purchased over the counter or by post with a cheque from many offline outlets, including libraries and family history societies. This voucher scheme has remained in operation but is now winding down. As of May 2008, no further vouchers were being sold to retailers, and the 1901 Census site says: 'You will be able to continue to purchase 1901 Census Vouchers from your local library/shop whilst their stocks last.' Vouchers can only be used on 1901censusonline, not on Genes Reunited. Six years on, online payment systems are widely accepted, so this is not really a surprising development. But it is nonetheless regrettable: the vouchers gave access for six months rather than the meagre seven days which online payment gives you.

Searching: Genes Reunited

The search facilities on Genes Reunited are rather basic. For the 1901 census the search form (Figure 10-1) has fields for forename, surname, birthplace, age, age range and gender.

Figure 10-1 Genes Reunited search form (1901)

The lack of any place field other than Place of birth is a real problem. Unless you are just using the site to fill in gaps in a pedigree, you are much less likely to know the birthplace of an ancestor than an approximate dwelling place. Since one of the main uses of the census is to supply birthplace information, this is quite a strange feature. However, the earlier census years have a more general 'Place keywords' field.

The Last name field accepts wildcards. The help pages say this is available only in the 1901 census, but it is in fact possible in all the census years. If you carry out a wildcard search which will produce a large number of matches, you will see the message, 'The query cannot be run as it will take too long. Input different values then try again.' The First name field also accepts wildcards for the 1901 census, but not for the other years.

When you click on the 'Search' button, you are presented with a page listing the first 30 search results. At the top of the page it will give you the total number of search results, unless it is over 300, in which case you will see a message 'There are more than 300 results for this search. View the first 300 matches below or refine your search.'

For the 1901 census this page (Figure 10-2) gives first name, year of

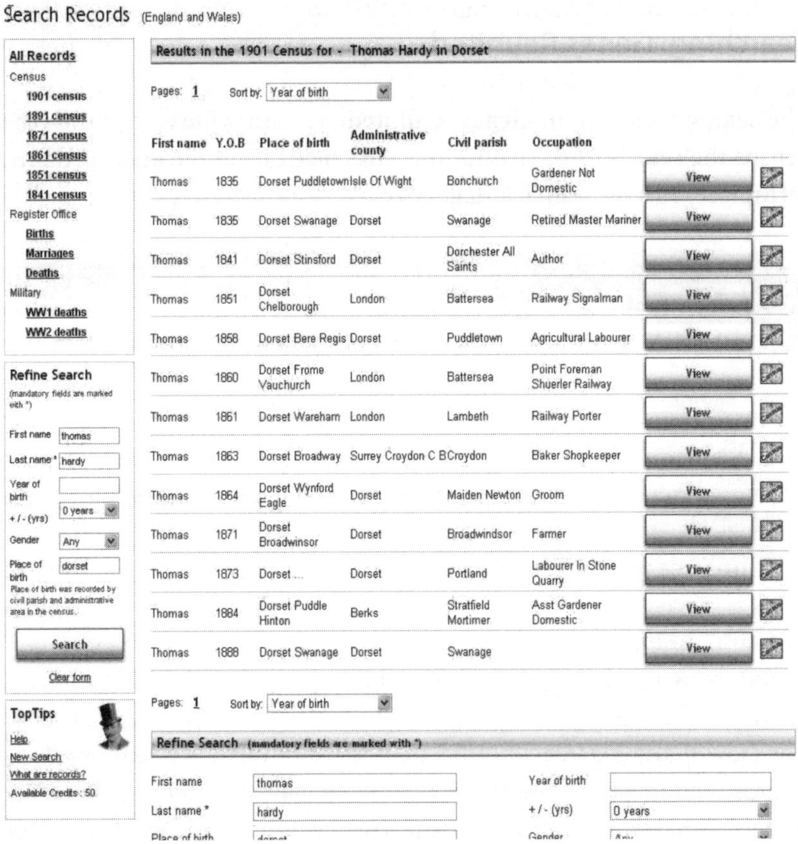

First name	Y.O.B	Place of birth	Administrative county	Civil parish	Occupation
Thomas	1835	Dorset Puddletown	Isle Of Wight	Bonchurch	Gardener Not Domestic
Thomas	1835	Dorset Swanage	Dorset	Swanage	Retired Master Mariner
Thomas	1841	Dorset Stinsford	Dorset	Dorchester All Saints	Author
Thomas	1851	Dorset Chelborough	London	Battersea	Railway Signalman
Thomas	1858	Dorset Bere Regis	Dorset	Puddletown	Agricultural Labourer
Thomas	1860	Dorset Frome Vauchurch	London	Battersea	Point Foreman Shuerler Railway
Thomas	1861	Dorset Wareham	London	Lambeth	Railway Porter
Thomas	1863	Dorset Broadway	Surrey Croydon C B	Croydon	Baker Shopkeeper
Thomas	1864	Dorset Wynford Eagle	Dorset	Maiden Newton	Groom
Thomas	1871	Dorset Broadwinsor	Dorset	Broadwindsor	Farmer
Thomas	1873	Dorset ...	Dorset	Portland	Labourer In Stone Quarry
Thomas	1884	Dorset Puddle Hinton	Berks	Stratfield Mortimer	Asst Gardener Domestic
Thomas	1888	Dorset Swanage	Dorset	Swanage	

Figure 10-2 Genes Reunited search results

birth, place of birth, census county and parish, and occupation. Note that it *does not* give the surname, so if you have used a wildcard there is no obvious way of telling what the surname of a particular individual is. However, there is a way to find out, though it's not something the site tells you. When you move your mouse over the 'View' button, the status bar of your browser (at the bottom of the browser window) gives you the web address of the page for the individual. This will be an enormous long string of characters (around 200), but the last two elements of the string will be the surname and year of birth, and even if you have searched with a wildcard, this will be the actual name of the record, not the name you searched for. For example, a search for 'Elizabeth Robins*' might turn up a link which ends *....first_name= Elizabeth&surname= Robinson&year_of_birth=1901*

For the other censuses the equivalent page does give the surname, and it gives the age rather than a calculated year of birth, but the only other information given is the district. There is no county, birthplace or occupation information given.

Clicking on a column heading allows you to sort the records: for the nineteenth-century censuses, you can sort by age or area; the 1901 Census offers year of birth, place of birth, administrative county, parish or occupation.

In the left-hand sidebar and at the foot of the page, there are Refine Search forms, already filled in with your previous search terms, so you can try to reduce the number of matches to a manageable level.

From the search results, you can click on the 'View' button or the census image on the right. It is not obvious at first encounter what these links do, but the 'View' button takes you to the View record page with a transcription of the census record, and the image takes you to the page image.

In both cases, the immediate response to your clicking on one of these is a page warning you that it will cost you 5 credits to view the page and asking you to confirm.

The View record page for the 1901 census is shown in Figure 10-3. The equivalent page for the earlier censuses is similar, though it does not show marital status.

From here, you can select to view the page image, or you can click on the 'View others' button to see the full record for all members of the household. As the page warns you, this costs an additional 5 credits.

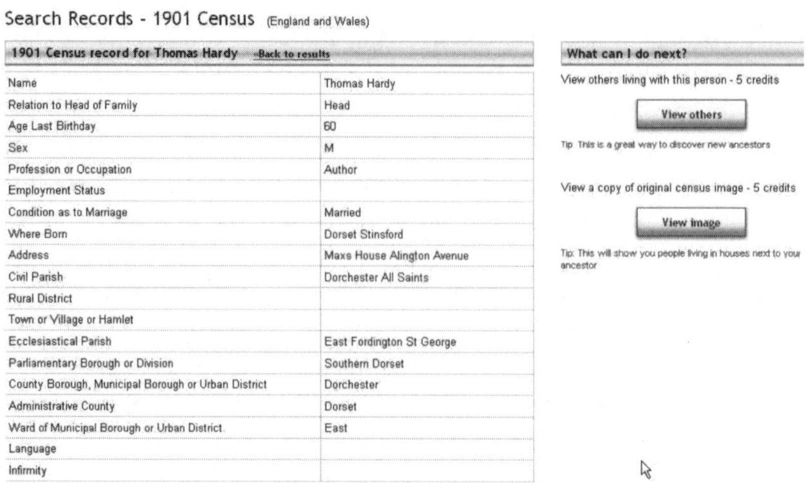
Search Records - 1901 Census (England and Wales)

1901 Census record for Thomas Hardy «Back to results

Name	Thomas Hardy
Relation to Head of Family	Head
Age Last Birthday	60
Sex	M
Profession or Occupation	Author
Employment Status	
Condition as to Marriage	Married
Where Born	Dorset Stinsford
Address	Maxs House Alington Avenue
Civil Parish	Dorchester All Saints
Rural District	
Town or Village or Hamlet	
Ecclesiastical Parish	East Fordington St George
Parliamentary Borough or Division	Southern Dorset
County Borough, Municipal Borough or Urban District	Dorchester
Administrative County	Dorset
Ward of Municipal Borough or Urban District	East
Language	
Infirmity	

What can I do next?

View others living with this person - 5 credits

View others

Tip: This is a great way to discover new ancestors

View a copy of original census image - 5 credits

View image

Tip: This will show you people living in houses next to your ancestor

Figure 10-3 GenesReunited view record

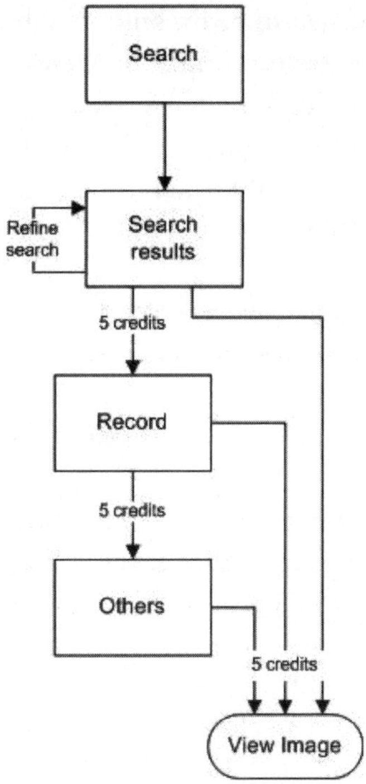

Figure 10-4 GenesReunited search flowchart

The images for this site and 1901censusonline are discussed below.

A flowchart for the census search facilities on Genes Reunited is shown in Figure 10-4. There is no address search, nor is it possible to make a specific search for individuals on vessels or in institutions.

One crucial piece of information that is not provided on any of these pages is the TNA reference for the records (compare Figure 10-11, see p. 180, where they are at the top of the details table). The piece number should always be visible on the page image, since it is supposed to be on the original microfilms from which the images were scanned, but you may or may not be able to see the folio and page number. Certainly it is very unfortunate for beginners that this information is not provided anywhere on the service, and they will be left unaware that this is needed to refer to a particular page in an enumeration book.

This omission, along with the limited person search options and the lack of any other types of search, make the Genes Reunited service poorly suited for any but the most casual use. Certainly, if you have sufficient interest in census records to be reading this book, you will find it frustrating to use. Given that the same data and images are available with similar pricing on the 1901 Census site, where the search facilities are far superior, there is no good reason to use this site for census data, unless you have already signed up to Genes Reunited for access to other data.

Searching: 1901censusonline

While the data and images at <**www.1901censusonline.com**> are the same as those on Genes Reunited, and the overall search process is very similar (see Figure 10-6), the search facilities are much more comprehensive.

The search facilities differ between the census years. The most comprehensive options are those available for the 1901 census, which offers person, address, location, institution, vessel and reference

Figure 10-5 1901censusonline home page

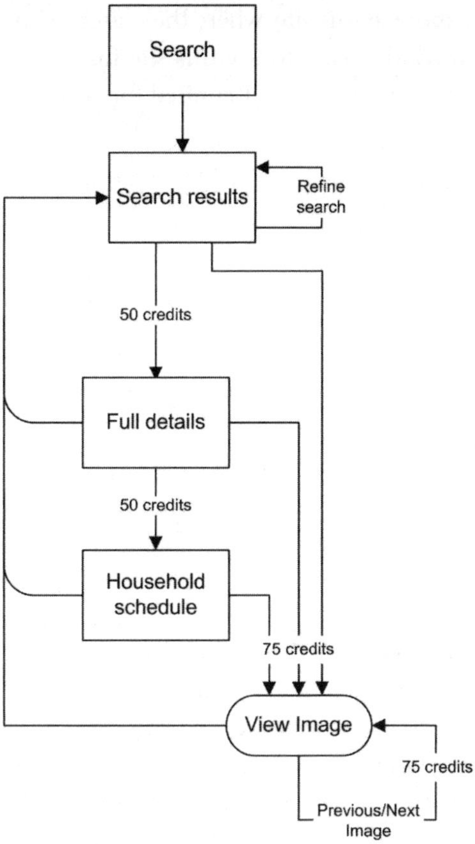

Figure 10-6 1901censusonline person search flowchart

searches (see Figure 10-7, p. 178). For the 1861 and 1871 censuses, person, address and vessel searches are available. For the 1841, 1851 and 1891 censuses only the person and address searches are offered.

For the 1901 census there are two levels of advanced person search. Clicking on 'Advanced search' at the bottom of the form (this link is not available for the earlier censuses) opens up a larger form with three additional fields for Other Name(s) (i.e. middle names), Marital Condition, and Relation to Head of Family, and a checkbox to limit searches to vessels.

This form in turn has a link 'See advanced place options', which allows you to specify the place much more exactly by distinguishing between the various types of administrative unit (Figure 10-8, see p. 179). However, unless you are very sure that you know which units are relevant to the place you are looking for, and have the correct

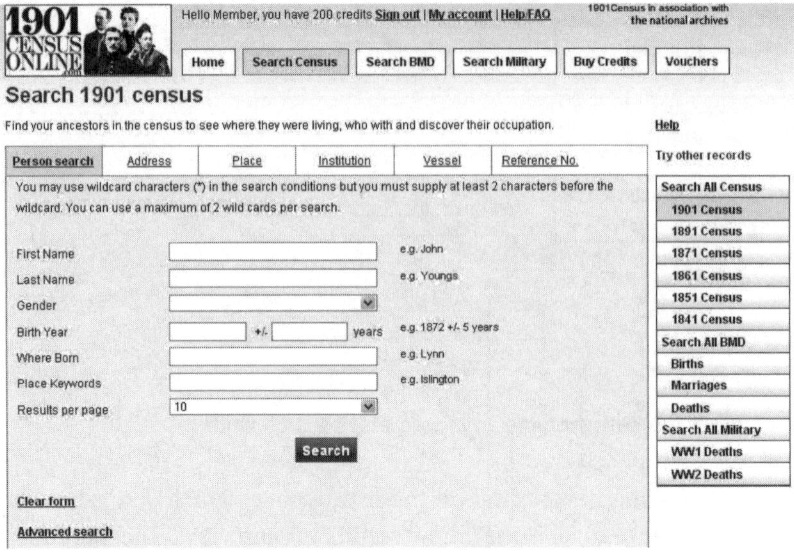

Figure 10-7 1901censusonline Person search form

information for them (perhaps from a birth certificate of similar date), these are probably best avoided, certainly for major cities. For example, a County Borough is its own Administrative County, and it is not part of the historical county in which it is geographically situated. Of them all, perhaps 'Town, Village, or Hamlet' is the only one that is more or less foolproof.

When you submit the search form, you will get a listing of the matching results (Figure 10-9). The number of entries on a page is determined by the Results per page option on the search form. As with Genes Reunited, the maximum number of results is 300 – if there are more you will only be shown the first 300. You can sort the results on any column by clicking on the column heading. When you do so a pointer icon will appear by the heading showing which order it is sorted in. In Figure 10-9, you can see that the results are sorted by decreasing order of age.

From the results listing, you have two main options: clicking on the name will take you to a page with the full census record for that individual (Figure 10-11, see p. 180); clicking on the graphic to the left of it will take you to the page image. Up to this point, all information has been free of charge, but both these options will deduct credits from your total, 50 for the details, 75 for the image.

From the details page, you can also pay 50 credits to see other household members' details. You can also go to the image from that page.

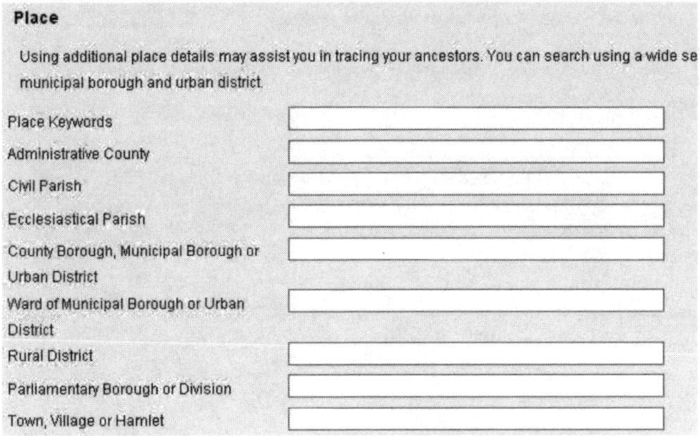
Place

Using additional place details may assist you in tracing your ancestors. You can search using a wide se
municipal borough and urban district.

Place Keywords
Administrative County
Civil Parish
Ecclesiastical Parish
County Borough, Municipal Borough or Urban District
Ward of Municipal Borough or Urban District
Rural District
Parliamentary Borough or Division
Town, Village or Hamlet

Figure 10-8 1901censusonline advanced place search fields

An interesting new option on the listing page, which you can see at the top of Figure 10-9, is the 'Show results in map view'. The 'beta' icon indicates that this is still undergoing testing. This option shows you a map of England and Wales (using Microsoft Virtual Earth), with markers at the locations of the individuals in the listing and a number identifying which is which (Figure 10-10, see p. 180). In the left-hand column is the same text as in Figure 10-9, and clicking on the numbered pointer on that listing will zoom in on the exact location on the map at a much larger scale. The map is modern and some locations can't be found

Person search | Address | Place | Institution | Vessel | Reference No.

Results: 1 - 10 of 13 Matches

beta Show results in map view

View	Name	Age△	Where born	Administrative county	Civil parish	Occupation
	Thomas Hardy	66	Dorset Puddletown	Isle Of Wight	Bonchurch	Gardener Not Domestic
	Thomas Hardy	66	Dorset Swanage	Dorset	Swanage	Retired Master Mariner
	Thomas Hardy	60	Dorset Stinsford	Dorset	Dorchester All Saints	Author
	Thomas Hardy	50	Dorset Chelborough	London	Battersea	Railway Signalman
	Thomas Hardy	43	Dorset Bere Regis	Dorset	Puddletown	Agricultural Labourer
	Thomas Hardy	41	Dorset Frome Vauchurch	London	Battersea	Point Foreman Shuerler Railway
	Thomas Hardy	40	Dorset Wareham	London	Lambeth	Railway Porter
	Thomas Hardy	38	Dorset Broadway	Surrey Croydon C B	Croydon	Baker Shopkeeper
	Thomas Hardy	37	Dorset Wynford Eagle	Dorset	Maiden Newton	Groom
	Thomas B Hardy	30	Dorset Broadwinsor	Dorset	Broadwindsor	Farmer

Figure 10-9 1901censusonline search results

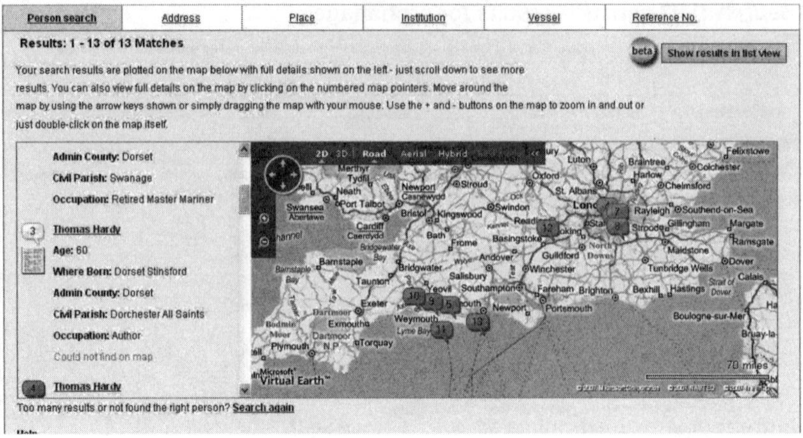

Figure 10-10 1910censusoline map view

(including the author Thomas Hardy's 'Dorchester All Saints'), but this is a good way to get a feel for the distribution of a name, if you do a search on surname only. It's also very helpful where you are unfamiliar with a place location listed in the parish column.

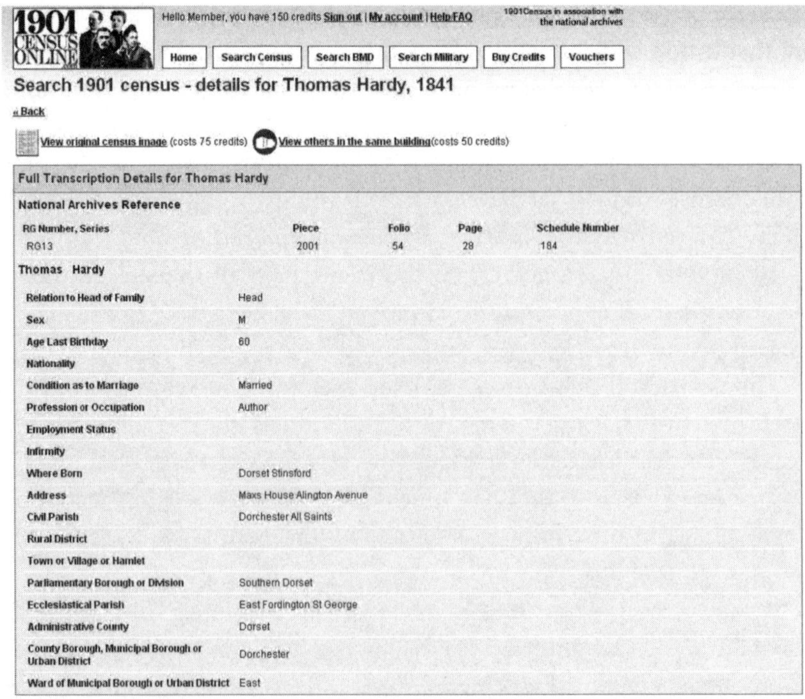

Full Transcription Details for Thomas Hardy

National Archives Reference

RG Number, Series	Piece	Folio	Page	Schedule Number
RG13	2001	54	28	184

Thomas Hardy

Relation to Head of Family	Head
Sex	M
Age Last Birthday	60
Nationality	
Condition as to Marriage	Married
Profession or Occupation	Author
Employment Status	
Infirmity	
Where Born	Dorset Stinsford
Address	Maxs House Alington Avenue
Civil Parish	Dorchester All Saints
Rural District	
Town or Village or Hamlet	
Parliamentary Borough or Division	Southern Dorset
Ecclesiastical Parish	East Fordington St George
Administrative County	Dorset
County Borough, Municipal Borough or Urban District	Dorchester
Ward of Municipal Borough or Urban District	East

Figure 10-11 1901censusonline Full Transcription Details

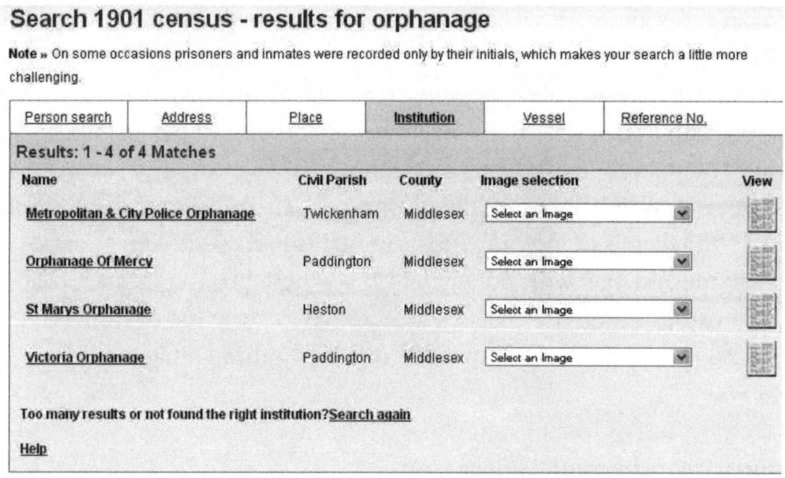

Figure 10-12 1901censusonline institution search results

Unlike Genes Reunited, 1901censusonline has not only a person search, but a range of other options. For all census years, there is an address search, which for the years before 1901 is flagged as a 'beta test'. For 1861, 1871 and 1901 there is a vessel search. The 1901 search has a separate place search (distinct from the address search). It also offers an institution search, and it is the only census year which has a TNA reference search. We do not have space here to explore all the options in the same detail as we have done for the person search.

When we attempted it (July 2008) the address search for the pre-1901 censuses did not seem to work at all – it just complained 'No street name entered', whether a street name was entered or not. The 'Who lived in your house?' search on the home page of the site produces results only for the 1901 census. However, if the 'beta test' tag has disappeared by the time you try it, you should have more success!

The vessel and institution searches look for a vessel or institution itself by name, not for the names of individuals enumerated within a vessel or institution. They work in basically the same way: you enter a name and location in the search fields and get back a list of matching vessels/institutions. Figure 10-12 shows the results of a search for 'orphanage' and 'Middlesex'.

If you click on the institution name you are taken to a list of individual names, with no other details. So far you have not been charged, but from the list of individuals it costs 50 credits to view full transcription details and 75 credits to view the page containing the entry for the chosen individual. However, there is often little point in viewing the full transcription details, first because your list of individuals does not contain a list of people with identical names the way it does with a person search, and second because there's no point in paying 50 credits to see the details first when you're going to have to pay 75 to see the image anyway. Also, be prepared for a certain amount of disappointment – the details of the individuals in institutions sometimes comprise only name and age, with no entry in the 'where born' column.

You can go direct to images without viewing the list of individuals. The Image selection drop-down list offers you three images to view:

- Description of Institution/Vessel
- First Page of Person Details
- Abstract of Totals (institutions)/People not on Board (vessels).

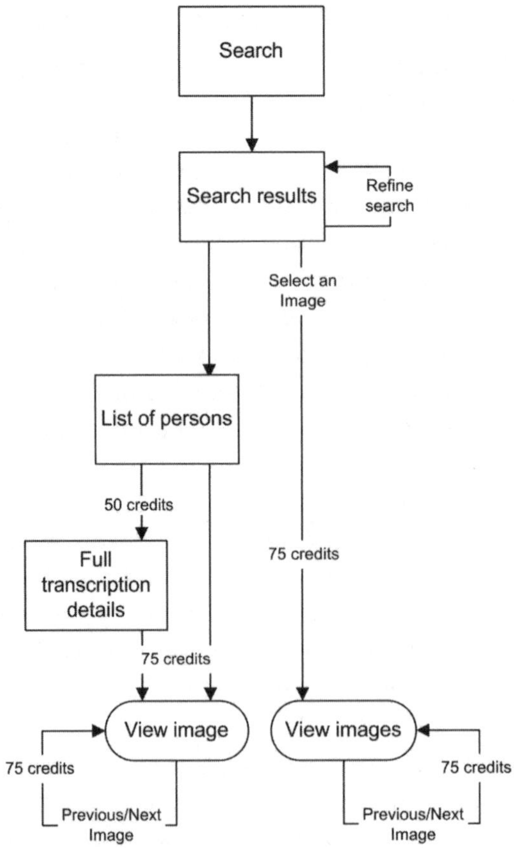

Figure 10-13 1901censusonline institution/vessel search

21 Household schedules and instructions for the 1911 census translated into German and Yiddish. (RG 27/8)

22 Abraham Shedletsky, Kosher butcher, and his family in Whitechapel in 1911. The children's ages and birthplaces suggest the Shedletskys came to England in the late 1890s. (RG 14/1459/30)

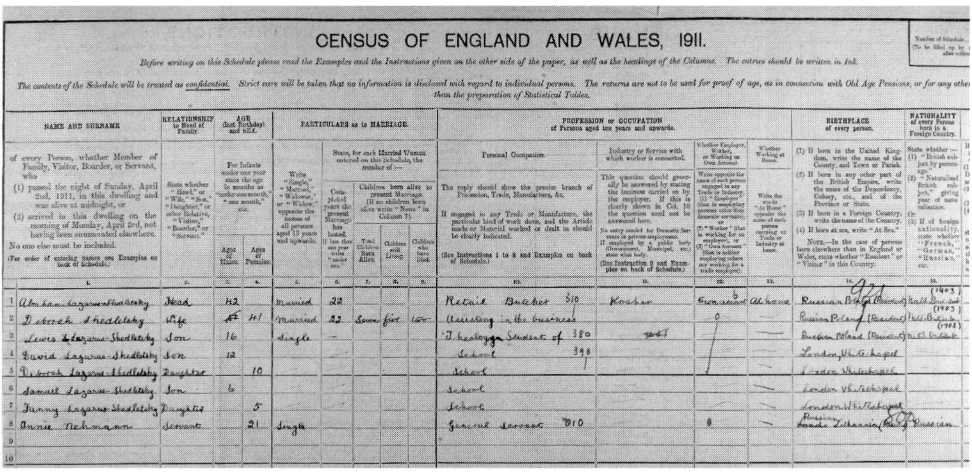

CENSUS OF ENGLAND AND WALES, 1911.

Before writing on this Schedule please read the Examples and the Instructions given on the other side of the paper, as well as the headings of the Columns. The entries should be written in Ink.

The contents of the Schedule will be treated as confidential. Strict care will be taken that no information is disclosed with regard to individual persons. The returns are not to be used for proof of age, as in connection with Old Age Pensions, or for any other than the preparation of Statistical Tables.

	1. NAME AND SURNAME	2. RELATIONSHIP to Head of Family	3. AGE: Ages of Males	4. AGE: Ages of Females	5. PARTICULARS as to MARRIAGE: Write "Single," "Married," "Widower," or "Widow"	6. Completed years the present Marriage has lasted	7. Total Children Born Alive	8. Children still Living	9. Children who have Died	10. PROFESSION or OCCUPATION: Personal Occupation	11. Industry or Service with which worker is connected	12. Whether Employer, Worker, or Working on Own Account	13. Whether Working at Home	14. BIRTHPLACE of every person	15. NATIONALITY of every Person born in a Foreign Country
1	Abraham Lazarus Shedletsky	Head	42		Married	22				Retail Butcher 310	Kosher	Own account	At home	Russian Poland (Resident)	(1903) Natd British sub
2	Deborah Shedletsky	Wife		41	Married	22	Seven	five	two	Assisting in the business			—	Russian Poland (Resident)	(1903) Natd British
3	Lewis Lazarus-Shedletsky	Son	16		Single	—				Theology Student of 380			—	Russian Poland (Resident)	(1903) Natd British
4	David Lazarus-Shedletsky	Son	12							School 390			—	London, Whitechapel	
5	Deborah Lazarus-Shedletsky	Daughter		10						School			—	London Whitechapel	
6	Samuel Lazarus-Shedletsky	Son	6							School			—	London Whitechapel	
7	Fanny Lazarus-Shedletsky	Daughter		5						School			—	London Whitechapel	
8	Annie Nehmann	Servant		21	Single					General servant 810			—	Russian Lithuania (Res)	Russian
9															
10															

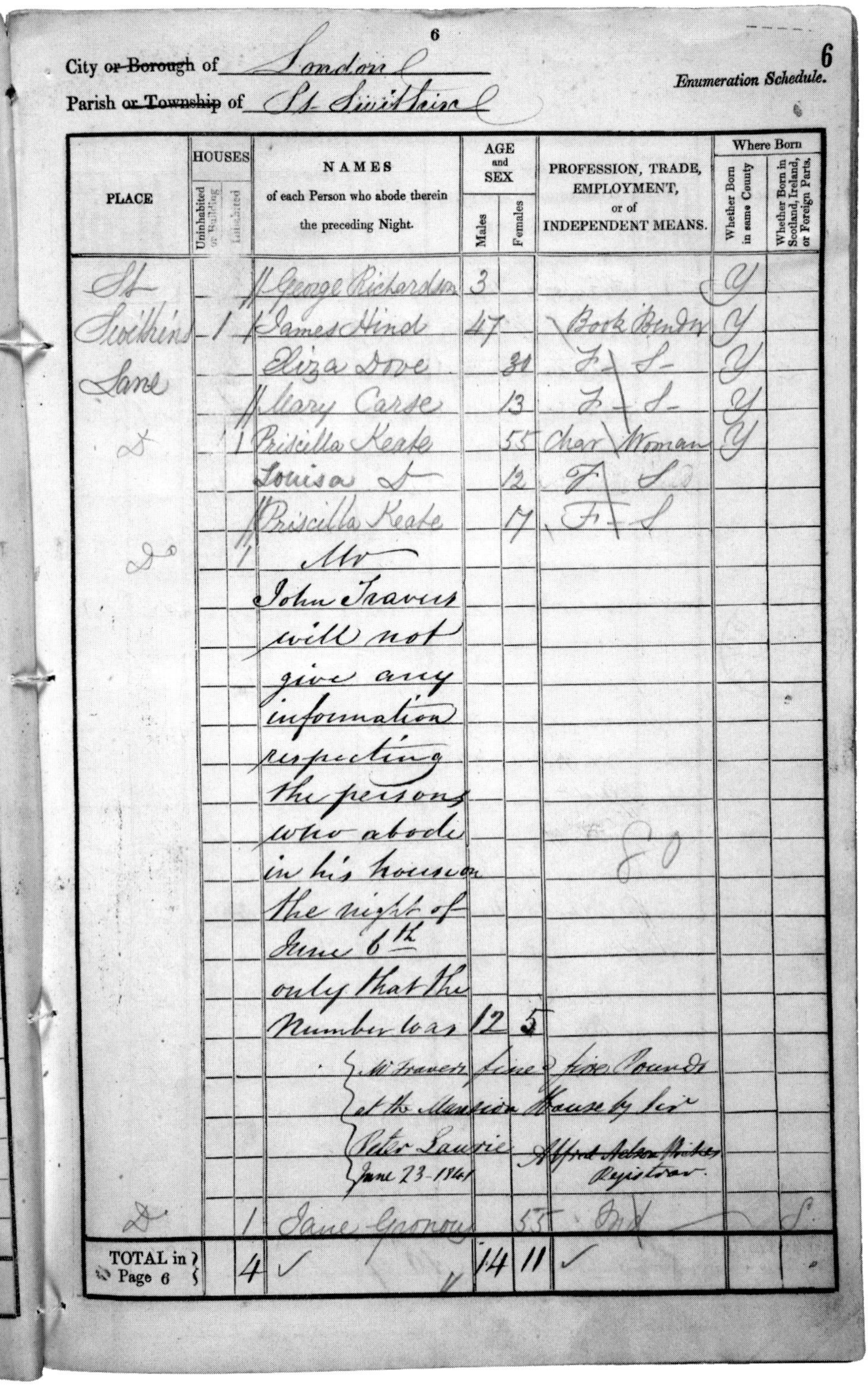

6

City or ~~Borough~~ of London

Parish or ~~Township~~ of St Swithin

6

Enumeration Schedule.

PLACE	HOUSES: Uninhabited or Building	HOUSES: Inhabited	NAMES of each Person who abode therein the preceding Night.	AGE and SEX: Males	AGE and SEX: Females	PROFESSION, TRADE, EMPLOYMENT, or of INDEPENDENT MEANS.	Where Born: Whether Born in same County	Where Born: Whether Born in Scotland, Ireland, or Foreign Parts.
St Swithin's Lane			George Richardson	3			Y	
		1	James Hind	47		Book Binder	Y	
			Eliza Dove		31	F S	Y	
			Mary Carse		13	F S	Y	
Do		1	Priscilla Keate		55	Char Woman	Y	
			Louisa Do		12	F S		
			Priscilla Keate		7	F S		
Do		1	Mr John Travers will not give any information respecting the persons who abode in his house the night of June 6th only that the Number was	12	5			
			Mr Travers fined five Pounds at the Mansion House by Sir Peter Laurie June 23-1841			Alfred ... Registrar.		
Do		1	Jane Gronow		55	Ind		S
TOTAL in Page 6		4		14	11			

23 John Travers in the City of London who was fined £5 for refusing to supply information about his household in 1841. (HO 107/723/12)

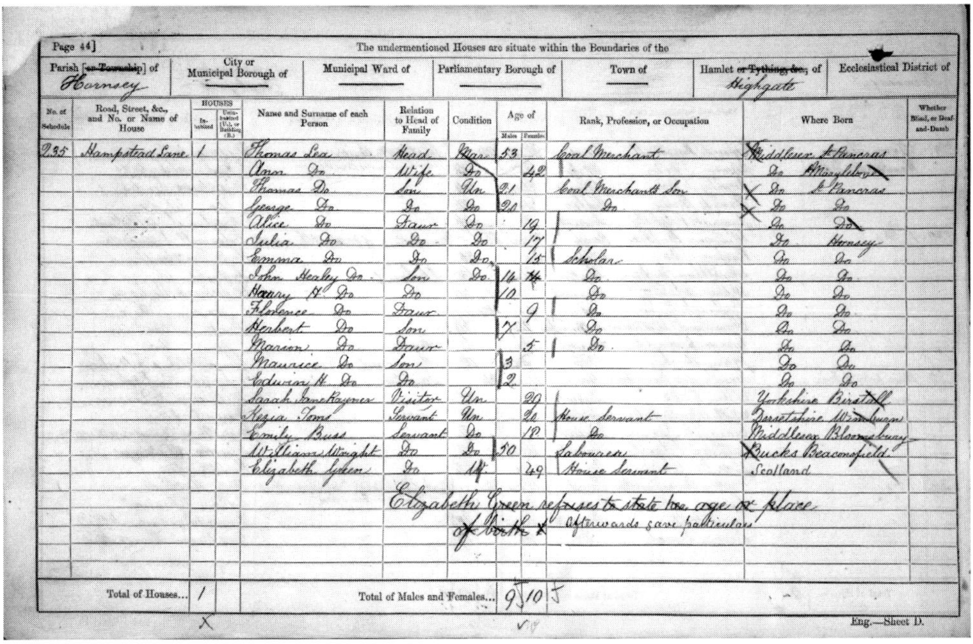

Page 44] The undermentioned Houses are situate within the Boundaries of the

Parish [~~or Township~~] of	City or Municipal Borough of	Municipal Ward of	Parliamentary Borough of	Town of	Hamlet ~~or Tything &c,~~ of	Ecclesiastical District of
Hornsey					Highgate	

No. of Schedule	Road, Street, &c., and No. or Name of House	Houses Inhabited	Uninhabited (U.), or Building (B.)	Name and Surname of each Person	Relation to Head of Family	Condition	Age of Males	Age of Females	Rank, Profession, or Occupation	Where Born	Whether Blind, or Deaf-and-Dumb
235	Hampstead Lane	1		Thomas Lea	Head	Mar	53		Coal Merchant	Middlesex St Pancras	
				Ann Do	Wife	Do		42		Do Marylebone	
				Thomas Do	Son	Un	21		Coal Merchants Son	Do St Pancras	
				George Do	Do	Do	20		Do	Do Do	
				Alice Do	Daur	Do		19		Do Do	
				Julia Do	Do	Do		17		Do Hornsey	
				Emma Do	Do	Do		15	Scholar	Do Do	
				John Healey Do	Son	Do	14		Do	Do Do	
				Henry H Do	Do		10		Do	Do Do	
				Florence Do	Daur			9	Do	Do Do	
				Herbert Do	Son		7		Do	Do Do	
				Marion Do	Daur			5	Do	Do Do	
				Maurice Do	Son		3			Do Do	
				Edwin H Do	Do		2			Do Do	
				Sarah Jane Rayner	Visitor	Un		20		Yorkshire Birstall	
				Kezia Toms	Servant	Un		20	House servant	Dorsetshire Wimborne	
				Emily Buss	Servant	Do		18	Do	Middlesex Bloomsbury	
				William Wright	Do	Do	50		Labourer	Bucks Beaconsfield	
				Elizabeth Green	Do	Un		49	House Servant	Scotland	

Elizabeth Green refuses to state her age or place of birth × afterwards gave particulars

Total of Houses...	1	Total of Males and Females...	9	10

Eng.—Sheet D.

24 Elizabeth Green, house servant, recorded in 1861. She initially refused to give her age and birthplace, but later supplied the information. (RG 9/792)

25 An unnamed 'Supposed Serjt Major in Army' and his family, from the 1891 census whose details the enumerator could only guess. (RG 12/471)

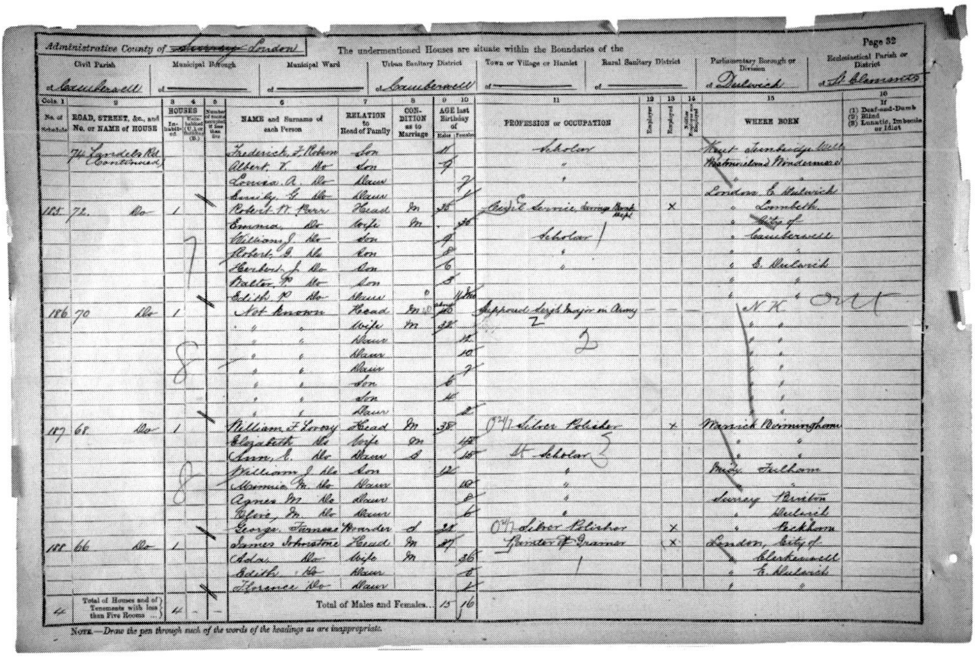

Administrative County of ~~Surrey~~ London — The undermentioned Houses are situate within the Boundaries of the — Page 32

Civil Parish	Municipal Borough	Municipal Ward	Urban Sanitary District	Town or Village or Hamlet	Rural Sanitary District	Parliamentary Borough or Division	Ecclesiastical Parish or District
of Camberwell	of	of	of Camberwell	of	of	of Dulwich	of St Clements

No. of Schedule	Road, Street, &c., and No. or Name of House	Houses Inhabited	Uninhabited	Number of rooms occupied if less than five	Name and Surname of each Person	Relation to Head of Family	Condition as to Marriage	Age Males	Age Females	Profession or Occupation	Employer	Employed	Neither	Where Born	Deaf-and-Dumb, Blind, Lunatic
	74 Landells Rd (Continued)				Frederick F. Robert	Son		11		Scholar				Kent Tunbridge Wells	
					Albert V. Do	Son		9		"				Westmorland Windermere	
					Louisa A. Do	Daur			7	"					
					Emily G. Do	Daur			2					London E Dulwich	
185	72 Do	1			Robert W. Barr	Head	M	35		Civil Service, Savings Bank Dept		×		" Lambeth	
					Emma Do	Wife	M		36					" City of	
					William J. Do	Son		9		Scholar				" Camberwell	
					Robert G. Do	Son		8		"				"	
					Herbert J. Do	Son		6		"				" E Dulwich	
					Walter P. Do	Son		3						"	
					Edith P. Do	Daur			4 Mo					"	
186	70 Do	1			Not Known	Head	M	40		Supposed Serjt Major in Army	—	—		N.K.	
					" "	Wife	M		38					"	
					" "	Daur			12					"	
					" "	Daur			10					"	
					" "	Daur			7					"	
					" "	Son		6						"	
					" "	Son		4						"	
					" "	Daur			2					"	
187	68 Do	1			William F. Lovey	Head	M	38		Silver Polisher		×		Warwick Birmingham	
					Elizabeth Do	Wife	M		40						
					Ann E. Do	Daur	S		15	Scholar					
					William J. Do	Son		12		"				Middx Fulham	
					Minnie M. Do	Daur			10	"					
					Agnes M. Do	Daur			8	"				Surrey Brixton	
					Elsie M. Do	Daur			6	"				" Dulwich	
					George Farmer	Boarder	S	28		Silver Polisher		×		" Peckham	
188	66 Do	1			James Johnstone	Head	M	37		Printer & Grainer		×		London City of	
					Ada Do	Wife	M		36					" Clerkenwell	
					Edith Do	Daur			6					" E Dulwich	
					Florence Do	Daur			2					"	
4	Total of Houses and of Tenements with less than Five Rooms	4	—			Total of Males and Females		15	16						

NOTE.—Draw the pen through such of the words of the headings as are inappropriate.

EARLY MORNING.—THE ENUMERATOR TAKING THE CENSUS IN ST. JAMES'S PARK.

26 An enumerator gathering information from vagrants who had spent census night in the open air.

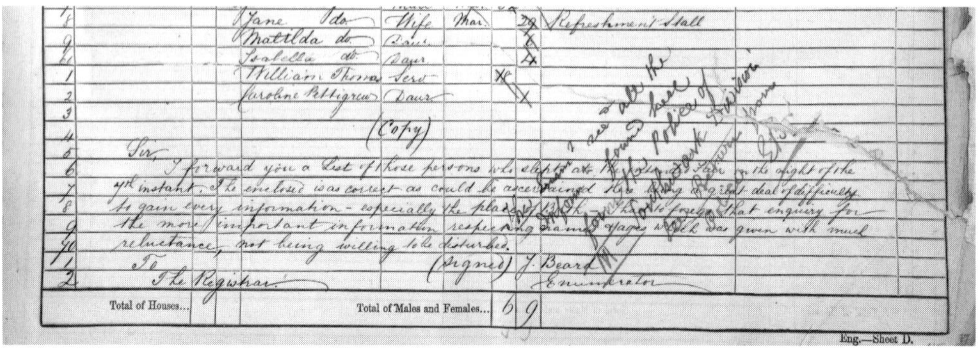
Jane do. Wife Mar. 29 Refreshment Stall
Matilda do. Daur 6
Isabella do. Daur 4
William Thomas Servt
Caroline Pettigrew Daur

(Copy)

Sir,
I forward you a List of those persons who slept at the ... Fair on the night of the 7th instant. The enclosed is as correct as could be ascertained there being a great deal of difficulty to gain every information – especially the place of Birth – the more important information respecting names & ages which was given with much reluctance, not being willing to be disturbed.
To
The Registrar
(Signed) J. Beard
Enumerator

Total of Houses... Total of Males and Females... 6 9

Eng.—Sheet D.

27 Enumerator's note regarding stallholders who spent the night of 7 April 1861 in a field in Deptford following a fair. Information was given with 'much reluctance'. (RG 9/396)

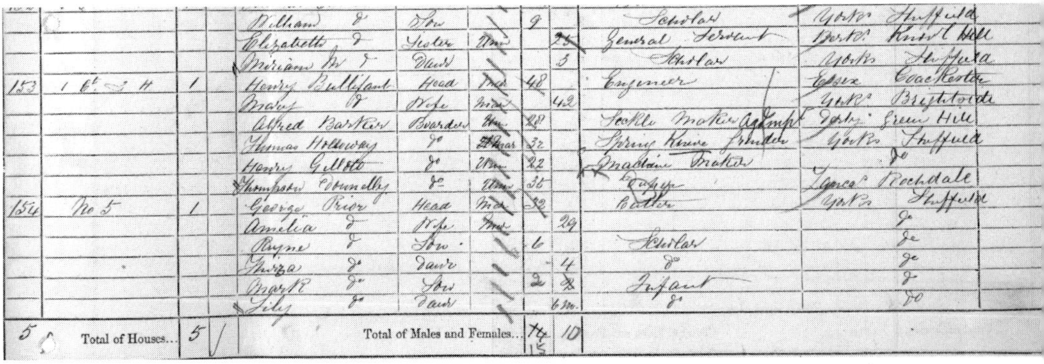

			William do	Son		9		Scholar	Yorks	Sheffield
			Elizabeth do	Sister	Unm		25	General Servant	Yorks	Knowl Hill
			Miriam M do	Daur			5	Scholar	Yorks	Sheffield
153	1 Ct. 2 H	1	Henry Bullifant	Head	Mar	48		Engineer	Essex	Coackerter
			Mary do	Wife	Mar		42		Yorks	Brightside
			Alfred Barker	Boarder	Unm	28		Sickle Maker	Derby	Green Hill
			Thomas Holloway	do	Mar	32		Spring Knife Grinder	Yorks	Sheffield
			Henry Gillott	do	Unm	22		Machine Maker		do
			Thompson Donnelly	do	Unm	35		Dyer	Lancs	Rochdale
154	No 5	1	George Prior	Head	Mar	32		Baker	Yorks	Sheffield
			Amelia do	Wife	Mar		29			do
			Ryne do	Son		6		Scholar		do
			Thirza do	Daur			4	do		do
			Mark do	Son		2		Infant		do
			Lily do	Daur			6m	do		do
5	Total of Houses...	5		Total of Males and Females...		14 15	10			

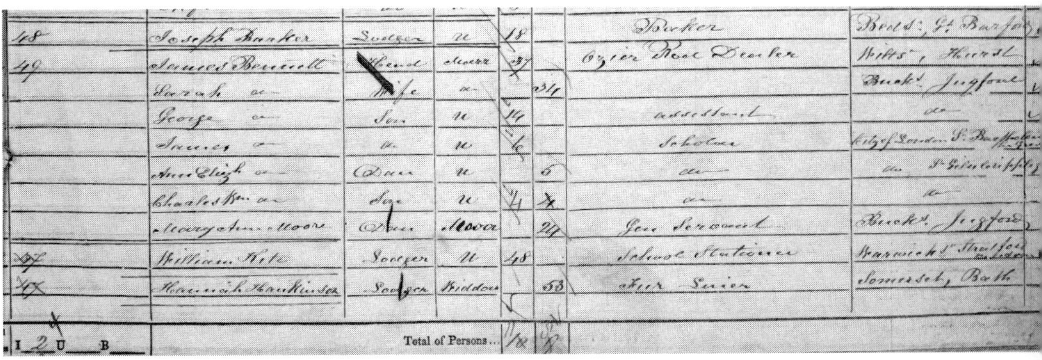

48	Joseph Barker	Lodger	U	18		Porter	Beds, Gt Barford
49	James Bennett	Head	Marr	37		Ozier Rod Dealer	Wilts, Hurst
	Sarah do	Wife	do		34		Bucks, Jugford
	George do	Son	U	14		assistant	do
	James do	do	U	6		Scholar	City of London St Bartholomew
	Ann Eliza do	Dau	U		6	do	do St Giles Cripplegate
	Charles Wm do	Son	U	4		do	do
	Mary Ann Moore	Dau	Marr		21	Gen Servant	Bucks, Jugford
47	William Kite	Lodger	U	48		School Stationer	Warwick St Stratford on Avon
47	Hannah Hawkinson	Lodger	Widow		53	Fur Sewer	Somerset, Bath
I 2 U B			Total of Persons...				

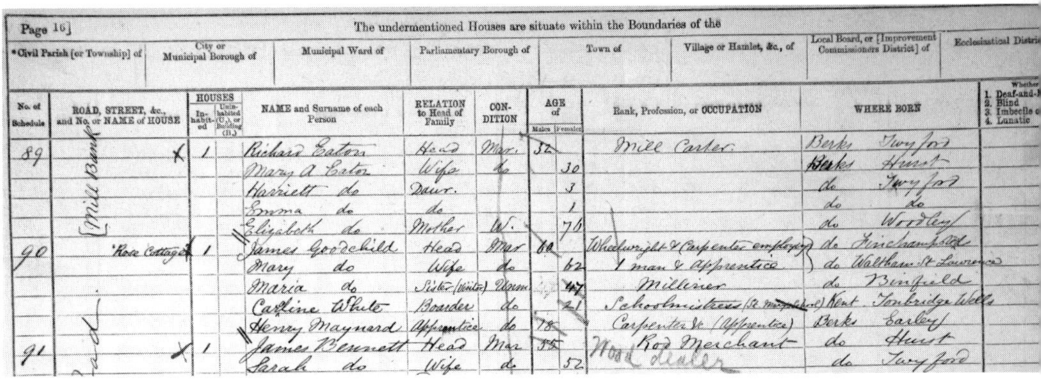

Page 16] The undermentioned Houses are situate within the Boundaries of the

No. of Schedule	ROAD, STREET, &c., and No. or NAME of HOUSE	HOUSES In-habited	Uninhabited (U.), or Building (B.)	NAME and Surname of each Person	RELATION to Head of Family	CONDITION	AGE of Males	AGE of Females	Rank, Profession, or OCCUPATION	WHERE BORN	
89	Mill Bank	1		Richard Eaton	Head	Mar.	32		Mill Carter	Berks	Twyford
				Mary A Eaton	Wife	do		30		Berks	Hurst
				Harriett do	Daur.			3		do	Twyford
				Emma do	do			1		do	do
				Elizabeth do	Mother	W.		76		do	Woodley
90	Rose Cottage	1		James Goodchild	Head	Mar	60		Wheelwright & Carpenter employ 1 man & Apprentice	do	Finchampstead
				Mary do	Wife	do		62		do	Waltham St Lawrence
				Maria do	Sister (Visitor)	Unm		47	Milliner	do	Binfield
				Carline White	Boarder	do		21	Schoolmistress	Kent	Tonbridge Wells
				Henry Maynard	Apprentice	do	18		Carpenter &c (Apprentice)	Berks	Earley
91		1		James Bennett	Head	Mar	55		Wood Dealer / Rod Merchant	do	Hurst
				Sarah do	Wife	do		52		do	Twyford

28 *Top:* Henry Bullifant's birthplace, Colchester, is rendered as 'Coackerter' by a Sheffield enumerator in 1881. (RG 11/4647)

29 *Centre:* Sarah Bennett's birthplace in 1851 appears to be the non-existent 'Bucks, Jugford'. (HO 107/1516)

30 *Below:* The same family was correctly located in 'Berks, Twyford' in 1871. (RG 10/1288)

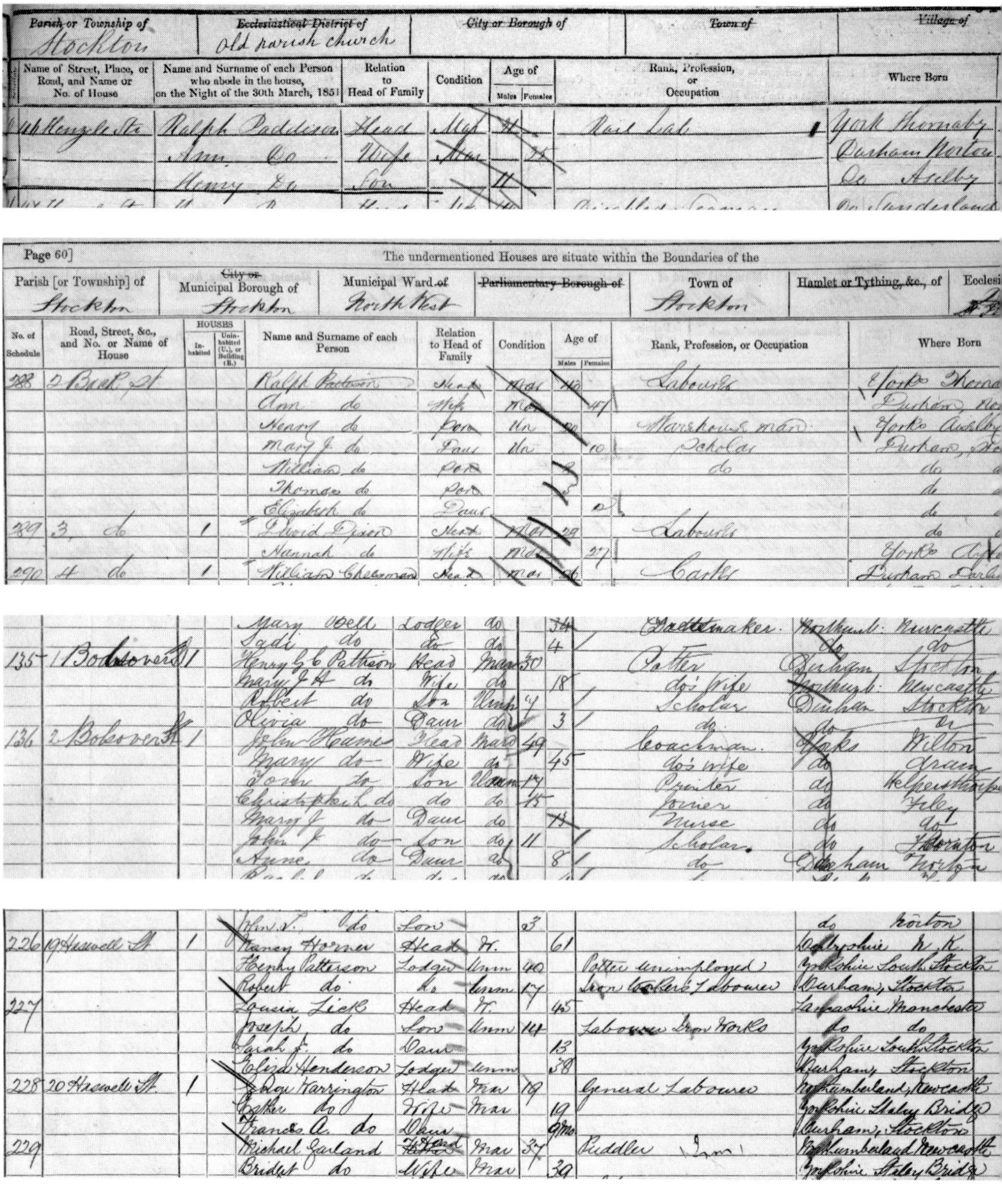

Parish or Township of	Ecclesiastical District of	City or Borough of	Town of	Village of
Stockton	old parish church			

Name of Street, Place, or Road, and Name or No. of House	Name and Surname of each Person who abode in the house, on the Night of the 30th March, 1851	Relation to Head of Family	Condition	Age of Males	Age of Females	Rank, Profession, or Occupation	Where Born
Henzle St	Ralph Paddison	Head	Mar	41		Rail Lab	York Thornaby
	Ann Do	Wife	Mar		37		Durham Norton
	Henry Do	Son		11			Do Aislaby

Page 60] The undermentioned Houses are situate within the Boundaries of the

Parish [or Township] of	City or Municipal Borough of	Municipal Ward of	Parliamentary Borough of	Town of	Hamlet or Tything, &c., of	Ecclesi[astical District of]
Stockton	Stockton	North West		Stockton		

No. of Schedule	Road, Street, &c., and No. or Name of House	Houses In-habited	Houses Uninhabited (U.), or Building (B.)	Name and Surname of each Person	Relation to Head of Family	Condition	Age of Males	Age of Females	Rank, Profession, or Occupation	Where Born
288	2 Brick St			Ralph Pattison	Head	Mar	48		Labourer	Yorks Thornaby
				Ann do	Wife	Mar		47		Durham Norton
				Henry do	Son	Un	20		Warehouse man	Yorks Aislaby
				Mary J do	Daur	Un		10	Scholar	Durham Stockton
				William do	Son		8		do	do
				Thomas do	Son		5			do
				Elizabeth do	Daur			2		do
289	3 do	1		David Dixon	Head	Mar	29		Labourer	do
				Hannah do	Wife	Mar		27		Yorks
290	4 do	1		William Cheesman	Head	Mar	26		Carter	Durham Darlington

			Mary Bell	Lodger	do		34	Dressmaker	Northumb. Newcastle
			Sadi do	do	do		4		do
135	1 Bolsover St	1	Henry G C Pattison	Head	Mar	30		Potter	Durham Stockton
			Mary J H do	Wife	do		18	do's wife	Northumb. Newcastle
			Robert do	Son	Unm	4		Scholar	Durham Stockton
			Olivia do	Daur	do		3	do	do do
136	2 Bolsover St	1	John Hoame	Head	Mar	49		Coachman	Yorks Wilton
			Mary do	Wife	do		45	do's wife	do
			John do	Son	Unm	17		Printer	do Helperthorpe
			Christopher do	do	do	15		Joiner	do Filey
			Mary J do	Daur	do		13	Nurse	do do
			John J do	Son	do	11		Scholar	do Thornton
			Anne do	Daur	do		8	do	Durham Norton

			Wm J. do	Son		3			do Norton
226	19 Haswell St	1	Nancy Horner	Head	W.		61		Yorkshire
			Henry Patterson	Lodger	Unm	40		Potter unemployed	Yorkshire South Stockton
			Robert do	do	Unm	17		Iron Roller's Labourer	Durham, Stockton
227			Louisa Lick	Head	W.		45		Lancashire Manchester
			Joseph do	Son	Unm	14		Labourer Iron Works	do do
			Sarah J. do	Daur			13		Yorkshire South Stockton
			Eliza Henderson	Lodger	Unm		58		Durham, Stockton
228	20 Haswell St	1	George Harrington	Head	Mar	19		General Labourer	Northumberland, Newcastle
			Esther do	Wife	Mar		19		Yorkshire Staley Bridge
			Frances A. do	Daur			9 Mo		Durham, Stockton
229			Michael Garland	Head	Mar	37		Puddler Iron	Northumberland Newcastle
			Bridget do	Wife	Mar		39		Yorkshire Staley Bridge

31 Henry Patterson's surname appeared with three different spellings in four census years: Paddison in 1851 (HO 107/2383), Pattison in 1861 (RG 9/3694) and 1871 (RG 10/4901) and finally as Patterson in 1881 (RG 11/4897).

32 Charles Darwin, naturalist and author (1809–1882).

33 *Below:* Charles Darwin in 1851, visiting his brother Erasmus. His daughters Annie and Etty, then in Great Malvern, were missed from the census. (HO 107/1476)

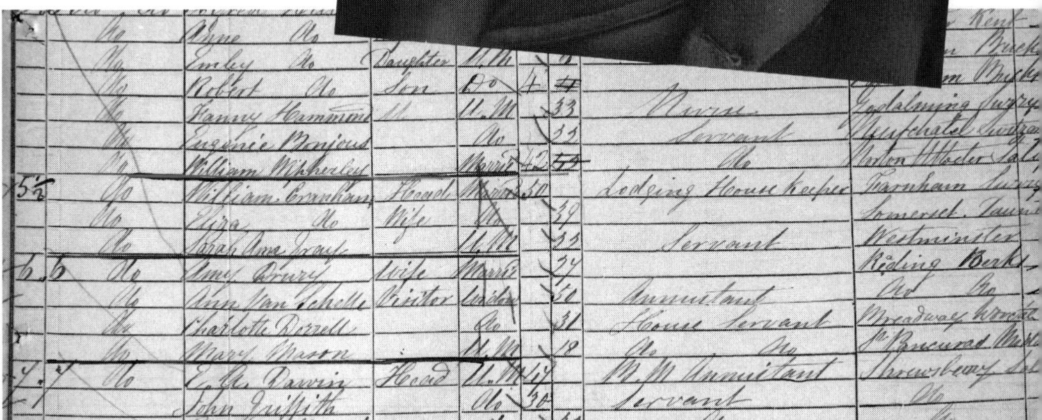

	Do	Anne Do					
	Do	Emily Do	Daughter	U.M			
	Do	Robert Do	Son	Do	4		
	Do	Fanny Hammond	Do	U.M	33	Nurse	Godalming Surrey
	Do	Eugenie Bonjour		Do	35	Servant	Neufchatel Switzerland
	Do	William Wycherley		Marr	42	Do	
5½	Do	William Farnham	Head	Marr	50	Lodging House Keeper	Farnham Surrey
	Do	Eliza Do	Wife	Do	59		Somerset. Taunton
	Do	Sarah Ann Gray		U.M	22	Servant	Westminster
6 6	Do	Amy Drury	Wife	Marr	37		Reading Berks
	Do	Ann Van Schelle	Visitor	Widow	50	Annuitant	Do Do
	Do	Charlotte Dorrell		Do	31	House Servant	Broadway Worcs
	Do	Mary Mason		U.M	18	Do Do	St Pancras Mx
7 7	Do	E. A. Darwin	Head	U.M	47	M.M Annuitant	Shrewsbury Salop
		John Griffith		Do	30	Servant	Do
		Emma Wiend		Do	32	Do	Do
		C. R. Darwin	Visitor	Marr	42	M. A. Proprietor & Land	Do

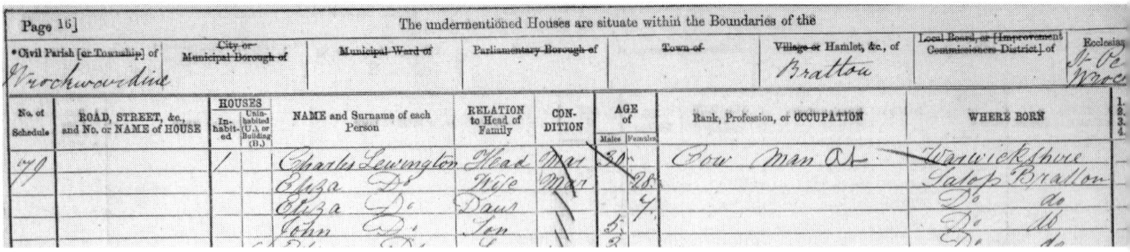

Page 16] The undermentioned Houses are situate within the Boundaries of the

Civil Parish [or Township] of	City or Municipal Borough of	Municipal Ward of	Parliamentary Borough of	Town of	Village or Hamlet, &c., of	Local Board, or [Improvement Commissioners District] of	Ecclesiastical
Wrockwardine					Bratton		[illegible]

No. of Schedule	ROAD, STREET, &c., and No. or NAME of HOUSE	HOUSES Inhabited	HOUSES Uninhabited (U.), or Building (B.)	NAME and Surname of each Person	RELATION to Head of Family	CONDITION	AGE of Males	AGE of Females	Rank, Profession, or OCCUPATION	WHERE BORN
79		1		Charles Lewington	Head	Mar	30		Cow man Ag	Warwickshire
				Eliza Do	Wife	Mar		28		Salop Bratton
				Eliza Do	Daur			4		Do do
				John Do	Son		5			Do do

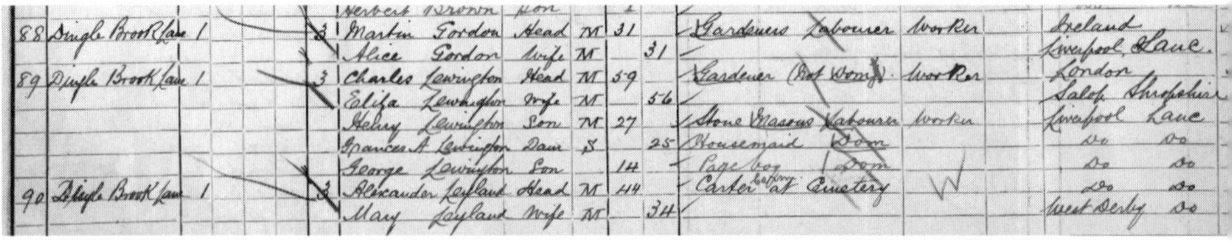

No. of Schedule	ROAD, STREET, &c.	Houses		Name	Relation	Condition	Age M	Age F	Occupation		Where born
				Herbert Brown	Son						
88	Dingle Brook Lane	1	3	Martin Gordon	Head	M	31		Gardeners Labourer	Worker	Ireland
				Alice Gordon	Wife	M		31			Liverpool Lanc
89	Dingle Brook Lane	1	3	Charles Lewington	Head	M	59		Gardener (Not Dom)	Worker	London
				Eliza Lewington	Wife	M		56			Salop Shropshire
				Henry Lewington	Son	M	27		Stone Masons Labourer	Worker	Liverpool Lanc
				Frances A. Lewington	Daur	S		25	Housemaid Dom		do do
				George Lewington	Son		14		Page boy Dom		do do
90	Dingle Brook Lane	1	3	Alexander Leyland	Head	M	44		Carter at Cemetery	W	do do
				Mary Leyland	Wife	M		34			West Derby do

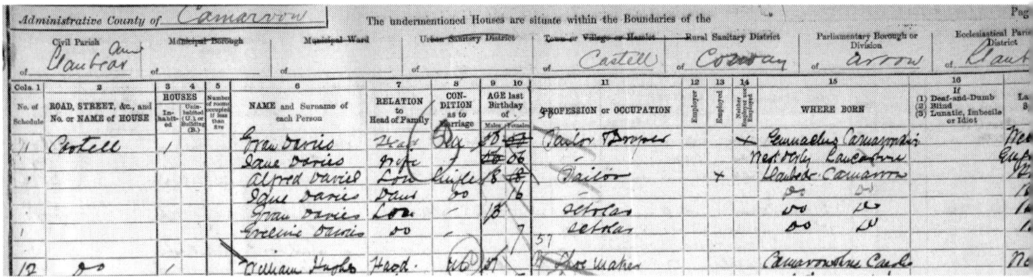

Administrative County of Carnarvon. The undermentioned Houses are situate within the Boundaries of the

Civil Parish	Municipal Borough	Municipal Ward	Urban Sanitary District	Town or Village or Hamlet	Rural Sanitary District	Parliamentary Borough or Division	Ecclesiastical Parish or District
of Llanbedr	of	of	of	of Castell	of Conway	of Arvon	of Llan[illegible]

No. of Schedule	ROAD, STREET, &c., and No. or NAME of HOUSE	Inhabited	Uninhabited	Rooms	NAME and Surname of each Person	RELATION to Head of Family	CONDITION as to Marriage	Age Males	Age Females	PROFESSION or OCCUPATION	WHERE BORN
71	Castell	1			Evan Davies	Head	Mar	58		Tailor & Draper	Llanarthney Carmarthenshire
					Jane Davies	Wife			56		West Derby Lancashire
					Alfred Davies	Son	Single	18		Tailor	Llanbedr Carnarvon
					Jane Davies	Daur	do		16		do do
					Evan Davies	Son		13		Scholar	do do
					Evelina Davies	do			7	Scholar	do do
72	do	1			William Hughes	Head	Wid	57		Shoe maker	Carnarvonshire [illegible]

"WHAT'S THIS?"

34 *Top and centre:* Charles Lewington was born in Eversley, in Hampshire, but his birthplace was given as Warwickshire in 1871 (RG 10/2808), Walton, Shropshire, in 1881 (RG 11/3714), Shropshire in 1891 (RG 12/3001) and London in 1901 (RG 13/3450).

35 *Below:* The Welsh question: according to this entry in the 1891 Census for Llanbeddir-y-Cellin, Caernarvonshire, Evan Davies spoke only Welsh and his wife Jane spoke only English (RG 12/4671).

36 *Left:* The census schedule was viewed with suspicion by many householders.

Select the one you want and click on the 'View' button on the right.

Figure 10-13 shows a flowchart for institution and vessel searches.

One problem we found consistently when using the site is that using the browser's 'Back' button to go from search results back to the search form doesn't seem to work – a message comes up 'Your search is now being processed. This might take a short period of time to complete', and in fact it seems never to complete. Instead, it is better use the 'Search again?' button – this takes you back to the form and preserves the fields you have already entered.

Images

The images on Genes Reunited and 1901censusonline are the same, though the viewing facilities are different. Both sites provide the images in PDF format. The original 1901 Census site used TIF images scanned at 300dpi, so these will have simply been converted to PDF. The images for 1901 are black and white, as are those for 1861, 1871 and 1891. Images for the two earliest censuses are greyscale.

On Genes Reunited, clicking on the image link loads the PDF file in a new browser window. On 1901censusonline, the only difference is that there is a header above the PDF image which provides links to the previous and next images and back to the search results.

Help and feedback

Help for Genes Reunited can be found by clicking on the 'Help Centre' button near the top of the page. This provides help for all the resources on the site, and you can get census help by looking at the 'Genes Reunited Records' area of the FAQ, or you can type a question in the Search box. At the bottom of each help page is a link to a form for submitting a query to the support staff, should you be unable to find the answer to your question on the site itself. There is no dedicated mechanism for reporting errors in the indexing or problems with the images, but there is a link to the Contact Us form via the 'Contact us' link at the bottom of the page.

1901censusonline has much more extensive help for those searching census records –the Help/FAQs page has detailed information about the different types of search and what to do in the case of problems. The search forms themselves have a 'Help' link with information on how to use the various search fields (this is in addition to the 'Help/ FAQ' at the top of the page). The Contact Us page has links to distinct forms for general feedback, payment queries and technical help requests.

The Full Transcription Details and Full Household Schedule pages have a link to an error reporting form, which displays the existing data and allows you to submit corrections for individual fields. You can request an email notification when the record has been updated. There is no mechanism, apart from the general Contact Us forms, for reporting image problems.

The original 1901 Census site published details of all corrections made and this information is reproduced at <**www.1901censusonline.com/main.asp?wci=census_static&item=changesindex**> (there seems to be no link to this page from elsewhere on the site). However, it stops in August 2005 and there seems to be no similar information for the period after Genes Reunited took over the data.

Other resources

Both sites have the same additional datasets: birth, marriage and death indexes for England and Wales 1837–2004, and military deaths for the two world wars. Credits purchased can be used for any of the datasets.

While 1901censusonline is purely a data service, Genes Reunited is in fact much better known as a social networking site where you can post your pedigree in the hope of getting in touch with distant or long-lost relatives. It also offers a number of message boards, which are good places to ask questions if you are having difficulty finding an individual in the census.

11

ORIGINS

Origins was the first UK genealogical data service. It was launched in April 1998 with Scottish civil registration data and images on a site called Scots Origins. Although the Scottish data subsequently moved to ScotlandsPeople (see Chapter 12), Origins by then had launched British Origins to host datasets from the Society of Genealogists. In 2005, it started to add census data for England and Wales. It also has an Irish Origins service with data for Ireland. All are accessed via the home page at <**www.origins.net**>.

The site's census data for England and Wales comprises the 1841, 1861 and 1871 censuses. Origins' 1841 and 1871 data has also been licensed to Findmypast (see Chapter 8), while Origins has in turn licensed the 1861 data from Findmypast.

Origins is currently the only commercial site to host Irish census data, offering the Dublin City census for 1851 and for the Rotunda Ward in Dublin for 1901. These are discussed in more detail on p. 240. Irish Origins also has separate datasets of Irish strays in the England and Wales census of 1841 and 1871. However, these are simply extracts from the census which include only those giving Ireland as a birthplace, and do not provide any data that is not already available on British Origins.

Charges

Origins started out as a pay-per-view site, but now offers only subscriptions. Access to the census records requires a subscription to the British Origins area of the site, and subscription prices are given in Table 11-1 (see p. 186). But Origins hosts an increasing amount of Irish data, including the census substitute Griffith's Valuation, and an Origins Total Access subscription gives access to this as well as the material on

British Origins. There is a separate Irish Origins subscription for those who don't need access to the data for England and Wales.

	British Origins	Total Access
72 hours	£6.50	£7.50
Month	£8.95	£10.50
Year	—	£47.00

Table 11-1 Origins subscription prices (summer 2008)

Since the annual Total Access subscription costs less than a six-month subscription to British Origins alone, the former is clearly the option to go for if you are going to be a long-term user. Subscriptions are payable only online with a credit/debit card. Monthly and annual subscriptions are automatically renewed unless the user cancels more than seven days in advance of expiry. The 72-hour subscription is not automatically renewed.

The site does not talk about 'units' or 'credits' – for the duration of the subscription you can access as much of the data as you wish. The site does not offer a free trial, though searches leading to the Records found screen (Figure 11-2) are available to non-subscribers.

Searching

Origins offers a global search across all three of its censuses and an individual search for each census. Since the global search allows you to specify only a last name and first name, its main use, unless you have an ancestor with a reasonably unusual name, is to provide initial information about how many matching records there are.

The search form for an individual census is shown in Figure 11-1. The only field you have to complete is the last name. Note that unlike some of the other sites, Origins does not have a basic and an advanced search form. You don't have to specify a county, but you can select one from the drop-down list; if you do this you will then be able to select a parish from the drop-down list below that, which initially says 'All Parishes'. This lists all the parishes in the county, so you don't have to worry about getting the correct spelling of the parish. The Birth Place field allows you to select from a list of English and Welsh counties and

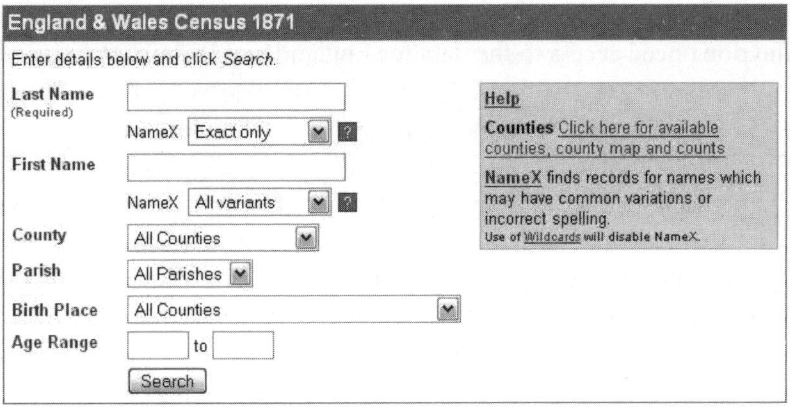

Figure 11-1 Origins census search form

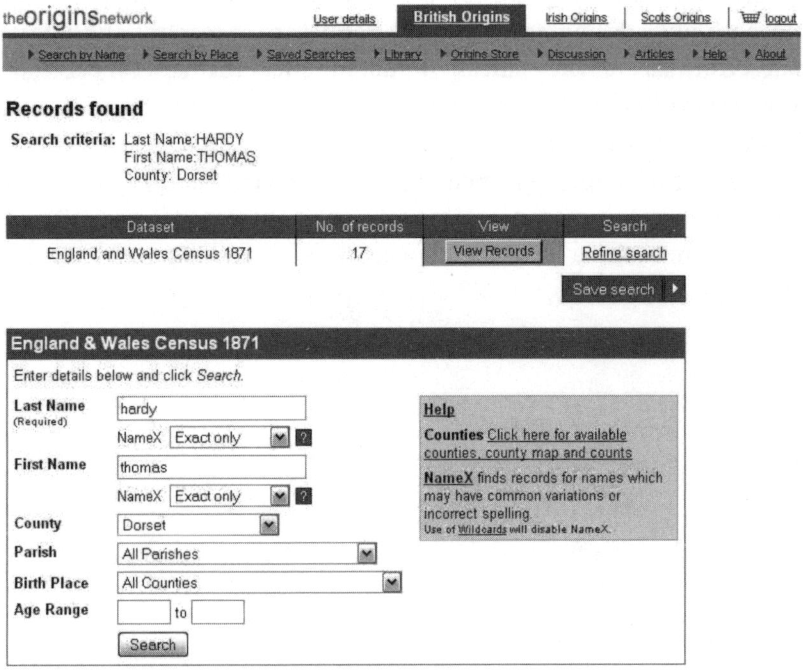

Figure 11-2 Origins Records found

other countries (including Scotland and Ireland).

Origins offers two ways of finding surname variants. The main one is NameX, discussed on p. 101. The default name search uses the NameX 'close variants' option, but you can switch NameX off by choosing 'Exactly only' or cast the net wider by selecting 'All variants'. The alternative is to use a wildcard (see p. 99, where the relative merits of the two techniques are discussed). If you want an exact match on the names you will need to select 'Exact only' for the two NameX fields.

When you click the 'Search' button on the search page, the initial results page, headed 'Records found', shows you only the total number of matches (Figure 11-2). The aim of this is to give you some idea whether you have got a manageable number of hits or whether you want to refine your search before looking at the matching records. The page actually has a link on it saying 'Refine Search'. However, this takes you back to the original *blank* search form from which you started and there is no real reason to use this. The best way to refine your search is to modify your completed search form, which is repeated on the Records found page.

Once you have refined your search as much as you think you need to, clicking on the 'View Records' button takes you to the View records page. This lists all the individual matching records, 20 to a page (see Figure 11-3).

For the 1871 census (shown in Figure 11-3), this page includes the main address and personal fields, excepting marital status and occupation. On the View records page for the 1841 and 1861 censuses, there is no Relation column. Also, because the 1841 census only asked whether

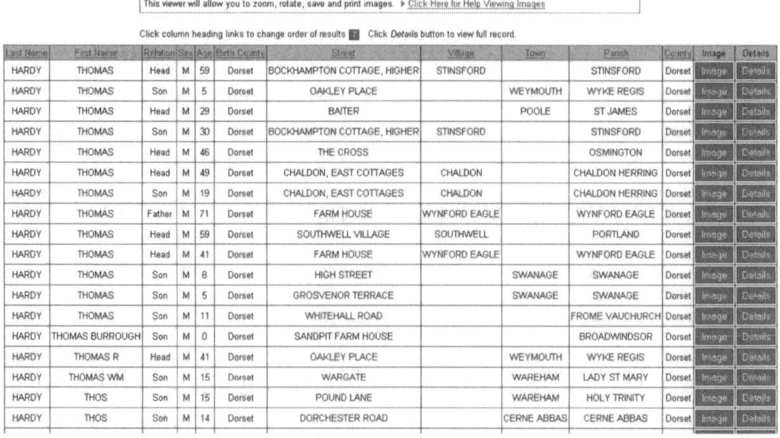
theoriginsnetwork User details British Origins Irish Origins | Scots Origins | logout

Search by Name · Search by Place · Saved Searches · Library · Origins Store · Discussion · Articles · Help · About

View records - England & Wales Census 1871

Search criteria: Last Name:HARDY
First Name: THOMAS + All variants
County: Dorset
Birth County: Dorset

Viewing Images

Please note: Without a *plug-in* you will be unable to view the TIFF images in your browser. If you are unable to view images, or if your default image viewer is Quicktime, please go to www.alternatiff.com and download the free image viewer. This viewer will allow you to zoom, rotate, save and print images. Click Here for Help Viewing Images

Click column heading links to change order of results. Click *Details* button to view full record.

Last Name	First Name	Relation	Sex	Age	Birth County	Street	Village	Town	Parish	County	Image	Details
HARDY	THOMAS	Head	M	59	Dorset	BOCKHAMPTON COTTAGE, HIGHER	STINSFORD		STINSFORD	Dorset	Image	Details
HARDY	THOMAS	Son	M	5	Dorset	OAKLEY PLACE		WEYMOUTH	WYKE REGIS	Dorset	Image	Details
HARDY	THOMAS	Head	M	29	Dorset	BAITER		POOLE	ST JAMES	Dorset	Image	Details
HARDY	THOMAS	Son	M	30	Dorset	BOCKHAMPTON COTTAGE, HIGHER	STINSFORD		STINSFORD	Dorset	Image	Details
HARDY	THOMAS	Head	M	46	Dorset	THE CROSS			OSMINGTON	Dorset	Image	Details
HARDY	THOMAS	Head	M	49	Dorset	CHALDON, EAST COTTAGES	CHALDON		CHALDON HERRING	Dorset	Image	Details
HARDY	THOMAS	Son	M	19	Dorset	CHALDON, EAST COTTAGES	CHALDON		CHALDON HERRING	Dorset	Image	Details
HARDY	THOMAS	Father	M	71	Dorset	FARM HOUSE	WYNFORD EAGLE		WYNFORD EAGLE	Dorset	Image	Details
HARDY	THOMAS	Head	M	59	Dorset	SOUTHWELL VILLAGE	SOUTHWELL		PORTLAND	Dorset	Image	Details
HARDY	THOMAS	Head	M	41	Dorset	FARM HOUSE	WYNFORD EAGLE		WYNFORD EAGLE	Dorset	Image	Details
HARDY	THOMAS	Son	M	8	Dorset	HIGH STREET		SWANAGE	SWANAGE	Dorset	Image	Details
HARDY	THOMAS	Son	M	5	Dorset	GROSVENOR TERRACE		SWANAGE	SWANAGE	Dorset	Image	Details
HARDY	THOMAS	Son	M	11	Dorset	WHITEHALL ROAD			FROME VAUCHURCH	Dorset	Image	Details
HARDY	THOMAS BURROUGH	Son	M	0	Dorset	SANDPIT FARM HOUSE			BROADWINDSOR	Dorset	Image	Details
HARDY	THOMAS R	Head	M	41	Dorset	OAKLEY PLACE		WEYMOUTH	WYKE REGIS	Dorset	Image	Details
HARDY	THOMAS WM	Son	M	15	Dorset	WARGATE		WAREHAM	LADY ST MARY	Dorset	Image	Details
HARDY	THOS	Son	M	15	Dorset	POUND LANE		WAREHAM	HOLY TRINITY	Dorset	Image	Details
HARDY	THOS	Son	M	14	Dorset	DORCHESTER ROAD		CERNE ABBAS	CERNE ABBAS	Dorset	Image	Details

Figure 11-3 Origins View records screen

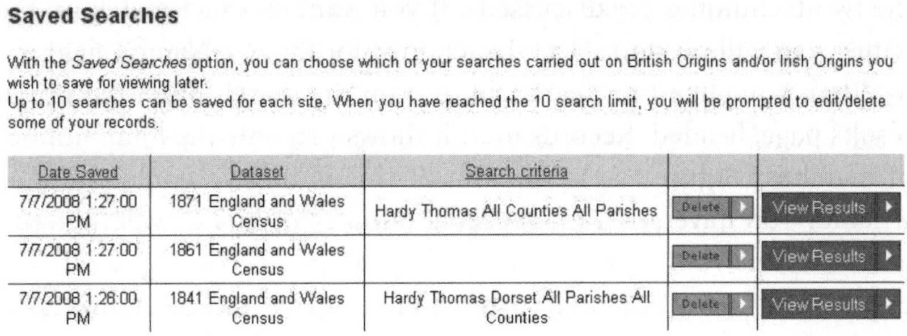

Saved Searches
With the Saved Searches option, you can choose which of your searches carried out on British Origins and/or Irish Origins you wish to save for viewing later.
Up to 10 searches can be saved for each site. When you have reached the 10 search limit, you will be prompted to edit/delete some of your records.
Date Saved
Dataset
Search criteria
7/7/2008 1:27:00 PM
1871 England and Wales Census
Hardy Thomas All Counties All Parishes
Delete
View Results
7/7/2008 1:27:00 PM
1861 England and Wales Census
Delete
View Results
7/7/2008 1:28:00 PM
1841 England and Wales Census
Hardy Thomas Dorset All Parishes All Counties
Delete
View Results

Figure 11-4 Origins Saved searches

a person was born in the same county or not, the Birth County column contains either the same county as the County column on the screen's right or the words 'OUT OF COUNTY', 'Scotland' or 'Ireland'.

The initial listing does not appear to be in any particular order, but you can sort on any of the columns by clicking on the column heading. Once you have sorted on a particular column, clicking on the heading a second time reverses the sort order. An obvious use for this is to sort by address, which will put family members together; or you can order the entries by increasing or decreasing age. In the case of the 1871 census, this also compensates for a search option missing from the original search form: you cannot search on relation to head of household. With a common name, this can be a good way of searching for the father of a family. Origins does not allow you to specify this when searching, but by sorting on the Relation column in the 1871 search results, you can at least group all the heads of household together for easier scanning.

If you want to keep the details of a search so that you can run it again, Origins provides a 'Save search' facility, which is available from the Records found and View record screens – click on the 'Save search' button at the bottom of the screen. To view your saved searches, you click on the Saved Searches link on the menu bar at the top of the screen. This brings up a list of all the searches you have saved, with details of date and time, dataset and search criteria (Figure 11-4). You can rerun the search from this screen and it will take you to the Records found screen. Many pages have a 'view all searches' link at the bottom, but this takes you to the main list of datasets, *not* to your own saved searches. At the time of writing, there is a bug when saving searches for the 1861 census: the 'Search criteria' field still remains blank, and any new saved search for 1861 replaces the old one.

From the View records screen you have two options – to view the details or to view the images. Clicking on the 'Details' button brings up the 'View full record' page, with three tables (Figure 11-5):

- the full TNA reference for the record, including piece, folio and page number
- details of the address and the administrative units in which it is located
- a repeat of the personal information on the View records screen.

View full record - England & Wales Census 1871

Reference details

Census	1871
TNA Ref	RG10-2011
Image No	138
Folio No	68
Page No	11
Entry No	17

Location details

County	Dorset
Superintendent Registrar's District	DORCHESTER
Registrar's Sub-District	DORCHESTER
Enumeration District No	10
Civil Parish	STINSFORD
City or Municipal Borough	
Municipal Ward	
Parliamentary Borough	
Town	
Village or Hamlet	STINSFORD
Local Board	
Ecclesiastical District	
Schedule No	47
Street	BOCKHAMPTON COTTAGE, HIGHER

Record details

First name	THOMAS
Last name	HARDY
Title	
Misc	
Relation	Son
Age	30
Sex	M
Birth County	Dorset

Image

View Census Image	Image

Figure 11-5 Origins View full record

Note this page does not give you the missing columns from the enumeration book – marital status, occupation and full birthplace; you can only get these by viewing the page image. The only real use of this screen is to give you the full TNA reference for the page.

You can call up the image display either from the View records or the View full record screen and this launches the image viewer with the matching page image. From the image viewer you can go to the next or previous page in the enumeration district, go back to the View records screen, or start a new search.

Origins does not have an address search; the 'Search by Place' link on the navigation bar at the top of the screen takes you to entries from

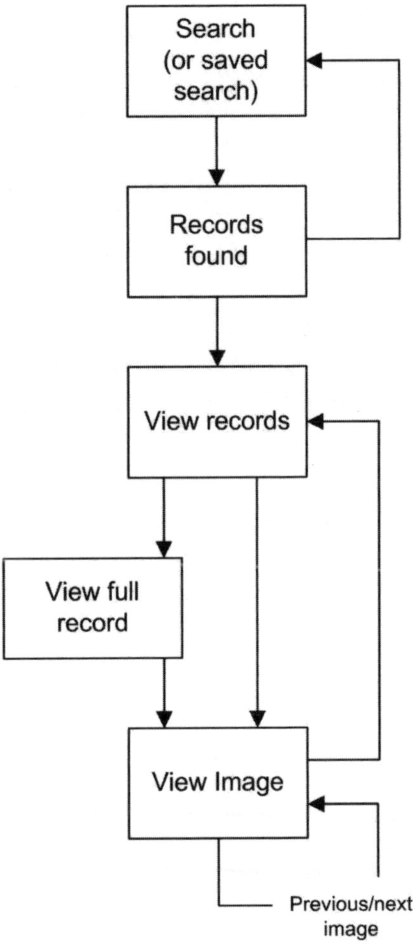

Figure 11-6 Origins search flowchart

the 1895 *The Comprehensive Gazetteer of England and Wales*. There is no facility to search by TNA reference.

Images

The resolution of the census images on Origins varies: most seem to have been scanned at 300dpi, but some are 200dpi. At the time of writing, all the page images for the 1841 and 1861 censuses and about one third of those for the 1871 census are greyscale. The remaining 1871 images are black and white, but these are in the process of being replaced and all images should be greyscale by the start of 2009.

The graphics format of all Origins images is the TIFF format. This is quite an important format for computer images but it is not a type of image that web browsers can display automatically. For this reason, your browser will need to use a plug-in, and if it does not already have one installed, you will need to install one. You will be able to tell whether you need to do this the first time you try to view an image on Origins because if your browser does not already have a suitable plug-in, you will not see the image.

For Windows users, Origins recommends the free AlternaTIFF viewer, and the 'can't view image?' link at the bottom of every image display page brings up information about this and how to install it. In fact, even if your browser already has a plug-in which displays TIFF images, it may be worth installing AlternaTIFF since it offers several useful tools for viewing: zooming, panning, printing and saving are all catered for. It can be downloaded free of charge from <**www.alternatiff.com**>. There are two different versions, one for Internet Explorer and one for other browsers.

The AlternaTIFF toolbar above every image (Figure 11-7) offers a range of options. The magnifying glass provides what is called 'zooming mode', which expands the image to full screen and allows you to move around it. However it only gives one level of zoom. More flexibility is provided by the 'fixed size button', four buttons further to the right. If you click on this button, the up and down arrows to the right of

Figure 11-7 Origins AlternaTIFF toolbar

it can then be used to zoom in or out, with twelve levels of magnification.

The 'Save as' icon (the floppy disk) allows you to save the image in either TIFF or BMP (Windows bitmap) format. Since a BMP file will be around ten times larger than the TIFF file, there is no good reason to choose this option (unless, I suppose, you want to use the image as your Windows wallpaper). A useful alternative is to use the 'Copy to clipboard' icon. Clicking on this saves the image to the Windows clipboard. In most graphics programs, you should be able to paste this as a new image. The Paste option is usually on the Edit menu, but some graphics software has an option under the File menu to create a new image from the contents of the clipboard. You can then save the image in any format that program offers. Note that the 'Copy to clipboard' icon copies the entire image to the clipboard, not just whatever is visible in the viewer.

If you are using Internet Explorer and you have Microsoft Office installed on your computer, the image will initially pop up in a Microsoft Office Document Imaging window, though you will need to rotate the image anti-clockwise to see it the right way up. If you want to use the AlternaTIFF viewer you will need to install the Internet Explorer version from the AlternaTIFF website. The AlternaTIFF viewer is slightly more convenient than Office Document Imaging, as it loads the image automatically.

If you are using a Mac, you should find that the image is displayed automatically using Apple's QuickTime plug-in. However, this does not offer any image controls to zoom or print the page. Origins' help page on image viewing at <**www.originsnetwork.com/help/popup-helpbo-images.htm**> offers some alternative suggestions for Mac users, though these require purchasing a software licence rather than just downloading a free product as with AlternaTIFF.

Help and feedback

Origins has an extensive suite of help pages, accessible from the 'Help' link shown on most pages or from the 'help & resources' link on the home page. There are articles on the census and other records, as well as a general introduction on 'How to Start Tracing your Family History'. The most important help page may be the one on 'Viewing Images and

Maps' at <**www.originsnetwork.com/help/popup-helpbo-images.htm**> – it is a good idea to have a look at this before you start viewing images on the site. There is also a link to this page from the image viewer.

There is a feedback link at the bottom of many pages on the site (apart from those which form part of the record search), which leads to an e-mail form, but there is no specific facility on the record pages for reporting transcription errors or on the images pages for reporting problems with the images.

Other resources

Origins has a wide range of other datasets for the British Isles, particularly for the period before the 1841 census and the start of general registration in 1837. The core of the collection is data from some important sets of records held by the Society of Genealogists, such as Boyd's Marriage Index, apprenticeship records, and will indexes and abstracts.

The site also has a library of digitized nineteenth-century books, including gazetteers, maps, guides books and other contemporary works providing an insight into eighteenth- and nineteenth-century life.

Future developments

As mentioned above, all remaining black and white images for the 1871 census are due to be replaced with greyscale images by the start of 2009. An interesting facility which is being considered is an option to go directly to the beginning of Enumeration District so that you can see the description of the area covered.

Origins expects to reintroduce a pay-per-view option alongside the current subscription service in due course.

12

SCOTLANDSPEOPLE

ScotlandsPeople at <**www.scotlandspeople.gov.uk**> was launched in September 2002 by the Scottish ISP Scotland Online, who had secured the contract from GROS to host the Scottish genealogical data. This had been available since 1998 at Scots Origins (see p. 185). At the time it took over from Scots Origins, the sited offered the 1881 Census Index (see p. 109) and an index and images for the 1891 census. Since then, all the remaining censuses have been added to the site – only the images for the 1881 census are not available. In January 2008, Scotland Online purchased Findmypast (see Chapter 8); in July 2008 it changed its name to Brightsolid.

For much of its existence, ScotlandsPeople was the only site with Scottish census data. However, in April 2007 Ancestry (see Chapter 7) launched a complete set of indexes to the censuses from 1841 to 1901, though without images because they had been unable to license the right to digitize them from GROS. As discussed on p. 85, in the summer of 2008 it was reported that GROS would start to grant non-exclusive licences to digitize the census and other records, so you can expect to see wider availability by 2009.

Charges

ScotlandsPeople is an exclusively pay-per-view site. In fact, you can do basic searches on the site without payment, but you need to register in any case – there is a prominent 'Register' button on the home page (Figure 12-1, see p. 197). Registering allows you to carry out searches, but *not* to view search results or images: when you carry out a search, the site always tells you free of charge how many search results there are and how many pages are required to display them. It also redisplays the search form so that you can refine your search to produce fewer results, requiring fewer page displays. But to view the search results you then have to purchase page credits.

An initial payment of £6 gives you 30 page credits (i.e. 20p each), and these are valid for 90 days from the day on which payment is made (not from the first search). If you still have credits unused at the end of the 90-day period, these will be carried forward to any subsequent purchase of credits – they are never lost but remain unusable until you make a new purchase. If you buy more credits before the initial 90 days are up, all the unused credits have their validity extended to the end of the new 90-day period.

- Searches are charged at 1 unit per page of search results (each page has a maximum of 25 results).
- Viewing an image costs 5 credits.
- For the 1881 census, where no images are available, viewing the full transcription costs 1 credit.

You can purchase larger numbers of credits, in multiples of 30, up to a maximum of 300. However, there is no discount on a larger number. Also, no matter how many credits you purchase, they all have a 90-day limit. If you really need more than 30 credits, then it will be much better to purchase additional credits when you run out – that way your access period will constantly be extended to 90 days from the last day on which you bought credits. Once you have logged in, the number of outstanding credits and their remaining validity are shown at the top of the screen (see the top of Figure 12-4, p. 199). However, the validity is given, precisely, in hours rather than days so a bit of mental arithmetic or a calculator will be required!

You can only purchase credits online with a credit or debit card. If you do not wish to pay online, or if you are giving page credits as a gift, you can print out an order form for any number of 30-credit vouchers and pay by cheque or credit card. Note that buying vouchers is slightly more expensive because you also have to pay a postage and packing charge (£1 within the UK). The vouchers are not available from retail outlets.

These page credits can be used for all the census, civil registration and parish register data on the site, but the wills and testaments have a separate payment system, which uses a shopping cart.

Searching

Once you have registered and logged in, the links to individual census years on the home page (Figure 12-1) will take you to the Search Census page for the chosen year. (If you click on these links without logging in, you will just get a page of information about that particular census.) The 'Search the Records' tab at the top of every page can take you to the search home page from wherever you are on the site.

The main search form, used for all the censuses apart from 1881, is shown in Figure 12-2 (see p. 198) and the initial search is free. Each field has a question mark button to the right, and clicking on this brings up help about using the field. The only compulsory field is the Surname. The Second Person Forename is for the name of another household member, though as the help text points out, this does not work if the household is split over two pages. All three name fields can have wildcards. Whereas most sites only use the * character to mean any number of characters (even zero), ScotlandsPeople also uses the '?' symbol to mean exactly one character. This is most useful where there are two variants of a name with a single difference of vowel. For example, 'B?rne' finds Byrne and Burne, but does not find the unwanted Blackbourne, Blanthorne or Bradbourne, which a search on 'B*rne' would turn up. Unusually, the wildcards can be used at the beginning

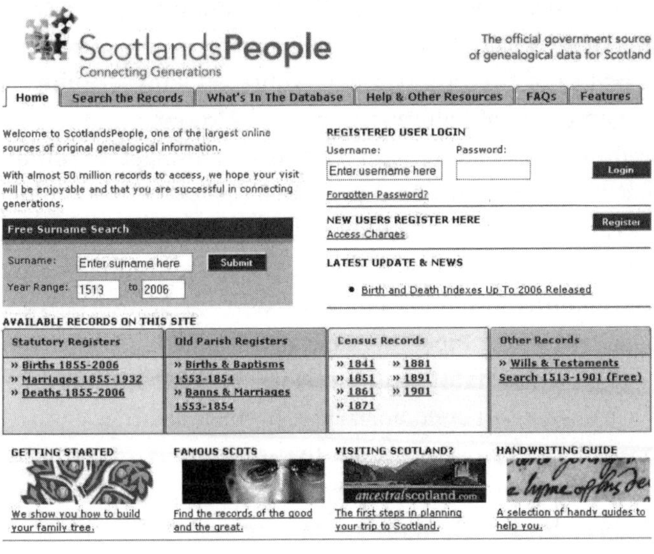

Figure 12-1 ScotlandsPeople home page

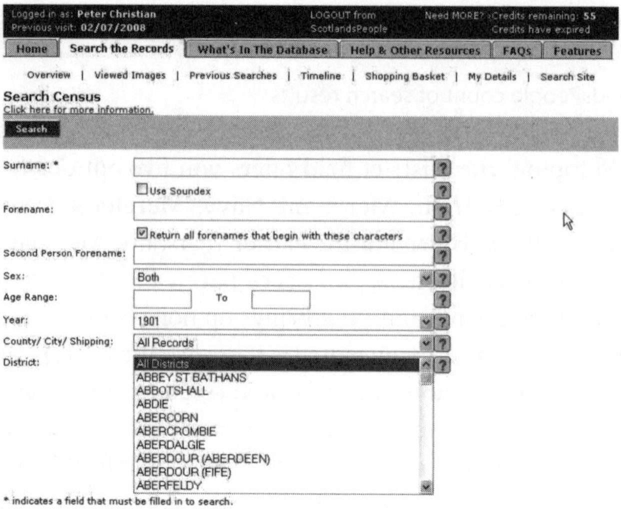

Figure 12-2 ScotlandsPeople search form

of a name. When searching for any patronymic surname in 'Mac' or 'Mc', using 'M*cDonald', etc., will find both forms.

For the surname field, variants can be found using Soundex (see p. 101) by selecting the Soundex checkbox beneath the Surname field. With forenames the only option for finding variants is to look for all names beginning with the letters entered, so 'Eliz' with this option selected will find both Eliza and Elizabeth, not to mention the occasional Elizth, but of course this is actually no different from doing a wildcard search on 'Eliz*'. The help text that comes up if you click on the forename help includes a link to the 'Forename Variants' page with useful guidance on Scottish forename variants, abbreviations, and nicknames.

There are two location fields from which you can select an option. From the County/City/Shipping field you can select a Scottish county, the cities of Aberdeen, Dundee, Edinburgh and Glasgow, and 'Shipping'. The District field initially lists all districts (i.e. Registration Districts), but if you select a county or city in the field above, the list is narrowed down to just the districts in the chosen county or city. Unless you are very sure of your geography and your ancestors' whereabouts (perhaps from the birth certificate of a child born close to the year of the census), this field is probably best avoided initially until you see how many results you have got when searching on just county or city. Unfortunately, these fields only apply to the census address, and there is no facility to search for a birthplace.

Figure 12-3 ScotlandsPeople count of search results

If you select 'Shipping', the District field offers you five options for 1901: English or Foreign, Irish, Merchant Navy, Merchant Navy (Supplementary), and Royal Navy. For the earlier years, just Merchant Navy and Royal Navy are available.

When you click on the 'Search' button it brings up not a list of search results, but information on how many matches there are and how many pages they will take to display (there are 25 search results to each page) – see Figure 12-3. The importance of this last piece of information is that *each* page of search results costs 1 credit to view. If you have more than a couple, then you will probably want to refine your search rather than use up lots of credits to view all the search results, unless, of course, you are conducting a one-name study.

From here you go to the first page of search results (Figure 12-4). These are sorted by surname, then forename, and show only the fields available on the search form. The lack of any address information more precise than city or county and the lack of the birthplace can make it difficult to identify the right individual, particularly with a common

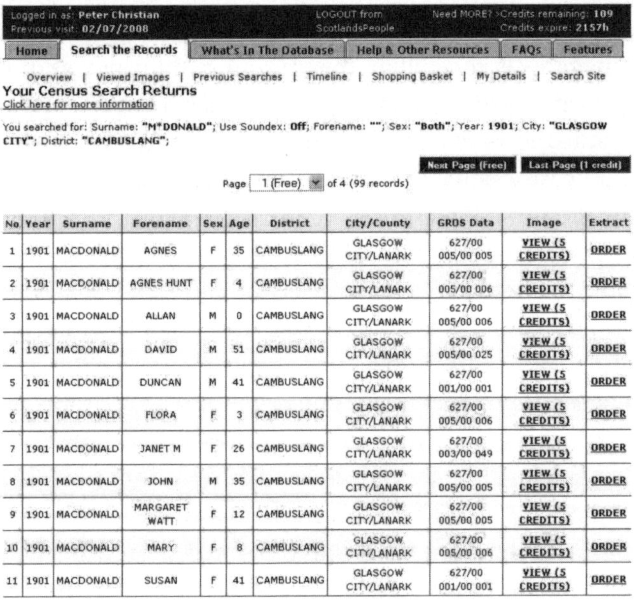

No	Year	Surname	Forename	Sex	Age	District	City/County	GROS Data	Image	Extract
1	1901	MACDONALD	AGNES	F	35	CAMBUSLANG	GLASGOW CITY/LANARK	627/00 005/00 005	VIEW (5 CREDITS)	ORDER
2	1901	MACDONALD	AGNES HUNT	F	4	CAMBUSLANG	GLASGOW CITY/LANARK	627/00 005/00 006	VIEW (5 CREDITS)	ORDER
3	1901	MACDONALD	ALLAN	M	0	CAMBUSLANG	GLASGOW CITY/LANARK	627/00 005/00 006	VIEW (5 CREDITS)	ORDER
4	1901	MACDONALD	DAVID	M	51	CAMBUSLANG	GLASGOW CITY/LANARK	627/00 005/00 025	VIEW (5 CREDITS)	ORDER
5	1901	MACDONALD	DUNCAN	M	41	CAMBUSLANG	GLASGOW CITY/LANARK	627/00 001/00 001	VIEW (5 CREDITS)	ORDER
6	1901	MACDONALD	FLORA	F	3	CAMBUSLANG	GLASGOW CITY/LANARK	627/00 005/00 006	VIEW (5 CREDITS)	ORDER
7	1901	MACDONALD	JANET M	F	26	CAMBUSLANG	GLASGOW CITY/LANARK	627/00 003/00 049	VIEW (5 CREDITS)	ORDER
8	1901	MACDONALD	JOHN	M	35	CAMBUSLANG	GLASGOW CITY/LANARK	627/00 005/00 005	VIEW (5 CREDITS)	ORDER
9	1901	MACDONALD	MARGARET WATT	F	12	CAMBUSLANG	GLASGOW CITY/LANARK	627/00 005/00 005	VIEW (5 CREDITS)	ORDER
10	1901	MACDONALD	MARY	F	8	CAMBUSLANG	GLASGOW CITY/LANARK	627/00 005/00 006	VIEW (5 CREDITS)	ORDER
11	1901	MACDONALD	SUSAN	F	41	CAMBUSLANG	GLASGOW CITY/LANARK	627/00 001/00 001	VIEW (5 CREDITS)	ORDER

Figure 12-4 ScotlandsPeople search results listing

surname in an urban area. Absence of the relationship and marital status fields here makes it impossible to identify whether a woman is using a maiden name or a married name. The only additional information given is the GROS reference (see p. 203).

At this point you can either choose to view the next page of results if there is more than one, or view the census image for an individual. (Although you can also order an 'extract', i.e. an officially certified copy of a census page, there is no reason to do this; it is really meant for ordering certificates from entries in the civil registration indexes.) Unlike many other sites, there is no page showing a transcription of the full record. Viewing the image is the only way to see occupation and birthplace information.

If you have already viewed an image, it will say 'View (paid)' instead of 'View (5 credits)' and you will be able to view the image again without further payment.

Unlike most other census data services, ScotlandsPeople does not recognize the unit of the household – there is no option to view all members of a household except by looking at the census page; if your family is at the end of a page, you need to check visually on the image whether or not there is an 'end of household' marker (see p. 124) after the last person or whether the household continues on the next page.

ScotlandsPeople provides only a person search. There is no facility to search for an address, nor can you use the site to locate a page image directly from a page reference. This means you cannot use search results from Ancestry's Scottish census indexes (see p. 123) to find a page image without going via the person search. However, if you already have an Ancestry subscription, there's a good case for using both sites in some instances: Ancestry's search can give you much more precise information about an individual than the search results listing on ScotlandsPeople (Figure 12-4) and, with a common name, it may be worth doing an initial search on Ancestry, so that you know the age and census location. With this information, you stand a much better chance of being able to keep the number of pages of search results on ScotlandsPeople down to one.

The search facilities for the 1881 census are different from the other years, because it is based on the pre-internet 1881 Census Index, described on p. 109. First, instead of county/city + district, the place fields are address and census place. Second, it also has a birthplace field. Finally, the search form allows you to leave the surname field blank, as long as you enter something in the address field. This means that the 1881 census is the only one on the site for which there is an address search. However, there are no images for this census on the site.

Figure 12-5 shows the search process for ScotlandsPeople.

The site keeps a permanent record of all the search results and images you have viewed, and this remains accessible whether or not you have any credits remaining. Once you have logged in, all the pages on the site have a 'Previous Searches' link near the top which brings up a list of the searches you have previously carried out – see Figure 12-6 (p. 202). Clicking on the 'View' link takes you to your original list of results, and indicates which records you have already viewed and which can therefore be viewed again without payment. Fields at the foot of the page allow you to filter your search by surname or location.

The previous searches can be saved to your computer in four different formats: PDF, Excel spreadsheet, CSV (comma separated values) for import into a spreadsheet or database, and plain text. This makes it easy to keep a complete list of all your searches on your computer

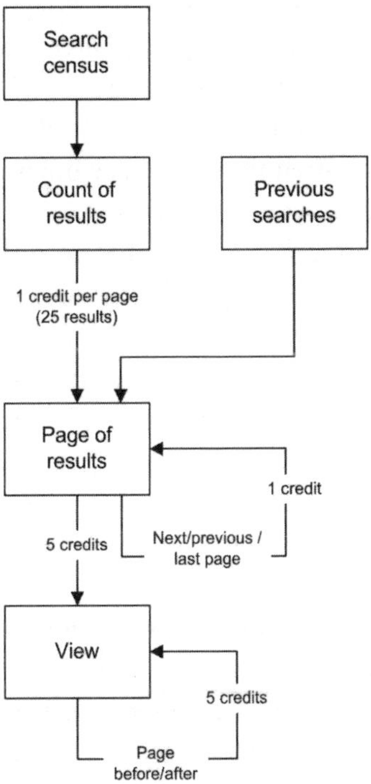

Figure 12-5 ScotlandsPeople search flow

Previous Searches

? Display as report Export as PDF file Export as Excel file Export as Spreadsheet file Export as Text file

1 2 3 4

Type	From	To	Page	Name	Sex	Location	Performed		
⊟ 08/10/2006									
Testament	01/01/1513	31/12/1901	1	FORRESTER, ROBERT*			19:22:48	VIEW	DELETE
Testament	01/01/1513	31/12/1901	1	FORRESTER			19:19:06	VIEW	DELETE
⊟ 20/06/2006									
Census	01/01/1871	31/12/1871	1	DOUGALL, CATHERINE		PARTICK	15:34:26	VIEW	DELETE
Census	01/01/1871	31/12/1871	1	DOUGALL, CATHERINE			15:32:31	VIEW	DELETE
OPR Marriage	01/01/1840	31/12/1854	1	DOUGALL			15:24:21	VIEW	DELETE
Census	01/01/1861	31/12/1861	1	FORRESTER, DAVID*			15:17:49	VIEW	DELETE
⊟ 19/06/2006									
SRI Death	01/01/1920	31/12/1920	1	MCCURRY, CHARLOTTE*			12:59:47	VIEW	DELETE

Figure 12-6 ScotlandsPeople saved searches

without logging in to the site. This does not download the actual search results, just the details you entered in the search form. To save the search results you would need to copy and paste the text from the results page.

Images

ScotlandsPeople has the most sophisticated set of image options of any of the commercial data services. On the Account Details page for your username you can choose between three different image viewers and six different levels of image compression.

For the compression levels, you should ensure that it is set to 'none', though in fact we could detect no difference in the file size of downloaded images between the 'high' compression setting and 'none'. Higher compression means lower quality, so it is best avoided. If you are connecting to the internet via a dial-up modem it might make a difference to your download speeds, but that is the only advantage of higher compression.

Another option is to have 'Descriptions In Images'. When this option is ticked, each image will have above it the name of the individual you searched for along with the piece, folio and page number, and this remains part of the image when you download. This means that each image automatically has the full reference attached to it so you know what to quote when using the image as a source in your family tree.

The viewer options are: direct download, Java Applet, ActiveX viewer. Direct download will work with any browser – it simply downloads the image to your hard disk. ActiveX is a feature of Internet Explorer and is not available with other browsers. The Java Applet option will work if your computer has Java installed and your browser has Java enabled. ScotlandsPeople recommends that Internet Explorer users choose the ActiveX option as the image will appear more quickly.

A link from the account page allows you to test the various options and see whether they work with your browser. If the Java Applet does not work, you can install it from <**java.com**>, which also has an option to test whether Java is installed on your computer. If it is already installed but not working in your browser, then your browser may not have Java enabled (this is sometimes done for security reasons). In Firefox, the option to enable Java will be found under Tools → Options → Content. In Internet Explorer under Tools → Internet Options → Programs → Manage addons.

There is further information about the image viewing options in the help section of the site: click on the 'Help & Other Resources' tab, select 'Technical Information', then 'Viewing Images'. It is well worth reading this before you start searching, to make sure you will be able to see an image the first time you select one for viewing.

Figure 12-7 (see p. 204) shows the Java viewer (with a page listing the one-year-old Arthur Conan Doyle in Edinburgh, 1861). The buttons along the top of the viewer allow for saving, printing and zooming. The remaining buttons are unlikely to be useful for the census images. The 'View Free Header' button is useful – it brings up (free of charge) an image of the front page of the enumeration district, which provides a description of the area the district covers.

The images themselves are black and white scans in TIFF format with a resolution of about 200dpi. This quality represented a necessary compromise when the site first launched in 2002 and download speeds were a fraction of what they are now.

But it now compares poorly in terms of legibility with the 300dpi greyscale scans available on some of the other data services. Now that the site has indexed and digitized all the censuses, it is perhaps time to look again at image quality. These issues are discussed in more detail in Chapter 14 (p. 221).

Unlike Origins, which also uses TIFF images (see p. 192), ScotlandsPeople does not offer any alternative file format for saving

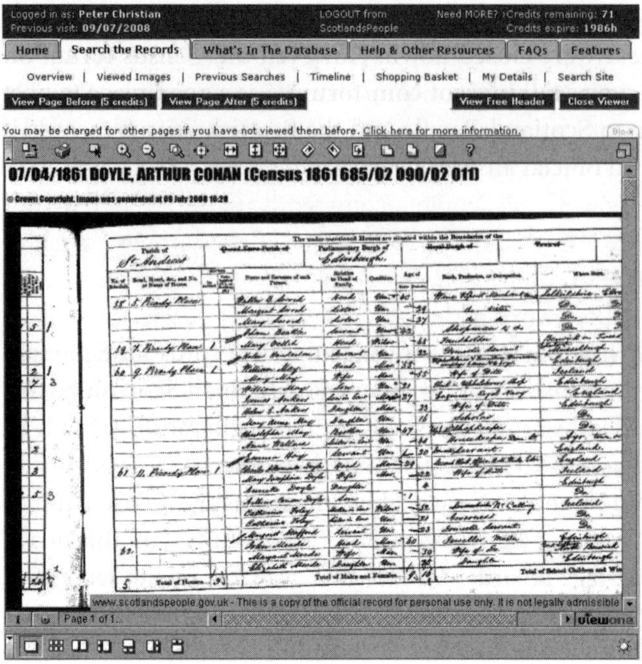

Figure 12-7 ScotlandsPeople Java viewer

images. However, any graphics software, whether a fully fledged graphics editor such as Photoshop or a simple image viewer like IrfanView or ACDSee, should be able to save a TIFF file in some other format.

Help and feedback

There are two places to look for help on the site: the FAQs and the Help & Other Resources area. Each of these is accessible by clicking on its tab at the top of the page. The FAQs are mostly about how the site works and provide brief answers to common queries about the records and indexes. The Help & Other Resources pages are more detailed and some of the most useful contents have already been mentioned, such as those relating to names and handwriting. This is the place to look for broader guidance rather than quick answers to basic questions.

There are no links to dedicated error reporting forms from the search results or image pages, but the 'Contact Us' link at the bottom of every page leads you eventually (after two more links) to a general form to report a problem.

The site originally had its own discussion forums, but after a number of problems these were closed down. However, the Census forum on TalkingScot at <**www.talkingscot.com/forum/**> is a good place to post queries relating to ScotlandsPeople and the Scottish census records if you don't need an official answer.

Other resources

ScotlandsPeople holds all the main genealogical records for Scotland. In addition to the censuses, it provides indexes to all Scottish births, marriages and deaths from the start of civil registration (which in Scotland was 1855) up to 2006. For the older records, images of the original registration books are available. It also has indexes to Church of Scotland parish registers 1553–1854, with images of the birth, baptism and marriage records. All these are available on the same pay-per-view basis as the census records and credits can be used to view any of the records.

The 'Features' area has biographies of over 100 famous Scots, and some are accompanied by images of their testaments, though there seem to be no links to the census entries or civil registration records. The 'Research Tools' area offers help if you have difficulty deciphering a word or an individual letter, as well as a glossary of occupations.

Future developments

The obvious questions about the future of census data on ScotlandsPeople are whether and when the 1881 census images will be added, and whether the current images will be replaced with superior versions. At the time of writing, there was no information about the possibility of either development (future plans for the site will normally be mentioned in the minutes of the User Group meetings – follow the link from the Help page). However, it does seem likely that the site will be affected by the impending loss of its monopoly, and these are two obvious enhancements that could blunt the challenge from new competitors.

The 1911 census for Scotland should be available on the site in April 2011 or shortly thereafter (Chapter 13, p. 213).

Case study 7 – The Lancasters

Throughout most of the recent history of the British Isles, the border between England and Scotland has presented a relatively minor obstacle to our ancestors in their search for work. Movement across the border has usually been a two-way affair and the census returns can be a very useful tool when it comes to tracking the migrations, providing a wealth of clues to follow up in other sources.

Ernest Frederick Lancaster was born on 1 April 1892 in Milton Street, Edinburgh. His parents, Edward James Lancaster and Rose (née Smith), had married the year before, just a few months after the 1891 census was taken.

Tracing the family through the Scottish censuses in the latter half of the nineteenth century is a fairly straightforward process. In 1901 the Lancasters (Edward, Rose and three children, Ernest, John and Edward) were living in the Canongate district of Edinburgh. Edward was a 31-year-old jeweller's salesman, and gave his place of birth as Cockpen in Midlothian.

Ten years earlier, the 1891 census finds Edward living at 241 Causewayside, Edinburgh, with his mother Agnes, sister Edith and brother Fred. His age is consistent with the age given in 1901, but this time his place of birth appears as Gorebridge, Midlothian. Further research reveals that this is only a minor discrepancy – Gorebridge (in the parish of Temple) and Cockpen are only a few miles apart – but it serves as a good example of the potential problems that birthplaces can present.

Agnes Lancaster's place of birth is given simply as 'England'. The enumerator's instructions were to record just the country of birth for people born outside Scotland (the same rule also applied in the censuses for the other parts of the UK), so this is not unusual. But it's interesting to note that whereas Edward's sister was born in Scotland (Hurlford, near Kilmarnock in Ayrshire), his brother was born in England. There's clear evidence here that the Lancaster family were moving back and forth between Scotland and England.

The 1881 census sheds a bit more light on this. The family were living at 3 Emily Place, Edinburgh, and consisted at the time of Agnes and five of her children: Mary Elizabeth, Edith Teresa, Agnes Gertrude, Frederick William, and finally Edward James, aged 11. Again, Edward's place of birth is given as

Gorebridge and Agnes's and Frederick's as 'England', while the three girls are all shown as having been born in Kilmarnock.

In both the 1881 and 1891 censuses, Agnes is listed as the 'Head' of the household, but also as 'married' rather than 'widowed', which suggests that her husband was still alive but living elsewhere. Sadly, the explanation is that he was a patient in Edinburgh's Royal Asylum for the Insane: he died there in 1893.

In 1871 the Lancaster family were living at Byrnhead, Bonnyrigg, in the parish of Cockpen. The head of the household was Edward Lancaster, a mining engineer. Also in the house were Agnes, their children Edith Teresa, Frederick William and Edward James, and a 'general servant'. Frederick, like Agnes, was born in England. The entry in the 1871 census and, indeed, Edward's birth certificate confirm that he was born in Cockpen and not, as the 1881 and 1891 censuses had suggested, Gorebridge.

Moving back to 1861, we find the family living in England – in the Lancashire township of Winstanley (RG 9/2782 f. 7 p. 7). We now get Edward and Agnes's precise places of birth (Radcliffe and Liverpool respectively) while the birthplace of their three daughters is given simply as 'Scotland'. They had evidently only recently moved down from Scotland, as we know from the later censuses that the youngest daughter, Agnes Gertrude, was born in Kilmarnock around 1860.

Although their first three children were born in Scotland, Edward Lancaster and Agnes Blount were married in Liverpool. The marriage took place on 24 July 1852 just over a year after the 1851 census was taken.

The whereabouts of Edward's father, William Lancaster, at the time of the 1851 and 1861 censuses is unknown. In 1851 his wife Elizabeth was living in Ince near Wigan with a large family consisting of five children (including our Edward aged 19), her husband's widowed mother, Rachel, two of his siblings and, finally, two servants (HO 107/2200 f. 62 p. 46–7). The youngest of the five children, Amelia, was aged just three months so it seems likely that William was still around at the time: the presence of his mother in the household would certainly tend to suggest that he was. Ten years later, in 1861, Elizabeth was living on the Isle of Man with three unmarried daughters, a grandson and a whole host of visitors. Elizabeth Lancaster is described as married but again there's no sign of William. Her occupation is given as 'Independent', suggesting that she had some sort of private income (RG 9/4412).

By 1871, Elizabeth is back in England, now living in Withington but, once more, with a large family comprising three of her children, a niece (who was born in Wales), two grandchildren and a servant (RG 10/3974 f. 7 p .7). Elizabeth is described as a widow, so whatever had happened to William since our last sighting of him, he was apparently dead by 1871. The explanation behind William's disappearance lies beyond the reach of the census.

Elizabeth, however, was on the move again. In 1881, aged 71, she was living in Hucknall, Nottinghamshire, where she was accompanied by three unmarried children, a grandson and a servant girl (RG 11/3333 f. 130 p. 24). This was the last census to record Elizabeth: she died in Salford in 1889.

The presence of at least one servant in each of the censuses provides ample evidence that the Lancaster family were not by any means poor – they were a fairly typical middle-class family with an agricultural background (William's father, John Lancaster, was a farmer). Like many similar families in the industrial north, they were nonconformists – William was baptized at the Union Street Wesleyan Methodist Chapel in Bury in 1812 – but what is remarkable about the Lancasters is their mobility.

From their early nineteenth-century roots in south Lancashire, the family moved extensively around the country, making their homes in such far-flung places as Nottinghamshire, Ayrshire, Paisley, Edinburgh, North Wales and the Isle of Man. But it's important to note that the moves that they made weren't necessarily permanent. Edward Lancaster did eventually settle in Scotland, as did his uncle, James, while his brother, William Henry, stayed in Nottinghamshire after his mother died, but Elizabeth herself seems to have spent most of her life on the move. It's somewhat ironic therefore that she eventually died just a few miles from where she had been born nearly eighty years earlier.

13

THE 1911 CENSUS ONLINE

Earlier chapters cover all the online censuses available as of summer 2008, but they will be joined in 2009 by the 1911 census for England and Wales. Chapter 2 looked at the 1911 census as a whole; the present chapter looks at the digitization project.

Information about this project (where it is not already in the public domain) has been provided by the 1911 Census site's development team and is, inevitably, subject to change before launch. Screenshots are taken from work in progress and the final design and features may be different from what is shown here.

In the wake of the Information Commissioner's decision that some access to the 1911 census should be permitted before the expiry of the 100-year closure period, The National Archives announced in December 2006 that it would digitize the 1911 census of England and Wales and offer an online service from 2009, with 'key sensitive information' withheld until 2012.[1] In 2007 the contract for the project was awarded to Scotland Online (now called Brightsolid), the company behind ScotlandsPeople (see Chapter 12).[2] With the subsequent takeover of Findmypast by Brightsolid in 2008, Findmypast became involved in the project.

The 1911 Census site is already up and running at <**www.1911census.co.uk**> with basic information about the project. As this book goes to press, the site provides basic information about the 1911 census and its digitization, and you can register to receive updates on its progress. The data will start to become available on the site in 2009. In order to avoid the problems which might be caused by heavy initial demand, such as led to the crash of the 1901 Census site (see p. 81), the plan is to release the data in stages, region by region, starting with the major urban areas. No date has been given for completion, but presumably it will be by the end of 2009.

Although some sensitive information in the census cannot be

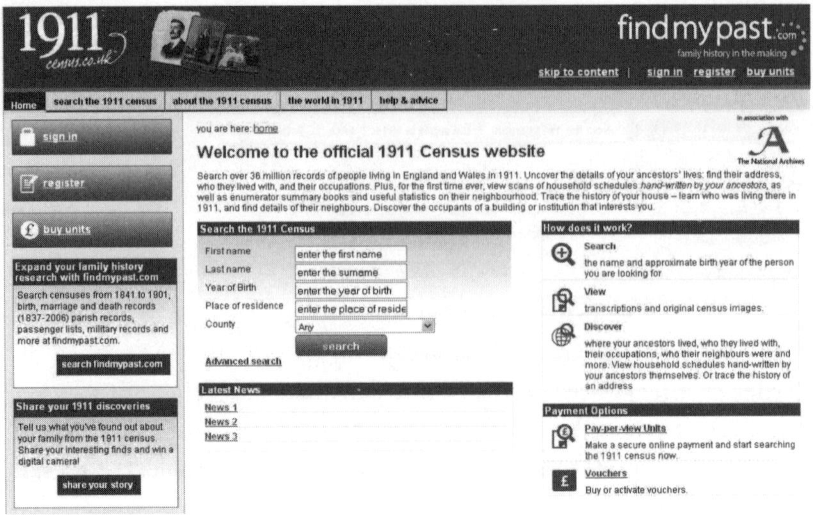

Figure 13-1 Provisional home page for the 1911 census (July 2008)

published at all until 2012, in line with the Information Commissioner's requirements, restrictions will in fact affect relatively few records. According to the minutes of the meeting of the Family Records Centre User Group in January 2007, 'information defined as confidential, or sensitive personal data would be redacted, e.g. details of infirmity or other health-related information; information about family relationships which would usually have been kept secret; and information about very young children who were born in prison.'[3] This means, for example, that any information on disabilities in Column 15 of Form A will be obscured until January 2012.

The 1911 Census site will work on a pay-per-view basis though there is no firm information on the charging regime as yet and there is likely to be a voucher option. There will also be free access in the National Archives.

From the provisional design of the search page, shown in Figure 13-2, you can see that there will be a comprehensive set of search options, with pretty well all the fields in the original records searchable. There are separate person and address searches; searching by TNA reference is provided on the person search form, and there will be a facility to list other household members to be included in the search.

Initially, the digital images will be available only on the 1911 Census site, but they will subsequently be available for licensing to other commercial data services, who will then be able to create their own

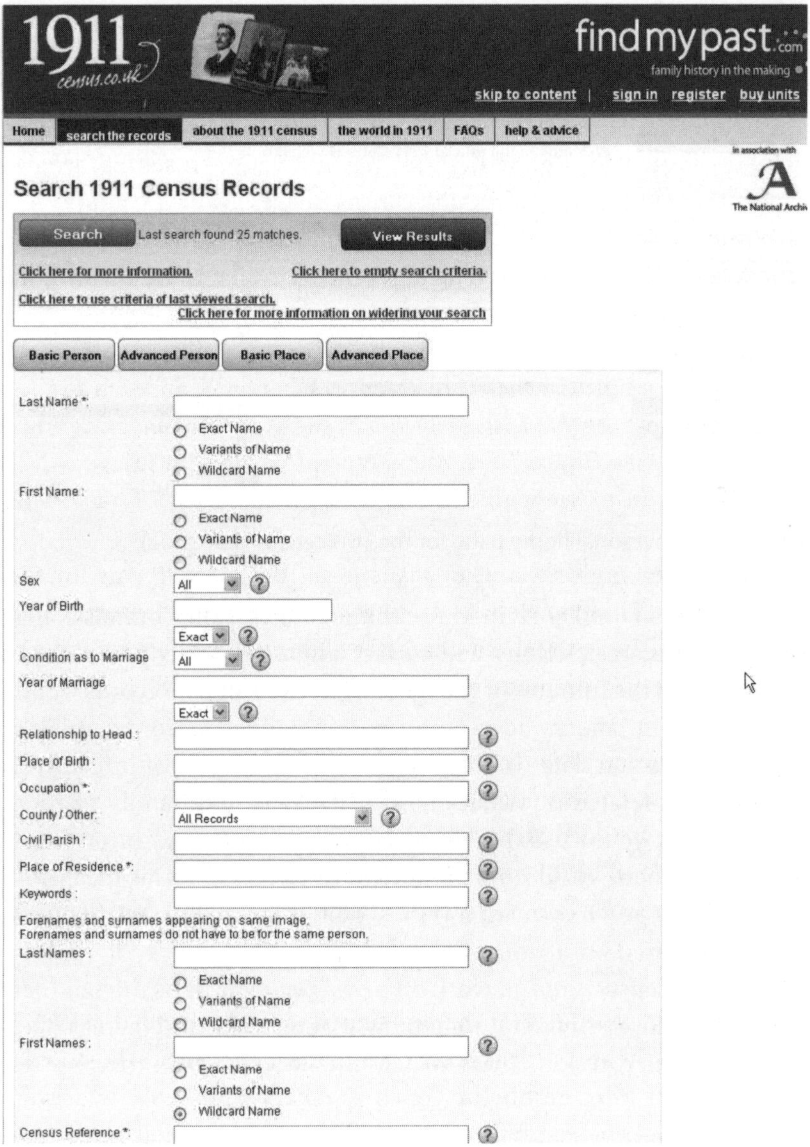

Figure 13-2 1911 census provisional search page (July 2008)

indexes. This will not be until at least six months after the complete release of the census, but presumably we can expect other sites to be offering the 1911 census by some time in 2010. Findmypast, which is owned by Brightsolid, has already indicated that it will be offering the 1911 census on a subscription basis as part of the site's Explorer subscription package (see p. 138).

Unlike earlier censuses, which were digitized from existing microfilms, the digital scans of the 1911 census have been made directly from the original documents and are therefore in colour rather than greyscale. The images have been scanned as TIFF files at 300dpi, and although the graphics format for online delivery has not yet been settled, we can expect these to be the best quality census images available online.

While earlier censuses are represented solely by the enumeration schedules, for the 1911 census the documents available are the original household returns (one per household) along with the Enumerator's Summary Books (ESBs) for the whole Enumeration District (see pp. 44–5). Examples of these are given in Chapter 2, and you can see further examples on the Irish 1911 Census site at <**www.census.nationalarchives.ie**> (see Chapter 15). The payment to view an image will in fact entitle you to view all the images associated with a particular address.

You can see high resolution scans of all the blank forms for this census on the Histpop website at <**www.histpop.org**>. Unfortunately the URL for these is a real 180-character nightmare, so here are longer-winded but less error-prone instructions on how to get there:

1. From the home page click on the 'Browse' tab.
2. Click on the arrow to the left of 'TNA Census – Other'.
3. From the expanded menu, click on '1911'.
4. Click on the 'Table of contents' link in the row 'TNA Census – Other – 1911 – Great Britain. Census of England, Wales and Islands in the British Seas, 1911.'

The household schedules for the 1911 census were also printed in Welsh. According to the 1911 census report, around 8.5 per cent of the population of Wales were monoglot Welsh speakers[4] and those who were heads of household might be expected to complete their household schedule in that language. The fields this affects are mainly those for relationship and occupation, which will naturally use Welsh vocabulary. The birthplace field will also tend to have the Welsh forms of place names (these are sometimes identical to the English forms but often not). As far as the search facilities go, Welsh entries in the relationship field will not affect searches on this field. However, place names in the birthplace field pose a much greater problem and it is not yet clear how the index will deal with these.

Welsh terms for occupations can be looked up in the online Welsh–English/English–Welsh dictionary created by the Department of Welsh, University of Wales, Lampeter, at <**www.geiriadur.net**>. For place names, you can consult the National Gazetteer of Wales at <**homepage.ntlworld.com/geogdata/ngw/places.htm**>. Where a place in Wales has an entry in the English Wikipedia at <**en.wikipedia.org**>, the Welsh form of the name will usually be given in the first line of the article. You could even try the Welsh language Wikipedia at <**cy.wikipedia.org**> – it has a list of Welsh town names at <**cy.wikipedia.org/wiki/ Rhestr_trefi_Cymru**>.

Alongside the official 1911 Census site, there are two other dedicated sites that may be of interest. <**1911census.org.uk**> is a personal site that offers basic information about the 1911 census and a message board. 1911 Census Info at <**www.1911census.info**> provides a facility for those who have paid for access to the 1911 entries for a specific address to post the results of their enquiry. It currently contains details of around 90 individuals.

There is already a mailing list devoted to the 1911 census at RootsWeb: UK-1911-CENSUS. Details and an archive of past messages are at <**lists.rootsweb.ancestry.com/index/other/Census-UK/UK-1911-CENSUS.html**>.

Scotland

As of July 2008, no formal announcement has been made about the release of the 1911 census in Scotland, but the minutes of the ScotlandsPeople User Group (all linked from <**www.scotlandspeople.gov.uk/content/help/index.aspx?r=551&973**> or, from the home page, click on 'Help & Other Resources', then 'User Group') make it clear that plans are under way for it to be made available at ScotlandsPeople in April 2011, when the 100-year closure period expires.

Scotland's Freedom of Information Act is different from that which applies to England and Wales, and specifically excludes census records. For that reason, the legal challenge which has led to the earlier release of the census for England and Wales could not succeed in Scotland. The ScotlandsPeople User Group minutes are the obvious place to look for up-to-date information as the project develops.

The availability of wider licensing for Scottish genealogical records (see p. 85) suggests that at some point in the future, perhaps by 2012, the 1911 census for Scotland might be available on other commercial data services.

Ireland

The 1911 census for Ireland is already in the process of being put online – see Chapter 15.

NOTES

1 The announcement is at <**www.nationalarchives.gov.uk/documents/13dec2006.pdf**>.

2 The press release is at <**www.nationalarchives.gov.uk/news/stories/156.htm**>.

3 <**www.familyrecords.gov.uk/frc/your_frc/ug-24-01-07.htm**>. This wording is based directly on the advice contained in the Information Commissioner's decision which led to the early release of the 1911 census, which can be consulted at <**www.ico.gov.uk/upload/documents/decisionnotices/2006/101391_dn_rt_changes.pdf**>.

4 The relevant section of the report is reproduced on the website of the Welsh Language Board at <**www.byig-wlb.org.uk/English/publications/Publications/638.pdf**>.

14

THE WEBSITES COMPARED

The obvious question which arises from the survey of commercial census data sites in the previous chapters is: which one should you choose? Of course, you may want to stick to free sites, initially at least, but these are unlikely to offer census images for the foreseeable future, so they can provide no verification for the entries in their indexes.

Unfortunately, there is no simple answer to this question, and even if there was at the time of writing, there can be no guarantee it would still hold by the time you are reading this – all the commercial census sites are constantly adding to their data holdings, extending their search facilities, correcting errors found in the data, improving image quality and viewing facilities, all in an effort to keep existing customers happy and get new ones.

Also, of course, your own requirements and budget will play a role in making one service preferable to another. If you can access one service free of charge at a public library, for example, any shortcomings of that service may be relatively insignificant compared to the savings involved.

However, it *is* possible to discuss the issues to be considered in deciding which of the commercial sites to use:

- coverage
- price and payment options
- search options
- index quality
- image quality
- support for full references.

Coverage

Table 14-1 shows which census years and regions the main commercial services offer, along with FamilySearch.

	Years complete	Regions	Notes
Ancestry	1841–1901	England and Wales, Scotland, CI, IoM	Scotland: index only
Findmypast	1841, 1861–1891	England and Wales, CI, IoM	1901 in progress 1881: free index, no images
TheGenealogist and RootsUK	1841–1871, 1891, 1901	England and Wales	Also London 1881 images
GenesReunited & 1901censusonline	1841–1871, 1891, 1901	England and Wales, CI, IoM	
Origins	1841, 1861, 1871	England and Wales, CI, IoM	
ScotlandsPeople	1841–1901	Scotland	1881: no images
FamilySearch	1841, 1861, 1881	England, Wales, CI, IoM	No images

Table 14-1 Coverage of commercial services

If you have Scottish ancestors, you will inevitably use ScotlandsPeople until data for Scotland starts to appear, with images, on other sites. Otherwise, Ancestry has the most complete coverage.

Charges

Full details of the charges for the various sites will be found in the seven preceding chapters. Table 14-2 summarizes the main options and their costs. The subscription column always gives the best-value subscription (i.e. the cheapest pro rata), but there are usually also shorter term subscriptions available at higher rates. The pay-per-view column lists the minimum purchases – larger purchases are sometimes cheaper pro rata, sometimes not.

'Best value' here is not simply a matter of relative prices. On the

	Subscription	Pay-per-view	Cost per search/image (in credits)	Notes
Ancestry	£79.95 p.a.	£6.95 for 12 record views (14 days)	0/1 (i.e. 58p)	Free trial available
Findmypast	£89.95 p.a	£6.95 for 20 credits (90 days)	1/1 (i.e. 35p)	
TheGenealogist	£68.95 p.a.	£14.95 for 75 credits	1/3 (i.e. 20p/60p)	Advanced searches 2 or 3 credits
RootsUK		£5 for 100	5/5 (i.e. 25p)	
GenesReunited		£5 for 50 credits	5/5 (i.e. 50p)	
1901censusonline		£5 for 500 credits	50/75 (i.e. 50/75p)	
Origins	£47.00 p.a.			
ScotlandsPeople		£6 for 30 credits (90 days)	1/5 (20p/£1)	Each page of results charged

Table 14-2 Charges for the main commercial census sites

subscription sites, your payment will entitle you to search all datasets, so one of the things you will need to look at is what other data the sites have which would be useful to you. On the pay-per-view sites, there is one very significant issue which is not apparent simply from the prices: the amount of information you get in your search results. On some sites, this is normally detailed enough for you to identify which is the entry you are looking for. On sites where it isn't you may end up using more credits because you need to check several details pages or images to find the right person. See the chapters on the individual services for details.

Search options

Table 14-3 summarizes the search options for all the commercial sites, as well as two free sites, the National Archives of Ireland and the 1881 Census Index at FamilySearch. Where a site has an advanced search, it

	Ancestry	Findmypast	TheGeneal-ogist	RootsUK	Genes Reunited	1901 census		Origins	Scotlands People	Ireland	1881
	Advanced	Advanced	Advanced	Advanced	Standard	1901 advanced	1841-91 standard	Standard	Standard	Standard	Standard
Name fields	2	3	2	2	2	3	2	2	2	2	2
Name variants	Custom	NameX	Custom	Custom	Wildcards only	Wildcards only	Wildcards only	NameX	Soundex		Custom
Age	Year	Year	Age	Age or year	Year	Year	Year	Age range	Age range	Age	Year
Birthplace	✔	✔	County	Place	✔	✔		County/ country			County
Residence	1 field, more addable	8 fields	County, district, address	County	Keywords	10 fields	Keywords	County, parish	County or city, district	County, district, street	Country, county, town
Occupation		✔	✔	✔							
Gender	✔	✔			✔	✔			✔	✔	
Marital status		✔									
Relation to head		✔	✔								
Family members	4 fields	1 member	Separate family fore-name search						1 additional forename		Head
Keyword	✔		Separate keyword search								
Address search	Yes – by leaving name field blank	Separate address search	Separate address search			Separate address search	Separate address search (beta)			Browse	
Reference		Separate ref. search									

is the details for this that have been given, in preference to the standard search. Even if you are a relative beginner and feel overwhelmed by some of the more comprehensive search forms, eventually you will be glad of them!

In principle, of course, the more search fields the better, because you then have more options for finding someone if a basic search on name, age and residence doesn't do the trick. But some of these fields are more useful than others. Lack of an occupation search field is not really a significant limitation; lack of a birthplace field is a considerable drawback.

We would suggest that the best suite of search facilities would include, in order of importance:

1. Some sort of surname matching beyond wildcards and Soundex (see chapter 5, p. 99).
2. Possibility of including a range of place names.
3. Ability to search for other family members.
4. Address search.

On that basis, Ancestry, Findmypast and TheGenealogist come off best in Table 14-3.

Index quality

While it's easy enough to compare the sites on the basis of their search facilities, and to find individual errors in the indexes, assessing the overall quality of a site's indexing is much more difficult.

There are a number of reasons for this difficulty. The main one is that differences between the various sites' search facilities mean that comparative searches can only be carried out for a small selection of the many error types. For example, most of the sites do not allow a search on forename only, which makes it impossible to gather any statistics for common forename mis-spellings. Also, many of the mistakes, even though they might be more prevalent in one index or another, are not in any way systematic; they're just a failure to a recognize a surname or a place name.

When the original 1901 census was launched, Jeanne Bunting and John Hanson analysed a complete enumeration book (for Rotherhithe

Table 14-3 (left) Comparison of search facilities

in London) checking for indexing errors. They sent a list of over 900 errors for correction to TNA. When Ancestry subsequently launched a 1901 census index, this too was checked against the originals. Here is what Jeanne had to say about the comparison:

> The Enumeration District consisted of 33 consecutive pages with 969 people. Just taking surname, first name and place of birth…, we sent in [to the PRO] a total of 378 errors (there were about another 150 occupation errors) made up from 63 first names, 192 surnames and 123 places of birth.
> Ancestry, on the other hand, had only 152 errors in total made up from 24 first names, 73 surnames and 55 places of birth. [1]

Although this survey has the limitation of being for a single district (and therefore could be looking at the work of a single transcriber in each case), it does at least suggest what level of error we might expect. The fact that even the better of these two sites had 7½ per cent of surnames misspelled is quite a frightening thought. Certainly, while errors on the part of transcribers are inevitable, it is a pity that quality control is not always as rigorous as it could be. We mentioned in Chapter 4 some of the oversights which marred the 1901 census, and Ancestry, too, has often been criticized for letting readily identifiable errors slip through.

In an attempt to replicate Jeanne and John's analysis for the wider range of indexes now available, we have made available on the website for this book some further statistics:

1. A comparison of the frequency of some typical surname mis-spellings (e.g. *Willaims* for *Williams*) on all the major sites.
2. A detailed examination of the errors found in the indexes at Ancestry, Findmypast and TheGenealogist for two complete enumeration districts:
   a. the 1861 census for Pevensey, Sussex (385 individuals), from a relatively clearly written enumeration book
   b. the 1891 census for part of Islington, London (496 individuals), the original less clearly written and with some idiosyncrasies to trap the unwary transcriber.

Since the other sites for English and Welsh census data all share it with either Findmypast or TheGenealogist, this latter comparison effectively covers all the relevant sites. The tables and some discussion will be found at <**www.spub.co.uk/census/tables/**>.

Although the results for the Pevensey and Islington enumeration books are in some cases better than those for the 1901 sample, they are sometimes very much worse, with error rates up to 40 per cent! And there is no clear winner, either, though the figures will at least give you a flavour of what can happen when census records are transcribed.

Several things emerge clearly from the comparison:

- Even from a single company some parts of the indexes can be very good, and others truly awful.
- The ability to recognize common English surnames and place names is essential for transcribers.
- You can't create a reliable index from a poor quality scan.

All in all, if this doesn't exactly help you decide which data service gives you the best chance of tracking down your ancestors, it certainly underlines the need for flexibility in your approach to searching which we stressed at the end of Chapter 5.

Image quality

An important issue on all sites which offer images is the quality of those images. This is mainly dependent on two things: resolution and colour depth. The reason for its importance is that it affects not just your ability to read the original census page, but that almost always the census indexes have been created from the digital image rather than the microfilms, so poor quality images may correlate with more transcription errors.

All census images seem to have been digitized at effectively 200dpi or 300dpi (that's dots per inch relative to the original documents, not per inch of the 35mm microfilm frame). Other things being equal, higher resolution is always better from the point of view of quality. However, it carries the price of larger files and hence longer download times. When the first census images went online in 2002, it was understandable that the preference was for lower resolution, as almost all users in those days had relatively slow internet connections. Nowadays, this is no longer an issue. The typical 300dpi image file should download in a few seconds over a broadband connection.

Colour depth is the term for how many shades are in the digital image. A typical greyscale scan has 256 shades of grey (strictly 254 grey, plus black and white), which is referred to as 8-bit greyscale ($256 = 2^8$, therefore 8 bits). Pure black and white, however, is 1-bit, so a black and white image will be an eighth of the size of a greyscale image of the same resolution. Again, this was a good reason to use black and white in the early days of online censuses. However, while black and white can be perfectly adequate for some purposes, such as digitizing printed text, it is poor for manuscript historical documents. When a document is digitized in pure black and white, every pixel is either black or white. But of course the document itself is in many shades and more than one colour, so the digitizer has to decide: how light does a mark on the paper have to be before it is regarded as white space and represented as white, and how dark does a mark have to be before it is regarded as part of the text and shown as black? Unfortunately, there is no right answer in the case of handwritten documents on paper which may itself be discoloured. Also, unlike greyscale where the digital image can subsequently be made darker or lighter to bring out contrast, once the shading information has been thrown away in a black and white image there is no way to recover it.

You can see the problem by looking at images of the 1841 census entry for Charles Dickens' household in Devonshire Terrace (HO 107/680, folio 14, district 12, p. 18). Figure 14-1 is the greyscale image;

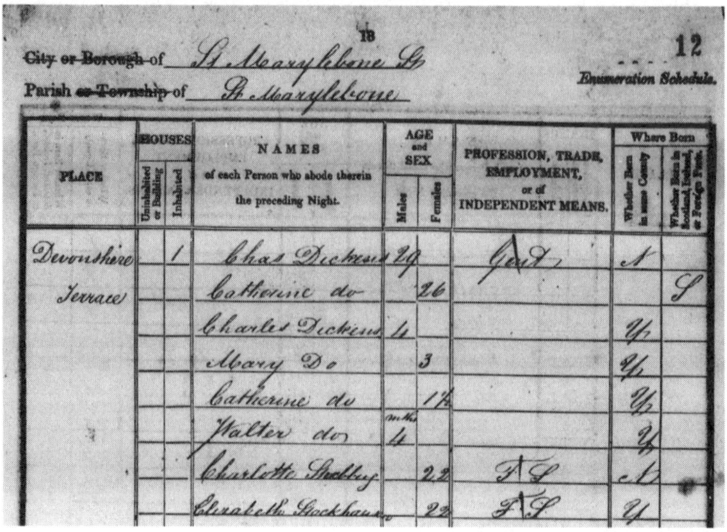
18

12

~~City or Borough~~ of St. Marylebone

~~Parish or Township~~ of St. Marylebone

Enumeration Schedule.

PLACE	HOUSES: Uninhabited or Building	HOUSES: Inhabited	NAMES of each Person who abode therein the preceding Night.	AGE and SEX: Males	AGE and SEX: Females	PROFESSION, TRADE, EMPLOYMENT, or of INDEPENDENT MEANS.	Where Born: Whether Born in same County	Where Born: Whether Born in Scotland, Ireland, or Foreign Parts.
Devonshire Terrace		1	Chas Dickens	29		Gent	N	
			Catherine do		26			S
			Charles Dickens	4			Y	
			Mary Do		3		Y	
			Catherine do		1½		Y	
			Walter do	4 mths			Y	
			Charlotte Shelley		22	F S	N	
			Elizabeth Stockham		22	F S	Y	

Figure 14-1 Greyscale image

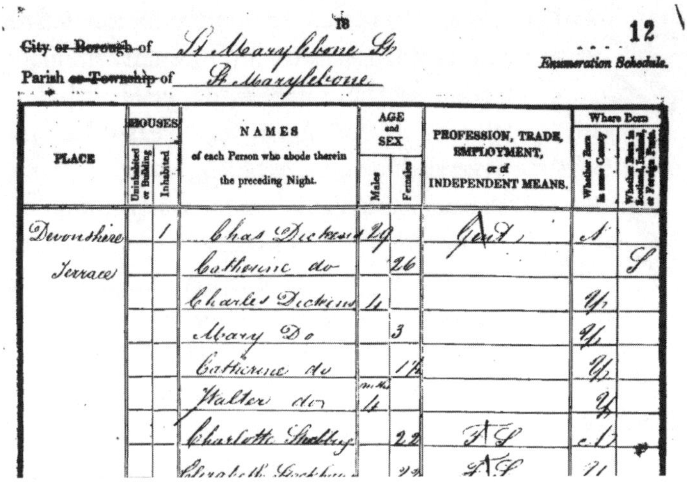

Figure 14-2 Black and white image with high threshold

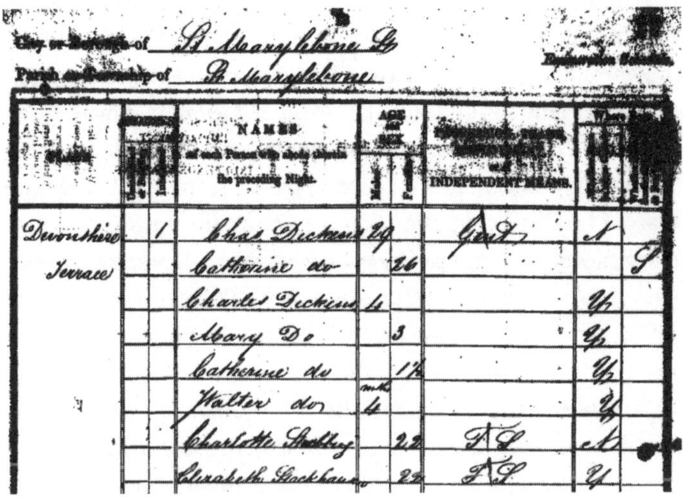

Figure 14-3 Black and white image with low threshold

Figure 14-2 has been converted to black and white with a high threshold, i.e. marks have to be quite dark to be treated as black; Figure 14-3 has been converted to black and white with a low threshold, i.e. marks have to be less dark to be treated as black. As you can see, neither of the black and white images is really satisfactory, with parts of the image too light or dark to be read.

The limitations of black and white are even more obvious if you zoom in on the problematic surname of the first female servant (Figure 14-4).

The lighter black and white image has lost large chunks of the lighter

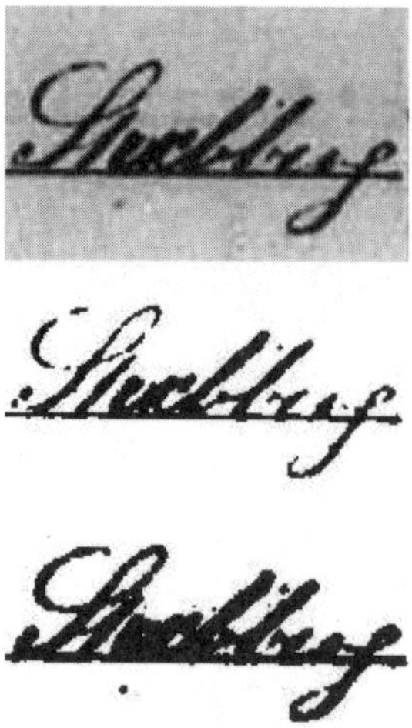

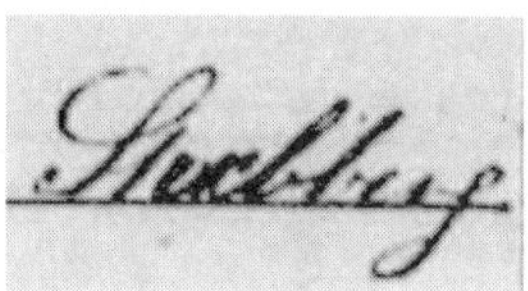

Figure 14-4 (top) Enlarged details of Figures 14-1 to 14-3

Figure 14-5 (bottom) Detail of Figure 14-1, enlarged and enhanced

strokes – look at the flourish on the 'S' and the tail of the 'g': while the darker image preserves these better, the letter or letters after St are completely illegible. Notice how even background marks in the paper (in the greyscale image these are clearly not handwritten) might be mistaken for ink, suggesting the presence of an 'i'. Even on the greyscale image, this name is hard to read, but you certainly have a better chance. And as already mentioned, it's not just a matter of whether you can read it. If the census index was created from the digital images rather than the microfilms, it should be clear which image is likely to give rise to a more reliable transcription. If your interest is in Charles Dickens, then the problem with this servant's name is minor, but if she was your ancestor, she might be hard to find.

Figure 14-5 shows the results of taking the greyscale image and tweaking the exposure level in a graphics editor to reveal details not previously apparent. The fact that the middle letters are 'bb' is now quite clear, though the preceding letters remain problematic.

Table 14-4 compares the image quality for the commercial census sites. Neither colour depth nor resolution is straightforward to specify here, since both are based on downloading sample images from the sites. In the case of the images in PDF format, the exact resolution is not possible to obtain with great accuracy as it is impossible to guarantee that an image extracted from a PDF is the same resolution as the one that was converted to PDF. However, visual inspection suggests this is broadly correct. Also, we cannot promise that we have not overlooked some black and white images on a mainly greyscale site or vice versa.

	Format	**Colour depth**	**Typical resolution (estimated)**
Ancestry	JPG	Greyscale	200dpi
Findmypast	DjVu	Greyscale	300dpi

TheGenealogist	PDF	Older black and white Newer greyscale	200dpi
Genes Reunited	PDF	1841, 1851 greyscale Others black and white	200dpi
Origins	TIFF	Mostly greyscale	300dpi
ScotlandsPeople	TIFF	Black and white	200dpi

Table 14-4 Image quality comparison

References

To include information from census records in your family tree, you need to be able to document the source of your information in a way which allows others to check it and follow it up. It is not enough just to say '1861 census', though in the absence of a full reference the census year and a full address might be adequate.

Although the reference can in principle be read from the scanned image, the folio number is only on alternate pages and the piece number is sometimes missing. Where the folio number is missing on a subscription site, it is simply a matter of looking at the previous page, but on a pay-per-view site this will count as an additional view, which you will have to pay for. But you should not have to pay extra to get an exact reference.

Some sites are better than others at giving you the reference. Those which give full references in the details of an individual are Ancestry, Findmypast, Origins and ScotlandsPeople. TheGenealogist and RootsUK give only the piece numbers reliably, while GenesReunited gives no references, and 1901censusonline only for the 1901 census index. Currently, Findmypast is the only one which actually allows a search on a TNA reference; Ancestry provided this facility on its old search form, but unfortunately it has been removed with the introduction of the new search.

Summary

As we suggested at the beginning of this chapter, there is no simple decision about which of the commercial sites is best. However, in an attempt to simplify your choice we have listed what we regard as the two best features of each, along with the two most significant limitations. Of course, it may be that by the time you are making your choice some of the limitations will no longer apply. Since most sites are making efforts to replace their poorer images with better ones, we have generally not included poor image quality as a limitation (though you may find comments on image quality in the individual chapter about a site).

	Best features	**Limitations**
Ancestry	Completeness of coverage Very flexible person search	Not very transparent ranking system Index quality variable
Findmypast	Good search facilities Good image quality	Special image viewer may give difficulties Some browser oddities
TheGenealogist	Good range of search facilities Good tools for saving searches and results	Need to search county-by-county can be tedious Incomplete TNA references
RootsUK	Very simple to use Link to civil registration search	Very basic search Need to pay for full details in search results
GenesReunited	Simple to use Easy to refine searches	Limited search facilities No TNA references
1901censusonline	Very good search facilities for the 1901 census Results mapping	Insufficient information in search results No TNA references
Origins	Good name matching with NameX Search results sortable	Only thee censuses County only for birthplace
ScotlandsPeople	Completeness of coverage Complete record of search results	Charged listings not informative enough Image quality

Table 14-5 Commercial census sites: best features and limitations

NOTES

1 The original message can be consulted at <**archiver.rootsweb.ancestry.com/th/read/genbrit/2004-04/1082370575**>. It is the start of a lengthy discussion thread and a number of other types of error which were found in the comparison are mentioned in later messages.

15

IRELAND

It is an undeniable and inescapable fact that many of the records that form the basic building blocks of our research into our English, Welsh and Scottish ancestors simply don't exist in Ireland. A combination of the ravages of time, a catastrophic fire and some regrettable decision making by the Irish government of the time means that, for most of us, the prospects of tracing our Irish roots back beyond the nineteenth century are frankly not good.

The legislation which set up the 1801 and 1811 censuses in England, Wales and Scotland made no provision for counting the population of Ireland. Of course, Ireland didn't formally become part of the United Kingdom until 1801 and, following an unsuccessful attempt to hold a census in 1813, it wasn't until 1821 that the first full Irish census was taken.

But after a slow start, things begin to look quite promising: unlike the equivalent census for the rest of the UK, the 1821 census of Ireland asked for names of individuals to be recorded along with their relationships, ages and occupations.

The 1841 census saw a further leap forward: the amount of information requested on each individual was quite phenomenal, particularly when compared with the relatively sparse forms used in England, Wales and Scotland. The householder's schedule included three tables: the first was to record the name, age, sex, relationship, marital status, year of marriage and occupation of each person living in the household at the time. An attempt was also made to gather information on literacy. The second table requested similar information on people who usually lived at that address but were temporarily absent, as well as asking for their place of residence, and, finally, the third table asked for details of all those who had died in the residence of the family completing the form within the previous ten years!

The Irish census continued to expand throughout the nineteenth century with additional questions on sickness and disease, and a wide range of forms being introduced to cover those in institutions and on board ships. Questions about religion also became both a significant part of the census and a matter of some considerable dispute; the predominantly Roman Catholic population was, perhaps understandably, reluctant to provide information which they felt could potentially be used against them by the largely Protestant ruling classes.

The bad news for family historians, of course, is that virtually none of this has survived. It is worth taking a few moments here to explode a popular Irish family history myth. Anyone who knows anything about researching in Ireland will have heard about the fire that destroyed 'all the primary source material' during the fighting at the Four Courts complex in Dublin in 1922. Well, first of all, not everything was destroyed: the Irish birth, marriage and death certificates had never been stored there and those records have survived, intact, from their starting date up until the present day. And most of the 'missing' census returns weren't lost in the conflagration either – the returns for 1861, 1871, 1881 and 1891 had already been destroyed by the government many years earlier. It's true that the pre-1861 censuses were lost, along with all the pre-1858 wills, large numbers of parish registers and a wealth of irreplaceable legal and historical documents, but fragments of these records (including some census returns) have survived and other sources that are unique to Ireland have been preserved and made accessible in an effort to redress the balance.

The good news is that the 1901 and 1911 censuses for the whole of Ireland survive in their entirety and can be seen at the National Archives of Ireland in Dublin (NAI). The Public Record Office of Northern Ireland has copies of the 1901 census returns (but not of the 1911 census returns) for the six counties that became Northern Ireland in 1922.

The situation with the digitization of these records could also hardly be more different from the rest of the British Isles – almost none of the material is online. This is all the more surprising since the 1901 and 1911 censuses for Ireland are not only currently open to the public but have been since the 1960s, which means they *could* have been among the first censuses to be digitized.

In fact, it was not until the end of 2005 that the NAI announced that the two surviving Irish censuses would be digitized under a cultural agreement with Library and Archives Canada.[1] The impetus for the Canadians was the large number of Irish immigrants to Canada and the importance of these records for Canadian family historians. In December 2007, the first fruits of this agreement went online, with the 1911 census of Dublin at <**www.census.nationalarchives.ie**>, which is described in detail below.

With the 2005 announcement promising free access, it is hardly surprising that the commercial data services have not made any move to digitize the Irish material, though Origins has a small amount of material from the Irish CD-ROM publisher Eneclann. However, for many years volunteers have been getting on with making up for the lack of an official digitization programme. The result is a number of small to medium census transcription projects, which also include indexes to some of the few surviving pieces of the nineteenth century censuses.

The National Archives of Ireland census site

So far, only the 1911 census for the City of Dublin has been digitized and indexed. It is available on the NAI's census site at <**www.census.nationalarchives.ie**>. The Dublin data is due to be followed by the rest of the 1911 census, county by county, and then the 1901 census. The order in which the counties will be digitized is published at <**www.census.nationalarchives.ie/about/futureplans.html**>. According to the project description at <**www.census.nationalarchives.ie/about/**> the project is due to be completed by mid-2009. However, since no further data has appeared in the six months since the unveiling of the Dublin data, it may be that this announcement was optimistic.

The site offers two ways to view the census: search and browse. A flowchart for the search process is shown in Figure 15-1 (see p. 230), and Figure 15-2 (see p. 230) shows the initial search form. The census year and county will become selectable once there is more data on the site.

One of the unusual things about the search is that you can leave both of the name fields blank. This means you can easily get a list of all the inhabitants of a street (making it effectively an address search) or even all those in a certain age range (109-year-old Henry Richard McGuiness is the oldest person in the Dublin census, if 109 is not a misreading of 69). The search treats any text you enter as a distinct word to be sought anywhere in the field, so a search for the forename 'John' finds 'Arthur John' and 'Michael John' too. All the text fields accept * as a wildcard, which stands for zero or more characters.

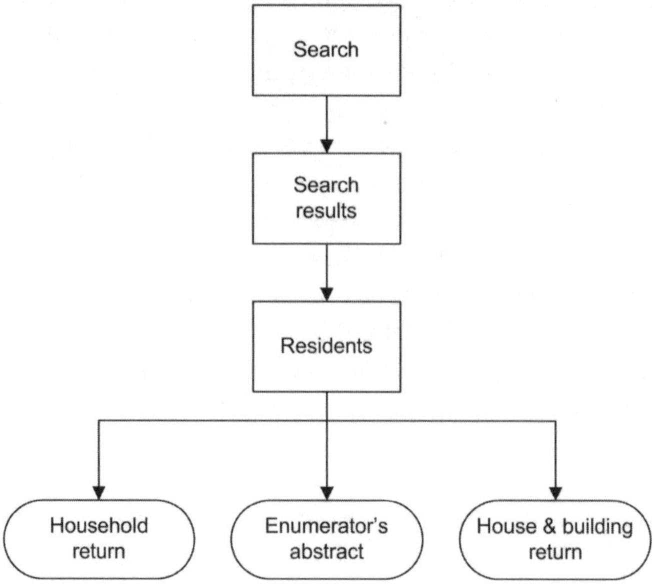

Figure 15-1 NAI census search process

If you enter two or more words in a search field, they are treated as an OR search, i.e. the results will comprise any entry in which any one or more of the words given is found. This gives rise to an unexpected trap if you enter a street name in the Townland/street field: if you search for, say, Iona Road you will find not only the 200 odd entries for Iona Road,

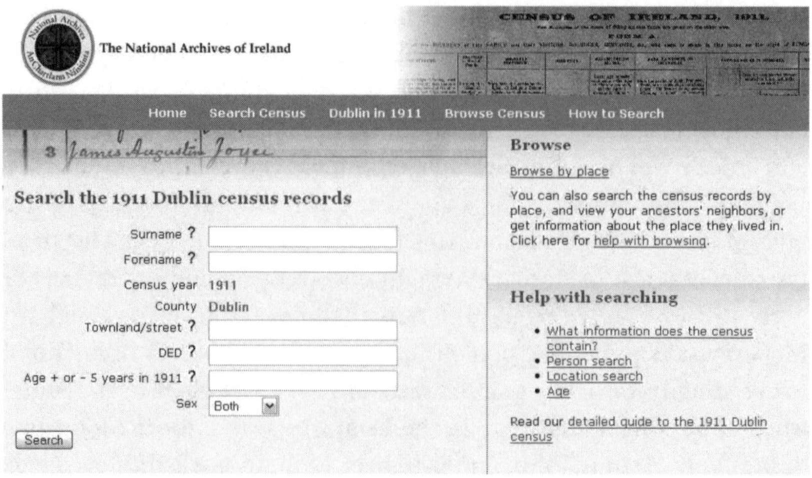

Figure 15-2 Search form for the Irish census

Search results

Displaying results 1 - 14 of 14. Records per page: 10 / **50** / 100

Sort by: Surname / Forename / Age / **Townland or Street** / District Electoral Division (DED)

Surname	Forename	Townland/Street	Age	Sex	DED
O'Brien	Edward	Ballybrack	58	M	Killiney
O'Brien	Edward F	Ballybrack	4	M	Killiney
O'Brien	Edward	Ballybrack	73	M	Killiney
O'Brien	Edward	Castleknock	14	M	Castleknock
O'Brien	Edward	Cork Little	9	M	Rathmichael
O'Brien	Edward J	Drumcondra Road Upper	23	M	Drumcondra
O'Brien	Edward	Fishamble St.	15	M	Wood Quay
O'Brien	Edward	Gracepark Road	19	M	Drumcondra
O'Brien	Edward	Harold's Cross Road	3	M	Rathmines & Rathgar West
O'Brien	Charles Edward	Leinster Avenue	10	M	North Dock Ward
O'Brien	Edward	Malahide Road West Side	9	M	Clontarf West, Part of
O'Brien	Edward D	St. Benedict's Terrace	6	M	Inn's Quay
O'Brien	Edward	St. Lawrence Road	25	M	Clontarf West
O'Brien	Edward	Western Square, Great	24	M	Arran Quay

Figure 15-3 Irish census Search results

but also all those for Iona Park and Iona Drive, which could be useful, not to mention every entry that has the word 'Road' in its street name, which is rather less helpful! You can get around this by omitting the word 'Road' or by putting the whole street name in inverted commas, 'Iona Road'.

Clicking on the 'Search' button at the bottom of the form brings up the first page of search results (see Figure 15-3). As you can see, the contents of the surname, forename, age and sex columns on the census form are given for the individual, as well as the District Electoral Division (DED) and the townland or street of the household. This list is initially sorted by surname, ten records to a page, but you can re-sort by any field except sex, and you can choose to display 50 or 100 results per page. If you have got too many results, the search form is repeated at the bottom of the page so you can refine your search.

You will sometimes see a name (usually male) which has no entry in the age or sex columns. This is not an error, but indicates that this is the name of the head of household entered on the outside of the household schedule by the enumerator (see Figure 15-7, p. 237). It's important to note that these entries will not appear in search results if you specify a gender and age. You might not think this matters, but there is one case where it makes a real difference. As explained later in this chapter, many householders, even in essentially Anglophone Dublin, entered their names in Irish, so you find James Casey recorded as Seámus Ó Cathasigh in the household schedule (as in Figure 15-5, see p. 235). However, the enumerator will have recorded the name in its English form on the outside of the schedule (see Figure 15-7, p. 237). If so, you will not find him if you search for James Casey, age 45, male, whereas if you search for just James Casey he will be included in the search results. Of course you will then need to look at the census image to check his age and make sure he is the person you are looking for.

From the Search results page, clicking on a forename or surname takes you to a listing of the household members (see Figure 15-4). Again, this listing gives only name, age, and sex, and its purpose is really just to help you establish that you have the right household. All the other personal information on the household schedule has not been transcribed and is only to be found in the digital image. The full address of the house is given at the top of the screen.

Below the household listing are links to the various images which have information relating to this household. Don't bother to click on the 'images' link – that just takes you to a page of general information about images on the site. More information about viewing the images is given below.

The browse is organized geographically, by county, then District Electoral Division (DED), then street. For each street, there is a page listing the houses with the surname of the head of household and links to a list of occupants and the image of Form A. For rural areas, the listing will be based on townland rather than street.

The site offers some basic tips on searching on its help page at

Residents of a house 33 in Ballybrack (Killiney, Dublin)

Surname	Forename	Age	Sex
O'Brien	Edward	58	Male
O'Brien	Ellen Frances	30	Female
O'Brien	Thomas W	5	Male
O'Brien	Edward F	4	Male
O'Brien	James F	2	Male
O'Brien	Susan Mary	0	Female
O'Brien	Edward	73	Male

View census images

Use our online form to report errors in transcription of names.

(Click here for help on image contents)

Household Return (Form A), Page 1

(Page 2)

Enumerator's abstract (Form N), Page 1

(Page 2)

Figure 15-4 Irish census household listing

<www.census.nationalarchives.ie/help/help.html>.

According to the help page, the indexes will be rebuilt at two- or three-monthly intervals, and the rebuild will incorporate any verified corrections. On the household page, there is a link to an online form for correcting transcription errors. One type of error we noticed, and which will not be corrected because the error is on the original form, is where both forename and surname have been entered in the forename field. If you can't find a surname, it might be worth trying it out in the forename field.

SURNAMES

One important issue with the Irish census is that surnames with the prefix 'O' (meaning literally 'grandson of', but more generally 'descendant of') are recorded in various ways. So O'Brien is sometimes 'O Brien', sometimes 'OBrien' and sometimes 'O'Brien'. This means there is no way to formulate a *single* search which will find all three forms. Just to make things even harder, there are even a few cases of 'O' Brien'. However, doing a search on 'Brien' alone will find Brien, O Brien and O' Brien. O*Brien finds OBrien and O'Brien. There are around 200 individuals whose surname is recorded with the Gaelic form of the prefix, 'Ua' and more rarely 'Ui'. No doubt there will be many more of these when the Gaeltacht districts are added. The Dublin census has just over 400 females who use the traditional feminine equivalent *Ní* (occasionally without the accent as Ni). In other families the girls have adopted English-style gender-neutral surnames. However, it would be natural to expect wider usage of 'Ní' names in the Gaeltacht, so these forms will probably be much more common in the data for some other counties not yet on the site. You will also see wives in Irish speaking families recorded sometimes as *bean Uí* X (wife of Ó'X), where the husband is called Ó'X. See, for example, Brigidh bean Uí Dhuinn at 5 Allingham Street, whose husband is Micheal Ó Dúinn. There are just over 80 of these in Dublin. In this particular household both parents speak only English, incidentally, and the husband's occupation of 'Ex-Policeman' is given in English, though he signs the Irish form of his name. On the reverse of the form his name is given as Michael Dunne.

With the patronymic prefix Mac, there are three forms: Mac, Mc and M'. A search for M*Donald finds MacDonald, McDonald and M'Donald. However, a search for 'M* Donald' is not entirely helpful for finding the forms which have been recorded with a space after the patronymic prefix – it finds every name with Mac or Donald as a distinct element. In fact the best approach is probably just to use the forename part: a search on Donald finds 'Donald', 'Mc Donald', 'Mac Donald' and 'M Donald.' Unfortunately you cannot use a wildcard at the start of a name, so you cannot use '*Donald' as a way to capture all the variant forms.

There is a detailed guide to Irish names and how they are constructed on the Nualéargais website at <**www.nualeargais.ie/gnag/ainm.htm**>.

THE IRISH LANGUAGE

An additional complication in the Irish census is that in 1911 over half a million people (almost 18 per cent of the population) spoke Irish, though the number of monoglot Irish speakers is naturally a good deal smaller.[2] In many cases, their Form A has been completed in Irish and using the Gaelic script, which is quite different from English scripts of the same period. Table 15-1 shows the letter-forms for this script, though bear in mind that handwritten letters may be significantly different from printed font. Irish does not use the letters J, K, Q, W, X Y, Z. Note particularly that the Irish 'i' has no dot. This can make it difficult to distinguish between 'm' and 'in' (m, ın), though in handwriting the 'i' often has a noticeable descender. Dots above letters are used for a quite different purpose in Irish, and are found only above consonants (see below).

A	B	C	D	E	F	G	H	I	L	M	N	O	P	R	S	T	U
A	B	C	Ꝺ	E	Ꝼ	Ᵹ	h	ı	l	M	N	O	P	R	S	Ꞇ	U
a	b	c	ꝺ	e	ꝼ	ᵹ	h	ı	l	m	n	o	p	ꞃ	ꞅ	ꞇ	u

Table 15-1 The Gaelic script

Some of the entries written in Irish have annotations in English in the family relationship and occupation columns, but the remaining columns may be hard to read if you are not familiar with the script, which you will need to be before you can look up the words in a dictionary. Figure 15-5 shows the entries for an Irish-speaking household in the Gaelic script. Figure 15-6 shows a transcription of the names from the household listing. Note the entry for James Casey mentioned above.

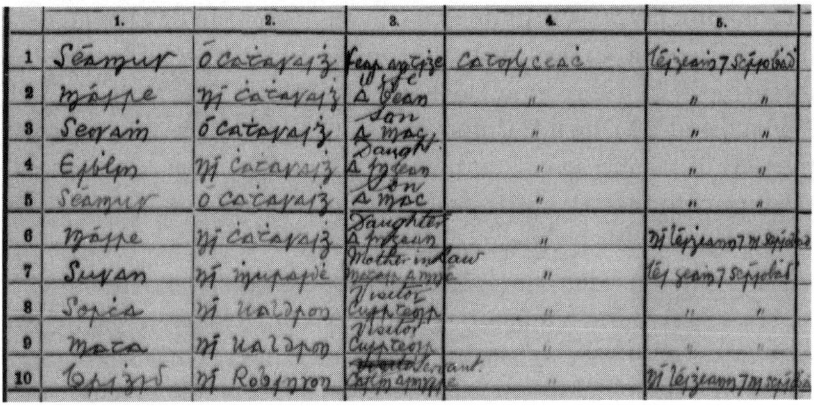

Figure 15-5 Entries for an Irish-speaking household

You shouldn't assume, incidentally, that all those with Irish names are Irish speakers: if you look up the family of Tomás O hAodha at 30 Leinster Street, North, you find both his wife Máire Ní Aodha and his youngest son Seaghán O hAodha speak only English. Occasionally, you will find both Irish and English names within the same family: Jeremiah Hayes has a wife and five children at 1 Mountpleasant Place, all called Hayes with the exception of a 22-year-old son whose name is given as Seosamh Ó hAodha, Seosamh being the Irish form of Joseph. In this case, it seems likely that the use of the Irish name represents a statement of national identity by an individual family member.

Residents of a house 49 in Iona Road, to Auburn (Glasnevin Ward, Dublin)

Surname	Forename	Age	Sex
Ó Cathasaigh	Séamus	45	Male
Ní Chathasaigh	Máire	37	Female
Ó Cathasaigh	Seosamh	13	Male
Ní Chathasaigh	Eibhlin	11	Female
Ó Cathasaigh	Séamus	8	Male
Ní Chathasaigh	Máire	4	Female
Ní Mhuraidhe	Susan	57	Female
Ní Ualdron	Sorcha	34	Female
Ní Ualdron	Mata	23	Female
Ní Robinson	Brighid	24	Female
Casey	James	-	-

View census images

Use our online form to report errors in transcription of names.

(Click here for help on image contents)

Household Return (Form A), Page 1

(Page 2)

Enumerator's abstract (Form N), Page 1

(Page 2)

Figure 15-6 Transcription of names in Figure 15-4

Where individuals have not got English or anglicized names, there are particular problems with searching, because the Irish vowels can also take an acute accent to indicate vowel length (the Irish term for this mark is *fada*). Padraig Ua Fagáin, for example, will not be found in a search for 'Fagain', you have to use the á spelling. This character can be entered at the PC keyboard by holding down the ALT key and typing 0225 on the numeric keypad (*not* the normal number keys on the top row of the keyboard). On the Mac, you can enter vowels with an acute accent by first holding down the Option key and the E key together, then releasing them and pressing the normal key for the vowel. The key combinations are show in Table 15-2.

Letter	PC (Windows)	Mac
á	ALT+0225	Option+e, a
é	ALT+0233	Option+e, e
í	ALT+0237	Option+e, i
ó	ALT+0243	Option+e, o
ú	ALT+0250	Option+e, u

Table 15-2 Entering *fadas* at the keyboard

Alternatively, you could use a wildcard instead of the vowel in question: *Fag*in* finds both the English and Irish spellings.

The older Irish writing system (prior to a reform started in 1948 and completed in 1957) also used a dot over certain consonants, indicating a linguistic feature called 'lenition'. In English transcriptions and in modern Irish spelling, this feature is indicated by an 'h' after the consonant, giving the consonant pairs bh, ch, dh, th, gh, mh, ph, sh, th. Although the dotted consonants are found in the actual census forms, the 'h' spellings are used in the census index, so you do not need to be able to enter the dotted consonants (just as well, as there is no way to do so!)

However, there is another complication: the initial consonant of a word can be affected by the final sound of the previous word (a feature also found in Welsh) – some forms have the consonant without and some with lenition. If you look at the family of Séamus Ó Cathasaigh in Figure 15-5 and Figure 15-6, you'll see that all the male family members are Ó Cathasaigh while the females are Ní Chathasaigh with a Ċ on the original form and 'Ch' in the index. The same distinction

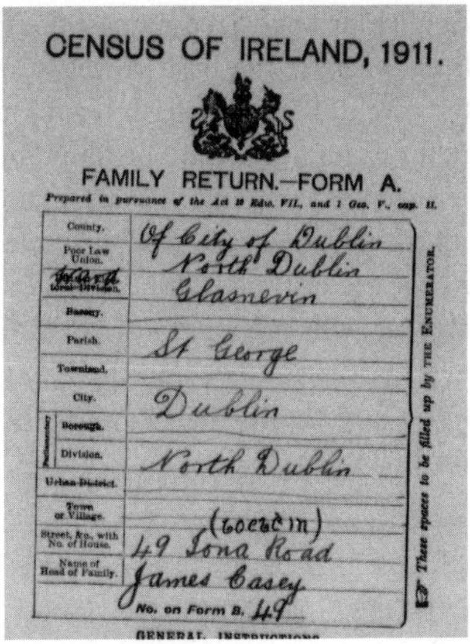
CENSUS OF IRELAND, 1911.

FAMILY RETURN.—FORM A.

Prepared in pursuance of the Act 10 Edw. VII, and 1 Geo. V., cap. 11.

County.	Of City of Dublin
Poor Law Union.	North Dublin
Ward.	Glasnevin
Barony.	
Parish.	St George
Townland.	
City.	Dublin
Borough.	
Division.	North Dublin
Urban District.	
Town or Village.	
Street, &c., with No. of House.	49 Iona Road
Name of Head of Family.	James Casey

No. on Form B. 49

These spaces to be filled up by THE ENUMERATOR.

Figure 15-7 The outside of Séamus Ó Cathasaigh's Form A

can be seen in the names of Micheal Ó Dúinn and Brigidh bean Uí Dhuinn mentioned above.

In general, Irish spellings correspond very poorly to English spelling conventions, so it is not a trivial matter for anyone but an expert to match up an Irish name with its normal anglicization. Most English speakers living outside Ireland have no hope of guessing the Irish spelling of a name on the basis of its form in English. Also, before the spelling reform there were many more 'silent letters'. For example, the modern name for the Irish language, 'Gaeilge', is spelled 'ᵹaeꝺılᵹe' (i.e. 'Gaedhilge') on the census forms.

Before you start using the Irish census, it is well worth consulting reputable reference works, such as the *Oxford Names Companion*, to check the surnames of any Irish (as opposed to Anglo-Irish or Ulster Scots) ancestors to see if they are anglicizations of Irish surnames, and what Irish spellings are attested. If you are searching for Casey ancestors, for example, you are unlikely to guess that they might be concealed behind the Irish surname Ó Cathasaigh shown in the extract above. Given that the Irish language had no agreed standard form until the 1950s, you should also expect that even the best surname dictionaries will not be familiar with all the spellings used for the same name as pronounced in the many local dialects, and spelt by householders who might be more or less literate.

Term	Older spelling	Modern spelling
head	ceann	ceann
wife	bean	bean
son	mac	mac
daughter	inġean	iníon
mother	máṫair	máthair
brother	derbráṫair	deartháir
sister	deirḟiúr	deirfiúr
visitor	cuairteoir	cuairteoir
married	pósta	pósta
single	aonta	aonta
widow	baintreaċ	baintreach
read and write	léiġeaṁ 7 scríoḃaḋ	léigheamh & scríobhadh
can't read and write	ní léiġeaṁ 7 ní scríoḃaḋ	ní léigheamh & ní scríobhadh
Irish	Gaeḋilge	gaeilge
Irish and English	Gaeḋilge 7 béarla	gaeilge & béarla

Table 15-3 The main Irish terms on census forms

While this problem is mainly one for surnames, it applies equally to forenames: Séamus Ó Cathasaigh would be anglicized as James Casey, and indeed that is the householder's name given on the outside of Form A for this family (Figure 15-7). Forenames are less problematic simply because there are fewer of them and the correspondences are well known and easy to look up. Even so, there may be surprises: even if you know that 'Seán' corresponds to 'John', you may not realize that there is an older spelling 'Seághan' which will be found on some of the census forms. A good online guide to the forename equivalences will be found on the Baby Names of Ireland site at <**www.babynamesofireland.com**> – follow the links to 'Girl Names' and 'Boy Names' at the top of the page.

Obviously it is important to be able to understand the terms used in the relationship and other columns on the household schedule. Table 15-3 gives some of the most common words. You will find a list of the main vocabulary of family relationships at <**www.irishgaelictranslator.com/articles/?p=30**>, though this gives the modern reformed spelling so there will be some differences from the 1911 records.

The Irish census site promises that: 'A list of Irish names and occupations, with translations, will appear on this site in the coming months.'

The birthplace column will usually give the name of an Irish county or city. You can find the (modern) Irish spellings for towns and cities in the Dictionary of Irish Terms at <**www.focal.ie**>. Geonames' Ireland page at <**www.geonames.de/couie.html**> gives the names of the present day county councils of the Republic of Ireland with their main towns in both Roman and Gaelic letters. The equivalent material for Northern Ireland will be found at <**www.geonames.de/cougb-sub.html#gbi**>.

IMAGES

For each household, there are several images:

- Household Return (Form A) – this consists of two pages, one with the list of inhabitants, and another with the details of the address. These are the only pages with information on individuals
- Enumerator's Abstract (Form N) for the whole street or townland
- House and Building Return (Form B1), with physical details of the house
- Out-offices and Farm-steadings (Form B2), with details of things like stables, barns, sheds.

In the case of the Forms N, B1 and B2, there are links to all the pages for the street and not just the pages which related to the one household, so in a long street or a large townland you may need to look at several of these to find the right one.

The page images are greyscale and are provided in PDF format with a file size of between 500k and 600k. Because of the nature of the PDF format it is not possible to be precise about the resolution at which the images have been scanned, but they seem to have been scanned at about 200dpi, though at very high magnification one can detect some distortion because of compression. On the whole, fine detail is easy to make out.

OTHER RESOURCES

The 'How to Search' link on the home page leads to the Help Menu with general information about the Irish censuses and basic help on using the search facilities.

There is a page on user feedback, linked from the home page, and this links to an online form for reporting errors.

The site has extensive supporting material about life in Dublin in 1911. Pages on each of 16 themes (transport, politics, religion, etc.) have a substantial essay on the topic with links to the images of the census records for the people and places mentioned.

Commercial sites

Although the NAI site will obviously be the main Irish census site, Origins (see Chapter 11) has two Irish census extracts available for subscribers to its Irish Origins service: the 1851 census for Dublin, and the 1901 census for the Rotunda Ward in Dublin.

While the 1851 census no longer exists, this Dublin index was created by Dr D.A. Chart before the records were lost. It gives only the names and addresses of heads of household (around 60,000). The forenames are usually abbreviated.

The 1901 census extract covers 13,556 individuals living in Dublin's Rotunda Ward. Origins offers a full transcription of all the fields in the original documents.

These sources are covered in the general search for census records on Irish Origins, or they can be selected for individual searching. Details of how to use the Origins search features will be found in Chapter 11.

In July 2008, a number of county sites started to make Irish census data available on a pay-per-view basis. All are part of the Irish Genealogical Online Record Search System, an all-Ireland initiative organized by the Irish Family History Foundation:

- North Tipperary Genealogy Centre at <**tipperarynorth.brsgenealogy.com**> (67,000 records for 1901)
- the Mayo Family History Centres at <**mayo.brsgenealogy.com**> (370,000 records for 1901 and 1911)
- the Mallow Heritage Centre (Co. Cork, North and East) at <**corknortheast.brsgenealogy.com**> (410,000 records for 1901 and 1911).

Searches are free, though you need to register first. Viewing the records costs €5 for one record, €40 for eight and €100 for twenty. These prices seem quite high, because the search results do not give any information to identify individuals other than what you have entered on the search form, so you may have to pay to view several records before finding the right person. You can use the same login on all sites and credits purchased can be used on any of the participating counties, which also have indexes of civil registration and parish register data. There are certain to be further census indexes available on the other county sites involved in this project, which has a home page at <**www.irish-roots.ie**>.

Volunteer transcriptions

During the long wait for any official plan to digitize the Irish censuses, many groups and individual volunteers set about indexing or transcribing the census for particular towns or areas.

The largest of these seems to be the Leitrim–Roscommon material for the 1901 census. This includes details of around 300,000 individuals in the counties of Roscommon, Leitrim, Mayo, Sligo, Wexford, Westmeath and Galway. Data for the first four of these is complete. There are no images, but the search results give family groups with the occupation of the head (see Figure 15-8).

The best way to find other county indexes is to consult the Ireland page on Census Finder at <**www.censusfinder.com/ireland.htm**>. Alternatively, consult the Genuki page for the relevant Irish county at <**www.genuki.org.uk/big/irl/**>.

The Leitrim-Roscommon 1901 Census Search Output

Townland	Parish	Barony	County	Description	Head of household Surname	Head of household Given	Head of household Occupation	Other occupants
Corracoggil North	Tibohine	Frenchpark	Roscommon	Household	Kelly	Joseph(34)	teacher	Bridget(34)-Eugene(6)-Mary(5)-Sharkey(16)niece-Ellie Sharkey(
Cuilleenirwan	Dysart	Athlone South	Roscommon	Household	Kelly	Joseph(48)	farmer	Bridget(36)-Mary A.(16)-Julia(2
Carrick	Cam	Athlone South	Roscommon	Household	Kelly	Joseph(74)	farmer/civil service pens.	widower-Mary Kate(34) teacher
Ballyardan	Ardcarn	Boyle	Roscommon	Household	Kelly	Joseph(39)	Superannuated Ins.RW Officer	Annie(46) wife-Mary(19)-Kathle Patrick(18) scholar-Kate McMa unmarried/servant

Figure 15-8 Leitrim–Roscommon 1901 Census Search Output

References

When you refer to Irish census records as sources in your family tree, you will want to enter a reference so that someone else can trace the original document. This is pretty straightforward for the census records for England and Wales: as explained on p. 48, each page of the census has a unique combination of piece, folio and page number, and these numbers can normally be seen on the digitized images. Around half of the main data services actually give the full reference in the transcripts/indexes (see, for example, Figure 11-5, taken from Origins). Although Scotland uses a slightly different referencing system, you can choose to view the full reference on any census image at ScotlandsPeople, as shown in Figure 12-7, and save the reference information with the image.

But references for the 1911 census of Ireland are quite different. In fact on the NAI census site no document references are explicitly given: there are none in the household listings (Figure 15-3) and neither the original microfilms nor the digital images made from them contain any reference information like that found on the microfilms for England and Wales.

The way in which the NAI refers to 1911 census documents is to cite the census year, county, DED number and townland number. Lists of the latter numbers are available in printed form at the NAI itself, but they do not seem to be available online. However, they can be found on the forms themselves and can be read off the digital images. Specifically they are found on the first page of Form N, the enumerator's schedule. At the top right of the form are details of the townland, below which is an oval with a thick bar across it. The number in the left half of the oval is the DED, the number in the right half, after the word 'File', the townland number. So the reference for the household of Edward O'Brien in Ballybrack, shown in Figure 15-3, would be 1911 Dublin 93/12. See Figure 15-9.

An alternative is to use the web address of the household schedule – for the household of Edward O'Brien this would be <**www.census.nationalarchives.ie/reels/nai000239889/**> for the image or <**www.census.nationalarchives.ie/pages/1911/Dublin/Killiney/Ballybrack/96653/**> for the transcription. The problem with this is that the web address will cease to be valid when the NAI decide to redesign their system. It may

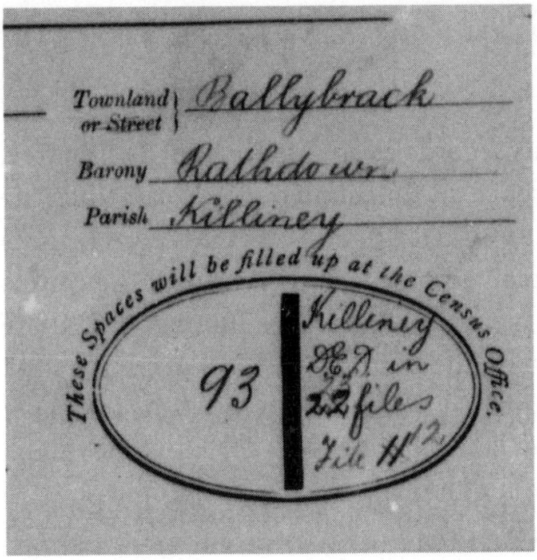

Figure 15-9 DED and Townland number from an Irish census form

still be valid in five or ten years, but it's unlikely still to be so in 50 years. The reference taken from the document itself, however, will always be correct.

At present, unfortunately, there is no way to use this reference to check a source in the online census – the only thing you can do is conduct your own search for the person. It would be nice to see this information included in the household listing and searchable.

NOTES

1 The press release is at <**www.arts-sport-tourism.gov.ie/publications/release.asp?ID=1138**>.

2 The Central Statistics Office Ireland provides historical data on the number of Irish and non-Irish speakers in the counties of the Republic (i.e. excluding the six Ulster counties which now make up Northern Ireland) since 1861 at <**beyond2020.cso.ie/Census/TableViewer/tableView.aspx?ReportId=1208**> (summary) and <**www.cso.ie/census/documents/vol11_entire.pdf**> (very detailed).

16

THE CENSUSES ON CD-ROM

While the web is now the most popular way to access census data, particularly if you need to search the whole country for your ancestors, there is still much census material on CD-ROM or DVD. This material is generally in the form of indexes only, though some suppliers include images, and most CD-ROMs cover only a county or in some cases a smaller area.

This might suggest that you should not bother with CD-ROM products. But there are several reasons why, even if you have already signed up for one of the commercial data services, it might be worth your while to see what is available.

The online services cover only the censuses from 1841, but there are a number of places for which earlier censuses include individual names (see Chapter 1, p. 6), and some of these are available on CD.

If you live close to the area where your ancestors came from, your central library, local studies library or county record office is very likely to have copies of census indexes published on CD-ROM for the local area. You will be able to consult these without signing up with a commercial data service.

If you are consulting the census as part of a local history or one-place study, it may make sense to have the complete data for that place available without going online. This is particularly the case if you haven't got a broadband connection. Also, it is generally quite difficult to use the online censuses for any sort of general analysis of the population of an enumeration district (e.g. what the main occupations are) – you would have to download and then merge the data for every individual household.

In the particular case of the 1881 Census Index (see below), the CD-ROM set includes Scotland, which the free online version of the index at <**www.familysearch.org**> does not.

Finally, there is an argument that CD-ROM census indexes will often be superior to their online equivalents. In particular, this ought to be the case for those produced by family history societies. While the data services outsource indexing to non-specialists without local knowledge, FHS census indexes have always been produced by local volunteers and have in many cases been in use by the society for many years before appearing on CD. That should mean that all obvious and many non-obvious errors will have been spotted and corrected.

Before CD-ROM replaced floppy disks (which had too little capacity for census indexes), many family history societies published census indexes on microfiche or in print. Some stocks of these are still available for purchase, but it would be unusual for new material to be published in these formats. However, they will still be available to consult in libraries with genealogy or local history holdings.

There are three main sources of census material on CD-ROM:

- The largest single CD-ROM product is the 1881 Census Index, which is available online at <**www.familysearch.org.uk**>, but it was previously published as a set of 25 CD-ROMs and these are still available.
- Many local family history societies sell census indexes on CD-ROM (and in some cases on microfiche or in print).
- A number of commercial genealogy suppliers publish ranges of census indexes on CD-ROM.

Each of these is discussed more fully below.

There is no comprehensive master catalogue of all the publications, but some of the commercial retailers discussed below source their products from dozens of different suppliers and browsing their catalogues will give you a good idea of what's available.

A very comprehensive online listing, on a county by county basis, is provided by Daniel Morgan at <**www.mit.edu/~dfm/genealogy/census-chart.html**>. Another source is the library catalogue of the Society of Genealogists, which is linked from the SoG home page at <**www.sog.org.uk**>. This is the largest genealogy library in the UK and the catalogue lists many census indexes in a variety of media.

1881 Census Index

The 1881 Census Index is described on p. 109. The CD-ROMs can be ordered via the FamilySearch Online Distribution Center (go to <**www.ldscatalog.com**> and select Family History → Software & Databases → Censuses. If you are located in the UK, it is better to order through the LDS Church's UK Distribution Centre at 399 Garretts Green Lane, Birmingham, B33 0UH, telephone 0121 785 2200. The current price is £7.85. (UK prices for all LDS CDs will be found at <**www.londonfhc.org/order_lds_cds.php**>.)

The constant swapping between CDs that is required can be very tedious, since there are eight CDs of indexes and 16 CDs of data, organized by region. However, it is possible to install all the data on your hard disk. Instructions on how to do this are given at <**freepages.genealogy.rootsweb.ancestry.com/~framland/framland/1881.htm**>. The process is quite complex and is not for the computer novice – some of the steps could damage your computer's operating system if you don't carry them out absolutely correctly. Unfortunately, you can't simply copy all the files on the CDs to a folder on your hard disk.

The CDs come with software called the Resource File Viewer which needs to be installed on your computer. This runs only on Windows systems. It was designed for Windows 95, and some people have experienced problems running it under Windows XP and Vista.

There is an excellent article on 'The 1881 British Census on CD ROM, Problems and Solutions' by Barney Tyrwhitt-Drake at <**globalgenealogy.com/globalgazette/gazfd/gazfd32.htm**>, which deals both with installation and with the search facilities.

The LDS Church also has the 1851 census for Devon, Norfolk and Warwickshire on CD for £4.70.

Note that these CDs are no longer being produced and will only be available until existing stocks are exhausted.

Family history societies

Many family history societies have published their census indexes on CD-ROM. Although some of these indexes are available online, many are not. With the closure of FamilyHistoryOnline, many of the FHS census indexes for 1851 will become part of Findmypast's 1851 census index (see p. 150), but others may no longer be available online. Even where a FHS index is online, it may be less expensive, if you are interested in many families in a county, to buy an index on CD than to pay for lots of searches online. Of course, since they are only indexes, you will still need to check the index entries against the originals. If your interest is more in local history than in genealogy, having a complete index for a town or village could be more convenient for you than carrying out place-name searches in the online census collections.

For census CDs, the obvious place to look is on the websites for the societies covering the area you are interested in. Few societies have their own online shop, but you can order from a society by post or from one of the commercial suppliers. You can find links to the websites of all the family history societies in the British Isles on Genuki's 'Family History And Genealogy Societies' page at <**www.genuki.org.uk/Societies/**>. GENfair at <**www.genfair.co.uk**> is the FFHS's online shop (actually run by S&N Genealogy) and is discussed below.

Commercial suppliers

The largest producer of census CDs is S&N Genealogy, whose online shop is at <**www.genealogysupplies.com**>. There is a link to the page for census CDs in the left-hand column.

Whereas almost all census products on CD-ROM are indexes only, S&N has concentrated on putting scanned images of the enumeration books on CD-ROM, with separate indexes released subsequently. Prices depend on the number of CDs in a set. The smaller counties cost £12.95 for each census year, while the largest (London, Lancashire and Yorkshire) with as many as 30 CDs or one DVD cost £24.95. The images are supplied as Adobe Acrobat (PDF) files; the indexes indicate the file and page number on which the matching entry is found. The image collections come with indexes of streets and areas, so if your information on where your ancestors lived is accurate for the year in question, you may not need the indexes. Likewise, if your interest is in the local history of an area rather than the individuals as possible ancestors.

The indexes require the installation of a program on your computer (Windows systems), which provides a very simple search facility – you can search on name and age only. For each name that comes up in the search results, the age, location and the TNA piece and folio reference are given. You can also get a listing of the other family members to check that you have the right person. Figures 16-1 and 16-2 show the results of a search for Charles Dickens in the 1841 census for London, and the household listing.

With the PDF file and page reference you can now load the relevant CD (there are 41 CDs in this particular set) and navigate to the relevant page. Note that the page number you need is the page within the PDF file (which appears in a small window at the bottom of the Acrobat Reader), and not the page number printed on the enumeration book.

Another major supplier of genealogy books and CDs is GENfair at <**www.genfair.co.uk**>. This is the online shop of the FFHS, which sells products from around 120 suppliers and which currently offers almost 5,000 products under the heading of census. The majority of these are from family and local history societies, but products from major producers like S&N are also included. To see the census products available, either click on the 'Census' link on the home page and then search on the county, or click on a county on the map on the home page, and search on census.

Parish Chest at <**www.parishchest.com**> sells census CDs from a range of suppliers (including family history societies). To see the census offerings, click on the 'Census' link on the home page and then select

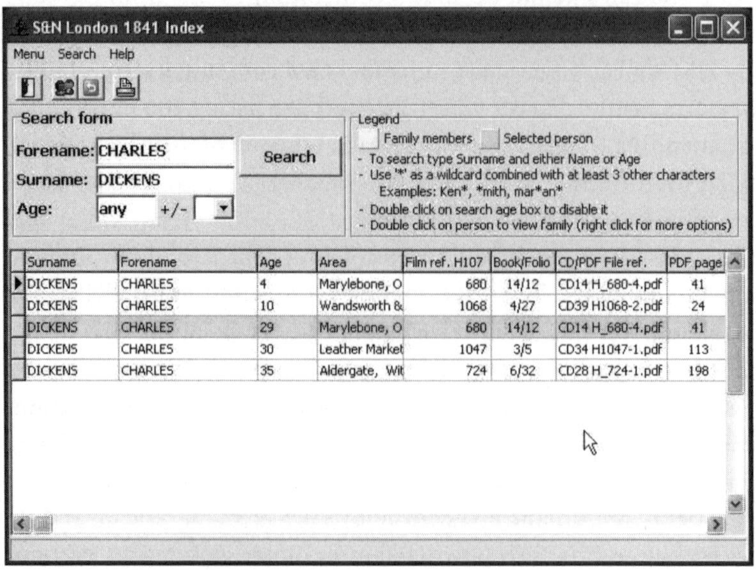

Figure 16-1 S&N London 1841 census index search results

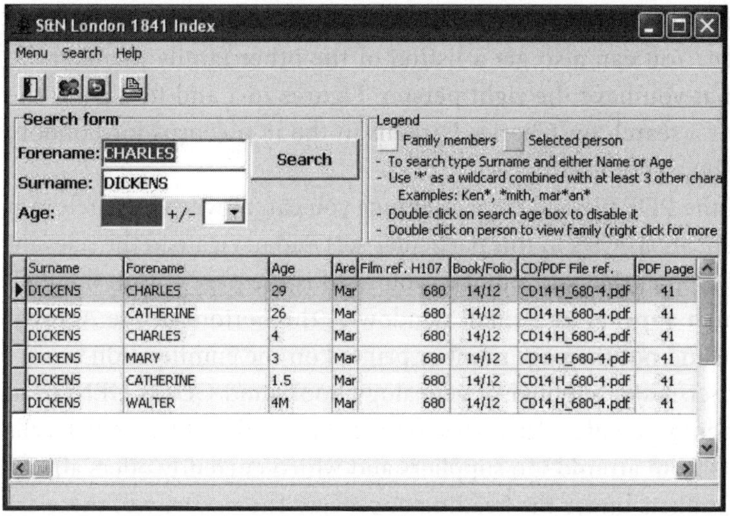

Figure 16-2 S&N London 1841 census index family listing

the county from the map. Unfortunately, within a county, the listings are arranged by supplier, so you may have to visit half a dozen sub-pages to see the full range of what is available for a county.

You don't need to go online to purchase census indexes on CD – a wide range will normally be found on sale at the various family history fairs around the country and at the open days of local family history societies. You can find out details of forthcoming events from Genuki's events calendar, GENEVA, at <**geneva.weald.org.uk**> and from the Family History Fairs website at <**members.aol.com/aquarterma/familyhistoryfairs.html**>. Parish Chest have a page listing the events they will be attending (click on the Events tab at the top of their web pages). A similar list for S&N can be found by selecting Events from the What's New menu on their site.

The largest fair, the Who Do You Think You Are? Live show at Olympia, is attended by all the major vendors and many FHSs. See <**www.whodoyouthinkyouarelive.co.uk**> for details of the next event.

A further source of census indexes on CD are online auction sites such as eBay at <**www.ebay.co.uk**>. A search on 'CD' and 'census' should bring up all the relevant items. There is one caveat about bidding for genealogy CDs in an online auction: check the normal retail price of a CD before bidding. Most genealogy CDs are quite cheap, and it's easy to end up paying above the retail price on an auction site, particularly if the seller has high postage and packing charges.

Cyndi's List has a page devoted to a list of CD-ROM publishers and suppliers (listed under 'Vendors') at <**www.cyndislist.com/cd-roms.htm**>, though this is not exhaustive.

New census CD-ROMs are regularly reviewed in the genealogy magazines.

Future prospects

Although there continue to be good reasons for using census CD-ROMs, it is likely that this type of product will become less common in the long term. The more family historians have internet access from home, the less need there is for local census indexes on CD-ROM. Most people will feel the need to subscribe to a data service for a wide variety of records and there is no need to spend money on duplicate data. Certainly, no one with an internet connection is going to buy several county census indexes on CD to track down a couple of families, when they can do national searches online for a fraction of the cost.

On the other hand, having the census images on CD-ROM is much more convenient for anyone interested in a whole town or village from the point of view of local or social history. It would be a very tedious business to download from the web all the images even for a single enumeration district, certainly at current domestic internet connection speeds.

CD-ROM is not necessarily doomed as a whole for genealogy – it remains a good way of distributing other types of digital material, such as scans of directories and similar books – but it is beginning to look less appealing for the census.

17

USING THE CENSUS ON MICROFILM

The various websites that we've looked at in Chapters 6 to 15 have one thing in common – they are essentially designed to help you find individuals in the census. As we've seen, some of them do allow you to search by place or even by address, but the emphasis is very much on the search for a person or a family.

For most family historians, this is fine – generally speaking, we can find our ancestors using one website or another and we have the undeniable bonus of being able to download images of the original census pages to our own PCs. The advantages of searching online are manifold and, we hope, obvious to all, but it's also true to say that there are times when what you really need to do is to go back to the originals – or at least to a microfilm or microfiche of the originals.

For that reason, despite the extensive drive towards digitization of the records, the National Archives still provides access to microfilms of the censuses in its reading rooms at Kew, and many libraries and local record offices continue to do likewise. There are no signs that this is likely to change in the foreseeable future, but for researchers who have come to family history quite recently the process behind finding the returns for a particular property using microfilm may be unfamiliar and potentially confusing.

There's also a small but significant body of researchers who either cannot or will not use a PC. Of course, we would encourage them to think again – help with using computer technology is not hard to come by: classes run by local libraries or adult education groups such as the University of the Third Age (U3A) are available all around the UK and most of us have friends or relatives who might be willing to offer some basic assistance, so there's really no excuse.

The structure of the records

If you do decide to view the census returns on microfilm, it's particularly important to understand the structure of the records and the referencing system that has been applied to them (see p. 31).

The records were arranged by the General Register Office into Registration Districts, sub-Districts (the same hierarchy used for the registration of births, deaths and marriages) and finally Enumeration Districts. There was never an exact match between this system and the ancient structure of counties, hundreds and parishes. A large parish could extend over several enumeration districts or alternatively a single enumeration district could include the returns for two or more small parishes. Also, many Registration Districts included parishes situated in more than one county, which gave rise to the rather confusing term 'Registration County' as opposed to the traditional 'Administrative County'.

All documents held by the National Archives have a three-part reference which uniquely identifies them, comprising a 'Department Code', a Series Number and a Piece Number. The first of these relates to the government department which created, maintained or inherited the records, so in the case of the census returns this was the Home Office (HO) for 1841 and 1851 and the Registrar General (RG) for all the others. The Department and Series references for each of the census years are as follows:

1841	HO 107	taken on
1851	HO 107	taken on
1861	RG 9	taken on
1871	RG 10	taken on
1881	RG 11	taken on
1891	RG 12	taken on
1901	RG 13	taken on
1911	RG 14 and RG 78	taken on 2 April

Before the census records were microfilmed, they were stamped with 'folio' numbers. It's important to note that each folio number relates to two pages: the numbers were stamped on the top right of every second page – this page is often referred to as 'recto' (Latin for 'right') – but the folio number also relates to the following page (the other side of the same piece of paper) which is referred to as 'verso' (i.e. 'reverse'). This is all much easier to understand when you imagine the sheets as pages in the original summary books.

As an example of how this works in practice, the full TNA reference for the page recording the Darwin family in the 1881 census is: RG 11/855, folio 83, page 1. We could also use the General Register Office hierarchy and say that the entry is in the Bromley Registration District, the Bromley sub-District and is on page 1 of Enumeration District number 5.

Finding aids

The biggest problem facing researchers in the long years of the pre-digitization era was how to locate the returns for a specific place or address and the solution was to produce a vast array of finding aids. Staff at the Public Record Office were for many years at the forefront of this venture, creating lists and indexes to hamlets, townships, chapelries, villages, towns and cities the length and breadth of the country. For the cities and the larger towns, street indexes were produced identifying the precise location of a given address in the records. These indexes have always been seen as 'work in progress' and this approach continues today with a plan to make the street indexes available online via The National Archives' wiki, *Your Archives*.

The first problem facing anyone compiling a place-name index is what to include and what not to. After all, when you start to think about it, what actually constitutes a 'place'? If, for example, someone asked you where you were born, you could give a variety of answers. You could give the name of the actual hospital or give the name of the town in which it was situated. You could name the district within that town or if you were born in a rural area you might say the name of the hamlet or village, or possibly even the name of the nearby market town.

A separate set of finding aids was created for each of the census years and they are now available in the reading rooms at Kew. You start by finding the name of the place that you're looking for in the alphabetical place-name index. The place-name indexes include the names of every Civil Parish, as well as the more significant hamlets, townships and chapelries.

Next to each place name you'll find the name and number of the relevant Registration District and the number of the sub-District. Using these numbers, you can then turn to the Reference Books, which are arranged numerically by Registration District and sub-District. These books will identify the microfilm which contains the census returns for the place that you're interested in.

The lists for 1841 work slightly differently – the number next to your place name is the page number in the Reference Book, not the number of the Registration District. But once you've found your place in the Reference Book, the process is pretty much the same as with the other census years.

You can also use the National Archives' Catalogue <**www.nationalarchives.gov.uk/catalogue**> to find places in the censuses. Simply enter the placename in the 'Word or phrase' box, and the relevant record series reference (see p. 252) under 'Department or Series code' and click on 'search'. This should give you the National Archives reference for the document or documents including the returns for that place.

This system works well for rural areas or for small towns. If, however, the address you're looking for is in a large town or a city, you'll need a more precise reference and for each of the most heavily populated districts in England and Wales a street index has been produced, listing all the streets, roads, avenues, places and terraces in alphabetical order. Each entry in the street indexes provides you with a range of folios within a particular piece number so that you can go straight to the relevant entry, without having to wind through a whole microfilm.

Finding addresses in London can be particularly difficult. Boundary changes, renaming of streets, renumbering of houses and long streets which stray into more than one Registration District can all make your search that bit more complicated. A huge amount of work has been carried out by, first, the Public Record Office and then the National Archives staff to help alleviate these problems, the result of which is a number of additional finding aids designed to help you trace that elusive London address. Again, these are available in the reading rooms at Kew.

In order to carry out an effective search of the census returns on microfilm, you need to have a pretty good idea of where your ancestors were living at the time of the census. There are a number of sources that you might use to get potential addresses for your ancestors: wills, newspaper reports, obituaries, electoral registers and trade directories can all prove useful, but by far the most important source comprises the General Register Office's birth, marriage and death certificates.

Armed with a contemporary birth or death certificate, finding the census returns for the address shown on the certificate is a relatively straightforward matter. As we've seen, the two sets of records use exactly the same hierarchy: so if a death was registered in the Watford Registration District, the address shown on the certificate will be found amongst the census returns for the Watford District. You might need to watch out for the occasional boundary change but generally speaking this direct correlation between the two sets of records works well. Addresses on marriage certificates are less useful – they tend to be less precise than those given on birth and death certificates and are often inaccurate or even invented!

Libraries and county record offices will all have their own ways of accessing microfilms of the census returns for their areas. Some of them may use National Archives' references, while others will have their own systems. You may find that your local record office has a copy of the relevant street index or, alternatively, they may have produced their own index.

Another option open to you is to use the worldwide network of Latter Day Saints' Family History Centers. You can order a microfilm of any census return (including Scotland and Ireland) to view at your local Center – details can be found on the Church of Latter Day Saints' website at: <**www.familysearch.org/Eng/Library/FHC/frameset_fhc.asp**>.

While staff at the Public Record Office were busy working on place-name and street indexes, members of family history societies up and down the country were embarking on the monumental task of creating surname indexes to the census returns. From the 1970s onwards, a huge amount of work was done by volunteers, producing indexes to some quite significant sections of the census. 1851 was the first year to be tackled in earnest, and long before the commercial census websites got in on the act thousands of indexes had been published. And it wasn't just 1851: family history societies and a whole host of dedicated individuals moved on to other census years as well. It's certainly true that some parts of the country were better covered than others, but there was something for every county and some counties had been fully indexed for certain years.

These surname indexes are still available to researchers today – mainly as printed booklets or on microfiche. The National Archives has a large collection, as does the Society of Genealogists in London.

Also, libraries and local record offices are likely to have copies of the indexes for their own areas of interest and may even have unpublished manuscript or card indexes, which are only available in their own reading rooms.

The indexes were produced by hundreds of different local and family history societies. There was no central body to establish conventions for transcribing the returns or to impose rules on how to create indexes, so the published results can vary greatly from county to county and from index to index.

Having said that, the transcription and indexing are generally of a higher standard than we've come to expect from the various census websites – they were usually created by people who had a good local knowledge of the names and places and a personal interest in the area.

One of the advantages of using census returns on microfilm is that you get a better sense of the context of the records you're looking at than you do in an online environment. Rather than dropping you in on a particular page, the microfilm forces you to wind through the returns, viewing a whole range of pages on the way. And by doing this you become familiar both with the physical structure of the records and also with the geography of the area in which your ancestors were living.

While searching online should always be your first choice, it's important not to ignore the possibilities that the microfilm alternative can offer.

READING AND WEBSITES

SELECTED READING

Colin R. Chapman, *Pre-1841 Censuses and Population Listings in the British Isles* (2nd edn, 1991)

Jeremy Gibson and Elizabeth Hampson, *Census Returns 1841–1891 in Microform: A Directory to Local Holdings in Great Britain* (6th edn, 2001)

Jeremy Gibson and Mervyn Medlycott, *Local Census Listings: 1522–1930* (3rd edn, 1997)

Jeremy Gibson and Elizabeth Hampson, *Marriage, Census and Other Indexes for Family Historians* (8th edn, 2000)

Edward Higgs, *Making Sense of the Census – Revisited* (2005)

Edward Higgs, *Life, Death and Statistics* (2004)

Susan Lumas, *Making Use of the Census* (2004)

Muriel Nissel, *People Count: A History of the General Register Office* (1997)

USEFUL WEBSITES

Histpop – The Online Historical Population Reports Website

Everything you need to know about the background to, and history of, the UK's census returns. <**www.histpop.org.uk**>

A Vision of Britain Through Time

Detailed historical information on places in Britain <**www.visionofbritain.org.uk**>

Sites with national census datasets:

Ancestry <**www.ancestry.co.uk**>
FamilySearch <**www.familysearch.org**>
Findmypast <**www.findmypast.com**>
TheGenealogist <**www.thegenealogist.co.uk**>
Genes Reunited <**www.genesreunited.co.uk**>
National Archives of Ireland <**www.census.nationalarchives.ie**>
Origins <**www.origins.net**>
RootsUK <**www.rootsuk.com**>
ScotlandsPeople <**www.scotlandspeople.com**>
1901censusonline <**www.1901censusonline.com**>
1911 Census <**www.1911census.co.uk**>

There is a web site for this book at <**www.spub.co.uk/census/**> with updates and additional material.

INDEX